TEACH-INS: U.S.A.

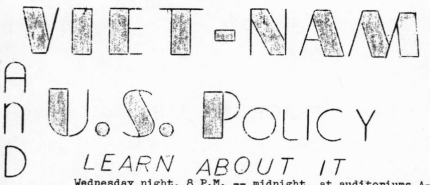

VIET-NAM

AND U.S. POLICY

LEARN ABOUT IT

Wednesday night, 8 P.M. -- midnight, at auditoriums A-D

Speakers:

1. JOHN DONAHUE - Anthropoligist who did his field-work in
   Viet-nam - Speaking on the background of Vietnam

2. ROBERT BROWN - Economist who spent 6 years as a State
   Department advisor in Vietnam - Speaking on the
   faklure of american policy in Vietnam.

3. ARTHUR WASKOW - of the Institute for Policy Studies -
   Speaking on alternative policies.

There will be an extensive question period

PROTEST IT

12-1:30   Torchlight protest rally on Diag. ProfessorsBergman and
          Boulding will speak.

1:30-3   Seminars focusing on Vietnam and the war.

3-4 AM   Break for coffee and refreshments.

4-6 AM   Seminars on mechanisms for changing U.S. policies.

6-7 AM   Plans for future activities.

7-8 AM   Diag rally and folksinging.

   All discussions will be informal. At the same time there will
be movies on Vietnam (including one made by the National Liberation
Front) , folksinging, and other activities for those who don't want
to talk all night.

   FACULTY COMMITTEE TO STOP THE WAR IN VIET_NAM

TEACH-INS: U.S.A.

Reports, Opinions, Documents

EDITED BY

LOUIS MENASHE

AND

RONALD RADOSH

FREDERICK A. PRAEGER, *Publishers*
New York · Washington · London

For
Sheila *and* Alice

FREDERICK A. PRAEGER, PUBLISHERS
111 Fourth Avenue, New York, N.Y. 10003, U.S.A.
77–79 Charlotte Street, London W.1, England

Published in the United States of America in 1967 by
Frederick A. Praeger, Inc., Publishers

© 1967 by Frederick A. Praeger, Inc.

Library of Congress Catalog Card Number: 67–16682

Printed in the United States of America

Frontispiece: Announcement of the first teach-in, held at the
University of Michigan, Ann Arbor, March 24–25, 1965.

Preface

From modest beginnings at a Midwestern campus one night in March, 1965, the teach-in movement went on to release vast amounts of moral and political energies from professors and students across the nation. Nothing quite like it has been witnessed before on American campuses, and few campus-based activities have ever had as immediate and widespread an impact on the surrounding community. The teach-ins remind us that teachers, like politicians, are practitioners of the arts of communication and that, when communication is blocked, they, like political leaders, seek new channels, sometimes with explosive results. The teach-ins sprang from the feeling of large sections of the academic community that Government leaders were no longer listening to criticism of U.S. policy on Vietnam and that the American public, subjected to the massive persuasive powers of the information media, would. soon stop offering it. In this situation, teachers turned to their most reliable constituency, their students. The students were not only willing listeners but also enthusiastic responders, and together, teachers and students built a movement.

This volume attempts to explore, with the aid of documents and opinions, the origins, development, and impact of the American teach-in movement. The editors have had the good fortune to join animated, bleary-eyed, but keen-witted, participants in many a teach-in session and have witnessed from within some of the dynamics of the movement. This experience has been especially valuable for putting together a work of this kind, for much of the "primary documentation" of the movement—the crumpled mimeographed broadsides, the intramural newsletters—was available either from the editors' personal collections or from those of colleagues.

The varied materials collected here provide a rich source for analyses on many levels—political, educational, sociological. The teach-ins grew out of earlier protests against the Vietnam war and, inevitably, they continue to thrive on foreign policy issues. But they also examine and reflect important problems and trends in other areas of American society. As political phenomena, for example, they might be viewed as expressions of a new political awareness and activism, largely anti-Establishment in orientation, seeking fulfillment through increasingly direct forms of political action. In the realm of higher education, the teach-ins may well prove to be methodological models for interdisciplinary approaches to controversial themes outside the traditional structured classroom situation. In this light, they satisfy at least two important educational needs: They bring subjects before large student audiences and, at the same time, preserve the informality and directness so vital to learning processes, but so rapidly diminishing under the impact of the IBM card and the televised lecture.

With these selections, we have tried to represent the movement as comprehensively as space will allow and with as much perspective as the first two years of a viable movement permit. The materials—many appearing in print for the first time—fall into four categories: 1) primary data originating from the teach-ins themselves—programs, announcements, speeches, background accounts by organizers and participants; 2) descriptions of teach-ins drawn from the press and other sources; 3) reflections of the teach-in's impact on Congress, the academic community here and abroad, the Administration, and the press; 4) evaluations and discussions of the movement, especially by those involved. The short introductions to the chapters are designed primarily to bring into focus some of the issues touched upon explicitly or implicitly in the selections and to provide background and connections where they are not necessarily evident. But the editors have, on occasion, injected their personal views.

The selections themselves have been edited and cut for reasons of space, clarity, and stylistic consistency. In some cases, a few extracts suffice, particularly where the complete original documents contain material not relevant to our subject, elaborations not necessary for basic illustrative use, or repetitions of information and views adequately presented elsewhere in this volume. In others, we have used documents virtually in their entirety. In all cases, of course, we have adhered to original meaning and flavor.

No general theme or point of view pervades the work, but we make this brief observation at the outset: While the teach-in movement has expanded, so has the war. To cite only one measurement, there were 25,000 American troops in Vietnam when the teach-ins began; as of this writing, the figure is pushing 400,000. To paraphrase Churchill, the teach-ins talked, talked, talked, while the Administration made war, war, war. And although Administration officials consented, after much pressure, to respond to the teach-ins, it is clear, as many in the movement have come to realize, that techniques other than those that have served so well to reach students and fellow teachers will have to be invoked if the New Protest is to influence the makers of U.S. policy.

* * *

In compiling this book we have been fortunate in receiving the help and critical advice of many of our friends and colleagues. Among these, special mention must be made of Professor Constance Sutton of New York University, who supplied us with many documents pertaining to the teach-in movement on her campus and elsewhere; the staff of the *National Guardian,* who generously permitted us to draw from their voluminous files of clippings on American protest movements; and Professor Marvin E. Gettleman, of the Polytechnic Institute of Brooklyn, who provided special materials, and whose *Vietnam: History, Documents, and Opinions on A Major World Crisis* has become a kind of *Robert's Rules* of the teach-in movement.

In addition, the authors have received suggestions, help, and materials from Mr. Paul Breines (University of Wisconsin), Professor Robert Buckhout (Washington University, St. Louis), Professor Dixon Bush (Antioch College), Mr. Isaac Deutscher (London, England), Professor John T. Dorsey, Jr. (Vanderbilt University), Professor Eugene D. Genovese (Rutgers University), Professor Helmut Gruber (Polytechnic Institute of Brooklyn), Professor Staughton Lynd (Yale University), Miss Marilyn McGregor (New York City), Professor David Mermelstein (Polytechnic Institute of Brooklyn), Miss Nadine Miller (Long Island University), Mr. Jack Monet (Paris), Mr. Fred Newdom (Columbia University), Professor James O'Connor (Washington University, St. Louis), Mr. Robert Randolph (University of California, Berkeley), Dr. Anatol Rapoport and his assistant, Mrs. Clair Adler (University of Michigan), Professor Murray Rothbard (Polytechnic Institute of Brooklyn), Professor C. Wade Savage (University of California, Los Angeles), Professor Donald Willmott (University of Toronto), and Mr. Jack Zaraya (City College of New York).

Mrs. Jean Lester, Mrs. Nita Woods, and Miss Myra Shapiro, of the Polytechnic Institute of Brooklyn, and Miss Elspeth Leacock graciously assisted in the preparation of the manuscript. Editorial supervision and help was warmly and effectively provided by Mr. Gilman Park, Mrs. Marian Wood, and Miss Sarah Brown, of Frederick A. Praeger, Inc. Sheila Menashe and Alice Radosh, our severest critics, helped in more ways than we can enumerate.

L. M.
R. R.

New York, January, 1967

Acknowledgments

For permission to reprint articles, speeches, and other materials, we wish to thank the following persons, publications, and organizations:

Arnold Beichman: "A Study in Academic Freedom," *The New York Times Magazine*, December 19, 1965.

Brandt & Brandt: "Priorities—Economic and Moral" by Seymour Melman; address delivered at the Columbia University Teach-In on March 24, 1966. Reprinted by permission of Brandt & Brandt.

George Braziller, Publishers: Transcripts of addresses delivered before the National Teach-In, May 15, 1965, by Hans J. Morgenthau, Arthur M. Schlesinger, Jr., and Eric Wolf.

Germaine Brée: "Sartre and Camus: Two Concepts of Commitment," address delivered at the University of Wisconsin Teach-In (April 1, 1965); later (April, 1966) it formed the concluding section of the Phi Beta Kappa Address and third Kathleen Morris Scruggs Memorial Lecture given by Professor Brée at Randolph-Macon Woman's College, and published by the college in the fall of that year.

Donald G. Brennan: "The Importance of American Intervention in Vietnam," address delivered at the Oslo Teach-In, April 16, 1966.

Art Buchwald: "Foreign Policy on Campus," syndicated newspaper column of May 16, 1965.

Bulletin of the Atomic Scientists: "Reflections on Protest" by Kenneth E. Boulding is reprinted, with permission, from the October, 1965, issue of the *Bulletin of the Atomic Scientists*. © 1965 by the Educational Foundation for Nuclear Science. "Some Social Implications of the Teach-Ins" by Richard Flacks is reprinted, with permission, from the October, 1965, issue of the *Bulletin of the Atomic Scientists*. ©1965 by the Educational Foundation for Nuclear Science.

The Canadian Forum: "Teach-In as Institution" by Arthur Pape, November, 1965.

The Christian Century: "Hudson Valley Teach-In on Vietnam by Charles Austin. ©1966 Christian Century Foundation. Reprinted by permission from the April 20, 1966, issue of *The Christian Century*.

CBS: CBS-News Special Report—Vietnam Dialog: Mr. Bundy and the Professors; extracts reprinted by permission.

Henry Steele Commager: "The Problem of Dissent," *The Saturday Review*, December 18, 1965.

Isaac Deutscher: "The Teach-Ins and the American 'Thaw,'" *The Statesman* (Calcutta), June 9–10, 1965. World © 1965 reserved by Isaac Deutscher.

Stanley Diamond: "The TV Debate," *Bi-Weekly Information Action Report*, July 2, 1965.

Gazette and Daily (York, Pa.): "Pseudo-Debate in the Teach-Ins" by William Appleman Williams, June 19, 1965.

Eugene D. Genovese: "American Imperialism Confronts a Revolutionary World," address delivered at the Rutgers University Teach-In, April 23, 1965.

Ernest van den Haag: "American Intervention Minimizes Violence," address delivered at the New York University Teach-In, and others, 1965–66.

Stanley Hoffmann: "The Syndrome of Oscillation," remarks delivered at an evening panel at the National Teach-In, May 15, 1965, and published by *The New Republic*, May 29, 1965.

Russell Kirk: "The Scholar Is Not a Lion or a Fox," The *New York Times Magazine*, May 1, 1966.

Staughton Lynd: "Nonviolent Alternatives to American Violence," address delivered at the University of California (Berkeley) Teach-In, May 22, 1965. Reprinted from *We Accuse*, published by Diablo Press, Berkeley, California, in 1965.

Herbert Marcuse: "The Inner Logic of American Policy in Vietnam," address delivered at the University of California (Los Angeles) Teach-In, March 25, 1966.

The Michigan Daily: "The Intellectual Community Begins to Stir," editorial, March 26, 1965; "Protest, Learning, Heckling Spark Viet Rally" by Roger Rapoport, March 26, 1965.

John D. Montgomery: "How to Stay in Vietnam," address delivered at the World Affairs Council Teach-In (Boston, Mass.), May 17, 1966; printed in *Vietnam Perspectives*, August, 1966.

The Nation: "Treason of the Experts" by Eric Bentley, December 13, 1965; "Teach-Ins and Walk-Outs" by the editors, April 12, 1965; "State Department on Campus" by Donald Janson, May 24, 1965; "Teach-Ins: New Force for the Times" by Arnold S. Kaufman, June 21, 1965; "Passion in Clear Reason" by David Krech, March 28, 1966; "New Curriculum for the Teach-Ins" by Christopher Lasch, October 18, 1965; "Teach-Ins: New Forum for Reason" by Webster Schott, May 31, 1965.

The National Guardian: "12,000 at UC Teach-In on Vietnam" by Robert Randolph, May 29, 1965.

National Review: "The Professors and the 'Teach-Ins' " by Will Herberg; permission from the *National Review* (July 13, 1965), 150 E. 35th St., N.Y., N.Y. 10016.

The New York Times: "Genesis of the Confuse-In" by Russell Baker, May 20, 1965; "London Teach-In Castigates U.S." by Clyde Farnsworth, June 12, 1965; "Vietnam Comes to Oregon University" by Mitchel Levitas, *The New York Times Magazine*, May 9, 1965; and "Decline of Serious Debate" (April 1, 1965), "Teach-In Could Become a Useful Tool" (May 17, 1965), and "Senator Fulbright's

Teach-In" (February 13, 1966), by James Reston. © 1965, 1966 by
The New York Times Company. Reprinted by permission.

Carl Oglesby: "Teaching-In in Tokyo," *Bi-Weekly Action Information
Report*, No. 4, Fall, 1965.

Marc Pilisuk: "The First Teach-In: An Insight into Professional Activism," *The Correspondent*, No. 34, 1965.

The Reporter: "After the Washington Teach-In" by Meg Greenfield,
June 3, 1965. © 1965 by The Reporter Magazine Company.

San Juan Star: "Puerto Rican Teach-In Marked by Violence" by Dimas
Planas, October 14, 1965.

Susan Sontag: "We Are Choking with Shame and Anger," address delivered at the Town Hall Read-In, February 20, 1966. © by Susan
Sontag.

I. F. Stone's Weekly: "What Should the Peace Movement Do?" by
I. F. Stone, June 28, 1965.

Studies on the Left: "Teach-Ins: New Force or Isolated Phenomena?"
by Peter Lathrop (V, No. 4, 1965); "The Teach-In: National Movement or End of An Affair?" by Joan W. Scott (V, No. 3, 1965).

Constance Sutton: "Introduction to Teach-In II," address delivered at
New York University's first-anniversary teach-in, May 3, 1966.

Time: "The Black Banders," May 14, 1965. Reprinted by permission
from *TIME The Weekly Newsmagazine*; © Time Inc. 1965.

Frank N. Trager: "The Struggle for Vietnamese Independence," address delivered at the Oslo Teach-In, April 16, 1966.

United Features Syndicate: "Campus Lefties' Field Day" by William
S. White, syndicated column of May 12, 1965.

Viet-Report: "A Protest Against the Draft and Death of Intellect" by
Tom Hayden, June-July, 1966, pp. 3–4.

The Village Voice: Joseph Barry column of June 2, 1966. By permission of *The Village Voice, Inc.*

Washington Post–Los Angeles Times Syndicate: "On Viet 'Teach-
Ins' " by Barry Goldwater, syndicated column of October 24, 1965.

Arthur Waskow: University of Michigan Teach-In address, March 24,
1965.

William Appleman Williams: "Our Leaders Are Following the Wrong
Rainbow," address delivered at the University of Wisconsin
Teach-In, April 1, 1965.

Contents

Contents

VIII. Escalation of the Teach-Ins

TEACH-INS: U.S.A.

To those of us who still retain an irreconcilable animus against war, it has been a bitter experience to see the unanimity with which the American intellectuals have thrown their support to the use of war-technique in the crisis in which America found herself. . . .

If our intellectuals were going to lead the Administration, they might conceivably have tried to find some way of securing peace. . . . They might have turned their intellectual energy not to the problem of jockeying the nation into war but to the problem of using our vast neutral power to attain democratic ends . . . without the use of the malevolent technique of war. . . .

An intellectual class that was wholly rational would have called insistently for peace and not for war. For months, the crying need has been for a negotiated peace, in order to avoid the ruin of a deadlock. Would not the same amount of resolute statesmanship thrown into intervention have secured a peace that would have been a subjugation for neither side? . . .

Criticism by the ruling powers will only be accepted from those intellectuals who are in sympathy with the general tendency of the war. Well, it is true that they may guide, but if their stream leads to disaster and the frustration of national life, is their guiding any more than a preference whether they shall go over the right-hand or the left-hand side of the precipice? . . .

Is there no place left, then, for the intellectual who cannot crystallize, who does not dread suspense, and is not yet drugged with fatigue? The American intellectuals, in their preoccupation with reality, seem to have forgotten that the real enemy is War. . . . There is work to be done to prevent this war of ours from passing into popular mythology as a holy crusade. . . . There must be some irreconcilables left . . . to call unceasingly for peace. . . . The intellectual who retains his animus against war will push out more boldly than ever to make his case solid against it.

—Randolph Bourne
("The War and The Intellectuals," The Seven Arts, II; June, 1917)

I

The Teach-Ins Begin

Editors' Introduction

"T-Day" at the University of Michigan—March 24, 1965—came less than two months after American warplanes had begun systematic bombing of North Vietnam. For many of the nation's scholars, the bombings initiated on February 7 were the most repugnant of all U.S. actions in the escalation of the Vietnamese war. They had been ordered by a President whose 1964 pre-election oratory had included the promise not to "go North," in marked contrast to the proposals of his Republican opponent. Academics had rarely demonstrated such political mobilization as in the months preceding the Presidential elections; they spoke, wrote, circulated petitions, and placed advertisements in leading newspapers on behalf of "peace candidate" Lyndon Baines Johnson. Now they felt betrayed. Their anger, coupled, ironically, with experience many had gained in working for Johnson, led professors and students to mount a new campaign—speaking, writing, circulating petitions, placing newspaper advertisements—against the Administration's Vietnam policies. This new campaign soon escalated into the American teach-in movement.

The development of the teach-ins out of debates over political action on one American campus is detailed in this chapter by two of the movement's organizers, Anatol Rapoport and Marc Pilisuk. Their accounts not only describe the background of the first teach-in and convey the exhilaration it produced among faculty and students, they also introduce an issue that later would confront teach-in organizers everywhere and that invariably split them into moderate and radical factions: the conflict between teach-in as debate and teach-in as protest. This issue will receive more attention in subsequent chapters.

Everywhere the teach-ins developed, they drew large and enthusiastic student-faculty audiences. Other accounts in this chapter depict the teach-ins in action. All were similar in their display of color, spirit, and concern, but each reflected local features and possessed a distinctive composition and "personality." Thus, the Berkeley Teach-In continued the radical traditions of that campus by assembling some of the nation's most vehement Vietnam critics for a mammoth two-day protest. The debate occasioned by this use of the teach-in for pure protest is illustrated here by an exchange between Professor Robert Scalapino, a leading academic supporter of Administration policy, and the organizers of the Berkeley sessions.

The description of the Hudson Valley Teach-In exemplifies the movement's thrust into unexpected areas. Teach-ins turned up not only at large campuses like Michigan, Berkeley, and Wisconsin, which have traditionally been oriented toward political action, but also at such unlikely schools as Kent College, Ohio; Goucher College, Maryland; Flint Junior College, Michigan; Marist College at Poughkeepsie, New York; and hundreds of other small, customarily placid retreats.

The statements concluding the chapter, issued after teach-ins at New York University and the University of Chicago, reveal that the political spirit behind the teach-ins did not simply evaporate with the morning hours, but was encouraged by, and continued well beyond, the actual meetings.

Dialogue or Monologue?

—ANATOL RAPOPORT

An organizer of the first teach-in, Dr. Rapoport is Professor of Mathematic Biology and Senior Research Mathematician at the Mental Health Research Institute of the University of Michigan. The following is part of a report distributed privately by Professor Rapoport; the second section of the report appears in Chapter IV.

Everyone had already done everything—chipped in for full-page ads, spoken at community meetings, written letters to the President, to the Secretary of State, and to Congress. The President did not reply. The State Department sent out pamphlets published by the Advertising Council of America, in which the evils of Communism were explained. (The pamphlets were somewhat out of date; "Communism" was illustrated by Khrushchev with a smirk on his face.) The senators replied in a somber mood to the effect that the final decision was with the President, and advised us to pray for divine guidance. An old woman in Detroit had just set fire to herself, but that did not stop the escalation either.

At one point [during discussions at the University of Michigan] some people went into another room and came out with the idea of calling a "work moratorium." Classes were to be canceled for a day, and students were to be invited to participate in a day-long analysis of historical, political, military, and moral aspects of the Vietnam war.

In future dictionaries of American English, the suffix "-in" may well be defined as referring to a technique of social protest characterized by a nonviolent occupation of premises. This technique goes back to the sit-down strikes of the thirties. The idea is to move the picket line from outside the premises, where it can be ignored, to inside, where it cannot be ignored. The now historic sit-in demonstrations of the civil rights movement were an adaptation of this idea.

In one variant of the work moratorium, the discussions on Vietnam were to take place in the classroom during the scheduled class periods—thus, the term "teach-in," which would properly apply to this sort of demonstration. However, as it turned out, the name stuck to a different type of function.

The call for a work moratorium at the University of Michigan, issued on March 12, 1965, was signed by forty-nine faculty members. Reactions ranged from enthusiasm among the students to "concern" among our colleagues, from misgivings in the university administration to denunciations in the state legislature. It quickly became apparent that the Vietnam issue was about to be completely submerged in the ensuing fight about the legality, the ethics, the prudence, and the effectiveness of the work moratorium as an instrument of protest by academics. The endemic debate on the "nature of academic freedom" was about to erupt and to drain the rhetorical energies of the university community. There was also talk of another Berkeley.

Then came the all-night meeting of March 17–18. This meeting was originally called to discuss the organization of the work moratorium. The program committee had prepared a full "class schedule," including the assignment of topics to faculty members. The publicity committee had prepared the press releases. A contingent of students sat on the floor, ready with its suggestions for recruiting student participants. It was in this charged atmosphere that the proposal to reconsider the work moratorium was introduced.

The anticipated reaction of the "militants" was immediate. After eight hours of nerve-frazzling, soul-scraping debate, consensus was reached at 4:00 A.M., and the teach-in movement was born. With it was born the political dilemma stated in the title of this article. Anyone who wishes to estimate the degree of success achieved by the teach-in movement, its possible effects, and the possible role it and its derivatives will play in American life, must understand the issues involved in this dilemma. Before I discuss these issues, I must say something about the difference in the way the teach-in was viewed by the militants and by others (who, I suppose, could be called the moderates, though this would be a misnomer).

Actually, the change from the original work moratorium to the accepted format was only a shift from regular working hours to night hours. By shifting to night hours, we undercut all the talk about "breach of contract," "propaganda in the classroom," "infringing on the right of the taxpayers," "depriving the students," and so on. The actual program of the teach-in remained essentially the same as that planned for the moratorium: lectures, seminars, and mass meetings.

Why, then, did the militants resist the change with such determination? Because the change looked like a retreat, a compromise, a fixation on the constraints of the academic tradition. In the eyes of the militants, the time for polite academic discussion of issues was past. Speaking out was no longer enough; it seemed useless to speak out and to be told that you had a perfect right to speak out, while the people who held the whole of humanity as hostages proceeded with their genocidal plans. Therefore, argued the militants, it was actually *necessary* (not just unavoidable) that the protest be imbued with some aspect of questionable legality. It would not do to act in the "approved" fashion.

I think that the militants finally yielded to the strength of two arguments. First, the moratorium (let's face it, the strike) was a protest against the wrong target—namely, the administration of the university instead of the administration of the United States; second, the teach-in idea had a greater chance of being picked up by other campuses. The militants were not impressed by what their opponents thought was the strongest argument against the moratorium—that it would raise issues entirely irrelevant to the situation in Vietnam. I think that, in the eyes of the militants, *all* issues were relevant—civil rights, the investments of the Chase Manhattan Bank in South Africa, Latin America, and academic freedom.

Consensus was reached on the understanding that, if the Michigan Teach-In were a "success," immediate plans would be made for a National Teach-In in Washington; otherwise, we would "escalate," that is, organize a moratorium. As I recall it, the success of the local teach-in was to be estimated on the basis of response by other campuses. Others, however, have a different recollection. Success was to be nothing short of a cease-fire in Vietnam.

After the change of hours was announced, the university administration extended to us its full cooperation. Four big auditoriums and several classrooms were placed at our disposal. Women students were given permission to stay out all night. The angry legislators were reminded that faculty members could be trusted to use good judgment in deciding the limits of academic freedom. Faculty support mushroomed. We revised our estimates of attendance from 500 to 1000.

At 8:00 P.M. on March 24, 3000 students showed up. About seventy to eighty of these constituted a counterdemonstration. There was also a contingent of some thirty who marched behind a flag . . . and a sign saying "Drop the Bomb."

Such was the opening of what one of our speakers called the Free University of Michigan.

The teach-in brought two innovations to American education. First, it established a genuine rapport between students and a segment of the faculty, thus alleviating, to some extent, the erosion of such rapport in the huge, mass-education institutions. Second, it effected a fusion of scholarly analysis and deep personal concern.

It was an exciting night. Imagine a professor carrying on in traditional classroom manner about, say, the history of Sino-Vietnamese relations; [but now] his class is a mass audience. Imagine a helmeted policeman handing him a note. The professor interrupts the lecture to announce, "I should not think this would happen in the United States, but there has been a bomb threat. We must clear the building."

So there is an improvised mass meeting outdoors in 20° weather (spring comes late to Ann Arbor). After the building is searched, everyone returns, and the "class" continues. Midnight . . . 2:00 A.M. . . . refreshment break . . . the 4:00 to 6:00 A.M. sessions . . . the bleak dawn . . . spontaneous buzz groups . . . the final mass meeting, again outdoors . . . everyone turning to watch the tower clock. 8:00 A.M. "We made it," the last "chairman" announces. The 600 survivors disperse to breakfast, bed, or classes.

The next night, while we were having the "counter teach-in" (the State Department's response was prompt), Columbia had its teach-in. The chain reaction was on: Michigan State, Western Reserve, Buffalo, Chicago, Pennsylvania . . .

The First Teach-In: An Insight into Professional Activism

—MARC PILISUK

At the time of the first teach-in, of which he was an organizer, Professor Pilisuk was on the staff of the Mental Health Research Institute of the University of Michigan. He has since joined the faculty of Purdue University. This article is from The Correspondent, *No. 34 (1965).*

It is interesting to speculate on the reasons why some Vietnamese professors and other professionals have thrown personal comfort to the winds and cast their lot with the National Liberation Front. The reasons may parallel, albeit remotely, the explanations for the recent behavior of American university professors who have discarded their publication and research proposal deadlines in order to engage in the marathon of protests now symbolized by teach-ins.

In both cases the protesters were [spurred on] by their government's sometimes arrogant disdain for just criticism. In both cases the inhumanity of many governmental actions made possible coalitions and conciliations among diverse factions that share only the intensity of their opposition. But perhaps most important was the germ of an idea which permitted the concerned professional to envision himself as the conqueror not of governments but, rather, of his own sense of impotence. This dimly formed vision of self, perhaps more than anything else, links the professor garbed as guerrilla warrior with the professor debating in a marathon teach-in.

On Thursday, March 11, a meeting of University of Michigan faculty members was called by a research psychologist who felt it was time for the Michigan faculty to express itself on Vietnam. Meetings of this type were not new in Ann Arbor. Many of the same faces were present again, veterans of a string of advertisements for the [nuclear] test ban, for a fair housing ordinance, for the election of Lyndon B. Johnson. But the attendance of more than twenty-five persons was somewhat better than usual, reflecting, probably, the outright horror over American bombings of North Vietnam. As people sat packed against the walls of the suburban living room, talk revolved around the usual insurmountable issues: Is a more critical statement with fewer signers more effective than a milder statement with many signers? Should opposition be directed to mass publics or to decision elites?

Lengthy discourse is the gift of the university professor; organizational efficacy is not. Rarely does his analysis include what the professor himself must do, aside from convincing other professors that his analysis is correct. More often, he lapses into an impotent state—away from the lengthy and indecisive meetings, the busywork of phone calls and fund solicitation. An example, par excellence, of the overcommitted professional, he is always a bit behind in his obligations and falls easily into devotion to daily duties. These accentuate his passivity in the face of a foreign policy he can neither stomach nor change.

But the March 11 meeting was not to result simply in a highly articulate frustration. The first breakthrough, a substantive gem, was offered by Bill Gamson, a sociologist, who asserted that the seriousness of this particular situation called for more than a local newspaper advertisement. He suggested that we declare a one-day faculty strike, replacing all normal duties and responsibilities with a special school to teach the concealed story of Vietnam. Almost immediately, fuel was added to this point by others. However, this broadening of the agenda to include activities out of keeping with the conventional professorial role soon aroused anxiety and drew fire. How effective would we be if we isolated ourselves or sabotaged the only legitimacy we carried? Since the arguments over mass public versus governmental elite appeals, and over dramatic versus more isolated actions seemed irreconcilable, we divided the meeting in half, with one group working out the ad petition while the other detailed the work moratorium proposal.

The *sine qua non* for the work moratorium was to obtain signatures from a sufficient number of faculty members to forestall a fizzle. There was some joking about being fired—a majority of the group lacked tenure—as we drew up the committees needed to recruit signers, plan and publicize the program, contact other universities, work with the community, and, finally, raise money.

Some signed before the pressure got rough. Others signed later, in opposition to an unfortunate statement by University President

[Harlan] Hatcher to the effect that we had to have faith in such competent leaders as Robert McNamara. The number reached forty-nine as the Governor and a handful of state legislators shouted for disciplinary action. The faculty senate considered censure but, in the absence of any direct knowledge, first sent a group to find out what was going on.

By Monday only three full professors had signed. Many, especially those who had been working on the ad, found the controversy distasteful and irrelevant to Vietnam. But the second meeting was packed with students as well as faculty, and the dissidents were partly beaten down and partly caught in the rush of organizational needs.

It was amazing that so few people could create such a stir. Probably every one of the original signers felt some pressures. Deans called department chairmen to see that missed classes would be taught. I know of only one case of direct threat of personal consequences, but the common accusation was, "You are hurting the University. Why?"

In daily arguments, we buttressed our resources against the onslaught of criticism. We explained carefully that we planned a work moratorium, not a strike. Participants agreed to make good on all obligations to students. Some offered to request a day's leave of absence. The issue of canceling classes had struck a vital nerve. Professors who constantly missed classes for conferences, speaking engagements, consultation, or personal reasons still would not sign up for the work moratorium. A few, rather ironically, followed their moralisms about responsibility to classes with statements like, "I'll be out of town on that day anyway." It was also interesting to observe how direct was the equation of the well-being of the university with the budget it could wrest from a reluctant legislature.

At this point, some felt that the plan to strike had already served its purpose. Others foresaw widespread support and active participation on a scale never before envisaged. On March 16, a group of those least happy among the signers met to reconsider. It was at this meeting that Marshall Sahlins, an anthropologist, suggested that if the complaints about our not teaching the students were just, then we could stay in our classes and teach them—all night long—about Vietnam. The teach-in was conceived.

Then the Wednesday (March 17) meeting was called. Attendance was absolutely restricted to signers. By 4:00 on the morning of March 18, the moratorium had surrendered to the first all-night teach-in. Its model was protest, not discussion; monologue, not debate. But that handful of signers did not miss their Wednesday classes.

Following this meeting, many students felt betrayed, the faculty felt relieved, and the administration was delighted. President Hatcher now praised those "brilliant young social scientists" who were seeking solutions for today's complex problems. The angry legislators were reminded of the responsibility of faculty judgment. College deans now assisted in getting university space and late permissions for the female students. For one week, a booth at the hub of the campus gave information. Ministers announced the teach-in to their congregations and Women for Peace planned to keep the participants fueled on coffee and doughnuts.

In a truly unprecedented move, the faculty invited themselves to the fraternity and sorority houses and the dorms to let the students know they were needed. Now it was an event, perhaps an historic one, and we took to the telephones and to the media with an air of inflated confidence. We expected to sell the plan at Wisconsin and Berkeley and Columbia. But Flint Junior College and the University of Miami in Coral Gables were not to be outdone. By T-Day, March 24, we knew of thirty-five other teach-ins that were in the works, and these proved to be only a beginning.

Hill Auditorium, the university's largest concert hall, was in other use that night, and even had it been available, no one really would have expected to fill it. So, when 3,500 people presented themselves in the vicinity of four modest-sized lecture halls, the atmosphere resembled Times Square during the rush hour. The opposition, seventy-five student marchers complete with drums and "Drop the Bomb" posters, paraded across the lobby. During the last of three lectures, a bomb threat carried the meeting outdoors into the 20° night.

The heart of the activity was clearly the fifteen or twenty discussion groups, which reached a depth of concern and an intensity of argument rarely seen at universities. One honors student later told me that this was her first educational experience provided by the university during four years' attendance. Another described this as the experience which destroyed the illusion of American omnipotence. Some who had hardly ever spoken in class before argued for an hour in the halls with white-haired full professors. Facts were demanded and assumptions were exposed. On that night, people who really cared talked of things that really mattered.

Following this remarkable episode, the pace seldom slowed. Calls for speakers came in faster than they could be met. Heavy involvement in the Washington lobby, in the proposed student march on Washington, and in securing of an antiwar resolution from the local Democratic Party all followed. By mid-April we were tired. I recall one depressing meeting, in early April, when we assessed our waning faculty participation and the hours we would have available to work on a National Teach-In. Many of us who said, at that time, that ten hours a week would be our new limit of activity were to find ourselves donating ten hours per frantic day as the network of contacts and responsibilities swelled.

What transformed us? For it seems obvious that we are not now wholly the same people we were before the teach-in. As social scientists, many of us had pursued a professional interest in the analysis of problems relating to the conditions of war in underdeveloped nations. Some were area specialists whose knowledge had not been called upon in forming Government plans. Some of the social scientists and philosophers among us believed that the dilemma was not in Vietnam but in the United States and that their knowledge was vital to an understanding of the crisis. But, for all of us, the most interesting aspect of our metamorphosis was the realization that our purely academic work was virtually irrelevant to American policy in Vietnam—unless we chose to make it count.

This heightened sense of responsibility offered a new line of attack on American foreign policy. The question of whether protest ought to be aimed at influencing elites or masses seemed much less important now. We had found a new power in the activation of ourselves beyond the capacities we had previously envisaged. The mistaken fear of tarnishing our credit as unconcerned academics largely evaporated.

Three factors stood out in the transition. The first was the involvement [brought about by] participation. Events moved so fast prior to the National Teach-In that it was well nigh impossible to get an open line on any of the four telephones in our rented office. Students as well as faculty had to make spontaneous decisions in the midst of long-distance phone calls and then answer to the group for the promises they had made to radio stations, to scholars in far off places, to hotel managers, to Government officials. When these commitments fell due, people did the work because it had to be done. However we might rationalize the new role as activists, it is important to note that the activation process moved more from task to task than from decision to decision.

A second factor involved the ineptness of the Government's response. Just as the sheriff's bullwhip helped to increase the number of civil rights demonstrators, so criticism by members of the state legislature helped to recruit new participants for the first teach-in. Dean Rusk's public criticism of many in the intellectual community and McGeorge Bundy's now famous letter to Washington University [St. Louis] provide similar examples [*see Chapter IV*]. The effect of the McCarthy era had been to leave the professional community largely without organization for partisan protest. When the teach-ins occurred, organization grew around specific tasks, a procedure which was hectic and inefficient but extremely productive. The Government, similarly deprived by the McCarthy era of experience in the control of such protest movements, blundered at several points. In forcing us to accept a nonprotest format for the National Teach-In, they helped us gain a hearing in the media. Charges of one-sidedness in the teach-ins were poorly timed, coinciding as they did with the refusal or inability of State Department personnel to accept invitations. These blunders did not enter into the professional scholar's ability to change policy, but they assuredly encouraged the activists to work harder. [*For a discussion on whether the Government did blunder, see Chapter IV, Part 5.*]

The third factor involved the acceptance of our own limitations. We were often unable, for example, to agree on what ought to be done. Accepting this limitation, we worked on tasks which conformed to a range of tastes and preferences. We also came to grips, somewhat, with our inability to run an activity perfectly. Facing this limitation, we were able to view criticisms as details which could be accommodated, rather than as outright obstacles. Many of us became aware that we were no more capable of an unmitigated disaster in our choice of activities than of an absolute success. The only true disaster would have been to do nothing.

We found, moreover, that we could not act effectively without students. Collaboration with students as equal status partners was a heavy price to pay. Students introduced a set of values related to protest action which frequently departed from faculty values. But many of us gained from this forced participation with students, as well as with clergymen, housewives, and faculty members outside of our own disciplines. The price in time and haggling was great, but we became aware that the professional as activist, unlike the professional as scholar, cannot go it alone.

In this sum of effects upon ourselves and upon society lie both the hidden strengths and the amazing changes wrought by the teach-ins.

Protest, Learning, Heckling Spark Viet Rally

—ROGER RAPOPORT

From The Michigan Daily [*University of Michigan
student newspaper*] *of March 26, 1965.*

"Get *The Daily* out of Vietnam, Defoliate the Arb, Deflower the
Thetas, Stop the senseless waste of human beings, Close the Union
Pool."

The sign stood high above a midnight Diag throng at Wednesday night's teach-in. But, aside from the few sarcastic onlookers,
most of the shivering crowd of over 2,000 listened closely to Professor Kenneth Boulding, of the Economics Department, saying,
"The poorest peasant in Vietnam should have as much right as the
richest American. The world has become much too small and
crowded for what we are doing."

The midnight rally was the highlight of the twelve-hour marathon teach-in.

Nearly 3,000 students came to hear one or more of the lectures
or take part in the seminars held in Auditorium A, B, C, and D of
Angell Hall as well as in six Mason Hall classrooms.

"We only expected 500 students," said Professor Arnold Kaufman of the Philosophy Department, one of the 200 faculty members who planned the event.

Women were given all-night permission to attend the teach-in
and, as Jared Stammel, '68, remarked, "This undoubtedly gave a
big stimulus to the event."

By 7:45 P.M., fifteen minutes before the teach-in began, Auditoriums A, B, C, and D of Angell Hall were packed to the walls.

Carl Oglesby [of Students for a Democratic Society], told students that revolutions in nations like Vietnam may be "inspired by
the monied few who exploit their power by universal bureaucratic
corruption, by governmental indifference to the condition of men,
by police-state suppression of honest dissent, by no work and no
wages."

Three bomb scares forced evacuation of Angell Hall and an
early start for the midnight Diag rally. Hecklers abounded in the
crowd. One athlete came dressed in an Alabama football shirt (No.

55). A group of seventy-five students marched through the crowd chanting "Better dead than Red." One sign read, "All the Way with LBJ"—underneath was a huge black bomb.

Nearby, a student said, "This thing isn't fair at all. They aren't presenting the other side. These people want another Munich." One of the faculty leaders quipped to a friend, "That guy is going to enlist tomorrow."

One student remarked, "Just look at who is leading this thing— the philosophy and psychology department. You don't see any political science people here, do you?"

At the back of the crowd a sophomore was parked on a Honda, his girl friend seated behind him. "I'd never really thought very much about this," he said, "but, after tonight, I think we should get out of Vietnam."

A few feet away the Fishbowl was overflowing. Amid the arguing and folksinging students, there were bulletin boards full of clippings on Vietnam, 50-cent buttons asking to "Stop the war in Vietnam," and a protest petition to President Lyndon B. Johnson.

In the midst of the turmoil was a boy collecting money for the United Jewish Appeal.

Many of the students wading through I. F. Stone's rebuttal to the State Department's "white paper" or talking to teachers did not appear to be activists. Many came, it seemed, for curiosity's sake.

In the early morning, seminars were held. The topics were not planned. They were led by students and centered on such issues as student involvement and on alternatives to student policy.

One professor noted that "We are, ourselves, to blame for the Vietnam predicament, for we were silent and did not let our voices be heard."

Ironically, it was Republicans who came to the defense of President Johnson's current Vietnam policy.

Chairman William Gamson, of the Sociology Department, noted that many sign-carrying hecklers "came into our seminars and engaged in intelligent debate. This was our purpose: to promote serious examination of U.S. policy."

Gamson added, "I learned something I should have known— how bright and serious our students are. The closeness between faculty and students was most moving."

Gamson said the faculty committee will send a delegation to Washington, on April 8, 9, and 10 to ask legislative action on Vietnam policy. They also plan to support a march on Washington scheduled for April 17.

One of the teach-in guest lecturers, Arthur Waskow of Washington, commented, "This teach-in is in the true spirit of a university, where students and faculty learn from each other and not from the calendar."

During a 3:00 A.M. coffee break, many of the students relaxed over a game of bridge or informally discussed the night's events. A second set of seminars began at 4:00 A.M.

In Room 433, Mason Hall, more than sixty students took seats, sat on the floor, or craned their necks inside the door to hear Professor Frithjof Bergmann, of the Philosophy Department, speak. Earlier that evening he had said, "We must allow the Vietnamese to be governed by the government they have chosen themselves— the Vietcong."

By 6:00 A.M., 325 students had gathered for the final sessions. One speaker said that the teach-in illustrated a new dimension in education; the barriers between students and teachers had been broken, and both were the better for it.

Toward the end, one student rose and said, "I'm just a lowly freshman, but this teach-in shows me what a university has to be."

Vietnam Comes to Oregon U.

— MITCHEL LEVITAS

Mr. Levitas is a member of the staff of The New York Times Magazine. This article appeared in that publication on May 9, 1965.

Never had the pleasant, placid campus of the University of Oregon been through anything like this. The Erb Memorial Student Union, usually deserted on a Friday night, was jammed with 3,000 standing, sitting, milling people. Raw freshmen argued fearlessly with senior professors. Platoons of "Greeks"—fraternity men—debated with intellectuals they ordinarily ignore as "smokies." "Between choosing one extreme or another," patiently explained a smokie, "there is another alternative—think."

As he spoke, one happily unthinking student waved aloft a sign on which was written nothing at all. A pert coed decorated her sweater with a card that carried the sensible entreaty: "Let's make love, not war." Carefully watching it all from the sidelines—and later in the thick of things—were two Eugene policemen, dressed in plainclothes for the evening.

The occasion was a marathon protest against U.S. policies in Vietnam, and for twelve straight hours nothing else seemed to matter. Finally, after 400 sandwiches, 60 gallons of coffee, 30 speakers, nine "seminars," three folk singers, two poetry recitations, and an edgy interlude of drunken jeering and brief violence punctuated by an exploding firecracker and a flying golf ball that narrowly missed its human target, the evening-till-morning demonstration stumbled to a weary finish. "This has been a great success as a campus event," anthropology professor David F. Aberle, 47, organizer of the meeting, told 250 survivors who stood beneath the cool gray morning sky. "As to its success as an event of national importance, that's a wide open question." . . .

Not for twenty-five years, since the nation and its halls of learning bitterly argued whether or not to intervene against the menace of Nazi Germany, have the campuses echoed to similar organized outcries on a foreign policy issue. . . .

The demonstration at the University of Oregon, on April 23–24, originated with a phone call to Professor Aberle from Marshall Sahlins, an anthropologist at Michigan, who had thought up the "teach-in" idea and who knew Aberle as a former colleague at Ann Arbor.

A slender man with thinning black hair fringed by strands of silver, Aberle feels "uncomfortable" picketing or marching for a cause. He is less concerned with ideology than with facing what he considers his moral and social responsibilities. . . .

Rather than call their protest a teach-in, the Oregon organizers decided at the outset to fly the banner of a "Faculty-Student Committee to Stop the War in Vietnam." "A teach-in," said Professor Lucian Marquis, Director of the university's Honor College, "suggests an immediate grievance, like a civil rights sit-in. To use that concept here, we thought, would be falsifying the situation." "Besides," added Professor George Streisinger, of the Institute of Molecular Biology, "the term suggests a protest against the university administration, which it certainly wasn't."

Oregon's President Arthur S. Flemming, who was Secretary of Health, Education, and Welfare under President Eisenhower, firmly supported the committee's right to protest. Enhancing the university's long-established reputation for protecting academic freedom, Flemming . . . made the Student Union available for the Vietnam demonstration, and, by officially "recognizing" the rally as a university event, he enabled coeds to stay up all night—if they attended (or said they did).

Meanwhile, Aberle's group plunged into the hectic job of signing up supporters, planning the meetings, and finding off-campus speakers. Everyone agreed that Oregon's senior U.S. Senator, Wayne Morse, a vehement critic of United States policy, would be the ideal big gun. The pacificists wanted one of their own, so they got David McReynolds of the War Resisters League. Professor Marquis had heard about Stanley Sheinbaum, an economist at the Center for the Study of Democratic Institutions, who had been on a University of Michigan technical-aid project in Vietnam under the Diem regime, and Sheinbaum agreed to speak. Someone, Aberle doesn't remember who, thought of Robert Scheer, a writer for *Ramparts* magazine, who had recently returned from Vietnam, and Scheer accepted, too.

The line-up was strictly anti-Government, as befits an all-out protest, though among the organizers and sponsors—five departmental chairmen signed up, along with 104 other faculty members and 190 students—opinions ranged all the way from those who thought the U.S. position in Vietnam was blatantly immoral to those who thought it was merely untenable. Within the inner circle, it was more important that the United States had helped obstruct free elections in Vietnam (specified under the Geneva agreements of 1954) than that there had never been free elections in Hanoi; anger over growing U.S. military involvement overshadowed parallel aid from China, the Soviet Union, and North Vietnam; doubts about a future U.S. role in Southeast Asia were louder than fears concerning Red China's aims for the area.

"Believe me," said Aberle, . . . "I'd much rather teach and do research than fight this thing. The kind of publicity I need [comes from] articles in professional journals. But what we have in Vietnam is a schizophrenic situation, a war that is not a war by a government that is not a government. And we refuse to recognize a stable regime in Peking, a stable regime in Hanoi, a stable National Liberation Front. This could lead us into World War III, but we're acting like the man who jumped off the Empire State Building and shouted, as he passed the twenty-fourth floor, 'So far I'm all right.' " . . .

Two groups of students, in particular, decided—at the last minute—to protest the protest demonstration. Paul Medlar, a sophomore pre-med student, initiated a petition urging those who favored the United States staying in Vietnam to show up at the all-night meeting wearing white shirts and blouses; more than 800 signed the petition. At the same time, two earnest freshmen, Bill McCarter and Jim Mead, organized a picketing cadre, thriftily using some signs imported from other campuses where similar opposing forces had already met.

"We disagree strongly with those who want to pull out of Vietnam," said McCarter, a lanky, trim figure in a suit and tie. "But we really respect the atmosphere of their demonstration. If it accomplishes nothing else, it at least will make a lot of people who didn't know or care about Vietnam really think about it. And that's what the democratic spirit is all about."

The democratic spirit overflowed the Erb Memorial Union the night of the rally, despite a light drizzle and threats of heavy rain.

At about 7:15, McCarter's pickets unloaded a pile of signs from the back seat of a yellow Cadillac convertible. There were rumors that some Law School students might show up with a supply of eggs to throw, and that the Greeks would come bearing tomatoes. The messages on the placards seemed to match the mood of uneasy expectation: "Welcome Comrades—Vietcong Headquarters Upstairs," "Reddish Professors Turn Out Yellow Pinks," "Oh Hell, Let's Pull Out—Who Cares About 15,000,000 Vietnamese."

The incoming crowd ignored the marchers, and after circling about for a few minutes, the pickets climbed a wide staircase to the second-floor ballroom. There they quietly took up positions on the fringes of the packed hall, dotted with white shirts and blouses. A thousand people occupied folding chairs on which pamphlets protesting the war in Vietnam had been placed along with the State Department White Paper and an analysis of that document by journalist I. F. Stone, whose credentials include a book accusing the United States of having plotted the Korean War. Outside the hall, hundreds of students stood shoulder to shoulder in the adjacent upper lobby, crowding a table [set up to collect] donations to offset the estimated cost of $1,500 to transport speakers and to pay for janitorial services and mimeographing.

The meeting began promptly at 7:30. In a few words of welcome, Aberle greeted "those who came to protest, those who came to be informed, and those who disagree with us." It was a mild prelude to a series of fiery speeches.

Senator Morse, former Dean of the Oregon Law School, was first up, and stayed up for ninety minutes. If words were bullets, he would have defeated the Administration singlehanded.

Morse gave credit to the teach-ins as the most important single factor behind President Johnson's Baltimore pledge to hold "unconditional discussions" on Vietnam. At the same time, he said that "a return to the Geneva accords is the last slim hope for peace." Otherwise, Morse predicted, "if we keep up our unilateral policy, twelve months from tonight there will be hundreds of thousands of American boys fighting in Southeast Asia—and tens of thousands of them will be coming home in coffins." The crowd leaped to its feet in a standing ovation, while the pickets jiggled their signs in silent disapproval. His speech over, Morse fielded a few hostile questions with ease ("Can we wait until China becomes a nuclear power?" "Why do you say we can't win the war in the air?"), then sat down to another ovation.

Thus primed for more protest, the audience attentively listened while *Ramparts* magazine's Scheer argued that Vietnam is "America's Hungary" because, like the Russians, "we are trying to push our way of life onto a people that want none of it." Economist Sheinbaum, who ought to know, reported that the staff of the Michigan State University aid program in Vietnam was heavily infiltrated with CIA agents. Pacifist McReynolds took the line that President Johnson deceived the voters by switching to a "Goldwater policy" in Vietnam after the [U.S.] election, an opinion widely shared among "teach-in" organizers.

The speeches continued until 12:20 A.M., with the ballroom crowd as large as ever. Meanwhile, on the main floor of the Student Union, a more personal form of education took place as a dozen informal debates were waged in the midst of a jostling mob. One student, carrying a sign that said "Stop Communism in Southeast Asia," was challenged by a social scientist. "Your sign says nothing about methodology," he argued, and the discussion was on.

In the glass-walled Fishbowl, a curved, spacious room with tables and a jukebox, Jim Peterson, a sophomore political science major, sat with pretty, blonde Carol Chislett, a freshman liberal arts student. "A lot of the students here don't know what they're talking about when they argue Vietnam," she said. "I didn't know anything and that's why I came." Added Peterson: "Now *this* is an education. I have no sympathy with the aims of this protest, but it would be a crime to miss it." . . .

Following a thirty-minute break after the main speeches, part of the demonstration was scheduled to move outside for more speeches (brief ones) and folk singing. Instead, it stayed indoors because of the threat of rain, the fear that students might drift away in the open air, and the belief that possible trouble from rowdy students would be easier to control in the ballroom. Trouble did erupt, but it was not easy to control.

Standing in the rear of the hall were about 100 students, many of whom had used the recess as a cocktail hour. No sooner did the speeches begin than heckling, jeering, and catcalls drowned them out. One speaker who had a German accent was interrupted by cries of "Heil!" Another, who was perfectly audible, was stopped by shouts of "We can't hear you."

The uglies were confronted by sweating Dean of Students Donald M. DuShane, who tried to mollify them. The hecklers laughed and went on booing. When a policeman tried to eject a blond youngster, his companions grabbed the youth by the arm and yelled, "You got free speech, man. Stand up for your rights." Instead, the kid defiantly went limp, telling the policeman, "I'm a juvenile. You better not hit me." Finally, in a desperate maneuver, the folk singers came on to quell the outburst. As they began to sing "Over Jordan," the cry went up "The Vietcong want to cross the Mekong."

After forty tense minutes, the atmosphere simmered down. The hecklers departed, and the speakers went on as before, denouncing the United States for "the most immoral actions it has ever taken," pleading for the recognition of Red China, and arguing that, like the French in Algeria, the United States would win the world's respect by pulling out of Vietnam "with no loss of face." "All this nauseates me," said Steve Munson, former president of the campus Young Republican Club.

If the early part of the formal program was only loosely "educational," the hours from 3:00 A.M. until dawn more fully redeemed its pedagogic aims. After another break for coffee and sandwiches, the participants [dispersed among] nine seminars. There, looking remarkably alert, they quietly argued various aspects of the Vietnam conflict: Was the "domino theory" a plausible forecast of eventual U.S. defeat in all Southeast Asia? Could the United Nations help to end the war? How relevant was the breakup of monolithic Communism?

Most seminars were led by sponsors of the protest, but they made no effort to control the discussion. "You can't duplicate this in a classroom," said Chuck Webster, a freshman. "I've learned an awful lot." Sophomore Jane Isaacs was amazed by the "frat types" who stayed to disagree. "There are 500 people in those seminars—and this is Oregon!" she exclaimed.

As the sun rose over Eugene, 250 sleepy souls trudged back to the ballroom to conduct the penultimate part of the program: hearing reports from the seminar leaders and voting on a "policy proposal" that summed up the night's work. The resolution preserved the polemic tone of the opening speeches. The United

States was condemned for military actions "not directed toward the welfare of the people of Vietnam," for its "unilateral intervention," and for "willfully misrepresenting the facts concerning the war."

As for proposals, the document demanded an immediate ceasefire, U.S. abandonment of its "policy of containment and confrontation of Communism for an active policy of coexistence based on extensive economic aid . . . ," and the convening of an international conference, including the National Liberation Front, to supervise "free elections in North and South Vietnam." The resolution passed, 233 or 234 (the bleary tellers couldn't be sure) to 9. With that, the group adjourned for another outdoor rally "to show our strength," as Aberle said, wearily. A few more remarks by students, faculty, and two members of the clergy, and the protest at Oregon was over.

But not forgotten. At the tables in the Fishbowl, in the wooden booths at Maxie's, a local beer joint, and through the hi-fi at the New World coffee house, the debate over Vietnam continued the next day. They were even talking about it at the Paddock, a dimly lit, upholstered watering place favored by the Greeks. "I know my parents are for the United States staying," said pretty Barbara Kimball as she eyed a pizza, "but the demonstration pretty well convinced me that we ought to go."

Though the speeches at some teach-ins may often be more shallow than profound, and the atmosphere perhaps more propagandistic than scholarly, the roots of protest are nurtured by legitimate longings.

One is the desire among academics for clarity—and Vietnam is an issue riddled by moral and intellectual contradictions. Another desire stems from the larger battlefield of the Cold War—the fear that [despite] the nuclear test ban agreement, Goldwater's defeat, and President Johnson's promises, the chance for a "reconciliation" with Moscow seems to be slipping away: according to this reading of events, bitter disappointment has bred angry discontent.

Then there is the question of the democratic process itself. Oregon's Aberle may be swayed by enthusiasm when he proclaims "a new form of citizen communication." But President Flemming is undoubtedly correct when he says that, regardless of whether the communicants are right or wrong, "If we don't have this kind of discussion and debate, if we don't encourage the trend of getting people involved, then our form of government is in trouble." . . .

No one among the protest leaders at Oregon claimed to represent a majority of faculty or student opinion. Many who attended the rally simply were curious or, like their elders, concerned and perhaps confused. Among those in the crowd who were undecided about the wisdom of U.S. policy in Vietnam, undoubtedly more people became critics than supporters, scarcely surprising after hearing twelve hours of mostly one-sided discussion.

Yet the real significance of the teach-ins lies deeper. They are catalysts, not only for the conversion of ideas, but for the dispersion of ideas. And when interest replaces apathy, the growth of a meaningful consensus will take care of itself.

The Teach-In: New Forum for Reason

— WEBSTER SCHOTT

Mr. Schott is literary editor of Focus/Midwest. *The following is from* The Nation *of May 31, 1965.*

Lyndon B. Johnson has lost the academic intellectuals and is in serious trouble with the student generation of voters.

Affiliated with the National Teach-In at Washington that failed to produce McGeorge Bundy [*see Chapter IV*], some 100 teach-ins were held at colleges and universities across the country on May 15. At Washington University in St. Louis, the teach-in began at 1:00 P.M. with a radio-telephone hookup to the Washington debate; it ended the next morning at 1:30. Professors and students then swept up cigarette butts, paper plates, leftover French fries, and rearranged chairs and tables for breakfast in Wohl Student Center cafeteria. . . .

Academia was to be seen in profile: beatle haircuts and beards; barefoot girls with elbow-length hair and Daisy Mae shorts; little old ladies in hairnets; professors pulling on their pipes; a man in overalls; middle-aged "adult education" women who might have been on their way to the A & P; and, outside Wohl, the inevitable baby carriages. Although Plato was invoked later in the day, only the Greeks stayed home: I saw just one fraternity pin. . . .

Everything except the sandwiches, Cokes, and smoke changed when the "live" teach-in started late Saturday afternoon. Ideas took on vitality because they came from identifiable personalities.

Faculty and students from Washington University, St. Louis University, Flat River Junior College, the University of Missouri at St. Louis, Maryville College, Eden Theological Seminary, and elsewhere delivered papers, made extemporaneous speeches, questioned and answered from the floor as the rotating panel rolled through the night. The interplay among panelists, faculty, and students revealed the teach-in as more than a phenomenon of protest and dissent. Could it become a permanent new technique of interdisciplinary education or a means of achieving a consensus of intellectuals on issues of national concern?

By the time the teach-in had taught itself out, approximately thirty panelists (some unscheduled and improvising hastily) and perhaps 100 five-minute speakers from the audience had discussed the State Department White Paper on Vietnam, national liberation movements in America and Asia, the Vietcong, Leninism, U.S. intervention in the Dominican Republic, Maoism, international law, the bankruptcy of liberal ideology, the Monroe Doctrine, Madison Avenue, civil rights, racism, capital punishment, Austria and Czechoslovakia, the French underground in World War II, social democracy and capitalism, Algeria, Walter Lippmann and James Reston, creeping involvement, managed news, Mussolini and Ethiopia, the nationalization of British industry, the student-professor relationship, dominoes and checkers, salami and baloney. I took sixty-one pages of notes and the only topic conspicuously absent was sex.

There were no good guys or bad guys during the live teach-in. Continually changing, as some 2,000 students came and went for eight hours, the audience of 500 to 600 responded unpredictably. Both defenders and opponents of the Government's foreign policy found support. The only speakers left hanging on threads of applause were those who lacked facts, took vague positions, or droned abstractions. Around midnight, Robert Buckhout, Assistant Professor of Psychology, asked whether someone didn't want to heckle, and someone did. Students came to the teach-in because they wanted to know.

The largest ovation of the day or night followed a long, detailed account of Indochinese social and political history by Jesuit Father Francis Corley, Professor of Asian Studies at St. Louis University. Students took notes on French colonialism, Bao Dai, the Geneva accords of 1954, the Diem family government, changes in Vietnamese regimes, the formation of the National Liberation Front, and the Vietcong. Father Corley called the last "both a gamble and a wonderful opportunity for the Communist Party of North

Vietnam." The enthusiasm for this painstaking presentation supported a point made at the start of the teach-in by Dr. Bernard Baumrin, Associate Professor of Philosophy and one of the teach-in organizers.

"There is nothing improper in what we are doing here," he said. "We are just covering up for, or updating a poorly designed curriculum. We forgot to have courses on Southeast Asian politics in the curriculum this year. The academic community failed in Germany during the 1930's. We are not going to let it happen here."

The audience and speakers wanted a discussion of foreign policy in Vietnam—and anything else entering their heads—not an old-fashioned revival meeting to convert the State Department. But tar and feathers were more or less always at hand.

Baumrin went on: "The United States is engaged in aggression against North Vietnam. Twenty years of economic improvement in North Vietnam is being wiped out while we talk. . . . Our whole policy of anti-Communism is clichés, not principles. (Applause.) The Administration has convinced itself that clichés *are* principles. . . . It's the principles, not the facts, which are the issue, even assuming the Administration has all the facts. . . . The right of open inquiry is a principle, not a cliché. . . ."

Successive academicians probed, attacked, and illuminated. The audience listened, applauded, ate, and lined up for questions. There was no typical speech. They ranged through history and, it seemed, through eternity. . . .

The professors argued. Richard Yang, an Associate Professor of Asian Studies, who sounded as though he had been flown in from Formosa especially for the occasion, demanded that the United States behave like a real tiger and stop the Communists. Stanley Spector, Yang's chief at Washington University, insisted otherwise. "Since 1949, we've pursued a vicious policy toward China. We've frustrated her industrialization, tried to consign the Chinese to oblivion in our imagination, if not in reality . . . and our omniscient President knows that China's goal is all of Asia despite the fact there's not a single Chinese soldier outside of China tonight. . . . What we fear about China is that the Chinese may have American responses. With American forces so near, they may become trigger-happy." China wants and must have neutral buffer states, he said.

Apparently, there is at least a little exoticism built into every teach-in. The casual decorum and rationality at Wohl Center (no folk singers, dancing, or fights) broke down as we approached early morning. Suddenly, at the speakers' table, there appeared a heavy-set young man wearing blue jeans, a T-shirt, and a Turgenev beard. A member of the Student Peace Association, he confessed over the public-address system that he had loved his country when he came to the university. But, since then, he had discovered that his mother was America, his father was Batista, and he himself was Fidel Castro. A few minutes later, Art Fillmore, a free-lance photographer and World War II bomber pilot recently returned from making a USIA film on the war in South Vietnam, unexpectedly moved onto the program. "I haven't heard a single suggestion tonight about what to do in Vietnam," Fillmore said with the look and stance of Gary Cooper. He said he had lost respect for Dr. Spector and all the speakers. "I've been anti-Government for twenty-five years. Our Government double-crossed me in World War II, and I don't trust them. . . ." Talk about U.S. withdrawal is "stupid because it's unrealistic," he said. The buzz of the crowd stopped. Someone dropped a glass. "I don't want to see any more Vietnamese killed; I've seen too many of them killed and dying. I love those people. . . . I am opposed to the war, too, but I don't know how else we're going to stop it except by the course we're following now." Professor R. Gene Burns leaped up to tell Fillmore his speech was "the least pertinent of any we have heard today." And Dr. Spector defended the whole teach-in idea: "I cannot imagine that you find this a humorous exercise. I, too, have seen friends die at the hands of Communists—in Malaya—but I do not believe it is just for this nation to be put repeatedly in positions where we must kill or be killed."

After these two brief emotional breakthroughs, I expected the spontaneity of group therapy to take over. But no. Resuming that academic tone, James O'Connor, who teaches economics at the university, described the failure of liberalism to provide an ideology to deal with change. The product of the urban middle class, liberalism has no relevance to the cultures of Southeast Asia, he said. A student wanted to know whether the academic community didn't have to reach the public to influence the Government? Yes, he was told by Baumrin, and this meeting, tied to a hundred others, was the way to do it.

Waiting for a cab in the cool St. Louis morning and listening to the students outside Wohl Center buttonhole the professors for still more words, I wondered whether the assorted pieces of the teach-in made a logical whole.

The Washington University Teach-In typified the national exodus of intellectuals from the Johnson camp. Among the real movers of the St. Louis teach-in—Buckhout, Baumrin, William Long

(Instructor in English), Peter Gaspar (Assistant Professor of Chemistry), Daniel Bolef (Professor of Physics), Barry Commoner (Chairman of the Botany Department)—were several who had organized the highly effective Missouri Scientists, Engineers, and Physicians for Johnson and Humphrey during the last election. For intellectuals, it had been a bad choice from the start—Lyndon Johnson or Barry Goldwater. To find Johnson fulfilling Goldwater's foreign-policy campaign promises seven months later is, as Dr. Gaspar said, "simply unbearable."

To make matters worse, the aides held over by Johnson from the Kennedy Administration appear to have sold out. The intellectual stronghold in the White House slipped to a toehold after November; now it's nonoperational. Adlai Stevenson defends the presence of 30,000 American Marines and soldiers in Santo Domingo. . . .

There are other frustrations. Buckhout and Baumrin got a Vietcong propaganda film, *Heroic South Vietnam*, from Boston University's May Second Committee and showed it, along with a film of Wayne Morse speaking at Yale, in an adjoining room during the teach-in. But the law prevented their showing a USIA propaganda film to balance the Vietcong harangue. USIA pictures cannot be shown in the United States.

Leadership of the teach-in at Washington University came from two groups: young professors and graduate assistants in physical and social sciences and the humanities; and older professors in the physical sciences. No one on the Washington University Law Faculty or in the Political Science Department signed the *ad hoc* Committee's letter [*to McGeorge Bundy; see Chapter IV*]. No one from the Political Science Department appeared as a speaker or panelist, though political scientists came from other schools.

Physical science leadership in the teach-in movement is evident everywhere. Gray Dorsey, Nagel Professor of Jurisprudence and International Law, says the physical scientists are troubled because they see the United States using force, a method they are not acquainted with as a means of achieving goals in international affairs. Furthermore, they are "reacting against the value aridity of methodology; until just recently you could be scientific only if you eliminated subjectivity." To some extent Dr. Bolef agrees. A former research physicist for Westinghouse, he says the atomic bomb put scientists into international affairs. More important, they can lead attacks on government foreign policy because their research grants are not made by federal agencies responsive to State Department pressure. Political science grants are.

Students who question our foreign policy are coming from the same social-action groups that have participated in civil rights demonstrations. Ronald Landsberg, the student who ran the projector for the Vietcong-Wayne Morse films, is active in SNCC. A busload of Washington University students went to Selma. On May 17 and 18, Landsberg's Student Speaker's Forum brought Claude Lightfoot, an American Negro Communist, to the campus for two days of debates. The teach-in carries a fervor, a grind, a provocation, and even a name derived from the civil rights movement. But the teach-in is different. This revolt against the existing power structure in the United States must have faculty leadership, organization, and participation. The physical requirements demand at least tacit administration approval. Thomas H. Eliot, Chancellor of Washington University, who rose to his post from the Political Science Department, was unavailable for comment on the teach-in. On several other occasions, however, he has defended academic freedom. The provost, George E. Pake, declined to comment on the teach-in directly, saying the university was neither for nor against it. However, he did say that "the university is in favor of anything which brings about a free and open discussion of national issues."

Several issues were resolved at the Washington University Teach-In. No one except Professor Yang wanted the war in Vietnam expanded; everyone else agreed the only solution was negotiation. A dozen other issues were clarified, including the *ad hoc* committee's original bone with McGeorge Bundy: "Members of the academic community called into Government service *as* academicians continue to have a responsibility to the principles of scholarly discourse: free and open debate, and principles which underline decisions." [*See Chapter IV.*]

Buckhout, Baumrin, Long, and the scientists stuck to this position. Theodore Von Laue, Professor of History, Earl Reeves, Professor of Political Science [University of Missouri at St. Louis], Dorsey, and Spector said otherwise. Highly critical of the State Department, Spector told me he had thought the letter "ill advised" but had signed it anyhow. Dorsey said that Bundy is responsible to the President and the President is responsible to the people. Von Laue said it was irresponsible for Baumrin to say that Bundy has pursued "an insane policy." And Baumrin replied, that, since Bundy could give no reasons for our Vietnam policy, it had to be irrational.

Thinking over the talkathon the next day, Buckhout was satisfied with the way it went. "I was especially pleased for the university," he said. There was "a level of involvement on the part of students and teachers I've never seen happen here before. . . . The students at Washington University listened to a balanced presentation. I was pleased by the contrast with other teach-ins; ours didn't become an anti-Government diatribe." The only thing that would have made it more instructive, he said, would have been the presence of people from the State Department. "For three weeks they sat on our request. The day before we began, they said they couldn't fill it because of the Washington [National] Teach-In."

Almost young enough to be a student himself, Buckhout is right. The campus Indians are restless on the plains. Someone should tell Lyndon Johnson to send more scouts out to talk with them. By letting them talk to themselves, he makes a mistake that may cost him dear. The country is eavesdropping.

The Teach-In at the University of California (Berkeley): A Refusal to Attend

—ROBERT A. SCALAPINO

Dr. Scalapino is Professor of Political Science at Berkeley.

The May 21 meeting on the Berkeley campus is symbolic of the new anti-intellectualism that is gaining strength today.

A few individuals, most of whom would not dream of treating their own disciplines in this cavalier fashion, have sponsored a rigged meeting in which various ideologies and entertainers are going to enlighten us on Vietnam.

Only a handful of the performers have ever been to Vietnam or made any serious study of its problems. The objective is propaganda, not knowledge.

To lend some respectability to the performance, the organizers sought to give a few of us "guerrilla" status in the show.

They urged us to appear, with ratios of up to 8 to 1 against us, and with our opponents being such individuals as the editor of the *National Guardian*, the international secretary of the Du Bois Clubs, the Mime Troupe, and assorted jazz singers.

Can we be blamed if we did not want to lend our names and reputations to that effort?

This travesty should be repudiated by all true scholars irrespec-

tive of their views on Vietnam. It can only damage the reputation
of Berkeley as an institution of higher learning.

Reply to Professor Scalapino

— MORRIS HIRSCH, STEPHEN SMALE,
AND JERRY RUBIN

*Professors Hirsch and Smale teach mathematics at
Berkeley; Jerry Rubin is a graduate student there.
Professor Smale and Mr. Rubin were co-chairmen of
the Berkeley Vietnam Day Committee, which, after
organizing the Berkeley Teach-In, continued to coordinate local activities in opposition to the war.*

Professor Scalapino, in slandering the organizers and speakers of
Vietnam Day, to be held Friday and Saturday on the Berkeley
Campus, has confused the purpose of the meeting to such an extent
that one must consider it deliberate.

The purpose of Vietnam Day is to present to the Bay Area Community alternatives to current U.S. policy. The information and
ideas that will be related on these days cannot be found in the mass
media, the State Department White Paper, or even in university
classrooms. We are contributing to democratic dialogue by expressing the views which, although widespread in Asia and Europe, are
rarely presented to American people. Professor Scalapino calls such
an objective "propaganda."

Professor Scalapino has implied that the only people who are
qualified to discuss Vietnam in public are academic or State Department experts on Vietnam. We do have such technical experts
on the program: Professor Stanley Sheinbaum, who designed the
strategic-hamlet program for the Government, but now regrets it,
is one example. But to restrict public discussion to "experts" leads
to a dangerous elitism because, in the end, decisions on foreign
policy are based on value judgments, not just on a simple recording of facts. The issues in Vietnam are too important to be settled
by Cold War gamesmanship or academic hairsplitting. One of the
purposes of Vietnam Day is to transfer the discussion from The
RAND Corporation to the streets.

But, more important than this, the problem of Vietnam is the problem of the soul of America. What the State Department is doing in our name in Vietnam is tied directly to Alabama, the Dominican Republic, the state of freedom of the press in America, and the scope of our literature. We think that people like Bob Parris, of the Student Nonviolent Coordinating Committee, Norman Mailer, and Dr. Benjamin Spock have much to say that is relevant to Vietnam.

Professor Scalapino makes much of the fact that we have included entertainers in the program. Had he bothered, he would have counted less than three hours of entertainment scattered throughout the main program. He conveniently juxtaposes speakers and entertainers and calls them all "performers." Which of our speakers does Professor Scalapino consider entertainers or performers? Senator Gruening? Isaac Deutscher, world-renowned writer on the Soviet Union? Bertrand Russell? Ruben Brache, the representative of the Dominican rebels in the United States? Professor Marvin, Chairman of the International Relations Department, San Francisco State College? Bui Van Anh, Counselor of the Vietnamese Embassy in Washington?

We offered Professor Scalapino and Professor [Eugene] Burdick, who attacked us yesterday, as much time as they wanted at any hour. If they fear the public will be misinformed, they do the public a great disservice by attacking the meeting instead of participating in it as others who support the State Department are doing.

They refuse to take part because they fear four aspects of the meeting:

1. Vietnam Day is giving a platform to intellectuals who are not favored by the State Department, as Professor Scalapino is, but who, nevertheless, have much to say about Vietnam: people like Robert Scheer, Staughton Lynd, Dave Dellinger, M. S. Arnoni, Edward Keating, and Felix Greene.

2. The meeting goes beyond the narrow definition of an academic expert and challenges the authority of professors Scalapino and Burdick.

3. The meeting will spread some dangerous ideas to masses of people.

4. The protest movement against the war is successful and is spreading.

One week the State Department, well aware of the nature of the program, promises to send speakers. The next week they back out, giving as an excuse "lack of balance," thereby helping to create the very imbalance they say they oppose. Why are professors Scalapino and Burdick and the State Department afraid to take the best time in our program and face an audience which has just heard fresh and unconventional ideas on Vietnam? Are they afraid that in this atmosphere their clichés, apologies, and academic excuses for injustice will be exposed?

12,000 at UC Teach-In on Vietnam

—ROBERT RANDOLPH

Mr. Randolph is a graduate student at Berkeley. This report appeared in the National Guardian, May 29, 1965. *Excerpts from the Berkeley Teach-In can be heard in the recording* Berkeley Teach-In: Vietnam, *edited by Louis Menashe, Folkways Records (FD 5765). Complete texts of the major addresses appear in the volume* We Accuse *(Berkeley, 1965).*

Speaker after speaker excoriated American policy at the massive Vietnam protest teach-in of May 21–22 on the campus of the University of California. Crowds, ranging up to 12,000 during the thirty-five-hour marathon, heard U.S. military operations in Vietnam attacked as "genocide" against a people seeking their own determination and as a cynical, brutal betrayal of the American heritage—a betrayal which has become obvious, as novelist Norman Mailer put it, to nations "bound to us by the depth of their hatred for us."

As originally planned, the teach-in was to be a dialogue between supporters of the Government's policies, led by representatives of the State Department, and nationally known critics of U.S. intervention in Vietnam coming from all sectors of the intellectual community. But, since the State Department decided not to participate in the program, and pro-Administration UC faculty members Eugene Burdick and Robert Scalapino "finked out" (as it was expressed here), the rally lost much of its dialogue quality. Empty chairs with a sign reading "Reserved for State Dept.," were placed on the platform, making it apparent to thousands present that the Government and its supporters were not interested in a basic dialogue on foreign policy except under carefully controlled conditions. Even spokesmen of the South Vietnamese Embassy in Washington withdrew, after originally agreeing to appear.

When the program opened at noon on May 21, gray skies threatened trouble for the thousands gathering in the open, but by the next afternoon the sky was sunny. It was a Chautauqua in the best tradition of democratic deliberation. Marxist historian Isaac Deutscher, who was one of the speakers, described the meeting as a sign of "the awakening of the critical spirit in America." Deutscher said later, "This is the most exciting speaking engagement I have had since I spoke to the Polish workers thirty years ago. It is extraordinary—simply extraordinary."

Speakers included the whole spectrum of criticism from Democratic Senator Ernest Gruening of Alaska, Dr. Benjamin Spock, Chairman of SANE, and Norman Thomas to spokesmen for radical and revolutionary student movements.

Gruening characterized the domino theory of Communist takeovers in Southeast Asia as "utter rubbish," to which Mailer added that a lot of the dominos had already fallen out of the U.S. domain anyway—such as Cambodia, Indonesia, and Burma, with its refusal to allow U.S. military staging operations within its borders. I. F. Stone said that "all of this miasma about wars of liberation is a reflection of the military establishment looking for work to do. . . . We don't want a democratic government in South Vietnam—we want a military base."

Other speakers included California Assemblyman Willie Brown; William Stanton and John Burton; editors Dave Dellinger of *Liberation*, James Aronson of the *National Guardian*, Paul Krassner of *The Realist*, M. S. Arnoni of *Minority of One*, Edward Keating of *Ramparts*, and Hal Draper of *New Politics*. Faculty participants included Professor Staughton Lynd of Yale, Gerald Berreman, Chairman of the UC Anthropology Department, and Aaron Wildavsky of UC, who supported U.S. policy in a debate with Robert Scheer [a writer for *Ramparts* magazine]. Others among the thirty-five or so speakers included Levi Laub of the Progressive Labor Movement; Si Casady, of the California Democratic Council; George Clark, of the British Committee on Nuclear Disarmament; Robert Pickus, of Turn Toward Peace (who supported U.S. military withdrawal only if tied to later political settlement); Bob Parris, SNCC leader; Jack Barnes, National Chairman of the YSA [Young Socialist Alliance]; Mario Savio, UC FSM [Free Speech Movement] leader; Paul Potter, president of Students for a Democratic Society; and Mike Meyerson, national head of the Du Bois Clubs of America.

Laub called for a greater recognition that the events of Vietnam were the inevitable consequences of the American system driven to imperialist penetration around the globe. Potter asked: "What kind of system is it that allows good and decent men to tolerate the deaths of tens of thousands of men, as in Vietnam? We must name that system; we must analyze that system; and we must control it, or it will destroy us. How do you stop the war if its roots are deep in the American system?"

Expressed many times was the question, "Where do we go from here?" Alan Meyerson, director of the participating San Francisco satirical theater group, said, "I can't sit and listen to debates all the time—so I'm going to sit-in with the group next month at the Oakland Army Terminal." (Large amounts of military hardware go to Vietnam through this depot.) Lynd said, "We're beginning to turn our thoughts toward action." He made the following action proposals: (1) Call for the retirement from office of the present Administration. (2) Burn draft cards. (3) Refuse to pay income taxes. (4) Establish a speak-in in the lobby of the Pentagon. (5) Set up in Washington a citizens "war crimes commission," made up of international religious and civil rights leaders, to review American crimes in Vietnam. At the end of Lynd's speech, the audience of 10,000 gave him an ovation. [*Professor Lynd's Berkeley address appears in Chapter II.*]

A climactic moment during the thirty-five-hour span occurred at 1:30 A.M. at the conclusion of Deutscher's address, in which he called for recognition of the role of the class struggle and declared that world peace was possible only with world socialism. His eighty-minute speech, delivered in the chill midnight hours to almost 12,000 people, was a penetrating analysis of the whole Cold War. He asserted that the "West is sick with the myths and distortions of the Cold War." The deafening ovation given him indicated that the policy of anti-Communism had lost its magic and that radical alternatives at last could be heard—at least on the campuses. Deutscher described the indicated U.S. desire to bomb China's nuclear facilities as a piece of "incredible, fathomless arrogance that future historians will see as an example of the degeneration of the human mind."

Bertrand Russell, British peace leader, sent a taped message to the teach-in.

The two-day meeting had its lighter side, with the wit of Dick Gregory and Paul Krassner, the satirical skits of The Committee, the topical songs of Phil Ochs and Malvina Reynolds, and the blues and folk music of Barbara Dane. Jerry Rubin, a co-chairman and originator of the event, said it furnished fun, politics, and ideas together, as an antidote to the vulgarized main culture of the society around it.

During the hours before dawn, numerous films were shown, including *Ballad of a Soldier* and CBS's film on Vietnam, *It's a Mad, Mad War*. Workshops were set up throughout the daylight and evening hours in the university's adjoining Harmon Gymnasium. They were conducted by leaders from civil rights and other groups.

Other speakers included Felix Greene, the China expert; Isadore Zifferstein, Los Angeles psychiatrist, who spoke on the psychological hazards of becoming used to bombings as part of daily life; and Stanley Sheinbaum of the Center for the Study of Democratic Institutions. U.S. involvement in the Dominican Republic was criticized scathingly by Paul Jacobs, labor journalist, James Petras, UC graduate student, and I. F. Stone in the second of his two appearances. After both of Stone's speeches, he received standing ovations, as did many of the others.

A telephone message was broadcast to the meeting from Ruben Brache, special ambassador to the U.N. from the Dominican rebels. The student movement of Japan, the Zengakuren, carried out supporting demonstrations throughout Japan to coincide with the Berkeley teach-in.

Rubin said the idea of the teach-in was broached in a conversation between himself and a friend about a month ago, and step by step it gathered momentum. After most of the program was arranged, they approached the university administration to notify it they were holding the teach-in on campus without the usual permits, and the administration told them to go ahead. Rubin said, "At the first planning meeting we called, four people showed up. We didn't have any workers, we didn't belong to any organizations. But interest developed at such a rate that at our second meeting there were eighty people. In the end, we had the sponsorship of two American Federation of Teachers [AFT] locals on campus and of the Faculty Peace Committee." He added: "The $11,000 we spent has just about been covered by donations from individuals and from the collections during the meeting."

Around the meeting area, a dozen tables were covered with the literature of as many organizations. Banners everywhere on the nearby university buildings decried the U.S. intervention in Vietnam and the Dominican Republic. The AFT sponsors set up, in the Sather Gate area, large pictures of dead and dying National Liberation Front guerrillas, scenes of government torture, and a photo of government personnel carrying heads of guerrilla leaders. Hundreds of students studied them closely and silently.

Coverage by the local press was spotty. The tone of some papers was that it was a big festival of sunbathers eating hotdogs, drinking Coca-Cola, and sleeping through speeches. The San Francisco *Examiner* ran a May 22 article headed "The 'Camp' Meeting at Cal," and, although 10,000 people listened to outstanding speakers until the 11:00 P.M. ending on May 22, there was not a word of it in the May 23 edition.

Hudson Valley Teach-In on Vietnam

— CHARLES AUSTIN

This report, on the teach-in at Marist College, by Charles Austin, of the Evangelical Lutheran Church of the Redeemer, Kingston, New York appeared in The Christian Century, *April 20, 1966.*

The first teach-in debate on Vietnam in New York's Hudson valley was sponsored by Marist College at Poughkeepsie on March 22. At a time when the academic freedom of some Roman Catholic schools is being questioned, it is notable that the teach-in, organized by an *ad hoc* student-faculty committee headed by Professor Oswald LeWinter and William Morrissey, a senior, almost at once received the blessings of the administration of the 1,000-student men's college operated by the Marist order of teaching brothers.

It is also notable that on short notice the teach-in was able to snare some of the most in-demand commentators on the Vietnam war: Fr. Daniel Berrigan, S.J.; Professor Staughton Lynd of Yale; Ambassador Henry Cabot Lodge; and the Rev. A. J. Muste, Secretary Emeritus of the Fellowship of Reconciliation. Among the other speakers were John M. Murphy and Joseph Y. Resnick, New York congressmen; General Bernard Yoh, a former adviser in Vietnam; James Rosenthal, former adviser to the U.S. aid mission in Vietnam; and Charles Wiley, free-lance war correspondent.

In his address, Ambassador Lodge advocated "defeating the military might of North Vietnam" through use of air power against all military targets in the north, mining of Haiphong harbor, and a blockade by the U.S. Seventh Fleet. Lodge's speech gave the day a vigorous beginning; he condemned peace demonstrators as "war demonstrators, because they make our enemies feel that we don't mean it when we say that we will not stand for aggression."

A highlight of the day was a debate in which Professor Lynd and Fr. Berrigan clashed with congressmen Murphy and Resnick. The soft-spoken Yale professor criticized President Johnson's peace offensive as a "public relations campaign." He noted that during the peace offensive there was no contact with the National Liberation Front, that during the bombing pause the ground war was escalated, and that the United States failed to respond to an apparent military slowdown in North Vietnam. Basing his remarks on observations made during his recent, controversial trip to North Vietnam, Professor Lynd said he feels that there is a desire to negotiate on the part of the North Vietnamese. "The U.S. has injected itself into what was essentially an internal rebellion," he said. "This is contrary to the policy of nonintervention in internal affairs of foreign nations."

The congressmen, both with military backgrounds (Murphy is a West Point graduate and a decorated Korean veteran; Resnick served in Italy in World War II), backed the war and President Johnson's policy. Resnick insisted that the morality of the war lies in consideration of our national interest. "We have decided that the Vietnam war is in our national interest," he said. "There comes a time when debate must end and we must all unite behind our Commander-in-Chief."

Fr. Berrigan criticized both congressmen for failing to keep open the alternatives to military escalation. "The American vocation is the international revelation of hope; we must consider every means of giving to others hope for peace in the world," he said. He termed the war "unhistorical in timing," quoting the papal declaration *Pacem in Terris*, which notes that war as a redress of grievance is absurd. He added that, since "the great goods of the world are being corrupted," the war is "against the people in its methods." He pointed out that other nations are not backing the U.S. action and declared that we have been distracted from the real issues of the conflict. . . .

Later in the day, the nearly 2,000 students, faculty members, clergy, and guests heard octogenarian Muste declare that the great problem is "the imprisonment of all of us in the militarism of the past." The great need, he said, is for a change in the psychological make-up of people that leads them to believe that the eternal conflict between "they" and "us" must be settled by military means. "The U.S. has not so much chosen evil as it has let itself be blind to the alternatives," he said. "We now have the faculty and perhaps the inspiration to abandon the course of the past and begin something new." The dignified pacifist emphasized his personal loyalty to the United States, noting that this loyalty does not remove his responsibility to indict his country for aggressive action.

Since the motive of the teach-in was education, a debate format was followed throughout. As one student commented, "We want to show what can be done by a small, Catholic, liberal arts college when students and faculty are concerned about what is happening in our world." In obtaining speakers representing the whole spectrum of opinion on the Vietnam war, the college was able to consider the moral, religious, political, and social aspects of the war. Many Hudson valley residents took notice of the Vietnam debate for the first time. And that the discussion took place on a Catholic college campus, with clergy attending and participating, was a witness to the renewal of the Church in this century.

New York University Teach-In

Statement of Ad Hoc Committee for a Teach-In on Vietnam, April 15, 1965.

April 15, 1965

James Reston wrote, "The first casualty in every shooting war is common sense, and the second is open and free discussion." As teachers and citizens, we are deeply concerned both with the implications of our present military actions in Vietnam and with the relative absence of information, debate, and public discussion of the reasons for our involvement there. Our teach-in of April 14, 1965, grows out of these concerns.

We seek to generate discussions based upon the best available information. We do this in the belief that this is one way in which the academic community can best carry out its responsibility for providing students with an informed basis for their opinions and actions on major issues.

Many topics and views were presented in our teach-in. The speakers were selected on the basis of their area of special competence. A serious attempt was made to present as many informed positions as possible. The conclusions reached by the Ad Hoc Committee do not necessarily represent the views of the speakers. Our major conclusions were:

1. The U.S. Government has not offered adequate information and arguments in support of the military risks we are continuing to run in Vietnam.

2. Our present policies in Vietnam have led to the spreading of the war from the South to the North and create a serious risk of involving the United States in a military conflict with China. We welcome the President's offer for unconditional negotiations, but our stepped-up military actions following the President's offer vitiate the possible positive effect of his gesture.

3. Therefore, we believe that the U.S. Government should cease bombing attacks immediately in the North and should attempt to arrange a cease-fire in the South. This should be followed by negotiations with whomever necessary—not excluding the Vietcong—to the end of ensuring peace throughout Vietnam.

4. We disagree that vital interests of the United States are involved in Southeast Asia and particularly in Vietnam and, therefore, we believe that the solution to the political, social, and economic problems of the peoples of this area should be determined by them, with the assistance of the United Nations, and should not be directed by the United States.

5. Finally, we feel that the technique of a "teach-in" is an effective device for providing the academic community with a forum for the public exchange of information and opinions in an atmosphere appropriate to the serious consideration of current, complex issues of national significance.

Teach-In Petition at The University of Chicago

Issued by Students' Emergency Committee for Vietnam, April 25, 1965.

April 25, 1965

On April 14, The University of Chicago, with a capacity audience in its largest auditorium, held a teach-in which lasted from 9:30 P.M. until 4:00 A.M.

At this meeting, the enclosed petition, drawn up by a student campus organization, the Students' Emergency Committee for Vietnam, was read to the audience. The petition deplores the U.S. Government's current policy in Vietnam and expresses a refusal to support such intervention. Approximately half of the audience signed their names to the petition and their number is recorded at the bottom.

We are addressing our petition to Secretary General of the United Nations U Thant, in the name of all mankind, and sending it to major newspapers all over the world. We hope that people of all lands will begin to hear of the growing multitude of dissenting voices in America—voices of desperate concern.

ARTHUR KAUFMAN, Coordinator
STUDENTS' EMERGENCY COMMITTEE FOR VIETNAM

The Honorable U Thant
Secretary General of the United Nations,
In the Name of the Peoples of the World

Dear Sir:

President Johnson is still not telling our country the truth about Vietnam. In his speech of April 7, the President indicated that, while American soldiers are fighting to defend sacred values, the Vietcong are no more than tools of outside interests. Published reports lead us to believe that this assumption is false—that the war is a civil war and not an aggression from Hanoi. We, as students, faculty, and concerned citizens, cannot support the United States' continuous military interference in this internal conflict.

How is our Government defending our sacred values? By denying the people of Vietnam the right to vote? By moving them from village to village at the convenience of the military? By bombing and torturing innocent people? Are these the values of the United States? We believe that values so desecrated cease to exist.

We believe that if the people of this country were informed about Vietnam they would ask the same questions. They would demand, with us, a more humane policy toward all of Southeast Asia, a policy which relied not on military might but on political and economic initiatives relevant to the people of that area.

They would share our fear that reliance on military solutions will destroy future alternatives for peaceful settlement in Southeast Asia —a fear that our policies will, instead, lead to a massive war which nobody wants.

We have faith in democracy. We believe that, if the public is adequately informed, rational policies will arise from the ensuing debate. As the situation exists now, only a few men, in possession of all the facts and all the power, are making decisions that affect all our lives. Surely this does not accord with the values for which we claim to be fighting in Vietnam. We will feel shamed if the Government does not indicate by its actions a faith in democracy, both at home and abroad.

(Signed by 398 students and faculty of the University of Chicago)

II

Voices of The Teach-Ins

Editors' Introduction

The heart of any teach-in is made up of the actual speeches delivered by faculty members, students, and invited guests. Some participants spoke from prepared texts, but—unfortunately, for our purposes—most spoke from rough notes or completely extemporaneously. While this may have been in keeping with the spontaneity of the teach-in, it means that some of the best and most moving addresses will be preserved only in the listeners' memories. Of the nine addresses reprinted here, four (by Waskow, Lynd, Trager, and Brennan) are transcripts of actual addresses, edited only for style and clarity. The remainder are reconstructions of teach-in addresses delivered from notes; in such cases, the editors asked the speakers to retain as much as possible of the original presentations, as they remembered them.

Two further general observations should be made about the material presented here. The first bears repeating whenever teach-ins are analyzed, especially by those hostile to the movement. The teach-ins were devised as a form of faculty-student *protest* against the war in Vietnam, not as neatly balanced debating-society forums. Teach-in sponsors generally felt that news and information media were conveying views almost completely favoring the Administration's case and that these views were being assimilated uncritically. The teach-ins were consciously structured to subject Administration policy to critical examination and to acquaint student bodies with analyses and opinions that did not normally fill the pages of the press or the air-time of radio and television. (However, teach-in sponsors repeatedly invited members of the Administration, and even representatives of the South Vietnamese

Embassy, to defend their positions in person. More often than not, either because of anticipated chilly receptions or because of obvious imbalances in programing, such invitations went unanswered.) Thus, in this chapter, we have actually departed from the real ratio of pro and con presentations; in order to provide a balance of opinions, we have included a greater proportion of speeches favoring Administration policy than usually was in evidence at any single teach-in.

Second, we think that the speeches here quite accurately represent the range and content offered by both critics and defenders of Administration policy at the teach-ins in general. On the whole, critics tended to range further than defenders from the immediate topic of Vietnam; they broached civil rights, unemployment, the structure of the American polity, and other questions of domestic policy as necessary correlatives of foreign policy analysis. The address by Staughton Lynd, perhaps the best known of the young antiwar intellectuals, exemplifies both the activist approach and the concern characteristic of nonviolent radicalism. Seymour Melman examines the question of what national priorities are being minimized or disregarded because of the allocation of funds for military purposes. Arthur Waskow emphasizes that the means being used in Vietnam betray the noble ends that most Americans affirm. William Appleman Williams and Herbert Marcuse offer substantive critiques of the *bases* of American policy abroad. From different angles, both scholars see the failure and incorrectness of American actions as the dialectical result of too much success. The problem is not merely one of bad means, they suggest, but one of underlying assumptions and institutions that support American policies and inevitably lead to those means.

On the other side, Ernest van den Haag defends American intervention in Vietnam, whatever suffering it causes, as part of a necessary effort to preserve what is defined as Vietnamese freedom. An estimate of the background and nature of the Vietnamese conflict is presented by Frank Trager, who traces the problem to the attempt of the Communist North to destroy an independent South Vietnam. Although critical of aspects of Administration policy, Donald Brennan and John D. Montgomery explain why they feel the United States must remain in Vietnam and make the best of an unpleasant situation.

It is apparent from these speeches that any pigeonholing of those favoring and those opposing U.S. policy in Vietnam can be somewhat arbitrary. Many who consider themselves opponents of the war, such as Arthur Waskow, refrain from comprehensive criticism of U.S. policy. They concentrate, instead, on criticizing tactics they feel are contrary to acceptable, over-all American aims. Similarly, many supporters of U.S. policy back away from complete identification with the Administration position. Brennan, for example, explains why he believes bombing of the North is unwise and will not result in the desired aim of bringing the North Vietnamese to the negotiating table. Brennan, Montgomery, and others with similar views argue that the United States, once committed to South Vietnam, has no alternative but to stay involved and do its best to bring a version of democracy to that part of Asia.

Such failure to approve Administration policy *in toto* puts certain supporters of the war effort in curious proximity to many of the critics; recommendations of some critics to apply massive economic aid instead of military measures to South Vietnam are also approved by many Administration supporters. Thus, the line between critic and supporter sometimes becomes quite thin. Perhaps the clearest example of this peculiarity has been in the development of the views of former Administration adviser Arthur M. Schlesinger, Jr. Appearing at the National Teach-In and taking a position of qualified support for U.S. policy in Asia, Professor Schlesinger revealed a certain amount of scorn for the academic critics. (See Chapter IV.) But, by late 1966, he had emerged, without too much difficulty, as a leading critic of the Administration, appropriating many of the very arguments posed by critics he had debated a year earlier. (See his "A Middle Way Out of Vietnam," *The New York Times Magazine*, September 18, 1966.)

1. ADDRESSES CRITICAL OF ADMINISTRATION POLICIES

Our Leaders Are Following the Wrong Rainbow

— WILLIAM APPLEMAN WILLIAMS

Dr. Williams is Professor of American History at the University of Wisconsin and author of The Tragedy of American Diplomacy. *His address, here revised, was delivered at the University of Wisconsin Teach-In, April 1, 1965.*

I think it might be useful, at this point, to take a few minutes to reflect upon what is happening here in Madison. For here we are, over 2,000 of us, after midnight, asking for more lectures and discussion after having been engaged for more than ten hours in a dialogue with some of the most high-powered minds in the country. If nothing else, we have exposed the fallacy of the fifty-minute hour, which seems to be the cornerstone of the educational system —as well as the therapy system.

But, of course, there is much more. We are here from the city and the country, as well as from the campus. There is even a brave contingent from the far reaches of the Greek [fraternity] enclave on Langdon Street. And there are people over fifty and under fifteen in addition to those of college age. We have the makings of a community, and I know that most of us have felt the crucial differences between being in this group and being part of a crowd at a football game or any other entertainment. The strength of this shared identity and involvement reached a rare intensity during the last hour as Germaine Brée stretched and exercised our minds and our moral sense with her discussion of what it means to be committed and of why and how we should examine very carefully the nature and implications of our commitments. [*Excerpts from Professor Brée's address appear in Chapter VI.*]

So I think we should take a look at why we are here, and at how we can accomplish our objectives. We are here, I suggest, for four primary reasons. The first is simply that the actions of our Government have provoked us to assemble as citizens. Some of us are more upset than others; but none of us came because we decided it would be fun to change American foreign policy for the pure hell of it, or because we had nothing else to do; and we are most certainly not a highly organized group dedicated to one particular program or proposal. We should not allow either ourselves or the public at large to be confused on these crucial points. For the cranks are already shouting that we are part of some conspiracy to overthrow the Government, and others, including some members of the Government, have begun sneering that we are over-excited in our psyches or undereducated in the ways of the world.

The hard truth is that we are here because of actions initiated by John Fitzgerald Kennedy and carried further by Lyndon Baines Johnson. The hard truth is that we are here because the Congress of the United States has failed to execute its duty and fulfill its responsibility. If our Government had a different policy, we would not be here. And if our elected representatives were meeting their obligations, we would in all probability be registering our concern and disagreement through them.

The actions of our Government in foreign policy are failing the pragmatic test, they are violating our own best traditions, and they are threatening grave harm to our highest moral ideals and aspirations. We are waging an ever-bigger undeclared war. We are conducting it in an increasingly nasty and brutal way. We are fighting in the name of self-determination, but we are using our power to thwart and abort an indigenous social and political revolution. We are told, finally, that this has to be done for our very existence and security. That is playing with the fire of a moral A-bomb; for, if we justify our intervention in Vietnam on the grounds that it is crucial to our national security, we will soon be able to justify using our power for whatever we happen at the moment to want, or against whatever at the moment we do not like. That kind of moral arrogance—that kind of playing at being God—will destroy any chance we have to construct a *good* society.

Notice that I said *good* society. We already have a great society, and I think that may be the source of much of the trouble with our leaders. For greatness has primarily to do with size, strength, and power. But we citizens who are gathered here are primarily concerned with quality, equity, and with honoring our potential for becoming more fully and truly human. Our leaders are following the wrong rainbow.

The second reason we are here involves the breakdown of representative government in our country. To be a citizen is to act on one's responsibility to participate in the process of self-government. The vast majority of us here tonight met that obligation last November by supporting a man who told us he would not widen the war, who promised us he would do everything he could to bring peace to Vietnam. We are upset that his idea of achieving peace seems to be limited to . . . using more and bigger bombs. We are upset that he acts without being candid and without dealing directly with and through Congress.

The dangers in his actions are very great and very clear. Our system is not based on the idea that the people hand over all their power to the President. We, the people, are the source of authority, but election by us is not yet a grant of divine power in the United States. Arbitrary government is dangerous government, and never more so than when it is justified in the name of an election victory. If Lyndon Johnson thinks we are in his pocket just because we voted for him, then it is time to bring him back to night school for a course in the elementary truths of American history.

Such education is the proper business of Congress, but our congressmen are sitting on their hands. They know the President is going beyond his authority, but they excuse themselves by saying they voted away their power. But their vague and fundamentally meaningless resolution did nothing more than authorize the President to act in keeping with his constitutional responsibilities. It did not change the Constitution. Congress cannot amend the Constitution by passing a joint resolution, and the Constitution charges congressmen with fundamental responsibilities that they are not meeting. We are here, therefore, in an effort to rouse Congress, to restore its pride and revive its spirit, as well as to provoke it to confront and discuss and act on the dangerous course the President is following. We are here, in short, to restore the reciprocal action in politics before it becomes a one-way exercise of power by men who tell us one thing and do another—or tell us nothing and do as they choose.

The third reason we are here is because we have relevant things to say and consequential proposals to offer. This is true in our fundamental capacity as citizens, and it is also true in our particular capacity as members of a great educational community. We are here as citizens to say that we do not approve, that we do not acquiesce, and that we are not satisfied with the performance of our leaders. We are here as citizens to demand that those leaders come out of the womb of secrecy and engage each other and us, as citizens, in an open and candid dialogue about their policies. And we are here, as citizens, to demand that our leaders honor our institutions and our ideals when making foreign policy and when putting it into operation.

We are here as members of this educational community because it is our responsibility to direct and focus our emotions on the basis of our analytical and moral judgments and to do these things openly and candidly. We are here to offer the information we have; to explain, by thinking out loud before you, how we make sense out of that information; and to indicate, through that same process, the alternate lines of action that we find relevant and moral and creative. We are here, in short, to make it clear that the Government has no monopoly of the data or of the brains or of the morality and, thereby, to encourage all of us, as citizens, to participate in the process of governing ourselves.

The fourth reason we are here is because we hope to have some effect on the world. We are trying to bring our Government back into a dialogue with its own citizens. We are trying to encourage Congress to meet its responsibilities and to function as a full partner in governing the country. We are trying to change our foreign policy so that it will be closer to the realities of the world and far more in keeping with our best traditions and highest ideals—and thereby make it pragmatically more effective. We have caught a revealing and exciting glimpse of what a real community involves, of what it is like in character and tone and style. This experience has given some of us the hope that we may, if we care enough, be able to initiate a revival of that spirit and practice and thereby generate the kind of changes that could transform America into a more humane and creative country.

We hope to do these things, but we should not be too optimistic. The system is very solidly established, and our leaders are deeply entrenched in their false syllogisms and mistaken analogies. It will be very hard even to make ourselves heard through the sound and fury of their rhetoric. And it will be extremely difficult to break through the armor of their self-justifying arguments and force them to confront alternative ideas and proposals. We also confront the normal tendency of citizens to support their government in a war. This is unhappily reinforced by a more general lethargy and apathy that stems from a sense of powerlessness.

For all these reasons, therefore, we have to do our homework.

We have to know what we are talking about. Our sense of danger and our moral uneasiness are not enough. We have to know why and how our policies are wrong, and we have to offer alternatives that are related to reality and grounded in our traditions and our ideals. As Peter Weiss pointed out a few minutes ago, this teach-in has to become a freedom school in the North if we are to have any chance of achieving our objectives.

In keeping with that approach, I would like to offer an explanation of how and why we are in this predicament and a few suggestions as to how we can evolve new and better policies.

The policy our Government is following, and the pattern of ideas that creates and sustains that policy, are a product of American experience and thought during the last part of the nineteenth century. Our leaders are in trouble, and have us in danger, because they are trying to cope with the reality of the mid-twentieth century with attitudes and policies that are almost one hundred years old. Since they are no longer relevant, the only way they can possibly be made to work is by using our tremendous power in an attempt to change present reality so that it corresponds in some measure with the reality that originally evoked the ideas. But the world is a huge and stubborn reality, with a strength and dynamism of its own, and that is why the war in Vietnam has constantly to be escalated. A few more men and planes are not sufficient to turn back the clock.

We would be wrong if we explained this deep commitment to old ideas and attitudes as the result of a perverse will or as the product of a psychological fixation. The cause is at once more simple and more complex. Our leaders are clinging to the old analysis and the old policy because these worked surprisingly well over a period of two generations, because they seriously believe that any change in these attitudes and policies would severely damage or destroy the essence of American democracy and the basis of American prosperity, and because they have enough power at their disposal to postpone the final and complete breakdown of the old outlook and policy.

This traditional foreign policy has generally been known as the Open Door Policy, because that phrase appeared in several diplomatic notes announcing it to the world in 1899 and 1900. In that correspondence, the United States declared its intention to use its influence and power to establish and maintain an "open door" for its economic, political, and cultural activities in the underdeveloped and colonial areas of the world. . . .

The United States further announced, in 1899 and 1900, that it would use its influence and power in support of three particular means to obtain and secure the open door. These means were the related principles of self-determination and territorial and administrative integrity. American policy-makers reasoned that the honoring of those principles would open the door for American power and that Americans would more than hold their own in the ensuing competition for economic, political and cultural influence. Although the phrase itself—Open Door Policy—has largely been dropped from official rhetoric in the last fifteen years, these principles are clearly the justifications used by the Government to defend its present actions in Vietnam and other areas of the world.

When it was formulated and announced, this Open Door Policy had a high degree of relevance to the realities of the world. It was relevant, in the first place, to the *internal* realities of the United States. Americans had come to believe that the overseas expansion of their economic activities was essential to their prosperity and that the similar expansion of their political and cultural institutions was good, in and of itself, as well as necessary for their economic expansion. We can argue, of course, that this belief was actually mistaken, that such expansion was not necessary. But we should not allow that kind of analysis to confuse us on the central point—the reality of this . . . belief at the time the policy was formulated. Right or wrong, Americans of that period thought it was right.

The Open Door Policy was relevant, secondly, to the *external* realities of the world. We are inclined to forget that the storm of colonial and social revolution that now engulfs the world actually erupted at the turn of the century in a series of smaller, separate outbreaks. American policy-makers were perceptive enough to sense this and astute enough to realize that the American position in the world would be strengthened by identifying *with* those movements rather than by flatly opposing them. The United States would benefit directly by appearing as the champion of nationalism and internal progress and, indirectly, by placing itself in a position to encourage, and take advantage of, divisions among other advanced powers. The Open Door Policy was relevant, in short, both to the rising power of nationalism and the pressure for social change and to the competition among the industrial nations.

It was also a policy that had great moral strength. The principle of self-determination is the cornerstone of development and maturity. Both individuals and groups have to evolve an identity of their own as a base for relationships—and, hopefully, for a community—with others. It is quite true, of course, that self-determination carried to an extreme produces an assertive and even aggressive self-centered ego that is dangerous and destructive. That is the risk inherent in self-determination. But that risk is the price of human existence—the earnest money we have to lay down, as it were, in order to have a chance to become mature and to develop a true community. The alternative is to embrace despotism and to content ourselves with making it as benevolent as possible. American leaders who spurned that course made a moral choice of which we can be proud.

The moral cornerstone of the Open Door Policy remains sound. That is what in large measure accounts, I would suggest, for whatever contemporary appeal and influence the policy itself still has with Americans and other people throughout the world. It offers Americans the rationalization that, if things are going badly, they are at least going badly in the service of a noble cause. And it offers foreigners the hope, however feeble and flickering, that the great power of America that they confront and endure may finally enlarge *their* area of freedom to determine *their* lives.

The other source of the policy's limited success is, of course, that power itself. The United States has fantastic economic and military strength. It is not omnipotent, but it does have the capacity to impose its will in many situations and to delay or prevent unwanted developments in many other circumstances. The difficulty, of course, is that our Government is using this power in an increasingly futile effort to impose a policy upon a reality that no longer has any relevance to the policy.

What has happened is simply that we have reified the Open Door Policy. It was originally a policy that had great relevance to the real world. It treated people as live human beings and it was an effort to deal with them in keeping with reality and in terms of a moral principle. But it now has little or no relevance to the real world, either at home or abroad; and the effort to follow it forces our Government to treat people as *things* to be manipulated and changed, so that the policy will bring the desired—and expected —results.

The main reality that has changed is the nature of the rest of the world. The colonial and underdeveloped areas of the world have now achieved the kind of independence that the Open Door Policy was designed to encourage and support. China, for example, is now a strong, independent nation, and that is precisely what we have said we wanted for almost seventy-five years. The problem, of course, is that China, in its exercise of the right of self-determination, did not choose to become what the ideas and beliefs behind the Open Door Policy had led Americans to want and to expect it to become. The Open Door Policy unquestionably facilitated the rise of a strong China—if only because we fought and defeated Japan as an action predicated on that policy—*but, in doing so, it changed the reality on which the policy was based.*

The only way the policy can continue to work is by forcing the Chinese to act in keeping with the other reality on which the policy was based. That means our Government has to use its power to make the Chinese "self-determine" themselves in keeping with [our old] ideas of the necessity of American expansion and the superiority of American institutions. The same is true of [our dealings with] the Vietnamese. The Open Door Policy undoubtedly helped them win their independence from France, but our leaders are bound to interpret that success as a failure until the Vietnamese embrace as *their* truth the conditions of American influence that the Open Door Policy was supposed to create and sustain. This makes the Chinese and the Vietnamese into things to be manipulated. To put [their reaction] simply, they do not like this and they do all they can to prevent it from happening.

Clearly enough, this reification of the Open Door Policy has resulted in a violation of the moral principle of self-determination. It has changed its meaning: it now means the acceptance and the emulation of *our* particular form of self-determination. We have thus transformed a principle into a prescription, and we are using force to make the patient take our medicine.

This confronts us with a clear choice. We can, upon serious and candid examination, conclude that we do indeed have to expand and that our institutions are the best for all; we can then embark upon a sober and informed imperialism designed to establish and maintain an American Empire of optimum size, efficiency, and benevolence. I do not outline this alternative in any joking or sarcastic sense. I oppose it vigorously on pragmatic as well as moral grounds, but I am quite aware that it is a real alternative. Approached openly and intelligently, it could be tried and might even be made to function for a period of time. More importantly, I honestly think it would be psychologically and philosophically healthier than our present struggle to square the moral circle by using force to redefine the principle of self-determination into our particular version of self-determination. If we keep this up, we will become hypocrites or psychotics. We shall also very probably lead the world into a nuclear war.

The other alternative is to honor our moral commitment to the principle of self-determination. I think this is also more practical. For I think that if we can discipline ourselves to respect the right of self-determination for others, then we will be more secure in the world and also able to determine our own development in a more positive manner. . . .

I think it is time to realize that we are trying to do the impossible, as well as doing the immoral. We are trying to deal with the rest of the world through a foreign policy that has no relevance to [the new] reality. We do not have to expand in the old imperial sense. We can meet our economic needs by trading with others as equals. We can defend ourselves without controlling Cuba and without bases in Vietnam. And we can improve our own society without making everybody follow our path. We can clearly learn a good deal from others if we will only give them a chance to teach us, if we will only give ourselves the chance to learn.

I would like to think that a good many of us realize these things . . . and that we are here because we feel it is time to tell our leaders that [we are ahead of them], that it is time for them to change their policy. And I would like to think that we will keep telling them, in whatever ways they make necessary, until they do change those policies.

That is, at any rate, exactly what I intend to do, because I want this America to be a *good* society as well as a powerful nation. I am radical enough, furthermore, to hope that we can become a community instead of a society; I know we will never become either unless we honor our principles. If we are to honor our principles, we will have to change our foreign policy. And, if we honor our principles, we will gain a security that guns and bombs can never provide.

Nonviolent Alternatives to American Violence

— STAUGHTON LYND

*An Assistant Professor of American History at Yale
University, Staughton Lynd is among the most
prominent academic members of the peace movement. Late in 1965, in violation of State Department
prohibitions, he made a dramatic journey to Hanoi
on a private fact-finding mission with Tom Hayden
(a founding member of the radical Students for a
Democratic Society) and Herbert Aptheker (American historian and a member of the American Communist Party). (See* Viet-Report: An Emergency
Bulletin on Southeast Asian Affairs, *January, 1966.)
This address was delivered at the University of California (Berkeley) Teach-In, May 22, 1965.*

First, a word to Professor Scalapino. [*See Professor Robert A.
Scalapino's statement attacking the Berkeley Teach-In, Chapter I.*]
I, too, believe in precise and responsible intellectual discourse.
But I think it exposes a very curious and revealing double standard
that a man who finds it possible to support the government of
South Vietnam—which indiscriminately drops napalm bombs on
unprotected villages, which tortures men, women, and children—
should find it impossible to meet with us because, God save the
mark, our program is "unbalanced."

I am employed by Yale University, the institution which produced the architect of the Bay of Pigs, Richard Bissell; the author
of Plan Six for Vietnam, W. W. Rostow; and that unagonized
reappraiser, McGeorge Bundy. Hence, if Professor Scalapino is an
expert on Vietnamese insurgents, I consider myself something of
an expert on American counterinsurgents. I think I know something
about the Ivy League training which these unelected experts receive: a training in snobbishness, in a provincial ethnocentrism, in a
cynical and manipulative attitude toward human beings.

Look at the American Secretaries of State in the twentieth century and I think you will find that, almost without exception, they
were former corporation lawyers. They were what the President of
Yale has called "public entrepreneurs," that is to say, corporation

lawyers who spend part of their time on Wall Street serving their private clients, and part of their time in Washington serving the general interests of their class. I think you need to say to your teachers, as I need to say to my colleagues, that annihilation in a Brooks Brothers suit is still murder.

I would like to say this, too, to Professor Scalapino. You say that no self-respecting intellectual would attend this meeting. The entire educational world now looks back with gratitude on those few professors who protested what was happening in Nazi Germany. I predict that some day the entire academic community of this country will look back on the few professors who have publicly protested our Vietnam policy and say, "They kept the spirit of truth alive."

We've been talking for a long time in this meeting and we should be beginning to turn our thoughts towards action. But there are two analytical points I would like to make, which I think bear on the action we should take.

First of all, I believe that we have to recognize that this country is not just in a foreign policy crisis, but in a constitutional crisis as well. This point has been made by *The New York Times,* which said, editorially, that a style of executive decision-making and news-manipulation hitherto practiced only briefly in times of temporary emergency has now become a permanent way of life—which means, I think, that the Johnson doctrine has *two* sides. It means, on the one hand, that we will not permit governments that we do not like to come into being overseas, even if they are supported by a majority of their people. But the Johnson doctrine *also* means that the Government will not permit the majority of the people of *this* country to have a responsible discussion and to determine their own policy. I think that means that people who have been working in the Freedom Democratic Party now have to realize that not only Negroes in Mississippi are unrepresented in the Government of the United States; in a situation where Congress has handed over its constitutional power to declare war and peace to the President, all of us are now unrepresented by our Government. I think this means, too, that the Free Speech Movement here, and other movements on other campuses which have been concerned with university reform must now concern themselves with the unelected Board of Regents who run this country.

The second analytical point I wish to make has really been made for me by this morning's newspapers. We are, I think, in a kind of pause now; the bombing of North Vietnam has been going on for so long that even those of us who most protest it somewhere within ourselves begin psychologically to acquiesce. If Ipana tooth-paste is mentioned enough times on television, you find yourself subliminally reaching for Ipana when you go to the drugstore; so somehow, too, bombing has become almost an accepted part of the scenery. But this situation isn't going to last; there's going to be a new crisis in this country by midsummer, I think, when tens of thousands of American ground troops are in full-scale combat in Vietnam. And we have to be prepared to deal with that crisis when it arrives.

Now, Professor Scalapino said [*at the National Teach-In in Washington*] that what we are doing is simply putting in a small number of American ground troops to check the Vietcong in its ex-pected monsoon offensive so that, by September or October, the Vietcong will want to come to the negotiating table. As a histo-rian, I think this is madness. Four hundred thousand French troops failed to defeat this nationalist movement. How can we expect that 20,000, 40,000, 100,000 American troops will bring them to their knees in one summer? The troops that are going in are going to be there for a long time.

Now, at Washington, Professor Schlesinger presented himself as a supporter of this policy with a difference, with certain infini-tesimal differences, designed to indicate that he was a supporter of Presidential candidate Robert Kennedy rather than Presidential incumbent Lyndon Johnson. I would like to remind Professor Schlesinger that, in February, 1962, the Senator whose Secretary of State he may hope one day to be, told Homer Bigart of *The New York Times*, "The United States is in a war in Vietnam. American troops will stay till we win." [*Professor Lynd is apparently referring to Senator Robert F. Kennedy of New York.*] That's hardly a policy of negotiation.

There will then be a new crisis, an escalated crisis, this summer, as tens of thousands of American troops go into full-scale combat and the casualty lists begin to mount. Public opinion in the United States will crystallize in either of two directions. Either there will be an escalation of repression and a limitation of debate and a rally-ing of the people behind the present Administration; or, conceiv-ably, if we play our part, the mounting casualty list could produce a new wave of revulsion in the American people that could bring our present policy to a stop. So I think we need to ask ourselves what is to be done to produce the one outcome rather than the other?

Now, one strategy of social change which has been widely rec-ommended to us in recent months by Bayard Rustin, . . . by Michael Harrington . . . and by others, is a strategy of coalition politics within the Democratic Party. Mr. Harrington said, in his *Partisan Review* article (and here I paraphrase his remarks): If there is an escalation of foreign policy crisis in Vietnam or else-where, all talk of the Great Society or the Antipoverty Program will cease. I think we need to say to Mr. Harrington—and Mr. Rus-tin—that that escalation has now occurred and that coalition poli-tics in this situation means coalition with the Marines.

Is there an alternative? I think the alternative is nonviolent revo-lution. For the benefit of the FBI men present, I would like to make it clear that what I mean is not the violent overthrow of the U.S. Government, but the nonviolent retirement from office of the present Administration. The way to bring this about is the creation of civil disobedience so massive and so persistent that the Tuesday Lunch Club that is running this country—Johnson, McNamara, Bundy, and Rusk—will forthwith resign.

We do not live in a parliamentary government like the British, where a vote of no confidence can compel a criminally irresponsible administration to resign. . . . Yet we cannot wait until the next Presidential election in 1968; therefore, I think we have to vote with our feet by marching and picketing; vote with our hands by burning our draft cards and refusing to pay income tax; and, if necessary, vote with our backsides by sitting in jail.

But is this what Bayard Rustin would call "merely a moral ges-ture?" Is there really any chance of success in such a strategy? I think yes. First of all, there are two spirits in conflict in this coun-try today. One is a spirit revealed by a quotation from yesterday's *Wall Street Journal*, which said, "Battle statistics are showing a dramatic change. Last month's 3,120 Vietcong dead was up from 1,965 in March." Death, too, is now listed on the stock exchange and goes up and down monthly for the *Wall Street Journal*.

But there is another spirit in this country. It is the spirit of the thirty-eight Columbia students who, when twelve were identified by the university [*for disrupting ROTC graduation exercises*] and threatened with expulsion, voluntarily came forward and told the university, "If you throw them out, you'll have to throw us out, too." I just don't think that spirit can be defeated in the long run. People may die, people may suffer. But, in the long run, stock-ex-change morality cannot defeat the ethic of solidarity.

There is another thing which gives me hope for a strategy of non-violent civil disobedience. World public opinion is on our side. One reason that I hope there will be civil disobedience in Washington this summer is because of its international visibility. I think that, in the Selma [Alabama] crisis, perhaps the most important single product of that situation was the sit-ins at the White House, because, prior to that time, we had all confronted a kind of thought-barrier to direct action in the nation's capital. Now we have passed that barrier, and I think we should devise new forms of such action. For example, professors—such as those who conducted the teach-ins in Washington last weekend—might set up a parallel Senate Foreign Relations Committee, which would hold hearings (since our present Foreign Relations Committee has not held them) on the Vietnamese war and would keep those meetings going until Bundy showed up.

The Committee for Non-Violent Action is planning, either in the first or second week of June, a "speak-in" in the Pentagon lobby. [*Such a speak-in was in fact held.*]

Others have been considering the idea of inviting to this country an international war crimes tribunal—composed of men such as Vinoba Bhave, Chief Lutuli, Pastor Niemoeller, Danilo Dolci, Michael Scott, and, hopefully, Martin Luther King—which would meet in Washington, hear evidence, and attempt to assess the moral responsibility for the horror of Vietnam. [*On June 18, 1966, Bertrand Russell announced the formation of a War Crimes Tribunal to meet in Paris to try President Johnson, Secretary of State Rusk, Secretary of Defense McNamara, Ambassador Lodge, and General Westmoreland on the basis of criteria developed at the Nuremberg Trials. Such figures as Jean-Paul Sartre, Simone de Beauvoir, Danilo Dolci, Lazaro Cardenas, and others have agreed to serve in the tribunal.*]

Some have even suggested that there might convene in Washington this summer or next fall or next spring, a new Continental Congress drawn from the community unions, freedom parties, and campus protests all over the country, which would say to one another, as Americans said in 1774: "This is a moment of crisis; our Government does not represent us. Let us come together and consider what needs to be done."

But finally, and most of all, I think that a strategy of nonviolent civil disobedience could be successful because I believe in the power of nonviolence. Thoreau said, in the 1840's, that one man who was prepared to die could stop slavery in the United States. I think this weekend we should all search our hearts and our souls for the courage and the clarity of spirit to go to the White House, to go to the Oakland Army Terminal on June 22, to go to Vietnam, if we could, and stand in front of the flame-throwers and say: "If blood must be spilt, let it be mine rather than the blood of Vietnamese children. If you need someone to search and destroy, let me save you the trouble, here I am. And if you are worried that the natives all over the world are restless, we want you to know that the natives here at home are restless, too, and maybe there should be a contingency plan to keep some of the Marines here to deal with us."

The New American Arrogance

— A R T H U R   I .   W A S K O W

Mr. Waskow is a Resident Fellow at the Institute for Policy Studies, Washington, D.C. These are excerpts from a revised version of a speech delivered at the first teach-in, March 24–25, 1965, which was held at the University of Michigan. The speech was interrupted by a bomb threat and completed in the snow outside of the evacuated auditorium (see the account of the Michigan Teach-In by Anatol Rapoport in Chapter I).

Before I address myself to foreign policy, I want to tell you how honored I am to have been invited to speak at the first teach-in, at the first session of what might be called the Free University of Michigan. I hope this Free University of Michigan holds many other sessions, and I hope they are not all held at night. Your being here tonight is in the greatest traditions of the university, in the tradition of *lehrfreiheit* and *lernfreiheit*—the freedom of the faculty to teach and of the students to learn whatever knowledge seems to them to be of great importance regardless of what has been set down in a course catalogue that was printed months before. And it is in the tradition that holds that great social issues are the legitimate concern of the academic community and that the university must serve as conscience of the community on such issues.

On the specific social issue that brings us here tonight, it may seem that I have no specific expertise. For I am no expert on the land, the people, or the history of Vietnam. My expertise is rather on America, since I have tried to study the relationships between American military strategy and American political purposes over the past twenty years. But I would venture to suggest that, if we are to understand our Government's behavior in Vietnam and to criticize that behavior effectively, we must study our own America at least as carefully as we study Vietnam.

The relationship between military strategy and political purposes is one between means and ends; it is precisely the relationship between means and ends that our Government has lost sight of in Vietnam—and not only in Vietnam, for our attitude there is symptomatic of a new and developing attitude toward the whole of the underdeveloped world. Before I try to characterize that attitude, let me sketch a few of the pieces of evidence that lead me to conclude it is increasingly important.

First, a piece of evidence that is not about Vietnam at all. I have talked with people active in the Agency for International Development and the Alliance for Progress who tell me that there is emerging in official Washington an attitude toward Latin America that runs something like this: Since the Alliance's New-Deal-style reform from the top in Latin America has proved so difficult, and since the United States certainly could not sponsor and probably could not stomach SNCC-style reform from the bottom, and since we can deal with Communists or proto-Communists by police action or a quick buy-off, the hell with economic development. After all, wasn't the only reason we were so interested in economic development the belief that without it Latin America would go Communist? So let's be prepared to use police action whenever there is danger of a Communist insurgency, or what looks like it to us. That is the first piece of evidence.

Second, let us look at the record in Vietnam itself and compare it to previous American standards of international behavior. In 1956, the United States condemned, as absolutely contrary to international law and the U.N. Charter, the action of Israel to punish alleged infiltration of guerrillas from Egypt not by a defense of Israel's own boundaries but by an attack on Egypt herself. Now, less than a decade later, we have done exactly what we condemned as contrary to international law and the U.N. Charter: Presumably in response to alleged infiltration across what we regard as the international boundary between North and South Vietnam, we have retaliated by bombing North Vietnam. We did not respond, as we insisted Israel should have responded, by asking for a U.N. peace force to patrol the border and prevent infiltration. Instead, we took the law into our own hands—the law of retaliation and punishment, not the law of self-defense.

Or let us look even nearer home. Perhaps it could be expected that any nation would ignore for itself the international law it would apply to others. But in 1943, in the midst of a life-and-death war against two great powers, the United States applied to itself a principle of international law that it has since ignored in Vietnam. It was proposed, in 1943, that the United States use some newly developed chemicals to destroy the rice crop in Japan—thus bringing an extremely dangerous enemy to her knees. But Admiral Leahy, the Chief of Naval Operations, refused indignantly on the grounds that such an act would be war against civilians, absolutely contrary to the laws of war. In the 1960's, we find our Government using similar chemicals to destroy the rice crop in Vietcong-held areas of South Vietnam, or countenancing their use by our allies and clients in the Saigon Government.

Again, we find respectable American magazines and newspapers publishing articles and photographs that show that American officers have been present while officers in the South Vietnamese Army —our allies and clients—use torture on Vietnamese adolescents to extract information about the Vietcong. We could have ended such behavior by refusing any help to any unit that behaved in such ways but, instead, we condoned the use of torture. It is often said—and truly—that the Vietcong and the North Vietnamese have also used torture and terror. But we expect this from totalitarians; indeed, torture is a technique that advances totalitarian goals. But you cannot create liberty by using torture.

And so we are back to the issue of means and ends. From the pieces of evidence that I have mentioned, it seems to me one can deduce the emergence of what might be called the new American arrogance, and it is an arrogance about the means we use to advance the ends we seek. The new American arrogance says that the ends we seek are so noble, so benign, that any means at all are legitimate to advance them. It says that, in the underdeveloped world, our dream of Western-style prosperity and liberty is so noble that we may use any means to suppress any threat to that dream. It says that the détente of the last two years between the Soviet Union and the United States can be turned into a corrupt deal—that, since the Russians will not want, or dare, to use their bombs on us in order to defend China or North Vietnam, we (and perhaps they) are free to do as we like to these and similarly annoying underdeveloped countries whose people have skin colors different from ours and whose governments have a philosophy hostile to ours. It says that perhaps we can stop bothering with economic aid to end the long night of poverty and despair that afflicts two billion human beings in Africa, Asia, and Latin America and, instead, simply use our superior firepower to shoot down any troublemaker who arises from that night of poverty and despair to shout his hatred into our well-lit, well-upholstered living rooms.

At the heart of this new arrogance lies an old assumption: that military means still apply to political ends. At the level of thermonuclear weapons, we have gone far toward teaching ourselves that military means cannot be used to advance political ends. For nuclear weapons mean genocide, and genocide is not victory. But we have not yet applied that lesson at the level of counterinsurgency warfare. The analogous equation would be that counterinsurgency means torture, and torture is not victory. But this second equation we have not yet learned. We have not yet learned that the political freedom of the Vietnamese people cannot be advanced by a military policy that relies on burning villages with napalm and on torturing the villagers for information. Tactics like this can produce chaos or advance totalitarianism, but they cannot protect or advance liberty. Only a policy that years ago approached the problem of Vietnam as a political problem to be solved by political means could have advanced liberty. Revolutionary guerrillas do not flourish where social reform is going on and liberty is advancing. Guerrillas only flourish when, as Mao Tse-tung put it, they can live among the people as fish swim in the sea. Our Government's attempt to put down political subversion and revolution with military suppression was doomed to failure from the start and could never have advanced liberty. A program of *massive* economic aid and *massive* social reform might have done the job, but we did not try it. . . .

There are some Americans who have responded to their own horror over the means we are using in Vietnam by denouncing the use of any means at all, who have responded to the difficulties we have discovered in the way of accomplishing our official noble ends in the underdeveloped world by condemning those ends as irrelevant to, or undesirable for, the underdeveloped world. They have responded to the new American arrogance with what, at first glance, looks like a new American humility: the humility that says we have nothing useful to offer the world. But humble as it may be in mood, a policy of true neo-isolationism would produce arrogance in action—an arrogance different from, but just as destructive as, the arrogance I have already described, which is based on policing the world as we like. If the first arrogance is that of the cop who shoots down the desperate poor man, the second, neo-isolationist arrogance is that of the man who simply shuts off his living room with walls and security locks, takes a cab to the office so as not to see the poor, and leaves them to rot in their misery. For if we offer no help of any sort to the underdeveloped world, we impose on them only two choices: permanent misery or the leap to industrialism through Stalinist techniques of capital accumulation. If they cannot get investment capital (in the form of money, food, educated people, and imaginative ideas) from those who are rich already—and only we are rich enough to help enough—they will have to get it from their own poor, squeezing every drop of blood and energy from a peasant today so that his grandchildren can own a steel mill. That is the choice neo-isolationism imposes on the hungry nations—hopeless but bearable misery forever, or an optimistic but terrifying misery for two generations. And that is why I say that neo-isolationism, too, is a policy of arrogance, though it may have the mask or the intention of humility. . . .

In world politics, as elsewhere, blindness and stupidity exact their cost; and if we have taken too long to learn the lesson that revolutionary change in Vietnam could not be stopped by military suppression, then we might have to pay the cost of our delay. That cost might be the loss of the war, in which case a graceful withdrawal, while we were still able to cut our losses, would be wise. But there may even yet be a chance to transform the war we are fighting, to shift our energy from the armed to the unarmed forces, and to win a real victory for liberty in Vietnam through libertarian means. Such a transformation would require a cease-fire—an abandonment of torture, napalm, and white phosphorus. It would require not only massive economic aid to Vietnam, but also the channeling of that aid to the villages rather than to Saigon. It would require the sending of hundreds of Peace Corpsmen, or members of a new overseas equivalent of SNCC, to be prepared to die without fighting back as they tried to activate the political energies of the peasants and tribesmen and slum-dwellers of Vietnam. As I say, it may be too late to win a victory for liberty by any means; but it is certainly too late to win a victory for liberty through military means.

If we took the course I have suggested, then the United States might make itself again what Jefferson once called it—the last, best hope of earth. But if we take the course of arrogance—either the arrogance of America as a world policeman or the arrogance of neo-isolationism—then we will find our arrogance suffocating and corrupting not only others but also ourselves. I fear the new arrogance is increasing among us, though it does not yet represent the majority opinion; and I suspect that something like it is increasing among Russians and West Europeans. When I meet it in *our* country, when I hear it in *our* country, I can only remember something else that Jefferson told us. He was talking, 150 years ago, of a remarkably similar arrogance that afflicted our domestic life, the arrogance of slavery, and he said, "Indeed, I tremble for my country when I reflect that God is just." Tonight, my fellow Americans, I tremble —I tremble for my country when I reflect that God is just.

The Inner Logic of American Policy in Vietnam

— HERBERT MARCUSE

Dr. Marcuse is Professor of Philosophy at the University of California, San Diego, and the author of One-Dimensional Man. The following is an edited text of remarks delivered at the Teach-In of the University of California at Los Angeles, March 25, 1966.

The official justification for the American policy in Vietnam is couched in Orwellian language; as such, it defies rational discussion. "We are fighting for freedom"—that is to say, on behalf of a military dictatorship which wouldn't last twenty-four hours without American bombs. "We are fighting for freedom" by protecting the social groups and interests whose power is based on exploitation and slavery. "We are fighting for freedom," in short, by supporting a military junta which fights *against* the economic and social changes which might create the very preconditions of freedom.

"We are fighting aggression"—by whom? The North Vietnamese are, after all, Vietnamese. The Chinese have not dispatched their military strength beyond their borders; they have not established military bases all over the globe; they have not succeeded in promoting the overthrow of established governments; they have even abandoned their meager economic support of socialist Cuba.

"We want to avoid another Munich." Here, too, the language is Orwellian, although the analogy is ultimately correct. The question is, who is the current appeaser? Who now boasts the most powerful war machine of all time? And who is now using it in foreign countries? Remember that Hitler, too, sometimes claimed that the German presence beyond German borders existed by "invitation."

Why is the war in Vietnam and the general policy of direct or indirect intervention in foreign lands justified in terms of the "na-

tional interest"? To answer this question we must turn from propaganda to reality. In spite of the heroic pronouncements from
Washington about defending freedom or stopping aggression, official definitions of the national interest insist on the necessity of
fighting and containing Communism wherever it appears. But, in
fact, our foreign policy deviates from this definition in two ways:
First, we do not wage war against the Soviet Union and the powers
associated with her; second, we engage in a convenient kind of cir-
cularity, since we usually define whatever we fight as "Communism." Who or what then, are we really fighting? We are fighting
a specific form of Communism in backward areas. We are waging
war against wars of liberation initiated by indigenous revolutionary
movements. These movements attempt to institute radical agrarian
reforms in order to abolish the exploitative domination of the traditional ruling classes; they attempt to eliminate the power of foreign capital; and, of course, they attack the native governments dependent upon that power.

Such movements are dangerous to us for three different reasons.
First, if successful, they would lead to the expropriation of foreign
investment and to the abolition of the corrupt and oppressive semi-
feudal regimes characteristic of the backward nations. They would
thus reduce the capitalist hinterland to a dangerously suffocating
area. I should add that I do not believe that the classical concept of
imperialism is applicable to Vietnam viewed as an isolated phenomenon. But it is essential to consider Vietnam within the global
context in the familiar "domino" terms: The defeat of the United
States would indeed be the signal for activating liberation movements in other colonial areas, much closer to home, and perhaps
even at home. In such areas, the stability of vested interests is indeed vital to the metropolitan economy. Seen in this perspective,
our Vietnam policy is only one aspect of a policy which extends
from West Germany to Indonesia, from Turkey to Japan—a policy
which is, perhaps, reflected in Mississippi and Alabama as well.

Second, the existence of a gigantic military establishment is an
integral, stimulating factor of the U.S. economy. This is something
that has been operative since the collapse of the New Deal in the
mid-1930's. The American economy may not require a war establishment, but any conversion at this point would necessitate sweep-
ing economic and political change.

Third, the affluent society is in need of an Enemy, against whom
its people can be kept in a state of constant psycho-social mobilization. As technical progress increases the possibilities for the pacification of the struggle for existence, the obsolescent character of the

social institutions, which perpetuate the profitable struggle for existence, becomes more apparent. Consequently, in order to protect and reproduce the established institutions, it becomes increasingly necessary to divert the available resources from rational employment to destructive and repressive use. This "surplus repression" activates a primary aggressiveness, which must be sublimated and channeled into activity on behalf of the national interest lest aggression explode within the established society. Such sublimation would be normal were it not for the novel factor of "technological" aggressiveness and its fateful consequences. The fact that aggression and destruction are carried out by a thing—a mechanism, an automated device—rather than by a person, impairs the satisfaction of the aggressive instinct, and this frustration prompts repetition and escalation of aggression. To the degree to which the agent of destruction is a thing and the person is removed from the victim, guilt and the sense of guilt are reduced. One of the most effective barriers against cruelty and inhumanity has thereby collapsed. The result is brutalization on a massive scale, a quality which is expressed also in our daily life at home in the form of violent language, images, and mass behavior.

The conclusion suggested by these tendencies is that the war against "Communism," waged on this basis of brutalization, becomes—by the inner logic of prevailing conditions—a war for reactionary military dictatorship. Revolutionary movements for social and economic change in the backward countries can be counteracted only by support of the old ruling classes. They, in turn, can maintain their dominion over the population only by means of constantly intensified suppression. There is no alternative, since a non-Communist, liberal "third force" cannot exist. It would lack an adequate economic and social base, and it would be unable or unwilling to carry through the radical changes necessary to bring backward areas onto the road to humane and modern forms of existence. Third force regimes succumb to either Communist or fascist dictatorships.

Thus, the reverse side of the domino theory—the side that actually exists in the contemporary world—is that, in one country after another, revolutionary and even liberal regimes are replaced, through bloody *putsches,* by counterrevolutionary dictatorships. The function of these regimes is to sustain or reinstate the very interests which kept the backward countries in conditions of backwardness and dependence. The American mission has become one of protecting reactionary regimes and refusing to accept any progressive historical changes.

The nation that was once the hope of all liberating forces the world over has become the hope of all counterrevolutionary forces the world over. The United States has become the advance guard of repression and reaction.

Priorities—Economic and Moral

— SEYMOUR MELMAN

Professor Melman teaches in the Department of Industrial and Management Engineering at Columbia University and is the author of Our Depleted Society. *This is a précis of remarks delivered at the Columbia University Teach-In, March 24, 1966.*

Senator J. W. Fulbright stated in an address, on March 22, 1966, at the University of Connecticut that "There is a kind of madness in the facile assumption that we can raise the many billions of dollars necessary to rebuild our schools and cities and public transport and eliminate the pollution of air and water while also spending tens of billions to finance an 'open-ended' war in Asia."

Government spokesmen have committed themselves to the proposition that the United States is an affluent society and can therefore afford as much military and space spending as may be desired —while also operating major programs of domestic betterment.

The rising gross national product ($700 billion) masks the major constraints on production capability—the finite stock of brain power and skilled hands. Priority allocation of skilled manpower, especially technical, to defense and space prevents fulfillment of the so-called Great Society legislative program. The crucial contrast between the nation's needs and federal allocation in the 1967 budget is summarized by the following data:

	Increases Proposed in Federal Budget	*Increases Required in the Nation*
Job Training Education	+ $0.2 billion	+ $25 billion
Health Care	+ 1 billion	+ 8 billion
Housing	+ 0.4 billion	+ 8 billion

The money made available for housing means that the people of the slum-ghettoes and their children are doomed to inferior housing for an indefinite future. The allotment for health care means continued decline in the number of physicians and nurses per thousand of population. The nation needs 150 new medical schools by 1975. The Johnson budget provides 13. The limitations on money for education mean continued priority use of talented men and women in the military and space industries.

Technological or economic depletion, or both, are found in many American industries, including house-building, ship-building, railroads, civilian electronics, typewriters, machine tools, sewing machines, ceramics, cotton textiles, et cetera. Failure in technological development, declining employment, or both, are found in these industries—with predictable long-term deterioration from continuation of present trends. No beginning of major repair is possible without moving skilled manpower from present use in military-space industries.

The shortage of skilled manpower in the country is so severe that faculties of present medical schools cannot be staffed properly. Metal-working firms now import machinists from Western Europe.

The low level of constructive civilian activity is sharply reflected in the revolt in Watts. The McCone Report on Watts recommended "adjustments on a scale unknown to any Great Society," including heavy spending for job training, general education, housing, and health care. None of the required investment has been carried out in Watts or in the twenty other American cities identified as locations for major Watts-type rebellions during 1966. None of these programs can be fulfilled because of priority given to defense and space. Thus, present priorities invite both economic deterioration and mass social rebellion in the great cities of our country.

The war on poverty has been transformed into war and poverty. Priority to the Johnson war in Vietnam now incites a racial rebellion within the United States.

Two years ago, the military budget of $55 billion was on the way down. Under Johnson, the military budget is being drastically enlarged. The present trend is toward a military budget of about $75 billion. A year ago, I predicted (*Our Depleted Society*, p. 307) that such a budget will mean: "Close government rationing of capital, technology, and skilled occupations for military work. Restricted civilian economy and massive tax burden. Major restraints on personal and political freedom. Military draft (heavy)." The promise of a Great Society is being transformed into a reality of a Greatly Depleted Society.

The prevailing madness in economics is matched, if not outdone, by a madness in morals. We are being deeply involved in a moral contradiction between preaching and practice, between behavior and ideals, that is now vividly mirrored in our Government's behavior in Vietnam.

We teach the value of human life and we kill six Vietnamese civilians for each Vietcong casualty.

We proclaim that government should be chosen by the governed and we deny that right to the people of South Vietnam.

We declare allegiance to rule of law, while the President and all who accept his orders violate international law and the Constitution in their undeclared war in Vietnam.

We teach that in a democracy public officials shall be public servants and not managers over the public, while the Government distorts news and repeatedly affirms a desire for peace while avoiding negotiations when the other side indicates its readiness.

The contrast between morals that are spoken and morals that are practiced generates bewilderment, a crisis of identity—especially among the youth. The unspoken question for millions is: Who am I? Am I the person represented by the morals we preach, or am I the person described by the morals we practice?

To whom should we give allegiance: to the men and institutions that teach the ideals of the Nation, or to the men and the activities that violate these ideals? Where the purpose of living is made obscure by a moral crisis and is not tacitly understood, or readily formulated in a way that is understandable—then we stand in danger of a moral vacuum. "Life without purpose" can become a mode of living for millions.

The future of our country will soon be determined by the choice we make in national priorities. The choice is essentially this: priorities to military systems of power and consequent weakening of the citizens vis-à-vis the extending power of the central state; or, priority to peace and people, and the chance to reverse the growth of state power while attending to human betterment at home and abroad.

The priorities and the politics of peace are not immune to the risk and uncertainty of all politics. Every man in a free society must take his chances; his choices are determined by his values. If the values accept the sacrifice of life, man's destructive potential, and a preference for authoritarianism, then he must look to the policies of war. If the values include high worth of human life, a desire to develop man's potential for peaceful living, and a will to maintain and extend freedom in society, then he must look to the morals of peace.

I choose the priorities of peace.

2. ADDRESSES SUPPORTING ADMINISTRATION POLICIES

The Struggle for Vietnamese Independence

— FRANK N. TRAGER

Dr. Trager is Professor of International Relations in the Graduate School of Public Administration, New York University, and the author of Why Viet-Nam? *These are excerpts from an edited transcript of an address delivered at the Oslo Teach-In, organized by the Norwegian Student Association, April 16, 1966.*

Where shall we begin this complicated story of Vietnam? Because I do want to talk to you about Vietnam. I spend all of my academic and professional life on Southeast Asia. I visit there on the average every two years; all of my work is concerned with it. Perhaps I see Asia a little more clearly than I see Europe. But if I do, it is because there is a need, especially in my country and in Europe, to get to "see" a little more of Asia, to understand that great part of the world in which we of the West have long since been known as the late imperialist conqueror. The struggle for Vietnam is a long-time struggle for independence, and now [it is fought] against a newer form of imperialism—the Communist variety. If you want a teach-in that adds more truth than fire, then let us look more closely at this struggle.

For one thousand years, the Vietnamese struggled first against imperialist China, then, having achieved their independence and unified their kingdom under their own dynasty, they lost their independence in the nineteenth century. For 125 years—more than the length of your own Norwegian struggle—the Vietnamese contended against the French. Their emperors like your kings, their mandarins (civil servants), like your civil servants, their people like you fought against the imposition of foreign imperial sway. Their struggles against the French began in the 1820's and ended in 1954—only, as we shall see, to begin again against a newer form of imperialism from another source. Now that is the broad context in which you can and should understand what Vietnam means: struggle against Chinese imperialism; struggle against French imperialism for generations before World War II; struggle against Vichy France and the Japanese during World War II—like your struggle against the Nazi occupation; struggle against the Gaullist and subsequent regimes that after World War II sought to reimpose French imperialism upon the states of Indochina, and almost succeeded—almost. . . .

At the end of World War II there were two clearly articulated forces in Vietnam, each of which were contending against the French. They had evolved as partly underground and partly aboveground revolutionary tendencies, which under one name or another occasionally united, but more often contested for leadership against the French. These two tendencies are today embodied in the Communist Democratic Republic of Vietnam (D.R.V.N.) and the nationalist, anti-Communist Republic of Vietnam (R.V.N.), struggling against a Communist rebellion and invasion.

In 1927 the nationalists were organized under the name of Vietnam Quoc Dan Dang (VNQDD), the Vietnam Nationalist Party. It has been well called the most significant non-Communist revolutionary nationalist organization. It was modeled on the Kuomintang and frequently supported by it. The Communists, under one name or another, such as the 1925, Canton-based Vietnam Revolutionary Youth League (Vietnam Cach Menh Thanh Nien Dong Chi Hoi) or the Indochina Communist Alliance (Dong Duong Cong San Lien Doan), were fused during January and February, 1930, in Hong Kong under the leadership of the Comintern agent now known as Ho Chi Minh. (Ho had joined the French Communist Party in 1920; was assigned to assist Borodin in China, 1924–1927; and has been in charge of Communist affairs in Indochina ever since.) The name for it has changed during the decades, but at or shortly after its founding it was called the Communist Party of Indochina (Dong Duong Cong San Dang). According to Ho Chi Minh, "since March 1951 [it has been called] the Vietnam Workers' Party" (Dang Lao Dong).

It may be worth noting parenthetically that the Stalinist Com-

munists in Vietnam assassinated or otherwise liquidated the Trotskyites, succeeded through the Pathet Lao in two or three northeast
provinces of Laos, but did not succeed in Cambodia. There Prince
Sihanouk (and his Popular Socialist Community Party) has been
and is the victor over the Communist remnants of Khmer Issarak.

As I have indicated, the Communists won out in North Vietnam, the nationalists won out in South Vietnam, and the country
was partitioned at roughly the 17th parallel by the Geneva Declaration and the agreements of 1954.

These documents have been the subject of much discussion and
debate. But I suggest that they are seldom read in their entirety. I
suggest to you as students that you read *all* the documents of Geneva, 1954. They include a Declaration of thirteen articles and
three agreements governing the "cessation of hostilities" in Cambodia (thirty-three articles), Laos (forty-one articles) and Vietnam (forty-seven articles). Nine states participated in the Geneva
Conference: Cambodia, the Democratic Republic of Vietnam
(D.R.V.N.—the Communist North), France, Laos, the People's
Republic of China, the U.S.S.R., the United Kingdom, the State
of Vietnam (soon to become a Republic, R.V.N.—the nationalist
South), and the United States. The Declaration contains the para-
graphs (Article 7) calling for free elections in 1956.

It is necessary to note that the Declaration of Geneva is an *unsigned* document. Each country "took note" of its contents and
stated its position with respect to it. It has no force in international
law. The State of Vietnam—South Vietnam—while agreeing to
abide by the terms of the cease-fire, explicitly rejected the Declaration. Its foreign minister (then, as now, Tran Van Do) had put
forth South Vietnam's position in the First Plenary Session in May
and in the concluding session in July 1954. South Vietnam proposed: no partition and free elections *then* under an international
supervisory body. The Communists—Russian, Chinese, and Vietnamese—rejected this. And since the French Government, under
Pierre Mendes-France, was anxious to cut its losses in Vietnam,
where it had been militarily defeated, and was also anxious to fulfill
Mendes-France's self-imposed timetable to bring about a cease-fire
"within thirty days or resign," France went along with the Communists on the Declaration.

What is more, France, not the State of Vietnam or Laos, signed
the cease-fire agreements with the D.R.V.N. (Cambodia signed its
own agreement with the Communist North Vietnam.) Obviously
France had no legal, moral, political, or military right to sign agreements with the D.R.V.N. *for* Laos and *for* the State of Vietnam.

These were *then* independent states by treaties with France. France could not commit them without their assent. And the government of South Vietnam, headed by Ngo Dinh Diem, who, whatever his shortcomings, was on record since 1933 as an ardent nationalist and Vietnamese patriot, opposed the deals made by France and the D.R.V.N. at Geneva.

Let me here insert a word about the role of my country. . . . The United States took modified note of the Geneva Declaration. Its representatives issued a unilateral declaration to that effect and indicated that though it welcomed the cease-fire, it would not take action which would contravene the policies of the independent State of Vietnam with respect to future elections and free determination by its government. The outgoing U.S. ambassador in Saigon, Donald Heath, had generally argued for the French position. The new ambassador, General J. Lawton Collins, initially had not made up his mind to recommend support for or against the new government of Premier Ngo Dinh Diem. Not until late 1954, and, more emphatically, not until early 1955 did the United States determine to support Diem's government (which became a republic in October of that year). By 1955 the United States, within its rights, and as it had acted earlier in Europe, obviously acted in order to aid this newly independent country, south of the 17th parallel, which had just adopted a democratic constitution and was proceeding to the elections of a national assembly.

Now to return to the 1954 Geneva articles. The agreement signed by France and Communist North Vietnam called, among other things, for a cease-fire, regroupment and evacuation of armed forces, respect for the democratic rights of the population, permission (for one year) for free movement of population, and an international supervisory body (later the International Control Commission, ICC, composed of India, chairman, Poland, and Canada).

What happened? I do not have the time to expand upon all these (and other) points in the agreement, but I shall illustrate with the following.

1. Movement of population. Oslo is a city of half a million people. Imagine, if you can, that all of you, twice over, were to decide to move to another country within one year. Imagine the dislocation in your lives. Now, almost one million people decided to leave their homes in North Vietnam. They quit the Communist dictatorship of the so-called Democratic Republic of Vietnam to go south. They left behind their homes, their agricultural holdings, everything but what they could transport in person. And we know that some 90,000 petitions of families who wanted to leave were

not acted upon during the year of grace from July, 1954, to July, 1955. These refugees were resettled and taken care of among the then twelve million South Vietnamese who were also facing great difficulties. Ponder that fact.

2. Withdrawal of armed forces. The regroupment and withdrawal of forces on each side of the 17th parallel was to be carried out in 300 days. The French completed their evacuation of North Vietnam by May, 1955. The regular forces of the Vietminh, the Communists, were also withdrawn (though not without considerable looting, destruction, and sabotage of public property, contrary to the agreement). However, despite arguments made by several governments at Geneva to include "irregular forces" as part of the armed forces withdrawal, the Communists at Geneva rejected any such inclusion. And the French acquiesced. As a result, Communist guerrilla forces were left in the South with arms cached in various hiding places. These "irregulars" formed an armed Communist network made up of southerners trained by the D.R.V.N. as well as northerners who came down as infiltrees.

3. The cease-fire. Immediately after the Geneva agreements were signed, the leader of North Vietnam, Ho Chi Minh, publicly vowed to bring about the reunification of his state with that of the Republic of Vietnam. There is nothing reprehensible in such views. Many Vietnamese, like many Germans and Koreans, are pledged to the eventual reunification of their countries. At issue are the methods employed to achieve the goal. In 1955, the Vietminh "irregular" cadres in the South organized what came to be called the Army of Liberation and began their military, assassination, terror, and kidnapping operations against the Republic of Vietnam. Their targets were the local leadership, whose destruction meant that the ordinary rice-farming family had to submit to the Communists, called later the Vietcong, or else not survive.

In mid-1956 I toured the Delta of South Vietnam to visit installations of the Philippine-manned Operation Brotherhood, a nongovernmental medical and social-aid effort, and the Cai San resettlement villages of northerners who voted with their feet against the Communist North. In both areas we had to have military protection because our jeeps and canal boats were subject to Vietminh fire. The country was at war with an enemy led, trained, inspired, and encouraged by Communists whose loyalty was to Hanoi and who were attempting to overthrow a legitimate government which had become a republic the previous year.

The "irregulars" . . . operated under various names, such as the "Patriotic Front" or "United Front" or "Fatherland Front." Estimates vary, but somewhere between five and ten thousand "irregulars" were thus available in the South to conduct warfare. And though the "armed forces" of the contracting parties were not to commit acts and operations, nothing was said in the agreements about infiltration, terrorism, assassination, and covert military operations—classic aspects of Communist tactics—which could be and were conducted by these irregulars. There was no cease-fire in Vietnam.

In sum, the Geneva agreements were inept, hopelessly ensnared in a mess of irresolution, ill-defined, with no policeman capable of handling any but the most unimportant complaints and minor violations. To go back to their "specifications," as has been proposed in some quarters, is to go back to a political sieve helpful only in advancing the Communist cause of warfare at the lower end of the spectrum: infiltration, subversion, guerrilla activity—the so-called wars of national liberation.

At that time and for some years neither my country, though obviously aiding South Vietnam, nor Ngo Dinh Diem's government paid sufficient attention to such wars. We did not study their strategy and tactics. We did not take seriously, as I am advising you to study and take seriously, its doctrine and consequent operations. The Communists did not conceal their plans. Mao Tse-tung has been putting them to paper since 1936. Marshal Lin Piao has recently (September, 1965) been reiterating them. General Vo Nguyen Giap of the D.R.V.N. published his own version some fifteen years ago. We initially treated the problems of Vietnam—and others—as we had the European ones: Provide economic and technical assistance to a country, and it will do the rest. But Vietnam is not Europe. The Republic of Vietnam had no national administrative machinery, had no industry or technology, had few trained citizens to man the many institutions of a government at peace, to say nothing of a government at war. Further, we did not really assimilate another fact: The great majority of the population of Vietnam—85 per cent—is rural. They have to be helped. Their security and stability are the main issues. Yet, we are mainly an urban people who tended to think that operations in the "city," particularly in the capital city, will find their way to the countryside. They do not, unless the countryside becomes the focus of one's effort.

But this is only part of the history of American aid to Vietnam, only part of what had to be learned. On the other side of the ledger there is the fact that every President of the United States since President Truman—Eisenhower, Kennedy, and Johnson—has made

and reaffirmed a commitment to support and defend the integrity and independence of a small country of fifteen million people living in 65,000 square miles. I suggest that you read a speech
that then-Senator Kennedy made in June, 1956. I have quoted in
my book *Why Viet Nam?* that speech in full. It is a speech with
which, in my view, no liberal, no democratic socialist can disagree.
It is directed toward the fulfillment of independence and freedom
for the South Vietnamese. [*For a critical evaluation of* Why Viet-
Nam? *and, indirectly, of some of the arguments in Dr. Trager's Oslo
address, see Bernard B. Fall's "The One-Eyed Hawk," The New
Republic, December 17, 1966.*]

Ten years ago—and even today—we in the West knew little of
such Asians as the Vietnamese. We are a white-skinned, basically
Christian civilization. We know little of the Buddhist-Confucian
traditions of such a country as Vietnam—though we are learning
and can learn if we will. For example, I know more about your
Ibsen, whose plays I read and reread as a young man, than I know
about such Vietnamese sects as the Cao Dai and Hoa Hao. I know
more about the Old and New Testaments than I know about the
Buddha or about Theravada and Mayahana Buddhism. These facts
of culture are foreign to our experience, but we neglect them at our
peril. As Bergson once said, "To understand you must install yourself in the flux of time." And we must install ourselves in the flux
of Vietnamese time and place if we are to understand why and how
these people have resisted for millennia the imposition of foreign
dictatorship. . . .

Thus I stand on the consequences of the policy adopted by my
country. The policy rests on a commitment to the Republic of
Vietnam made by three Presidents—Eisenhower, Kennedy, and
Johnson. The commitment is not only an executive promise. It has
been buttressed by a treaty, the Manila Pact of September, 1954,
which created the Southeast Asian Treaty Organization; and by
other congressional enactments. We once made such a commitment to Europe, and I heard few voices raised originally against
that commitment. Briefly and succinctly, the commitment to Vietnam was to help preserve its independence, to help it in the event
of Communist aggression. That is what we are doing. It is a commitment not to destroy North Vietnam, not to take over any Indochinese territory. We have no imperialist ambitions. Believe it or
not, Americans want to get out of Vietnam, want to go home.
Americans like to travel, but they prefer to live at home. We shall
get out of Vietnam when the job which we share with our allies in
Vietnam and above all with the Vietnamese people is done. That

job—expressive in full of U.S. policy in Vietnam—is based on three central ideas.

1. We are in Vietnam to preserve its independence by assisting its leaders to provide security against aggression and so-called wars of national liberation.

2. We are in Vietnam to help the Vietnamese achieve the stability in their domestic life that they want.

3. We are in Vietnam to help the Vietnamese improve the conditions of living for all the Vietnamese who wish to enjoy a full and free life.

I submit that these are three worthy propositions of policy—and they govern our presence in the Republic of Vietnam.

American Intervention Minimizes Violence

—ERNEST VAN DEN HAAG

Excerpts from a revised text of remarks originally delivered at New York University and other teach-ins, 1965–66. Dr. van den Haag is Adjunct Professor of Social Philosophy at New York University and the author of Passion and Social Constraint.

If you abhor suffering and premature dying, you will wish to minimize both, as I do. As you are aware, sometimes we must accept the risk—even the certainty—of much pain and of many premature deaths, to prevent (or at least reduce) the probability of more pain and of more casualties. Surgeons often advise operations for such reasons; a patient would be irrational to consider only the pain and the danger of the impending operation and not the greater pain and the greater danger he may have to endure later without it. So would we be irrational were we to direct our compassion solely to the cruelty, the horror, the casualties, and the dangers of the war in Vietnam without paying heed to the anguish, the grief, the dangers, and the casualties we might invite if we retreat from Vietnam now. Whatever the answer, certainly we must focus on the main, if not the only, question before us: Is the danger to future world peace greater if we continue, or if we halt the local war and abandon Vietnam?

A world without war is desirable, though unlikely in the foresee-able future. But a world with less, or even with less extensive, war is preferable to one with more, or more extensive, war. Just as not undertaking a comparatively minor, though still dangerous and painful, operation may ultimately cause more of the danger and pain the shortsighted patient tried to avoid, so unwillingness to fight a local, though still dangerous and cruel war, may make an immensely more cruel and world-wide war more probable. Cer-tainly World War II could have been avoided had it not been for the wooly-headedness, the misplaced goodwill, the well inten-tioned pacifism, and the utter shortsightedness of the English, French, and American peoples—all too faithfully reflected by the governments they elected. We all have paid an immense price for our illusions: Our reluctance to run a small risk, and suffer some casualties, caused millions of deaths and untold agony. Our com-passionate intention turned out to have cruel effects.

The circumstances in Vietnam are different. History does not re-peat itself—if we learn from it. Surely some lessons can be learned from our mistakes with Hitler. We might realize, for instance, that the answer to the question, would abandoning Vietnam now in-crease or decrease the probability of bigger and better wars?, does not depend on whether the Saigon Government is as weak, cor-rupt, unrepresentative, and reactionary as our journalists tell us. Possibly the governments whose territories Hitler infiltrated and conquered were as bad. But Hitler would have invaded Poland had it been governed by democratic angels. And Ho Chi Minh would infiltrate and try to conquer South Vietnam if it were run by an-gelic democrats. (To be sure, he would have a harder time. But the Apocrypha tell of attempts to subvert even paradise, stopped only by God's violent intervention.) . . .

At any rate, if Saigon is corrupt, unstable, or weak, it can be re-formed from within, whereas Hanoi—because it is strong, incor-ruptible, and irremovable—cannot. If both governments are bad—in whatsoever different ways—the future, even the present, is certainly better with corruptible than with incorruptible evil, with a bad government that is removable than with one that is not. The Vietnamese seem to think so, if the net immigration to the South means anything.

The power of the Vietcong in the countryside, often taken as evidence of popular support, may be evidence of ability to terrorize and intimidate. We know now that this was the case in an analo-gous situation in Malaysia. At the time, we were told that the Ma-laysian guerrillas were successful because they had the unanimous support of the people—as we are now told about the Vietcong. Our journalists and ideologues are so busy professing their love for Clio they do not notice that their sentiments are unrequited.

All this does not answer the main question: Is the reduction, if any, of the probability of worse clashes with the Communist powers sufficient, with what other grounds there may be for it, to justify our present policy in Vietnam? We must deal with at least a few of the irrelevancies which encumber this basic issue, before we explore it directly.

1. Should we have intervened in Vietnam in the first place? It is quite possible—though far from demonstrated—that intervening was one of President Kennedy's many mistakes. But the issue before us is not: Should we start the operation?—Mr. Kennedy decided that question—but, should we continue it? Objecting to the past is no substitute for confronting the present.

2. What right do we have to interfere in a faraway civil war? This, too, is a moot question now. The effects, moral or material, of continuing or discontinuing our present policy do not depend on whether we were right, wise, or justified, to start it. Once a promise has been made or an action started, the question is whether to keep or break the promise to continue or discontinue the action.

Further, Saigon (or Berlin, Moscow, Peking, or even the moon) no longer is far away, militarily or politically. And, partly for this reason, civil wars are no longer intranational conflicts, whether in Spain, Yemen, Hungary, or Vietnam. Therefore, China and the Soviet Union are allied with Hanoi and the Vietcong, and we are with Saigon. The policy of the government of one country affects other countries, which may attempt to influence, support, or overthrow it by diplomacy or force. Legally, governments are independent of each other. But, in fact, this is so in some cases, partly so in others, and not so at all in, say, East Germany or Yemen. I do not foresee any purely intranational civil wars in the future. There have been some in the past. There are none in the present. The world does not become different by wishing that it were; and to pretend that it is better than it is, is likely to make it worse.

3. Aren't we violating the Geneva accords? These accords were violated by North Vietnam, which was a party to them. Neither South Vietnam nor the United States subscribed to or is bound by these accords, though we did support them. But we also made it clear at the time that a "renewal of aggression" would not find us complacent. Anyway, the Geneva accords are as dead as the victims of the war they did not prevent.

4. What about the "free elections" provided for in the Geneva

accords? There is no indication that Hanoi will permit *free* elections—with opposition free to oppose and replace the government.
And most of the population of Vietnam live under the domination
of Hanoi—hence, election Communist-style would be an automatic
victory for Hanoi. Free country-wide elections are desirable, but
possible only when democracy has been established. The whole
idea is quite irrelevant to the recent circumstances.

5. What is the role of the U.N. in all this? None, of course. The
U.N. takes the side of all participants, since it is no more than a
name for all the nations together—a deceptively wishful one, since
the nations are not "united," and the U.N. cannot act independently of them; it simply reflects whatever conflicts or agreements
there are, causing neither. To presume that the U.N. can do anything the nations cannot do is absurd. Therefore, if you want to
think seriously about international relations, forget about the U.N.
It is as relevant to war and peace as the Metropolitan Opera Company, though more expensive and less enjoyable.

6. World opinion and our allies disapprove. Possibly. But foreign policy is not a popularity contest: We may be right though
disapproved of (world opinion usually favors appeasement of ag-
gressors and usually is wrong). Most likely, most things we will do
will be disapproved of; we cannot hope to be wealthy, powerful,
and popular. We can hope, though, to be respected and influential.
I doubt that abandoning Vietnam would increase the respect of
our friends and enemies, or our influence.

Further, there is no such thing as "world opinion"; there is a
relatively free public opinion in democratic countries, a govern-
ment-manipulated journalism in the nondemocratic ones, and cocktail gossip at the U.N. . . .

Now let me turn to more relevant questions:

1. Isn't there a danger that the war will degenerate into a wider
conflagration? I suspect that our intervention reduces the danger of
more extensive wars. China gives no indication of a wish to intervene directly, nor does Russia. Logistically, and in terms of its general situation, Chinese intervention would be ineffective and would
threaten disaster to both North Vietnam and China. Russia is in a
similar position. A widening of the war seems therefore most unlikely, provided that we continue to deny victory to Hanoi without
threatening either the existence of North Vietnam or of China.

2. Doesn't our intervention in Vietnam unite China and the Soviet Union against us, their common enemy? History has demonstrated that the conflict between China and the Soviet Union has
been exacerbated and the world Communist movement split wide

open during the Vietnam war. China's world-wide influence is declining. That of the Soviet Union is not increasing.

3. Can we win without escalating and greatly increasing the risk? I believe we can deny any semblance or hope of military or political victory to North Vietnam and its supporters, including the Vietcong, without spreading the conflict. As long as we do so, we are winning—for this was and is our aim. Once our resolve, ability, and persistence are beyond a reasonable doubt—beyond even the unreasonable doubts of some of our enemies—a reasonable truce along Korean lines is likely. This is not yet the case. (Peace demonstrations in United States, however legitimate and well-intentioned, do not help in this matter and do encourage false hopes in Hanoi, which prolong the war.) We have to live with war until this is achieved—not an attractive prospect. The alternatives, however, are even less enticing, indeed far more cruel and dangerous. . . .

If we were to discontinue our military action in Vietnam without having secured South Vietnam against being taken over by Hanoi, the following effects are probable:

1. South Vietnam would be united to North Vietnam under Ho Chi Minh's totalitarian rule. Countless South Vietnamese who placed their faith in our commitment, and helped us, would be slain. The chances for a nontotalitarian regime, for economic prosperity, and for individual freedom would be extinguished in South Vietnam for a long time to come.

2. Laos and Cambodia, now precariously independent, would become satellites of China: There would be no effective power in the area to check the Chinese. The reunified Vietnam would be entirely dependent on China. This is probably not the desire of any parties in Vietnam, and certainly not of the people. But it would be the effect of our withdrawal.

3. Neither Thailand nor Burma could hope to resist Chinese pressure; both countries would become satellites of China. Indonesia and Malaysia would be under increasing pressure. If we refused to help them, they would have to yield. If we supported them, we would be confronted with infiltration, subversion, and the same "civil war" from which we withdrew in Vietnam.

4. Chinese influence throughout Asia would increase and ours would decline. The Chinese would dispose of populations and resources not available to them now.

5. Our allies throughout the world, and the countries which relied on our support for their neutrality, would be forced to realize that American policy-makers, after having committed themselves to the defense of an area, and after having induced others to rely

on this commitment, may change their minds when the going gets rough without being compelled to do so by military defeat. Our promises would be regarded as unreliable. This would weaken the fabric of our alliances throughout the world.

Although our own actual power may not be decreased, the doubt thrown on our resolution and reliability will diminish its weight in influencing other nations. We may then have to exercise it to make it credible—we may have to go to war to defend positions that previously could have been defended merely by the promise to defend them if the need arose.

6. Within the Communist world, there has been a widening split between the Soviet Union, followed by its satellites, and China, followed by its client states; many of the Communist parties in the world are split now, but Soviet leadership has prevailed in most instances.

One of the issues in the Sino-Soviet conflict has been the strategy to be adopted toward the United States and its allies. The Soviet Union decided that attempts to conquer by external violence, or to support internal violence in countries now independent or allied to the United States, are unpromising as well as risky. Although not renouncing its ultimate aims either formally or in fact, and while no doubt hoping for a Communist world, the Soviet leaders now rely on political subversion, economic support, diplomacy, threats, blandishments, maneuvers, bluff—anything other than direct or indirect military confrontation with U.S. power. The Chinese accuse the Soviet leaders of betrayal, un-Marxist accommodation, cowardice, etcetera. They adhere daily to the ideology which Moscow now solemnizes only on Sundays (and has reinterpreted for everyday use in terms of "peaceful coexistence").

The Chinese believe that capitalism is on its last leg, and can be toppled by an aggressive Communist strategy. Unlike Moscow, Peking professes to believe that the United States is irresolute, divided, and beset by domestic difficulties which would paralyze it in case of war. Further, Peking insists that American power is overestimated and actually no match for Communist determination. Hence, Peking advocates a policy of confronting the U.S. with "revolutionary" power even at the risk of war; an aggressive policy of "liberation" should be pursued in Asia, Africa, and wherever possible.

7. The policies of imperial China had limited objectives and, most of the time, left its neighbors undisturbed. Communist China, however, has shown in Korea, Vietnam, Tibet, India, and Africa

that the talk of unlimited liberation is more than rhetoric. In time, more cautious counsels may prevail—but not if the dogmatic world-conquering ideas, which grossly underestimate our abilities and our will to resist, are—or seem to be—successful. In that case, an all-out war to defeat China may become unavoidable if the world is not to be surrendered to Chinese domination.

8. Should we abandon Vietnam now, we would immensely strengthen the Chinese and weaken the Soviet leadership within the Communist world. We would also create, or increase, pressure on the Soviet leadership to follow more aggressive policies. We would strengthen the fanatically aggressive wing of world Communism, which does not shrink from a military confrontation with us and which believes it can "win" such a cataclysm. We would have given the impression that the United States is weak or irresolute enough to retreat when confronted with determined revolutionary military force. Nothing could be more likely to bring about the world-wide disaster which those who propose to abandon Vietnam wish to avoid as fervently as I do.

9. Although it is fraught with "blood, sweat and tears" and the end is not in sight, our present policy in Vietnam seems vastly less dangerous and, in the end, less painful than any alternative. Politically, it has been successful beyond expectation. I do not think that the Chinese influence over the world Communist movement would have declined as it did had we not persisted in Vietnam. Nor would the uprisings in Africa, which replaced pro-Chinese with anti-Chinese governments, have happened. To be sure, these changes depended very largely on local factors. Yet, I doubt that they would have occurred, had the United States presented itself as a weak and unreliable ally.

If we allow the Chinese to impress the world as the wave of the future, their influence will increase. The destruction of the pro-Chinese Communist Party of Indonesia—which came near to ruling the hundred million Indonesians—would hardly have occurred had the Indonesians felt that the future belonged to China and that the United States was in the process of abandoning Asia.

The sacrifices made in defending Vietnam against Communist domination have already prevented the Chinese from taking over vast territories and have reduced their power in many areas and respects while increasing the power of our allies and the strength of our alliances. Continuation of our present Vietnamese policy is the best hope for world peace without surrender—the best policy to minimize violence and to avoid another world war.

The Importance of American Intervention in Vietnam

—DONALD G. BRENNAN

*Dr. Brennan is a member of the professional research
staff of the Hudson Institute (Harmon-on-Hudson,
New York), which conducts studies of policy problems in the areas of national security and international order. This is an edited transcript of an address
delivered at the Oslo Teach-In, April 16, 1966.*

In view of the unpopularity of escalation, I'm delighted to be
able to bring at least one particular form of escalation to an end—
namely, the escalation of the speeches. [*There had been six preceding speeches.*]

I probably should explain to you, briefly, the basis for my speaking to you on this subject. I am not a primary expert on Vietnam. I
haven't been there, I don't speak the language, I haven't interviewed Vietcong prisoners, and so on. I am primarily a student of
national security affairs, and I have spent a good deal of time thinking about Vietnam in terms of arms control and general strategy . . .

Let me begin by saying that I don't like the Vietnam war. It has
a great many bad effects. For example, it degrades the previously
growing détente between the United States and the Soviet Union.
It creates a bad image and some ill will for the United States elsewhere in the world. It diverts U.S. resources from other important
programs, and it generates divisiveness in the U.S. political system.
Moreover, apart from not liking the Vietnam war, I should question the wisdom of several of the past major U.S. decisions that
have brought us to the present state in that war.

First of all, I think it was unwise not to make a serious attempt
to achieve free elections throughout Vietnam in the 1954–56 era. I
think it very doubtful that it would have been possible to bring
about free elections in the North, which was one of the parts of the
election that was envisaged in the Geneva accord, but we would
have been in a much better position today if we had made a very
serious effort to try to get free elections in the whole of Vietnam

and had then found them impossible to obtain. I think it may have been a mistake to expand our role in Vietnam from an advisory role to a combat support role, somewhere around 1960, and . . . later on, to expand it from a combat support role to a combat role. I think the degree of the American commitment . . . in Vietnam at the time of those earlier decisions was considerably less than it has become since *because* of those decisions. I think it is quite clear that the implication of having had those decisions go the other way would have been bad for South Vietnam in ways that I shall discuss presently. But the cost of taking those decisions has also been quite high. Most especially, I should question the wisdom of the decision to bomb North Vietnam, both originally and after the relatively lengthy pause of a few months' duration.

In spite of all these differences with past policies and decisions, I believe there are very important reasons for continuing the American intervention in Vietnam. First of all, the United States has said it will continue that intervention. Whether it was wise or not, that was a very important commitment. . . . The matter is not one of prestige. It is a matter of commitment . . . of the sort that was made to Western Europe; and U.S. guarantees in many parts of the world would surely be much more suspect than they are at present, whatever one might think of the wisdom of our involvement in Vietnam, if it were not honored, and loss of the confidence that the commitment does engender would be a very large cost, not only for the United States, but for the entire Western world.

Second, as an important reason for continuing the intervention, I think it is clear that [South Vietnam] would get an oppressive regime if we were simply to withdraw. In the case of Vietnam, I, personally, do not much care about the Communist label—and, in this matter, I am not sure that Professor [Hans] Morgenthau accurately described the source of the motivation for remaining in that conflict as a somewhat theological one. [*Professor Morgenthau spoke at the Oslo Teach-In. See Chapter IV for excerpts from his address at the National Teach-In.*] In some minds, it undoubtedly is. I, personally, do not feel the least theological about that. I think that Communism (in terms of Marxism-Leninism) does not mean very much . . . [to] the Vietcong cadres. . . . There are, surely, some Communists there—such as Ho Chi Minh—but I doubt that there are many classical Communists of that type in the Vietcong cadres. Nevertheless, I think [the South] would truly have an oppressive government if the Vietcong were to take over, and it is clear that that oppressive government would, in fact, be directed by Hanoi. Dissidents of all sorts would be suppressed.

Another very important reason—perhaps the most important—for supporting continued intervention in the South is that one does not wish to encourage the techniques that the Vietcong and North Vietnamese have used in that conflict by rewarding them with success. I'll come back to that point later.

Finally, . . . I think it quite reasonable to continue the intervention [because] many of the main costs of that intervention have already been paid. We have taken something of a licking because of that involvement, and because of some bad decisions in the past, but it's not at all clear that many additional costs of that same kind must be paid before the conflict must be resolved in one way or another. Therefore, for all these reasons, I think it would be unwise for the United States simply to withdraw from the present situation, and I would not even think it unreasonable to strengthen that involvement. Sometimes such intervention has succeeded in very satisfactory ways.

I would point out, for example, the case of Greece, where the manner of life of the Greek people since the successful termination of the Greek conflict, in the late 1940's, has been very different from what it would have been if the Greek Communist insurrection had succeeded in capturing control of that country at that time. Many countries in Eastern Europe are quite different today from what they were in the early 1950's, but there was a long period during which those countries were very badly off, and I think it predictable that it will be a long time before North Vietnam and China and some other Communist countries will be well off.

If we continue that intervention, and especially if it is in any form strengthened, I think it is important to do so with wisdom and good judgment; I am not sure that we have, in the past, always displayed these. I would refer again to the bombing of the North. It seems to be unwise, in part because it doesn't do very much, so far as one can see in *The New York Times*. It is not at all apparent that carrying out bombing operations in the North makes a significant difference in the military effectiveness of the Vietcong. It certainly does do some things by the way of strengthening the North; it strengthens the hand of the Hanoi regime in their domestic political situation, and it strengthens the Soviet support of the Hanoi regime. And I think that the bombing is especially costly in terms of a new and dubious tradition.

Let me explain what I mean by the bombing being costly in terms of a new and dubious tradition. It has not been traditional, in military conflicts in modern times, to use pure reprisal attacks against foreign countries whose forces were intervening in some local situation. It is true that there has been a good deal of talk about retaliation as a military technique, but in point of fact there has been no significant use made of it outside of . . . Vietnam. I think it is a bad tradition to establish, in part because I think that the technique could easily be used against the West in other settings in which we would find it much less congenial to have it available as an established technique. But our own actions are making the tradition that such techniques are usable. And this is what I mean by saying that I think the bombing of the North is costly in terms of a new tradition.

But these reasons for opposing the bombing of the North, I want to point out explicitly, are essentially calculations in nature; in particular, it is very relevant in my own mind, and in the minds of many with whom I associate, that that bombing accomplishes very little. If you could be sure of bringing the war to an end in six months by that technique, very few people would find it so questionable, because most people who are concerned with international affairs share the view that it is perfectly proper to oppose the North Vietnamese intervention with force. I just happen to believe that the costs of this particular application exceed its likely gain. I think there is no question about the morality of this use of force. I think that it has been at least as moral to oppose the establishment of an oppressive regime in South Vietnam by forceful means as it has been to use military force in other contexts to oppose other uncivilized actions.

Obviously, it is unclear whether one can create a viable alternative to an oppressive regime in the South. It is unclear for several reasons. The relevant traditions in the South are mostly lacking. South Vietnam is not a country with a long tradition in modern times of governing itself. Briefly stated, [the South Vietnamese] don't know how. In particular, there seems to be little inclination of native political groups to submerge their differences on behalf of some larger common interest. Finally, and not least important, many of the competent potential leaders in the countryside—village mayors, police chiefs, teachers, and so on—have been systematically exterminated by Vietcong. A relevant leadership cadre is largely missing. This is the technique to discourage I was speaking of earlier.

I think that the systematic murder of the local leadership in the countryside practiced by the Vietcong is the most uncivilized technique of warfare employed in recent history—and I think one should not, if at all possible, crown that technique with success. Perhaps we cannot drive the Vietcong out right away but we can

certainly inhibit their success—at least if the South Vietnamese political situation does not disintegrate completely. And perhaps we
might ultimately get a reasonable government there that will not
be oppressive. I at least believe that one should hang on and try.

How to Stay in Vietnam

— J O H N   D.   M O N T G O M E R Y

*Dr. Montgomery is Professor of Public Administra-
tion at Harvard University. These are excerpts from
a revised version of a talk given at a teach-in conducted by the World Affairs Council in Boston, May
17, 1966. The full text appears in* Vietnam Perspectives, *August, 1966.*

If, in the months ahead, the Vietnamese people do miraculously
produce a constitutional government that can provide the means of
national political survival, it will be possible for the United States
and its allies to continue offering support along present lines and,
gradually, to replace military with economic priorities. But if this
does not occur, it may well be necessary for them to undertake
more direct political and administrative measures.

I believe that four alternative "models" of action will cover the
major contingencies. The first two—military government and constitutional dictatorship—might be necessary if no constitutional
order emerges at all. The third—supervised elections—would be
possible if a constitution is agreed upon. The fourth—a revolutionary directory—would serve in both of these contingencies and also
provide a means of establishing a working government if at anytime
the government failed to achieve a national consensus. All of these
models have precedents in American history, but any one of them
would require the United States to exercise various degrees of influence and to use its power and its wisdom for political purposes.
Each of them assumes that the United States is prepared to accept
primary responsibility for the establishment of international order
in South and Southeast Asia. Yet they do not make any assumptions about the nature of the internal political forms that may
eventually emerge in Vietnam itself. Indeed, I am convinced that
American foreign policy is best served not by attempting to impose

a specific form of government on other nations but by preserving (or creating) an international order which permits individual peoples to make their own political choices. The U.S. political commitment is to order and process, not to form and organization.

In considering these four alternative courses of action, the United States will have to weigh the probable domestic responses in both the United States and Vietnam; the international implications; the moral considerations that provide a fundamental rationale for the American involvement; and, most important of all, its own vital national interests. Such a choice cannot be carried out successfully until these implications have been carefully considered and presented to the public view.

The first, and harshest, model is an imposed military government. It would involve establishing an occupation or dominium in Saigon, to be supplemented with civil affairs teams posted in other areas as these are recovered from enemy hands. If this model were followed, the United States would assume maximum sovereign authority, with the exercise of its force being limited only by international convention and military factors. Such an action should be considered a last resort, to be taken only if there were no immediate prospects for stable government in Vietnam. Its practical justification would lie in its technical superiority over any mixed sovereignty's capacity to wage war; its ultimate purpose would be to install stable national political institutions. Many Americans would strongly resent such an action: They did not readily accept the responsibilities of military government even in Italy, Germany, and Japan after World War II. And the tasks in Vietnam would be politically much more difficult than those in the defeated Axis countries, whose governments had been at war with the United States. A closer parallel would be found in the occupation of France following the withdrawal of German troops, when civil authority was established under military discipline as occupied zones were liberated by advancing Allied forces. Similar developments occurred in southern Italy as the Allied troops moved northward in pursuit of first Mussolini's and then Hitler's armies. This approach also succeeded in establishing a viable order in South Korea. But resort to true military government under civil affairs conditions would require a kind of operation which has not been undertaken by American armies in recent years. It is one for which the Pentagon is notably ill-prepared at present, although there is, theoretically, plenty of experience and competence both inside and outside the Army, which could be invoked if a decision of this sort were made.

The duration of such a military occupation is difficult to forecast, since Vietnam is much less a nation than Japan or Germany were in the aftermath of defeat. Even after an adequate sense of national identity and coherence is developed, probably its first manifestations would be through a repudiation of the American presence. An American occupation would be deemed a form of imperialism and self-righteousness, both in this country and abroad; it would be resented by our Allies and exploited by our enemies. True, an imposed military command would reduce some of the complications of establishing stability in the short run, and it might even permit a gradual improvement in the indigenous political institutions. But it remains, nevertheless, the least desirable and least probable of all of the courses of action which would permit a continued American presence in Vietnam.

The second model . . . is a U.S.–sponsored Vietnamese constitutional dictatorship. Under American tutelage, a military dictator appointed and protected by the threat of force could doubtless retain major elements of sovereignty in domestic matters while executing war-related policies assigned by the senior partner. This dictator would have to be willing to accept limitations on his authority to make any decisions that would tend to commit American forces and prestige. He might be a Chiang Kai-shek, possessing personal vigor, and perhaps some elements of political support of his own, and capable of maintaining resolute government in the face of opposition (a skill, incidentally, which Chiang himself did not develop until after he had been evicted from mainland China). Not all such "constitutional" dictators are necessarily autocrats: Magsaysay, in the Philippines, was trained, chosen, and supported by American forces, and if he had survived, he might well have succeeded in his ambitious plan of introducing a viable democracy into that country. American support to abhorrent dictators like Batista shows the danger of being too generous in maintaining such creatures if they fail to respect the legitimate rights of their own citizens. Governments established with strong American support in Panama, Guatemala, and even Bosch's Dominican Republic, all give evidence of the wide range of political regimes which external forces can theoretically protect and maintain. The power actually wielded by the United States under such an arrangement would undoubtedly by greatly reduced from that of the first model, but the moral position and international prestige of the United States would be significantly better than if it operated a military government of its own. It is also possible that the long-term political prospects of creating indigenous institutions capable of maintaining themselves would be better under this second model.

The main difficulty with this approach is that no Vietnamese candidate for the post has shown the necessary qualifications. Diem, in spite of his virtues, was shortsighted and ill-advised, imprisoned by his distrust of everybody outside his own family. His successors lacked the stature, the personal stability, and the wisdom and self-restraint for the task. Unless a dark horse emerges in the next few months, the United States will probably have to abandon this model.

The third model assumes that the constituent assembly of 1966 is able to produce a constitution and hold some form of national elections. The role to be played by the United States would be to supervise these elections and, if necessary, accept an active part in determining their outcome. This kind of interference would be explained in terms of an undoubtedly benevolent purpose: to reduce the influence of those who would destroy the prospects of constitutionalism, and to offer logistical and communications support to those individuals and groups whose political record and purposes would seem to comport with eventual movement toward a viable indigenous institution.

There are three possible outcomes of such an election. First, it might permit a government to emerge that would seek to reduce American presence, perhaps by reaching an accommodation with the Vietcong or by vacillating among other forms of compromise. Since such an outcome would constitute a means of withdrawing from Vietnam, the United States would presumably use all of its influence against it unless the decision to withdraw had already been made in Washington. A second possibility is that the election would produce no government at all, but a continuous jockeying for power. Such a resolution would be intolerable and would eventually force a reversion to one of the other three models. The presumption of this third model is, therefore, that the United States would use the election as a means of weakening Communist or neutralist claims to power while establishing a basis for stability. At a minimum, this would require efforts to protect the privacy of the polling booth, but it is doubtful that voting safeguards alone would be enough to insure the outcome, given the determination, cunning, and violent tastes of so many Vietnamese factions. Quite possibly it would be necessary to provide some mechanism for screening and licensing parties and candidates or to offer logistical support to preferred groups. And, most certainly, there would have to be some means of guaranteeing civic order following the election. The United States would thus have to participate indirectly in "rigging" the election or, at least, consent to practices that would be so interpreted. But to expect any real resemblance to an American election is absurd. External surveillance will be necessary in any significant election that occurs in Vietnam today. Few countries in Asia use suffrage as the normal means of changing governments. Where elections do take place, the contests are usually unequal, the parties under surveillance, the competition restricted, and corruption rampant. Usually, the question to be asked in evaluating the outcome of such an election is "Who rigged it?" rather than "Was it rigged?" One may assume that any election in Vietnam today would be influenced by actions that would not be tolerated in the United States and Western Europe, in spite of any surveillance that could reasonably be placed upon the proceedings.

This option is, thus, the riskiest of all. On the surface, it might seem to be the one most likely to accommodate the political sensibilities of the American and Vietnamese people. But, in spite of the symbolism of electoral democracy, this model carries the largest element of hypocrisy among the possible solutions; it would involve the greatest administrative confusion of any of the four models; and, it might permit some future Vietnamese government to revert to the irresponsible gamesmanship characteristic of the Diem regime. The U.S. Government may have to opt for this model but, if it does so, it should be prepared to play a supervisory role beyond mere poll-watching—unless it intends to use elections as a means of withdrawal. And, after the elections, there would remain the uncomfortable prospect that American political participation would have to continue, through the use of national and local civil affairs teams. The result would thus be a resort to some other model after all.

The fourth model is a revolutionary directorate representing major elements in Vietnamese society, with a temporary mandate, specific functions, and close liaison with American civil affairs teams attached at national and local levels. Present U.S. support of the military junta is a somewhat uncertain experiment moving in the direction of this model, except that the Americans have never really tried to make political decisions in Vietnam. A directory would permit some sharing of political responsibility and would encourage local political contests over any issues that did not interfere with military operations. A true fourth-model approach would not eliminate the short-term causes of disorder and instability, but it would control the symptoms while working out a cure. In creating a directory, the United States would agree to help choose a special emergency coalition, sustained by force of arms, that would hold power under specific conditions. The military class has supplied the Vietnamese interregnum heretofore, but it has produced nothing more stable than a truce among war lords. If a collegial government were established temporarily by distinguished citizens in both civil and military life, including leaders from the Buddhist, Confucian, and Catholic elements, the United States would not need to be as halfhearted in its political support as it has been in the past. Elements in the new government, for their part, would have to accept the necessity for continued internal cooperation for the duration of the war and reconstruction, while the United States provided a demonstration of sufficient authority and determination to carry conviction with the political opposition. At the same time, the United States would have to retain some visible marks of authority and maintain civil affairs teams in provinces and districts in much the same manner as it did for the U.N. military government in Korea.

If the provisional directory were to be self-liquidating, a specific term of office would have to be assigned in advance, based on *time* or the accomplishment of designated *tasks*. Specific authority would have to be exercised under some written or informal agreement or treaty, and conditions regarding the eventual establishment of constitutional government would have to be specifically announced.

In imposing such conditions upon a coalition government, the United States would have to display greater decision and play a more affirmative political role than it previously has in South Vietnam. But the degree of actual interference in the internal politics of the government need be no greater than has attended less purposeful American influence there in the past. The protection of citizens against violence by the state and a limited recognition of civil rights would have to be guaranteed by the United States in order to fulfill the obligations of its commitment to eventual constitutionalism.

Part of the difficulty with the operation of this fourth model is that the United States has shown a tendency to support experimental coalitions in Vietnam without setting forth any generally understood conditions in advance. Surely, by now, we should have learned the danger of unconditional support of even a friendly coalition. The American prestige would be so heavily committed to the outcome of a revolutionary directory that the ultimate decisions would have to be made in the White House, with the full support of congressional leaders. Thereafter, choosing, briefing, and controlling the coalition leaders, once these constitutional decisions had been made, would require as much wisdom and forbearance as the United States has been able to field anywhere in the world.

American policy in Vietnam drifted in this direction following the dismissal of General Thi, but the United States has not yet been willing to set the ground rules that will be necessary to provide long-term political improvement. The major weakness of previous directories was the absence of either internal or external political support. Like the others, this fourth model demands a greater political commitment than the United States has yet made in Vietnam. It could offer great promise for the future, if the United States accepted its full implications.

All of these models would be improved by some form of internationalization. . . .

[They] give us no real insight into the form of government that might eventually emerge in Vietnam. They do not even guarantee the destruction of an indigenous Communist movement after a period of stability: Vietnam might conceivably produce the first national Communist movement to come to power by popular consent (though there is no reason to suspect them of having this much support at present). But, as I have said before, the vital interest of the United States is not to prevent Ho Chi Minh from legitimately taking power (a matter which would probably have been of indifference to us had it occurred a dozen years ago). What the American action is primarily designed to prevent is the success of movements of subversion, assassination, and sabotage, leading to an irreplaceable regime of Communist professionals determined to duplicate their successes elsewhere.

The United States has the power to prevent that from happening, but, so far, it is not using it very purposefully, except on the battlefield. If it is the highest interest of the United States to preserve an element of stability in parts of the world coveted by Peking or Moscow, it must accept more forthright responsibility for political measures to deny Communist success in Saigon.

In the present interim before the war is won, and then in that next interim before Vietnam can become a truly independent, self-governing state, government in cities and villages not actually under fire must provide security, render the services necessary to survival, transmit local desires to Saigon, and, finally, link communities together into a nation. Merely restoring local institutions to power will not do these things, nor will village self-help or greater religious tolerance or economic improvement. What is required is a structure that will permit the central government to extend its authority to the peripheries and the local citizens to register their needs and desires in the capital city. The Vietcong could doubtless have established such a structure, but only at a cost that neither we nor the South Vietnamese were willing to pay. If the Vietnamese cannot now establish it, the only sure alternative is for us, with our Allies, to do so. It can be done by organizing civil affairs units from personnel and communications facilities already in the region, once the necessary commitment is made.

There may well be no other way to stay in Vietnam—except to keep on fighting, indefinitely.

III

Response: Pro and Con

Editors' Introduction

The teach-ins had arrived; a new expression had entered the vocabulary of American education and politics. Most important, the teach-ins, whether applauded or denounced, were provoking something approaching a national debate on Vietnam. Even the Administration, as the next chapter will show, at length had to take notice of the movement and confront its critical thrust.

The opinions on the teach-ins presented in this section range from lofty praise to ridicule and vituperation. Response from students—perhaps the response that will count most—was generally favorable to the teach-in *idea*, although not always in accord with the anti-Administration content. Teach-in audiences often included students who hissed the critics, questioned them aggressively, and applauded minority speakers defending the Administration case. The earnest tone conveyed by the University of Michigan *Daily*, in evaluating the first teach-in, was typical of campus press response, whatever the particular political point of view.

The politeness that university authorities generally accorded the sessions is reflected in Dean Knedler's message of congratulations to an organizer of the first New York University Teach-In. Whether they appreciated the educational purposes served—as Dean Knedler did—or feared unmanageable consequences were they to oppose the movement, school administrations generally cooperated to the extent of providing classrooms, auditoriums, sound equipment, and the like for the meetings.

The teach-ins quickly attracted the attention of the nation's press; here were American educational happenings comparable in interest to the Berkeley eruption of the previous semester. Teach-in

sponsors welcomed the publicity, although they would have preferred a little less focusing on the trimmings—the hour of night,
the freewheeling style, the garb and hair styles of the students,
etcetera—and a little more on the content of the sessions. In the
wake of the news stories came evaluations by editorial writers and
columnists, and here political alignments came into play. The liberal weekly *The Nation*, critical of the Johnson Administration's
war policies and aware of mounting frustration among the academic opposition, saluted the teach-ins for both political and educational reasons. On the other hand, Will Herberg, writing in the
conservative *National Review*, was unimpressed by the quality of
professorial criticism and scolded academics for what he interpreted
as special pleas to be heard by the Administration (an argument
foreshadowed in McGeorge Bundy's grouchy reply to an invitation
from Washington University professors to discuss Vietnam policy;
see Chapter IV, Part 3). As practiced by William S. White and
former Presidential candidate Barry Goldwater, analysis of the
teach-ins becomes mudslinging of the most primitive type.

Predictably, red-baiting and intemperate charges of giving "aid
and comfort to the enemy" marked the reaction of critics on the
right both in and out of Congress. (See, for example, Senator
Dodd's evaluation of the teach-ins, in Chapter VII.) Senator Gale
McGee of Wyoming, though a supporter of the Administration's
war effort, was moved on several occasions to speak on the dangers
of leveling reckless accusations at teach-in critics. We have included
here one of Senator McGee's statements defending teach-ins as an
extension of academic freedom; a fuller discussion of this subject
appears in Chapter V. Other members of Congress responded so
favorably to the teach-ins that they joined them. Senator Wayne
Morse of Oregon and Ernest Gruening of Alaska, who had been
waging a lonely battle from the floor of the Senate against U.S.
Vietnam policies, now used the teach-ins to amplify their offensive.
Still other congressmen organized public hearings on Vietnam,
modeling them on teach-ins and inviting academics and laymen
from their constituencies to participate. (The transcript of one
such event, organized by Representative Robert W. Kastenmeier
of Wisconsin was published privately as *Vietnam Hearings—Voices
from the Grass Roots* by Representative Kastenmeier, 1965.) Such
efforts foreshadowed the long-overdue open hearings on Vietnam
conducted by the Senate Foreign Relations Committee in February, 1966 (Chapter VIII).

It is difficult to estimate with precision how many scholars the
teach-in movement represents. Critics of the movement have

spoken deprecatingly of a "noisy minority." However, the hundreds of teach-ins that have taken place since the inception of the campaign in March, 1965, the thousands of signatures on advertisements and petitions from the universities, and the volumes of letters to the press from academics across the nation leave the impression that professorial participation and support is widespread. Here and there, certain scholars have tried to counter this impression. One such attempt—a statement signed by twenty specialists—is reprinted here.

We must give special attention to what might be termed the middle-ground position on the teach-ins, particularly as taken by a dean of American political commentators, James Reston of *The New York Times*. Mr. Reston's first reaction to the teach-ins, reprinted here, in a way reflected the mixed feelings of large sections of the American public toward the whole subject of the war: a tremendous anxiety about our involvement and its potential consequences, coupled with a certain degree of faith (born, perhaps, more of hope than of confidence) in the Administration's constant reminders that it actively sought disengagement and a peaceful settlement. Teach-in critics of the Administration, particularly those who pulled no punches about the barbarism of the war or the incredibility of Administration pronouncements, were, in the Reston view, undercutting Government peace efforts. (President Johnson had just delivered his Johns Hopkins address offering "unconditional discussions," on April 7, 1965; ironically, the day Mr. Reston's evaluation appeared, *The Times* carried a front-page story by its military editor, Hanson W. Baldwin, revealing—accurately, as it turned out—that the Administration was planning a major ground build-up in South Vietnam and an intensification of the bombing in the North.) Mr. Reston's writing on the policies and personalities of the Johnson Administration has been consistently ambiguous. Not surprisingly, his response to teach-in criticism of those policies and personalities was to prove equally equivocal; for reasons examined in the next chapter, he was later to applaud the teach-in as a "useful tool." We reprint here a sampling of the many published and unpublished letters from the pens of scholars written in reply to Mr. Reston's original, plainly hostile estimate.

The Intellectual Community Begins to Stir

Editorial from The Michigan Daily, *March 26, 1965.*

The usually unorganized and ineffective intellectual community is beginning to stir. With the phenomenal success of yesterday's Vietnam protest and the burgeoning plans for similar activities on campuses across the country, it is clear that at least some faculty and students are seeking a greater role in shaping American policies.

These activities must continue. In general, the larger the number of people openly expressing opinions on policy issues—whatever their views—the more viable our democratic processes will be.

Specifically, this particular series of protests raises some fundamental questions about U.S. policies in Vietnam, and, if the protests do not affect policy, they can at least pressure the Johnson Administration into presenting a full defense of its position.

But the success of yesterday's protest should not preclude more radical actions in the future. Faculty and students at the university should not forget the issue which originally confronted them when they were planning a teaching strike instead of a "teach-in." That issue is whether teachers have the *de facto* as well as the *de jure* right to make final judgments on the relative value of different educational activities and whether this right extends, without legislative or administrative sanctions, to political protests which require class time.

Given the original faculty group's deeper immediate concern for Vietnam, however, we feel the decision to cancel the teaching strike is tactically justified. The faculty group would not have been able to present as large and effective a program as it did yesterday if it had had to fight on a second front at the same time.

With respect to Vietnam, a number of questions raised at Wednesday's protest deserve serious consideration. . . .

The very fact that these basic questions are being raised with such vigor points to the possibility that our policy in Vietnam is not in the best interest of the United States or the Vietnamese. The war there has tremendous military, economic, and humanitarian implications about which everyone should be concerned and about which the academic community should have much to say.

A Message from the Dean

—J. W. KNEDLER, JR.

Dean Knedler's message was sent to Professor Philip Zimbardo, an organizer of the first New York University Teach-In.

April 19, 1965

I could not attend all of the teach-in from 8:00 P.M. to 4:30 A.M., but I got there for about an hour and a half in the middle of the night. The lectures I heard were certainly of the first quality, and so was the reception given by the audience to the lecturers.

Here are my congratulations to you and the members of the Ad Hoc Committee on the excellence of the arrangements, the obvious skill involved in the planning, the authoritative cooperation in the execution. I admire the stamina and the devotion you all showed. It was an occasion of which . . . you and I and the college can proudly boast. Quite simply, you handled the evening so that it became an important part of the education of the participants.

Teach-Ins and Walk-Outs

Editorial from The Nation, *April 12, 1965.*

If necessity is the mother of invention, one may say that the all-night teach-in was born of desperate necessity. The chief opposition to the developing all-out war in Asia has centered in the academic communities, students and professors alike; and in the conventional forms of meetings, demonstrations, petitions, telegrams to the President, etcetera, it has had precious little effect. Mr. Johnson remains totally insulated from outside criticism, and nothing bores the average reporter more than a meeting which is not sponsored by the local millionaires and made bearable by libations for the press. So the backlog of frustration among critical members of the faculty and student body kept mounting—and then came the teach-in.

Teach-in! The very term inspires interest. It reminds the journalist of marathon dancing, flagpole sitting, and other honored American contests of endurance. So the reporters come and bring photographers with them, and the headlines follow. The reasons may be bad, but the results are good. Without publicity, nowadays, the best cause is lost.

The overriding merit of the teach-in, of course, is that it is truly educational, and even a university cannot object to education. The protesting students, some of whom may have protested intuitively without really knowing what it was all about, get background and facts, usually from the best-informed instructors on the campus. . . .

Columbia University held one, in cooperation with other New York City institutions, on March 26, and Professor Seymour Melman expressed the general feeling when he said: "I think the students of the universities are coming out of a long sleep."

The walk-out is briefer and less constructive, but President Harry D. Gideonse inspired one at Brooklyn College when he laid down the law to a few hundred students who complained about what they called the absence of academic freedom at the college. "We are leaving as a formal protest against the philosophy and methods of this administration," said the leader. "By all means go," Dr. Gideonse replied, and out they went to demonstrate in the rain. Perhaps Dr. Gideonse would profit by attending a few teach-ins.

The New Estate: The Professors and the "Teach-Ins"

—WILL HERBERG

From the National Review, *July 13, 1965. For different views on the role and qualifications of the scholar, see Chapter VI.*

There is no need to take the recent rash of university "teach-ins" on American policy in Vietnam too seriously. With very few exceptions, the protesting professors were not particularly distinguished either by the scope of their knowledge or by the cogency of their arguments. Nor have these professors had anywhere near the following attributed to them by the press, foreign and domestic. In no case did they enjoy the support of a majority of the faculties involved; mostly, it was no more than a small minority of teachers and students that made all the noise. Even the confusion they created was not particularly impressive—probably because Washington had already managed to confuse the facts and issues so thoroughly that even the most confused professor could not improve it.

Under the present circumstances, there would be little gained, and perhaps something lost, in pretending that arguing with the professors on Vietnam could concievably amount to a rational discussion.

There is, however, something about the university teach-ins that has been overlooked, yet seems to me to deserve serious consideration. In these "protest" activities, for the first time I can think of in our history, the professoriat—or, rather, small cliques speaking for the professoriat—came forward not simply as undivided citizens, not simply as professional groups, but as a substantially new Estate of the Realm, with a legitimate claim to be consulted on government policy and a special right to help determine it. Not as scholars in relevant fields but as professors, simply as professors. By virtue of being professors—professors of biology, assistant professors of English, instructors in Romance Languages—they claimed the right to challenge the Government to public debate on whatever issues they pleased. No one would maintain that plumbers, just by virtue of being plumbers, had any such right, or physicians, lawyers, engineers, merchants, bankers, or labor leaders, except perhaps where the issue touched on their special field of interest and competence. But professors—some of them seem to think—are different. They feel that they are entitled to demand that the Administration justify its policies before them in particular, and engage with them in formal debate: the Administration *versus* the Professors! A new estate has apparently emerged in our body politic—the Professoriat!

The fact of the matter is that a sizable group of our professors do not like to think of themselves simply as scholars and teachers in their various fields. They yearn to be recognized as *philosophes* in the eighteenth-century sense, that is, as self-appointed journalistic publicity-makers, freewheeling policy-makers responsible to no one and to nothing, except their own good opinion of themselves. This is not only to mistake their vocation, and to betray their academic responsibility; it is also to befuddle the minds of the students, not just on this or that issue, but on what a university is, or ought to be like. "If they want to be preachers"—I am adapting the late Justice Frankfurter's advice to judges—"let them dedicate themselves to the pulpit. If they want to be primary shapers of policy, the Legislature is their place . . ." The truth is that some of our professors, in their presumption, would like to be all of these things, without a thought as to competence, authority, or responsibility.

There is another reason why it is so disturbing to see professors make such pretensions. It is that they are peculiarly unfitted to play such a role: They have generally been so notoriously wrong in their judgment of public affairs, especially foreign affairs. As Reinhold Niebuhr pointed out with some exasperation a decade ago,

> It does not become intellectuals to speak so contemptuously of the practise of statesmanship, particularly since their own record since the eighteenth century has been so dismal. It has consisted in dreaming up utopias, both harmless and dangerous. . . . But vain dreams are never harmless if they prompt us to evade duties, or if they induce attitudes of contempt for people who do not share their illusions. Considering the vanity of these schemes dreamed up by the intellectuals, one is almost persuaded to thank God for the wisdom of the traditional "man in the street." I would substitute the taxi-driver for the man in the street. For the taxi-driver is superior to the ordinary intellectual in dealing with the complexities of politics, including international politics, because a shrewd awareness of human foibles prevents him from engaging in vain dreams or in self-pity. ("A Century of Cold War," *New Leader*, August 2, 1954.)

What our teach-in professors would like, apparently, is to have this proclivity to "vain dreams" and "self-pity" become *institutionalized* by getting themselves recognized as an Estate of the Realm, entitled, in their corporate capacity (the Professoriat), to be consulted by the Government for advice and consent in major policy decisions. There is, perhaps, no section of the American people that could make such a claim with worse credentials.

Campus Lefties' Field Day

—WILLIAM S. WHITE

From the New York Journal-American, *May 12,* 1965.

Washington: The neutralist and appeasement-minded college professors and their strident followers have, for months, dominated all discussion, among people of intellectual bent, of this Government's happily firm policies in Vietnam and Latin America.

Because those who howl in "protest" predictably attract more attention than do those who quietly support the clear necessity to resist the new Communist aggression, however prettied up it is by clever slogans, the campus lefties have had a long field day.

To a regrettable degree, they have been able to leave the impression in many minds abroad that the authentic intellectuals and true sensitives of this country are in sympathy with Communist terrorists demonstrably having blood in their nostrils.

It would be absurd to suppose that all or most of these screeching pedagogues, these leaping and lamenting boys and girls, are in thrall to the new international Communist conspiracy. For this is a mixed bag, indeed. Within it, to be sure, are professors and students with observably close ties to undeniably far-left movements who faithfully speak the harsh, twisty jargon that passes for Communist logic.

Within this bag are mere frustrated beatniks and middle-aged show-offs who would enter any "demonstration" anywhere so long as it would put their pictures in the papers and on the television screen. But within it, too, are youngsters of the greatest decency and the most generous ideals. It is these boys and girls whose nobleness of intention for peace in this world is being exploited by the hard, tough, hating intellectual tricksters and confidence men who all too often lead them.

Thus, there is posed a national problem of enormous difficulty and subtlety. Clearly, it is necessary, without further ado, to disperse this pinkish cloud from the campuses that spreads abroad a fallout of slander of honorable American policies and purpose. . . .

On Viet "Teach-Ins"

—BARRY GOLDWATER

From the New York Herald Tribune, October 24, 1965.

The thoroughly disgusting roots of the so-called teach-ins protesting our efforts in Vietnam have been exposed. It has been reported that several protesting professors have fully supported the Vietcong side of the fighting and have even said they would welcome a Vietcong victory.

For a time, it seemed that this raggle-taggle protest was being made by a bunch of beatniks and pacifists scrawling naughty words across the political fence in a "hey, look at us" effort to shock their elders.

But it went deeper than that. Some of these laughable fanatics seem to have had a far from laughable motivation. They don't just hate America's policies; they actually like the other side. Communism seems to appeal to them. The Vietcong does not repel them —their tyranny does not appall them, neither does their terror.

They must hate capitalist America—that's a virtual credential for their exploitation of everything capitalism makes possible, including the opportunity to spout-off endlessly about every subject under the sun. They seem to hate the United States enough to admire those who would smash it, not with an argument, but with a sword, a gun, or grenade.

In hoping for a VC victory, they are wallowing in violence—in effect, condoning the planned, purposeful slaughter of the anti-Communist Vietnamese and their wives and children. They are condoning captivity and cruelty in their rawest, most barbaric forms.

Unctuously, these protesting professors say they do not condone the killing of American soldiers by the Vietcong. But they welcome a Vietcong victory. They say they want a political victory, but prefer not to discuss whether a political victory would be any different from a military victory in fastening the chains of totalitarian government on all the Vietnamese people or in supporting a regime that has been committed to killing, torture, and assassination as routine political tools.

The right of these people to yammer ahead with their almost obscene support of a regime that is actually at war with the United States is not in question. We are not formally at war. Presumably, the laws regarding aid and comfort to the enemy do not technically apply.

But, surely, it is the right, the responsibility of every person who has a forum available in the proximity of these teach-ins (what a travesty even the name becomes) clearly to oppose those who would welcome a defeat of freedom and a Communist victory in Vietnam.

The right to speak is open to all. We cannot complain that it is being abused by those who hate America and love Communism if we do not take advantage of it ourselves.

Every American who remains silent when he could speak, in the face of such a slap as the hope for a Vietcong victory, betrays the brave men who now are dying so that freedom may live.

On Academic Freedom

—GALE MC GEE

Senator McGee is a former teacher of American history at several high schools and colleges in the Midwest. These are excerpts from remarks delivered in the Senate, July 27, 1965.

In the past few years, much to my delight, the university and college students of the nation have begun to take an increased interest in the state of the nation around them. During the years following the Korean conflict, it had been difficult to interest students in the affairs of the nation. They were interested in their personal surroundings and in the search for a job with status and security. But in recent years—sparked, in large part, by the magnetic personality and shining example of the late President John Kennedy—the students of America have become interested in the world around them. They have worked long and hard in the civil rights movement, in helping to teach and train the dropouts and the children of the poor and neglected minorities, and in projects, too numerous to mention, which aim at the improvement of society. It is from the ranks of our college students that we have drawn the majority of the recruits for the Peace Corps, and in that endeavor they have justly earned and received the acclaim of a great portion of the world.

Now, in the great debate on Vietnam, the students have entered these lists with the enthusiasm typical of all their endeavors. And on this issue they have been joined, again as seldom before in recent history, by the members of our college faculties. All across the nation we see the results of this interest, this concern for the future. A new word—teach-in—signifies a tactic to generate interest and enthusiasm and, I hope, instill knowledge. To this ferment I add my wholehearted and complete support.

In giving this support, Mr. President, I am well aware that this movement and its manifestations across the country represent no Arcadian discourse, with student and teacher contemplating the problems of state in the calm surroundings of the halls of ivy. I know full well that this debate has taken on many of the aspects of a protest movement, that in this movement there are professional revolutionaries and malcontents as well as bona fide academics and students. I realize that perhaps there are even a few persons who take orders from Moscow or Peking working to turn this activity to their advantage. And, too, there may be found in this movement a few individuals whose mode of dress and whose lack of enthusiasm for bathing cause concern among more traditional members of society. These are all facts which I acknowledge.

But emerging from the emotional extremes of the controversy on Vietnam have been harsh charges and even more dangerous assumptions from fringe groups on both sides. There have been certain groups on a few campuses, for example, who sought to shut out debate and controversy and to conduct a monologue their way. As these critics have attacked our nation's policies in Vietnam, they have described the policy-makers as "new imperialists," "power-mad militarists," and "warmongers" out to conquer the world.

In the Senate, earlier this year, I suggested that the campus debates would be better received and would better serve the traditional concepts of academia if dissent on this issue among the academics was not only tolerated but even encouraged and promoted. Whatever else in the realm of human knowledge, there has surely emerged full appreciation for the right to be wrong and the right to think "otherwise."

Likewise, I expressed the fear that, if the campuses didn't make a conscious effort to maintain a dialogue rather than a monologue, the consequence would be a distortion of the true face of the modern American college campus. In all fairness, the voices from the campus have not been as one-sided as the headlines and the newscasts would suggest. We all know that protest often gathers more attention than support. Willfully or otherwise, there has been a distortion of the state of mind in the halls of ivy. The fact remains that the vociferousness of the protests from both students and faculty have succeeded in exciting those who peddle patriotism professionally as well as those who may be wrongfully disturbed by the origins of the dissent.

What concerns me is that this normal, if sometimes wrongheaded, ferment on the campus is already being seized upon as an excuse to launch new witch-hunts, new predatory forays into the realm of academic freedom—all in the name of Americanism, of course, but with the purpose of stifling the differing points of view. It threatens, in fact, to shut the doors on free inquiry and free expression.

Given then the re-emergence of extremist groups during the past few years, it should not be especially surprising that the anxieties engendered by Vietnam, when added to the atmosphere of hate, smear, and fear, should increase the tempo of fringe groups both to the left and the right. The classroom, in particular, has always been an area of suspicion in their lexicon of conspiracy and, thus, it is not unusual that it becomes a prime target now. The cases of new attacks being launched against the campus are becoming numerous enough, however, to cause us all to become concerned lest it get out of hand.

It is more than a little disturbing that a teach-in on the campus of the University of Miami in Florida not long ago should have evoked the use of one of the newer weapons of the extreme right wing. This is the recorded telephone message. . . .

In the University of Miami case, people throughout the community were called by unnamed voices the night after the teach-in, asked if they knew what was going on on the campus, and told that if they didn't know, to dial 221–6767. A recorded woman's voice then said,

> This is "Let Freedom Ring." Last Tuesday night, at Miami's own little red schoolhouse, there was a strange assortment of pinks, punks, beatniks, and left-wing educators assembled for the unashamed purpose of pleading for a soft line against the Communists.

An extended diatribe then proceeded to link anyone who had participated in the affair with specifically named individuals who were accused of being socialists, Communists, and pacifists. The U.S. Senator who participated was likewise described as being "shoulder to shoulder with a Marxist who advocates selective assassination." Finally, the voice concluded the canned message with, "Thank you for calling. Call us Monday for a new weekly message. 'Let Freedom Ring.'"

Needless to say, this sort of irresponsible and reckless mish-mash of character assassination and name-calling readily excites the fears of well-meaning citizens and sometimes triggers additional actions which threaten to impinge upon fundamental freedoms. A former member of [the U.S. Senate], Senator Harry P. Cain, said, "The attack on the University of Miami and its encouragement for debate and free inquiry among its students and faculty was cowardly, scurrilous, distorted, misleading, and inaccurate." Those shortcomings, however, never deter the extremist groups. In fact, they become more often than not their stock in trade.

But not all of the outbursts of late have come from little-known spokesmen for secret societies. The temptation to find conspirators and plotters in the midst of our complex problems has spilled over into the halls of Congress. Just recently, a member of the [U.S. House of Representatives] questioned whether a professor who had engaged in a teach-in and was critical of the Administration's Vietnam policy should be allowed to conduct research supported in part by the federal government. To that congressman, for a professor to continue to receive federal aid under those circumstances was a "shocking inconsistency." Mr. President, the only thing about this that is "shocking" to me is that this grant should be questioned in the first place—and on such grounds. It has always been part of any federal involvement in education that such participation did not, should not, and must not involve any attempt to influence the thought or direction of the inquiry. To demand political conformity before hiring whatever talent and training a man may possess, to me would establish a precedent which contains the potential for the destruction of our system of higher education and academic freedom as we know it. . . .

To those who are concerned that—as one editorial writer put it —"the cockeyed professors and pacifists and anarchists" are destroying the nation and the culture that has given them sustenance, I would suggest that, while we should not glory in the fact that some dissent on the campus is erratic and irresponsible, to seek to enforce conformity (thought control is a better phrase) upon our institutions of higher learning would do far more damage to our civilization and our nation than can the fulminations of the most radical of students and professors. . . .

Let us hark back to a bit of the eternal wisdom which flowed so generously from the pen of Thomas Jefferson when he wrote, in his First Inaugural Address: "Error of opinion may be tolerated where reason is left free to combat it."

Experts Reply to Critics of United States

This statement appeared in the New York Journal-American, *October 20, 1965.*

We, the undersigned, write as scholars and specialists, most of whom have devoted much of their adult lives to study and work in South and East Asian affairs. Included in our number are most of this nation's nucleus of specialists on Vietnam. Many of us have lived in Vietnam itself.

We feel compelled to write in response to what we consider the distortions of fact and the emotional allegations of a small but vociferous group of fellow university teachers regarding the war in Vietnam. We must first observe that those who have signed advertisements and petitions represent a very small proportion of all university professors. Further, the petition signers include disproportionally fewer scholars in the fields of government, international relations, and Asian studies. To our knowledge, no acknowledged expert on Vietnam itself has signed the advertisements appearing in *The New York Times* protesting U.S. policy in Vietnam. A mere handful of scholars with Far East credentials identified themselves with these protests.

Quite apart from the merits of American policy—past or present —we believe the manner in which the petitions and many "teach-ins" have been presented is a discredit to those who would call themselves scholars. The Vietnamese war and its related political context are enormously complex. Even the most qualified experts disagree on important facts or the meaning of those facts.

It serves no useful purpose, therefore, to engage in name-calling, distortion, emotionalism, and gross oversimplification. Many of our fellow scholars, no doubt eminently qualified in their own fields, are in our view guilty of unacademic behavior in their protests of Vietnam policy. . . .

DR. WESLEY R. FISHEL
Michigan State University

PROF. P. J. HONEY
University of London

WILLIAM P. MADDOX
New York City

PROF. RALPH L. TURNER
Michigan State University

DR. CHARLES WOLF, JR.
The RAND Corp.

DR. GEORGE E. TAYLOR
University of Washington

PROF. WILLIAM B. DUNN
University of the State of N.Y.

PROF. J. D. MONTGOMERY
Harvard University

DR. CHAS. A. JOINER
Temple University

WILLIAM HENDERSON
Socony Mobil Oil Co.

DR. FRANK N. TRAGER
New York University

REV. F. J. CORLEY, S.J.
St. Louis University

DR. CHESTER L. HUNT
Western Michigan University

DR. LUCIAN PYE
Mass. Institute of Technology

DR. DAVID A. WILSON
University of California

DR. AMROM H. KATZ
The RAND Corp.

DR. JOHN T. DORSEY
Vanderbilt University

DR. I. M. SACKS
Brandeis University

DR. R. H. SMUCKLER
Michigan State University

GEORGE K. TANHAM
The RAND Corp.

The Decline of Serious Debate

—JAMES RESTON

From The New York Times, *April 21, 1965.*

Something is happening to the process of political debate in America. It is lagging far behind the events it is intended to influence, and a good deal of the time it takes the form not of serious intellectual inquiry but of one-sided headline-hunting and even of physical defiance of the law.

The debate on U.S. policy in Vietnam is a case in point. For almost a decade, there was hardly any debate at all. Those of us who protested against the deepening involvement of the nation in that country during most of the Eisenhower and Kennedy Administrations raised scarcely an echo in the country or even in the Congress.

Now the mood is swinging from indifference to violence. Since the U.S. bombings of North Vietnam, the protest movement against the Johnson Administration's policy has swept the campuses of the country. There was a sit-in on the driveway of the White House today, and marathon protest meetings, usually dominated by teachers opposed to the Administration's Vietnam policy, have been held all over the nation.

Some of these meetings have been exemplary. For example, at Principia College in Illinois last week, students from sixty colleges engaged in a serious discussion of the possible courses of action now open to the Government. They read the basic documents. They heard all sides of the question, analyzed the evidence, questioned sharply, and went away with some understanding of the complexity of the dilemmas now facing the Government.

Over 2,000 students took part for most of one whole night last week in a teach-in at Harvard, where most of the speakers protested against Administration policy, but at least the other side was argued by Samuel Huntington, Professor of Government, John Kenneth Galbraith, Warburg Professor of Economics, and Professor Harold Isaacs, of M.I.T.

At many other colleges, however, these nocturnal marathons have not been debates at all, but anti-Administration demonstrations disguised as "teaching" and, in many cases, backed by propaganda of the most vicious nature.

The Committee to Oppose the War in Vietnam, with headquarters in San Francisco and Berkeley, for example, circulated a leaflet with a photograph of a soldier plunging a knife into the stomach of a mutilated and half-naked man. The caption read: "Getting the Point: South Vietnamese Rangers interrogate a prisoner." It urged University of California students to "join the march against the war in Vietnam." [*The March on Washington, organized by Students for a Democratic Society, drew some 25,000 protesters to the capital on April 17, 1965.*]

Another mimeographed leaflet, circulated at the University of California on behalf of the March on Washington, said: "The war in Vietnam is a hideously immoral war. It is a losing war. It is a self-defeating war. It is a terrifyingly dangerous war. And it is a civil war in which the only outside forces are those of the United States. . . ."

The Young Socialist Alliance, with headquarters at Cooper Station, New York 3, New York, is circulating a pamphlet calling for "immediate withdrawal of all American troops." Another organization entitled "The Minority of One," with headquarters at Box 544, Passaic, N.J., is sending out "an appeal to the people of the United States" by Ho Chi Minh, the Communist leader of North Vietnam. [The Minority of One *is a monthly publication, not an "organization."*]

All this is vaguely reminiscent of the antiwar movement in the British universities in the mid-1930's and, oddly, it seems to have become more intense since President Johnson offered unlimited negotiations.

As an avowed protest movement, it is fair enough. There is plenty to protest about, but for professors to organize it in the name of "teaching" is something else again, and for officials here not to take it seriously enough to counter the campus revolt could be irresponsible.

For this is no longer a casual form of campus spring fever. The zeal of the civil rights movement is being transferred in some places into a get-out-of-Vietnam campaign, and this, in turn, is being widely distributed by Communist countries to the detriment of the Administration's effort to force a negotiated peace.

The basic question now is not whether the Administration has made mistakes in the past—it obviously has—but how it is going to make its way through the delicate process of diplomacy toward an honorable settlement. It is a serious discussion and debate, but this is not what it is getting from many university campuses, where the tradition of responsible inquiry is supposed to be strongest.

Replies to Reston

From Marvin E. Gettleman, Assistant Professor of History, Polytechnic Institute of Brooklyn, to The New York Times; *unpublished.*

April 21, 1965

As a participant in, and enthusiastic supporter of, teach-ins on the Vietnam crisis, I must write in reply to James Reston's attack on them.

Mr. Reston attacks the one-sided nature of the teach-ins, but had he inquired further he would have discovered that the most serious problem faced by the organizers of these meetings is the lack of speakers who defend the Administration's position.

We are further accused of contributing to a "decline of serious debate" on the basis of the literature distributed at the teach-ins. But the actual content of the teach-ins that I am familiar with consists mostly of historical analysis of the nature of U.S. involvement in Vietnam. If audiences are moved to denounce the morality of our role in Vietnam after being exposed to the actual text of the Geneva accords of 1954, this can hardly be credited to insidious propaganda.

Those of us who have addressed these meetings have needed to do very little more than inform our students of the nature of brilliant and courageous *New York Times* reporting from Saigon. And even James Reston himself has informed readers of this newspaper that escalating the war in Southeast Asia to a point where the United States can attack Chinese nuclear installations has been actively under consideration in Washington. No wonder we raise doubts that the Administration is actually straining to achieve a just and honorable settlement in Vietnam.

Attacks on the conclusions that academics reach after seeking to inform themselves on the issues is another melancholy sign that the Vietnam crisis is beginning to put out the lights here at home.

MARVIN E. GETTLEMAN

From Richard B. Du Boff, Bryn Mawr, Pa., to The New York Times, *April 30, 1965.*

April 21, 1965

James Reston's column . . . comes as a shock. It vividly shows how the whole peace movement, sadly enough, is being thrown on the defensive—and not mainly by the right wing.

Why do we have such vigorous, and at times even desperate, protest coming from both student and faculty quarters? Is it in response to a unique situation or not? Mr. Reston implicitly feels that it is not.

Yet it is in response to a situation in which a citizen can no longer expect the truth to emanate from his own Government; in which our major press services have criticized the Administration for exerting controls and secrecy "beyond anything known in the darkest days of World War II"; in which a small coterie of advisers has given the President consistently poor advice; in which these "tough-minded" intellectuals seem bent upon provoking a conflict with China to salvage their reputations and hide the fact that their "anti-insurrection" guerrilla policies have failed.

But Mr. Reston himself, over the last three months, has made all of these same observations in his own columns. Is he so inconsistent as to think that the resultant protest can or should be kept in "nice" and "noncontroversial" channels?

RICHARD B. DU BOFF

From faculty members of the Ad Hoc Committee on Vietnam, New York University, to The New York Times; *unpublished.*

April 26, 1965

As faculty members of the Ad Hoc Committee which sponsored a teach-in on Vietnam at University College, New York University, on April 14–15, we wish to protest James Reston's characterization of such events. . . . Our teach-in was orderly, informative, and wholly serious. More than one-third of the student body of 2,000 on this campus, as well as many faculty members, were present during the course of the all-night session. All those points of view for which we could find willing speakers were presented. We contacted many scholars known to be supporters of the Administration position; most of these declined to participate for one reason or another. We asked the military science professors on the campus to speak; they replied that they could not mount a platform without the prior approval of the Secretary of Defense.

The teach-in itself was evidence of serious debate and has further stimulated informed discussion on the campus. The tradition on many American campuses has, all too often, not been one of responsible inquiry since the beginning of the McCarthy era. Both faculty and students have concentrated upon private and narrow concerns. Scholarship has been most safely pursued in matters which bear little relationship to the major problems of the world. Our teach-in, at least, was an attempt to reassert the public role of the intellectual in the community, and to ascertain truth about vital issues, even if this proved unpopular and politically inconvenient.

The conclusions of many of the participants in the teach-in—that the present escalation of the war in Vietnam risks the most frightful consequences beyond any apparent justification; that the continued bombings of North Vietnam do not invite negotiation and may, on the contrary, make it nearly impossible; that we must be prepared to negotiate with the Vietcong as well as with other interested parties; and, that the American public has been given inadequate and often misleading information about the situation in Vietnam—are hardly irresponsible. They are shared by leading publications and statesmen of every political persuasion throughout the world.

Philip G. Zimbardo, Constance R. Sutton
Co-chairmen, Ad Hoc Committee on Vietnam
Robert D. Burrowes
Edwin S. Campbell
James T. Crown
Joan Fiss
H. Mark Roelofs
H. Laurence Ross
Thomas W. Wahman

From Norman K. Gottwald, Lowry Professor of Old Testament, Andover Newton Theological School, Mass., to The New York Times, *May 15, 1965.*

May 9, 1965

James Reston's valid point, in his April 21 criticism of the academic-based protest against the war in Vietnam, is that responsible political debate on Vietnam is lagging far behind events. His error is to blame the vehement Administration critics when the Administration itself has stifled debate, and when the long-term efforts of milder critics have, as he says, "raised scarcely an echo in the country or even in the Congress."

No recourse has been left to the doubters and critics except to take to the university lecterns and to the streets. As in civil rights, the place to look for resolution of the problems is not to the demonstrators but to the thwarted democratic process.

A handful of men are edging the United States into a major war in Asia, disregarding the socio-political realities of that continent as well as the limits of American wisdom and power, without giving constructive dissent any public channels for expressing reservations, criticisms, and alternatives.

There is wide discontent with, and considerable outright opposition to, our Vietnam policy in Congress. Nevertheless, with few exceptions, silence has settled over the legislative branch. The silence is largely due to Administration hypersensitivity to public criticism and resulting strong-arm political pressure and manipulation of news about the war and about deeper socio-political trends in Asia.

The President's passion for consensus is employed to impose the impression of near unanimity where it does not in fact exist.

Especially regrettable in Reston's appeal to stop the protest by showing that Communists make use of it for their purposes. With similar reasoning, patriotic Germans were silenced against the wrong policies of the Nazi Government and civil rights demonstrations are opposed in our country. Have we considered that the peaceful settlement of the war in Vietnam might be to the advantage of all parties involved, Communist and non-Communist?

Shall we cease to use the instruments of debate, petition, peaceable assembly, and even, in extremity, of civil disobedience, because to use them would be to appear divided as a people? Shall national unity be purchased by abrogation of democracy?

The only way for the Administration "to counter the revolt" is to let the issues be fully debated in Congress, to answer the doubts and protests with something more than slogans and superficial White Papers, and to give signs that among the President's trusted advisers are men who understand the realities of Southeast Asia.

NORMAN K. GOTTWALD

IV

Critics and Confrontations

Editors' Introduction

The Administration could not long ignore the critical barrage from the academic community. In a period of one month, local teach-ins had mushroomed throughout the nation, and with each, the voices demanding that Government representatives reply to the critics grew louder and more insistent. But the Government, in counter–teach-in strategy as in war policy, showed that it was not to be stampeded into situations not of its own choosing; in confrontations with the critics, the Administration very carefully picked the time and terrain for giving battle. This section documents those encounters and demonstrates how policy-makers turned them to their own advantage. In this context, the teach-ins offer yet another illustration of the formidable problems facing protest movements in the United States; in particular, they demonstrate that criticism runs the danger of losing strength, not by being muzzled, but by being nominally tolerated—and thus neutralized.

Secretary of State Dean Rusk fired the Administration's opening shot in a characteristic way. In a major foreign policy address to the American Society of International Law, on April 23, 1965, he turned unexpectedly from his main topic to jab at the critics. "I continue to hear and see nonsense about the nature of the struggle [in Vietnam]," he said. "I sometimes wonder at the gullibility of educated men and the stubborn disregard of plain facts by men who are supposed to be helping our young to learn—especially to learn how to think." He then went on to other matters.

Implying as it did an arrogant indifference to academic criticism in the upper levels of the Administration, Secretary Rusk's brush-off had the effect of spurring the critics to greater efforts and provided them with more ammunition for their claims that policy-making was suffering from insularity. The letters by William Appleman Williams, Vera Micheles Dean, and others capture some of the anger kindled by the Secretary's remarks.

Administration representatives made sporadic attempts to meet criticism directly on campus (as when Ambassador-at-Large Averell Harriman faced the jeers of a Cornell University audience), but the first concerted effort came with the visits of "truth teams" to selected Midwestern schools early in May, 1965. These encounters, as described here, often turned into hooting sessions when audiences felt they were simply being handed repetitions of the Administration's standard policy justifications. The accounts by Donald Janson, the editors of *Time*, and truth-team leader Thomas Conlon are supplemented by the humor and insight of Art Buchwald.

The third section of this chapter provides a fascinating revelation of the mind and manners of then Presidential Assistant McGeorge Bundy as well as a glimpse into the problems besetting genuine attempts to communicate with the Administration. In his reply to faculty members at Washington University and in his correspondence with Anatol Rapoport (here published for the first time), Mr. Bundy demonstrates not only something of his own quick temper but also a measure of the very attitudes of the Johnson Administration that had helped crystallize the teach-in protest in the first place.

The National Teach-In held in Washington, May 15, 1965, represented the crest of one phase of the teach-in movement—the academics' attempt to engage key members of the Administration in debates that would, the professors hoped, produce policy shifts. Here, for the first time in print, are the addresses of Eric Wolf, who outlines the motives and principles underlying the National Teach-In; Hans Morgenthau, who details the contradictions between reality and Administration policy; and Arthur Schlesinger, Jr., who emerges as a leading spokesman for the group of critics within the Establishment taking shape around Senator Robert F. Kennedy. Also included is an excerpt of panel remarks made by Stanley Hoffmann (in an exchange with W. W. Rostow, Administration policy-planner), on approaches to developments abroad. (For transcripts of addresses of George Kahin, Robert Scalapino [who substituted for McGeorge Bundy], Mary Wright, and others at the National Teach-In, see *Vietnam: History, Documents, and Opinions on a Major World Crisis*, edited by Marvin E. Gettleman.)

The Washington event was certainly a success if measured by the amount of attention received. The debates were televised and broadcast nationally, and all major press organs covered them extensively. Yet many teach-in organizers had deep misgivings about the value of the whole effort. They were disturbed, not simply because the chief Administration defendant, McGeorge Bundy, became a teach-in drop-out (on account of the latest crisis in the Dominican Republic) and because the much-heralded confrontation between Critics and Power did not come off. The problem went deeper, as indicated in the post-mortems reprinted here. Anatol Rapoport, William Appleman Williams, Joan Scott, and, to a certain extent, reporter Meg Greenfield in her breezy coverage of the event, all recognized that, in tailoring the format and choice of speakers to suit the Administration's conditions for participation, the organizers had jettisoned the very soul of the teach-in; student-faculty *protest* had been sacrificed to the enticements of engaging in "dialogue" and effecting a "consensus."

Reflective of this turnabout was the response of James Reston. Earlier, Mr. Reston had chided teach-in critics for abandoning "responsible inquiry" (see Chapter III). Now, after observing the balanced debates in the Sheraton Park Hotel Ballroom, he revised his estimate; the teach-in had become "an honest search for answers" undertaken jointly by academic and political leaders. For many in the teach-in movement, Mr. Reston's conclusions were the sort of damning with faint praise that characterized the Administration's whole attitude. "Nothing," he wrote, "was really resolved in the process [that is, policy remained unaffected], but an important technique of serious discussion was discovered."

Perhaps the most telling summary of the Administration's manipulation of public and professors alike is offered in the short satirical fantasy by Russell Baker.

The concluding section of this chapter features excerpts from a televised confrontation in which McGeorge Bundy debated (and baited) Professor Hans Morgenthau. Stanley Diamond's assessment of the confrontation supports the conclusion that, once again, teach-in organizers had been taken.

(Curiously absent from the confrontation episodes was the figure of President Johnson himself. Some viewers have attributed this, in part, to the President's supposed insecurity among, and hostility toward, intellectuals. And, of course, he had several lieutenants with academic credentials—Rusk, Bundy, Rostow—to handle confrontations for him. Perhaps indicative of the waning of the whole "confrontation campaign" and of the Administration's growing sense of confidence that criticism, particularly from academics, could be readily contained was the President's decision to address himself, at Princeton University, May 11, 1966, to the subject of Vietnam and the role of scholars, urging them to back the war. For the text and a discussion of the address, see the forthcoming volume *Lyndon Johnson's Great Society*, edited by Marvin E. Gettleman and David Mermelstein.)

1. PROFESSORS REPLY TO DEAN RUSK'S "GULLIBILITY" REMARKS

From William Appleman Williams, Professor of History, University of Wisconsin (Madison), to The New York Times, *May 2, 1965.*

April 25, 1965

Permit me to suggest that Secretary of State Dean Rusk could profit from some intensive homework before he launches another wholesale counterinsurgency attack on the teaching community's critique of American policy in Vietnam.

His own gullibility and stubborn disregard of plain facts is apparent in his acceptance of biased and partial reports of what the teaching community has been doing and saying and in his refusal to discuss the facts and issues that the teaching community has been raising.

I helped organize and participated in a two-day teach-in at the University of Wisconsin, and his accusations are absurdly wide of the mark. The people who participated were (and remain) deeply concerned about the triple crisis in American foreign policy.

They are concerned about the moral crisis involved in justifying American action by reference to the actions of others instead of by reference to our own moral heritage and tradition and in blatantly invoking a double standard of judgment.

They are concerned with the crisis in representative government involved in the Administration's policy of secrecy, its persistent refusal to engage in candid, open debate with its critics, and its regular disregard of facts which undercut its own rationalizations.

And they are concerned with the increasingly dangerous practical consequences of escalation and self-righteousness.

The Secretary might have learned something from listening to Germaine Brée discuss the nature and consequences of the different kinds of commitment, from hearing others explore various alternatives to his own policy, or from considering several analyses of how men get into serious difficulties from making policy on the basis of false analogies.

For, surely, the Secretary is not offering a very persuasive example of how to think when he defends his policy with an analogy to isolationism, Munich, and other aspects of the late 1930's. A false analogy is one of the most dangerous intellectual errors known to man, and the Administration's policy is based on just such a false analogy between the situation in Europe during the 1930's and the present situation in Vietnam.

Secretary Rusk and other Administration leaders are not thinking about the existing situation; they are merely reacting to it in terms of an irrelevant stereotype.

And that, to borrow his own phrase, is considerably more apt to lead to "sure catastrophe" than the actions of the teaching community.

WILLIAM APPLEMAN WILLIAMS

From J. Rogers Hollingsworth, Associate Professor of History, University of Wisconsin (Madison), to The New York Times, *April 29, 1965.*

April 23, 1965

Never in American history has a Secretary of State made such a sharp attack on a large segment of the academic community as did Dean Rusk in his comments of April 23. It is no wonder that United States policy toward South Vietnam has been so devoid of alternatives and clear thinking, given the proclivity to vitriol displayed therein.

His denunciation of those who have expressed disagreement with the Administration is suggestive of increasing unwillingness on the part of the Administration to communicate with critics—whether they be drawn from the ranks of government or from the academic community.

It is disheartening to contemplate the deterioration of the dialogue over foreign policy into a round of name-calling. However, by his expressions of contempt and dismissal, Dean Rusk has indicated his desire to move in just that direction.

Such rigidity of mind can hardly convince or enlighten critics within this country. More important, however, such rigidity is obviously not conducive to negotiations with other countries.

J. ROGERS HOLLINGSWORTH

From Klemens von Klemperer, Professor of History, Smith College, to The New York Times, *May 16, 1965.*

May 9, 1965

In Vietnam our Government has become involved in a singularly complex situation and, therefore, in highly controversial policies. In these circumstances, the difficulties of obtaining correct information to serve as a basis for independent opinion are, as your editorials have repeatedly stressed, great. But they must be overcome without, of course, jeopardizing national security.

President Johnson should not have to depend on a shallow consensus, which, in effect, eliminates all statement of independent opinion in Congress as well as in society at large. A consensocracy (to use Russell Baker's felicitous term) of this nature is dangerous. It threatens the vital political and social controls of Government policy.

There must be those who doubt and warn, however upsetting they may be, and their moral concern and expert knowledge ought to get a hearing in Government circles. Clearly, their usefulness and their ability to obtain a hearing will be all the greater the better they are informed.

I am writing not to argue about the merits of our Government's policies but to voice deep concern over what strikes me as the breakdown of communications between the Administration and the American academic community over the question of our foreign policy. Petitions are being signed, sent to Washington, published in the press—largely with the objective of immediate withdrawal from Vietnam. They have, in practice, remained unheeded and seemingly unheard.

At the same time, I feel that I must turn the searchlight on my own community. I have been appalled by the tenor of most petitions which have appeared on Vietnam. To judge by them, the American academic community is ill-informed (which, in this situation, is not altogether its fault), hasty, and sanctimonious (which is largely its fault).

I might go one step further and suggest that among those who now advocate our immediate withdrawal from Vietnam are those who, in 1947, fiercely attacked the Truman Doctrine (which, in re-trospect, has proved sound policy) and advocated that we abandon Greece and Turkey to Communist domination.

I see in such advice, such petitions, little that Washington can learn from. In short, I dread the fact that the academic community should be represented by those who are predisposed to see fault at home and who tend to give all the benefit of the doubt to the other camp.

The relative silence of independent critics among academics has allowed a vociferous minority to appear as representatives of the academic profession. This has dangerously broadened the gap be-tween, on one side, the university and, on the other, the Adminis-tration and, indeed, society at large.

I lament in the university the drowning out of responsible voices by a minority driven by a questionable and passionate intensity as much as I dread a corresponding toughening up on the part of the Administration or in the country at large and a rejection of the in-tellectuals as such. The result would be the end of every dialogue, a polarization of opinions, indeed of ideologies, over the heads and at the expense of the many sober and searching citizens of this Re-public.

KLEMENS VON KLEMPERER

From Vera Micheles Dean, Professor of Interna-tional Development, Graduate School of Public Ad-ministration, New York University, to The New York Times, *May 31, 1965.*

May 20, 1965

For those who remember the McCarthy period, the most poign-ant moment in the CBS television program of April 30 must surely have been Edward R. Murrow's eloquent statement: "We must not confuse dissent with disloyalty."

This reminder was particularly timely, following as it did the address of Secretary of State Dean Rusk to the American Society of International Law. . . .

Having met Mr. Rusk in his early roles of history professor and college dean, I cannot but wonder at the transformation that pub-lic service seems to have wrought in his concept and practice of intellectual freedom and at the effect this transformation is having, and may continue to have in the future, on free discussion of for-eign policy in the United States.

It may well be desirable, in fact necessary, for Government officials to see only the point of view of the Administration they serve —although it is difficult to believe that for some, at least, of the highly trained and experienced personnel of the Department of State there is one side, and one side only, to such multifaceted crises, deeply rooted in history, as those of Vietnam and the Dominican Republic.

But, for our Government to expect—and, even more serious, to demand—comparable one-sidedness from private citizens is to introduce into our lively democratic society, under the guise of national consensus, the very concepts and practices of official authoritarianism which we are urged at all costs to defeat in other areas of the world.

If there is one function educated men and women must perform in a democratic society, it is to discuss freely with young students who are being called on to live—and die—for democracy not only the advantages, which we all recognize and support, of our own institutions (based, as we sometimes seem to forget, on the heritage of Europe's English and French revolutions) but also the circumstances under which comparable institutions can be expected to emerge in developing areas of the world.

The most important of these circumstances is that Western democratic institutions not only took centuries to develop but were the product of economic and social changes which, in their day, were regarded as painful and even cruel. Yet, when in this century comparable changes occur in nations the United States regards as essential to its security, Washington's immediate official reaction is to view them with dismay and apprehension as inspired solely by Communism—thereby, incidentally, giving Communists more than their due.

Yet, as becomes increasingly clear, our very resistance to such changes leaves many new national leaders little or no choice but to accept Communist support at home and abroad and, ironically, fosters not democracy but anti-Americanism. Nor, in contrast to wars between nations, are social and economic revolutions negotiable at the conference table as we appear to assume can be done in both Vietnam and the Dominican Republic.

President Johnson generously gives of his time to consult business and labor leaders, as well as members of Congress, about foreign policy. He might consider giving equal time to representatives of the university community, many of whom, contrary to Mr. Rusk's strictures, are often better informed about the peoples of developing nations than Administration officials and are animated by the same patriotic concern for the welfare and security of the United States.

VERA MICHELES DEAN

> *From the Greater Boston Faculty Committee on Vietnam, Cambridge, Mass. This statement appeared in The New York Times, May 9, 1965, and was signed by over 750 faculty members from thirty colleges and universities, mainly in the New England area.*

In his address, on April 23 . . . Secretary of State Dean Rusk attacked academic critics of the Administration for talking "nonsense about the nature of the struggle" in Vietnam. He continued: "I sometimes wonder at the gullibility of educated men and the stubborn disregard of plain facts by men who are supposed to be helping our young to learn—especially to learn how to think." This abusive language suggests that the Administration wants to silence its critics. . . .

It is easy to see why the Secretary of State is angry. The reasons have nothing to do with "gullibility" in the academic community. He is angry because the facts and wider considerations brought up by these critics have contradicted so many official pronouncements. It is not the scholars but the leaders of the Administration who have shown a "stubborn disregard of plain facts."

For example, on March 25, 1965, President Johnson said, "We seek no more than a return to the essentials of the agreements of 1954—a reliable agreement to guarantee the independence and security of all in Southeast Asia." But the "plain fact" is that the Geneva agreement did not provide for a division of Vietnam into two nations. On the contrary, the agreement spoke of the two parts of Vietnam as "regrouping zones" and said that "the military demarcation line is provisional and should not in any way be interpreted as constituting a political or territorial boundary." It provided that ". . . general elections shall be held in July, 1956, under the supervision of an international commission. . . ." No such unifying elections have been held. The Saigon regime, with United States approval, refused. Ever since, the United States has insisted that Vietnam remain divided.

On April 7, 1965, the President gave another description of the Administration's goals. He said, "Tonight Americans and Asians are dying for a world where each people may choose its own path to change," and further on: "Our objective is the independence of South Vietnam, and its freedom from attack. We want nothing for ourselves—only that the people of South Vietnam be allowed to guide their own country in their own way." The "plain fact" is that the scale of American intervention is incompatible with the goal of self-determination. North Vietnam has, to be sure, intervened by helping the Vietcong. But, at every stage of the war, the scale of American intervention has been far greater. The manner of combat shows that we have saturated South Vietnam with every kind of military equipment the terrain allows. We airlift troops and supplies continually. We drop napalm on civilian populations intermingled with guerrillas. We burn and defoliate crops and forests. We have resorted to incapacitating gas. An intervention as massive as this does not furnish a choice to the people. It deprives them of one.

If American actions in Vietnam are defensible, Administration attempts to defend them should square with the "plain facts." Self-deception about American intervention can be a greater peril than discriminating protest. Only by recognizing the ambiguities of the situation can we reach accord with the deepest levels of the American conscience and with the common conscience of mankind. The Administration may have contrived the discreet silence or the grudging lip service of some foreign governments and of some U.S. Senators, but the hazards and inconsistencies of the present policy are widely recognized both at home and abroad.

The situation in Vietnam raises serious moral questions, not merely diplomatic and tactical ones. As a nation, we hold immense power. To permit it to be used in reckless and barbarous ways is to imperil the entire basis of American leadership.

Let us make known to the Government and to our compatriots that we oppose the disastrous policy of continued bombardment of North Vietnam. Continuation of the present policy makes it impossible for Americans and Russians to talk further about peaceful coexistence and encourages all Communist nations to close ranks in opposition to the United States.

World opinion does not support United States military operations in Vietnam. Throughout the world these operations appear increasingly to be a campaign in the self-interest of a Western power rather than in the interest of that stricken Asian nation.

Indochina has been macerated by twenty years of anticolonial, nationalist, and Communist warfare. The United States has the military might to defeat the Vietcong. But, unless we show immediate restraint, and show humane imagination in bringing interested parties to the peace table, we risk the loss of the respect and sympathy of men and nations far beyond the present theater of war.

Citizens must speak out on issues of national policy. We will not be intimidated by charges of gullibility or disloyalty.

We demand that the Administration return to the "plain facts" and make an earnest attempt to obtain a negotiated peace. Reiteration of the phrase "unconditional discussions" is not enough, especially because the condition attached to it is that the rebel forces in the civil war are not to appear at the conference table. Peaceful intentions can be made plainer than this. We must arrange for an immediate cease-fire and offer to negotiate with the principal combatants, including the Vietcong; we must cease our air raids on North Vietnam; we should use the good offices of the United Nations in bringing about these ends; and we must assure the world that we will not use nuclear weapons in the pursuit of victory or in the "pursuit of peace."

2. THE STATE DEPARTMENT VISITS THE TEACH-INS

The "Truth-Teams": A View from the Podium

—THOMAS F. CONLON

Mr. Conlon, a Foreign Service Officer serving in the Department of State, prepared the following especially for this book. The views expressed are his own and should not be regarded as necessarily those of the Department of State.

During the spring of 1965, the growing seriousness of the war in Vietnam led to an increase in the number of requests from community and citizens' organizations and from colleges and universities for speakers from the Department of State and other Government agencies to explain and discuss U.S. policy toward Vietnam. In May, 1965, it was decided to send a three-man team to visit a number of midwestern colleges and universities. The team, called the Inter-Departmental Speaking Team on Viet-Nam Policy, consisted of Mr. Thomas F. Conlon, of the Department of State, as chairman; Mr. Earle Young, of the Agency for International Development; and Lt. Col. Thomas Waitt and Lt. Col. Rolfe Hilman, U.S. Army, who split up the appearances. The members of the team had recently served in Vietnam, and it was felt that their varied experience in that country would help to satisfy the interest of their audiences in the Vietnam question as a whole.

The team visited the State University of Iowa, Drake University, the University of Wisconsin (both Madison and Milwaukee campuses), the University of Indiana, and the University of Illinois, speaking to university convocations and to meetings of *ad hoc* student and faculty groups specially interested in the Vietnam question.

For the most part, the team was well-received, and, although the discussions were occasionally warm and spirited, the atmosphere was appropriate to a serious, searching discussion of a major question facing the United States. On two occasions, however (at the State University of Iowa and at the University of Wisconsin in Madison), the team was subjected to emotional outbursts and displays little in keeping with the traditions of academic discipline and the respect due to another person who expresses a point of view. The element critical of Government policy on Vietnam was best organized at the University of Wisconsin in Madison, and national television programs carried extended excerpts of some of the exchanges between members of the team and critics in the audience. Since standard "news" criteria dictated selection of the hottest exchanges in the evening, the televised portions overplayed the extent of the opposition to the Government expressed at the meeting in Madison.

It was apparent to the team that the Vietnam question, although in the news in one form or another for the better part of a generation, had not received sufficient attention from either students or faculty. Accordingly, the academic community did not appear to be particularly well-informed regarding critical aspects of the question when the scale of hostilities increased sharply early in 1965. It was evident, for example, that many of the critics the team met, including both students and faculty, had uncritically swallowed large doses of straight Communist propaganda regarding the nature of the Vietcong, the origins of the so-called National Front for the Liberation of South Vietnam, the course of events in Indochina from 1945 to 1965, and, in particular, the facts regarding the Geneva accords of 1954.

The problem had been worsened, the team felt, by the holding of a substantial number of teach-ins at various American universities during the spring of 1965, at which interested faculty and student leaders had sought to "explain" the situation in Vietnam to their satisfaction. Surprisingly superficial and inaccurate statements were made at the various teach-ins and in the literature prepared in connection with them. This literature, evidently passed along from one teach-in to the next, perpetuated the same factual errors in striking fashion.

Two examples may illustrate the point. First, Mr. Walter Lippmann, the well-known columnist, in a column written in the spring of 1965, evidently misquoted President Eisenhower regarding elections in Vietnam. Mr. Lippmann alleged that, in President Eisenhower's book *Mandate for Change*, the President said that if elections had been held in Vietnam in 1956, Ho Chi Minh would have won 80 per cent of the vote. What President Eisenhower actually said, however (see *Mandate for Change*, p. 372), was that if elections had been held as of the time of the fighting (that is, necessarily prior to the armistice of July, 1954), possibly 80 per cent of the population would have voted for the Communist Ho Chi Minh as their leader rather than Chief of State Bao Dai . . ." Obviously, an election in 1954 between Ho Chi Minh and the playboy Emperor Bao Dai is one thing. An election in 1956 between Ho Chi Minh (who had just carried out a bloody agrarian "reform" in which perhaps 100,000 North Vietnamese were killed) and any other candidate is something else. A question related to President Eisenhower's book, usually citing page 372 and repeating the misquotation, was asked at each of the meetings the team addressed. Second, few of those in the audience were aware of the fact that neither the United States nor the government of South Vietnam had signed the Geneva accords of 1954 on Vietnam. In fact, most of the audiences were evidently unaware of the distinction between the Agreement on the Cessation of Hostilities (signed by representatives of the French and Vietminh high commands only) and the Final Declaration of the Geneva Conference (signed by no one and not approved at any plenary session of the conference). Yet the reference to elections throughout Vietnam, to be held prior to July, 1956, appeared only in this unsigned Final Declaration. Questions reflecting this basic misunderstanding were hardy perennials throughout the university appearances.

A factor which may explain some of the unusual features of the teach-in movement was evident in the audiences the team spoke to. For the most part, the faculty and student elements most critical of Government policy were those that might have been expected to be relatively apolitical. For example, an open letter was sent to President Johnson by 172 members of the faculty of the University of Wisconsin and was published in the student newspaper, *The Daily Cardinal*, on May 6. An overwhelming majority of those signing the letter were from the exact sciences, sociology, education, English literature, and even from the more exotic fields of mathematics research and Scandinavian studies. In other words, the most vociferous critics of Government policy were very often the least prepared, by virtue of their training, their reading, or their experience, to discuss Vietnam policy in an informed fashion.

This factor may explain the highly emotional tone of some of the discussions. That is, what some of the academic critics lacked in factual knowledge and understanding, they made up for with emotional denunciations of "immoral" policy actions, "criminal" bombings, etcetera. The critics never defined what kind of moral standard they were using, and the team had the feeling that, for at least some of them, this was the most transparent kind of hypocrisy.

For my own part, I continued to speak to community groups and colleges on Vietnam policy in 1965 and 1966, and I found that public opinion had largely clarified on this issue, crystallizing into a substantial majority in support of the President. I think this conclusion has been supported by the major public-opinion polls which have been taken. My colleagues on the speaking team and I would like to think that we, personally, contributed to this result, even if only in a small way.

Sit Down and Shut Up

—DONALD JANSON

Mr. Janson is a midwest correspondent for The New York Times. *Abridged from* The Nation, *May 24, 1965.*

Since February [1965], the State Department has been deluged with demands for explanation of a policy that risks world conflict. William Jorden, Deputy Assistant Secretary of State for Public Affairs, puts the number of letters at 20,000 in the last six weeks. Thomas F. Conlon, a State Department specialist on Vietnam, says this mail has been supplemented by telephone calls almost hourly since February.

Frequently, the requests for explanation display a sharp edge of disbelief that America is motivated by an altruistic desire to pave the way for self-determination in South Vietnam. Who invited us to defend whom? Was it a popular government or our puppet? Is not the conflict in South Vietnam a civil war, a legitimate revolution against dictatorship, rather than aggression from the North? Are we not there solely to contain Communism under the domino theory? Is not our insistence on making Vietnam safe for free elections a sham to draw the line against any further expansion of Communism, popular or otherwise? Why not end hypocrisy, permit elections under United Nations auspices now, pull out, and abide by the results in the true spirit of democratic self-determination?

At first, the reaction of top policy-planners was curt. The tempest in academic circles was written off as naive, impractical idealism, the work of a small but vocal minority of peaceniks and left-leaning liberals ever-present on university campuses. . . .

Last month, the State Department decided the ferment could no longer be ignored. On April 26, David Bane, a Foreign Service Officer for twenty years who is currently stationed at the University of Iowa under a limited (to three universities), new State Department program to keep its staff in touch with the country, received a call from Washington. Could forums be scheduled immediately at Iowa and other midwestern universities so that a team of Vietnam experts might bring the truth of the situation to representative campuses?

William L. Boyd, Vice-President for Academic Affairs and Dean of Faculties at Iowa, was delighted to give a hearing to a question that had stirred not only the campus but a considerable segment of townspeople in Iowa City. He said later that this was the first time in his memory that the Government had asked to come to the universities to discuss an issue. He wondered if it meant the State Department might finally be interested in learning what others thought about controversial elements of American foreign policy.

As it turned out, the Washington team was not open to suggestions. It was interested only in making sure that the "truth" was dispensed, so that students and others subject to influence by campus "extremists" would have the ammunition they needed to better uphold the Government viewpoint on Vietnam. Conlon, leader of the three-man team explained privately that the Department had already heard and rejected the type of suggestions being offered by spokesmen of the protest movement.

Accommodation before "aggression" ceased, he told students and faculty at Iowa, Drake, Wisconsin, Indiana, and Illinois universities, would confirm China's view that the United States is "a paper tiger" and lead to unrestricted infiltration and conquest of other vulnerable nations in Southeast Asia. The articulate, forty-year-old former Chicagoan with a background of service in Vietnam, justified escalation of the war on the ground that captured prisoners and arms proved control of the South Vietnamese revolution had been usurped by Communist North Vietnam. But neither the team's figures on numbers of Communists and Communist weapons captured nor those of the recent White Paper of the Defense Department were accepted as adequate by opponents of escalation, who contended that the conflict was civil war and American intervention was unwelcome.

At Drake, in Des Moines, and at the University of Wisconsin branch in Milwaukee, sessions were relatively calm, in part because sponsoring campus groups used debate and panel formats that precluded barbed questions, speeches, and attacks from the floor. But the veneer of politeness vanished in some of the question-and-answer sessions at the larger universities. The great majority of questions were hostile, and the smooth Government team had to smother temptations to snap back. Several times, Conlon found himself shouting down questioners and hecklers to make his points.

Stormy sessions punctuated the team's trip from the first day. In Iowa City, the Iowa Socialist League and others picketed, and faculty members charged that it was "idiotic" for a Government team to travel to the Midwest "only to listen to themselves." The biggest demonstration of hostility to U.S. policy came at the University of Wisconsin [Madison]. When the team entered the hot, sticky auditorium in the Social Science Building, on the night of May 6, they found more than 200 students standing against back and side walls despite scattered empty seats on the floor. All wore black arm bands of protest. The students, members of the Student Committee to End the War in Vietnam, continued the stand-in until the meeting ended at 11:00 P.M. They defied an order to sit from a professor who supports Government policy but cleared an aisle to the doors when asked to do so by a faculty member associated with their group.

They held aloft signs mourning "the death of American morality." They hooted and hissed when Conlon insisted that the United States was in Vietnam to help oppressed people establish social,

economic, and political institutions of their own choosing. They
jeered when he said it would probably be some time before elections could be held, because a Communist reign of terror made
them impossible now. They chortled in disbelief when told that
torture and murder of fellow Vietnamese was most commonly perpetrated by Communist forces.

Nor were all the protesters students. One hundred and thirty-
four faculty members that day published a full-page advertisement
[*which sharply criticized Administration policies as self-righteous
and brutal*]. . . .

The meetings frequently boiled over in heated exchanges between floor and platform.

"Why do prisoners we take confess to infiltration only after a
month of interrogation?" a Wisconsin student asked.

Conlon: "Have you ever had anything to do with interrogation?"

"No, and I don't want to."

"Sometimes it takes a long time before a prisoner wants to talk."

"Torture!" shouted another youth.

"Do you also charge the North Vietnamese with torture?" Conlon asked.

"I condemn torture, whoever does it!"

"The Americans do not torture," Conlon said when the pro-
longed applause had died.

"But we run the show," a student in the crowd shouted.

"We do not run it," said the team man.

"Aw c'mon," came shouts from all over the floor, "let's be
honest."

When the tumult slackened, a girl who asked how the State
Department defined a Communist triggered a line of questioning
designed to pin down the team on whether it could prove Vietnamese revolutionaries were Communists.

"I'm sure in your studies of political science you have learned the
definition of Communism and I see no point in repeating it,"
Conlon said.

This was greeted with sighs of "Oh no!"

"All right, it is Marxism-Leninism. . . . In the ranks of the Vietcong, the bulk are not Marxist-Leninist ideologues. But they fight
under Communist control, in support of Communist objectives, so
they might just as well be Marxist-Leninist ideologues in terms of
the terror they spread. . . ."

"The lack of elections in East Germany has not prevented holding them in West Germany," a student said after Conlon told the

audience elections could not be held in Vietnam because conditions were not conducive to free elections in North Vietnam.

"Why not hold them in South Vietnam?" the student continued. "Do we really want them?"

"This is a matter the South Vietnam Government itself has to decide," Conlon said. "Otherwise it is not sovereign."

The students hooted. One student began an impromptu speech telling why he thought no elections were being held. He was stopped in mid-statement.

"Can't this be a dialogue?" he shouted. "Do you want this audience to hear only one side?"

"If you want to make statements, you can send them to me in the State Department," Conlon said. The offer brought hisses. . . .

While few minds seemed to have been changed on either side by the trip, some State Department officials feel the effort buttressed pro-Government views that might in time have wavered under the persistent arguments of the protest movement.

As an exercise in Government public relations, the truth-team technique was of doubtful value. The team members radiated charm and self-confidence as each day began, but the aura dimmed whenever Conlon, backed to the wall by hostile questions, began telling people to "sit down!" or to send their arguments to Washington. The team did enjoy hearty applause when it struck down naive exaggerations by opponents who had not done their homework, but most of the time it was on the defensive.

If the team reinforced views of supporters of present policy, it also strengthened those of opponents. Many had hoped for a hearing and felt their views had fallen on closed ears. Listening to the same pat, undeviating, Government-line answers that they had been receiving for months without benefit of a truth team, they renewed their resolve to speak up. . . .

The Black-Banders

From Time, *May 14, 1965.*

The Government team had been given a thankless assignment: explaining the U.S. presence in Vietnam to college students and professors. . . .

They had been to the State University of Iowa, in Iowa City, and to Drake University, in Des Moines. At Iowa City, where the team met with 200 students and faculty in a campus building that once was the state Capitol, they were picketed, hooted, and jeered at by the largely hostile audience.

Now, the team arrived at the University of Wisconsin in Madison. They had been invited by a recently formed campus Committee to Support the People of South Vietnam. Opposing their appearance was a Committee to End the War in Vietnam. They were hailed by a declaration, signed by 132 faculty members and carried in a college newspaper, attacking the United States for creating in Vietnam "a triple crisis—moral, domestic, and practical."

At an informal preliminary session, over coffee and cookies with professors and graduate students, the team got a taste of what it was in for. "You State Department people," complained Fred Ciporen, 25, a history graduate, "are coming here on the assumption that we students don't know what Government policy is. Well, we do know, and we disagree with it." Replied Conlon: "No, we don't make that assumption at all. We only intend to share our experience with you. We are interested in, and respect, your views and hope you will respect ours." Retorted Ciporen: "Come on! Why not be honest with us? Like Johnson, you think we're a bunch of babbling idiots." Said Conlon quietly: "We want to shed light, not heat."

That night, some 650 students and faculty members showed up for the full-dress question-and-answer period. Many of them carried placards saying such things as, "The War in Vietnam is an Immoral War, a Dirty War, a Futile War." About a third of the audience wore black armbands.

The black-armbanders refused to sit down, stood hooting and hollering around the edges of the hall. The chairman of the meeting, Angela Mischke, 23, a graduate in Russian history, pleaded in vain, "Please sit down." Cried Fred Ciporen: "These people are standing for a reason! If you ask them to sit down, you're missing the point." Finally, a semblance of order was achieved, and Conlon began by comparing the meeting to a bullfight where the crowd had just shouted "Let the bull come out!" Asked for a general statement of the U.S. position in Vietnam, he said simply: "The over-all aim of the U.S. Government is to assist a legal government, recognized by over fifty countries in the world, to resist aggression from North Vietnam."

Lt. Col. Hilman was asked by an armband-wearer: "What do napalm or gas do to a person when used in Vietnam?" Said he:

"The gas you speak of is a misnomer as we normally understand gas. It is better described as an incapacitating agent, one already in use in the United States by police and Army . . ." Yelled a heckler: "Does it work against Negroes?" Continued Hilman: "To answer the rest of the question, what does napalm do? It burns."

A student from Ceylon wanted to know about "what goes on in the month of torture" undergone by captured Vietcong guerrillas. Said Conlon: "American interrogations in Vietnam—and I have participated—do not include torture . . . But if you want examples of torture, why do you never condemn the well-documented tortures carried out by the Communists?"

At times, reason seemed about to prevail, as when Robert Gordon, 20, a psychology student, arose and pointed at a placard proclaiming the death of U.S. morality. Said he: "I have always been led to believe that good manners are a prerequisite of morality. I'd like to ask what these students are doing here, standing against a wall, protesting loudly, and generally enjoying a right of freedom that would be denied them in any Communist society."

But that was one of the few bright spots. And when Conlon was leaving, he was accosted by Arnold Lochin, a 26-year-old biochemistry graduate, who sneered: "Get this straight, sweetie. We're not going to fight your filthy fascist war. Go fight it yourself."

Foreign Policy on Campus

— ART BUCHWALD

From the New York Herald Tribune, *May 16, 1965.*

U.S. foreign policy is going through its most difficult phase. Not only are we having trouble convincing our Western allies and our South American friends that we are doing the right thing, but we're having a heck of a time persuading our own university students and professors.

The President has ordered truth squads sent out to American college campuses, and it is only the first of many plans in the works to get the students and professors back on our side.

The Under Secretary of State in Charge of University Relations recently made his report to the Cabinet. I managed to get hold of a transcript.

He said, "Gentlemen, I am happy to report that West Point and the Colorado School of Mines are supporting our action in the Dominican Republic."

"What about the University of Wisconsin?" someone asked.

"They're still holding out, as is the University of Michigan."

"What are we going to do about it?"

"The Air Force is planning to drop 80,000 leaflets on their campuses this morning. Radio Free America has gone on a twenty-four-hour schedule and the psychological warfare people are now on the scene stirring up rumors about a left-wing takeover of the schools."

"That's all well and good," someone said, "but it seems to me we should bomb the schools with more than leaflets, just to show them we mean business."

"We've thought about it, but don't forget we have our own truth-squad people there and, besides, we have to think of public reaction from Harvard, Yale, and Princeton."

"Couldn't we have the U.S. Marines occupy the campuses under the guise of protecting American lives and property?"

"That's been discussed, but if the other universities revolt, we'll run out of Marines in no time."

"Suppose we broke off diplomatic relations with Wisconsin and Michigan?"

"The CIA is against it. If we recalled our people they would have to pull out and it would interfere with their plans."

"What plans?"

"They're planning to put in military juntas at Wisconsin and Michigan, made up of cadet colonies from the ROTC."

"Say, that's a good idea," someone said.

"If it works. If it doesn't work, we're going to have to deny we had anything to do with it."

"Don't you think the overthrowing of student governments is a dangerous business?" one of the doves said.

"Not if we have proof that they're left-wing controlled. I'd rather have an ROTC junta than a rabble of leftists running the school."

"Will we notify the American Association of University Professors of our plans?"

"We don't have time. Once the juntas are in, we'll ask the professors to come in and help us. But if we ask them first, they'll debate the question to kingdom come."

"How can we persuade the schools that supporting our policies is to their best interests?"

"By giving each university $1 billion if they go along with us."
"And if they don't?"
"Then we escalate. We will start by bombing the football stadiums and the highways leading to the schools."

3. DEAN BUNDY AND THE PROFESSORS

An Invitation to McGeorge Bundy

—ROBERT BUCKHOUT

From Robert Buckhout, Secretary of the Ad Hoc Committee on Foreign Policy, Washington University, to McGeorge Bundy, Special Presidential Assistant for National Security Affairs. For a brief discussion of the Ad Hoc Committee's letter, see the article by Webster Schott in Chapter I.

April 10, 1965

My Dear Mr. Bundy:

In a speech to the American Management Association, on January 31, 1962, you asked for citizen "interest, action, understanding, and support" for our Government's efforts to better international relations. Writing as private citizens and as members of the nation's academic community, not as representatives of our particular university, we agree that our Government should work urgently for improved relations with other nations and that all citizens ought to make serious efforts to understand and to support such a program. But, at this critical moment, we find ourselves unable to fulfill this important duty because we are unable to understand our Government's stated policy in Southeast Asia.

As educators, we feel a special responsibility in this regard because our duty to society requires us to help our fellow citizens understand the role of the United States in the world today. We have, moreover, an added responsibility because several members of the nation's community of scholars, yourself among them, who serve the Government at the policy-making level, do so in fulfillment of the intellectual and moral standards which the public rightfully associates with the academic community. As scholars, we are accustomed to questioning and discussing our colleagues' views, the better to understand them. Yet we, together with the entire American public, have had no opportunity to hear fully, and to examine critically, the views of yourself and other scholars who now help to guide our Government's policy in Southeast Asia.

Nevertheless, we are determined to exercise our right to examine this policy critically and to discuss it publicly. For this reason, we, the undersigned, urge you to come before the academic community in an open meeting here and explain and discuss with us the assumptions, intentions, and goals which guide the United States and its conduct of the war in Southeast Asia. If the evening of April 19th or 20th is a convenient time, we would appreciate an early acceptance of our invitation or, if this date proves inconvenient, we would be obliged if you would suggest another at your earliest convenience. We are aware, of course, of the urgent demands on your time, but we believe that a public accounting of the Government's policy in Southeast Asia represents a prior claim on the time of those who guide this policy.

We believe that such an accounting will allow us, in fact, to discuss with you at least the following questions as well as others raised by the recent White Paper [*put out by the State Department in February, 1965*].

Who is the enemy? Although we have not declared war, we are engaged in military action against insurgent groups in South Vietnam and against the territory of North Vietnam and Laos. In some instances, U.S. aircraft have attacked or supported an attack on undisclosed targets, so that the specific enemy is not even indicated.

Who are our allies? On September 30, 1963, before the World Affairs Conference, Albany, New York, you said that ". . . it would be folly for the United States to neglect, or to regard with indifference, political developments of recent months which raise questions about the ability of the Government and the people of South Vietnam to support each other effectively in their contest with Communism. . . . It is and must be the policy of the U.S. Government to make clear its interest in whatever improvements it judges to be necessary, always, of course, with a proper regard for responsibilities which rest in the first instance upon the people of South Vietnam." What "improvements" in the popular base of the South Vietnam Government, clearly required now more than ever, do you judge to be necessary? How are they likely to come about? Is it possible that the Liberation Front (Vietcong) and the people of South Vietnam *do* "support each other effectively?"

Under what conditions would the United States support the

participation of the Liberation Front in a future government of South Vietnam or encourage negotiations toward such participation? Would we continue, for example, to support the Mekong Delta project in the event that the Liberation Front participated in a future government of South Vietnam?

What kind of proof must North Vietnam provide to convince us that that country is not intervening, or has ceased to intervene, in South Vietnam? How will this proof be validated? Is the United States willing and able to offer some kind of *quid pro quo*?

President Johnson has said that "no negotiated settlement in Vietnam is possible as long as the Communists hope to achieve victory by force." On another occasion, he said that we seek no more than a return to the essentials of the Geneva agreement of 1954. Does this mean that, if the Communists should seek victory by the ballot box, we would support all-Vietnam free elections in accordance with these agreements?

According to the Office of Public Services, Department of State document *Situation in Viet-Nam*, "our and the Vietnamese response (to the provocations ordered and directed by the Hanoi regime) was carefully limited to military areas which are supplying men and arms for aggression in South Viet-Nam and was thus entirely defensive in nature." Why has this military policy in South Vietnam recently undergone a change? Why do some bombings of North Vietnam fail now to be even so limited? How does this policy justify the bombing of radar installations at the northern border of North Vietnam, a direction which has no bearing on military action in South Vietnam? Some commentators have concluded that the hidden agenda of our policy is to provoke China into action which would allow the United States to bomb targets in that country. Is there any substance to this assertion?

We look forward to hearing from you.

ROBERT BUCKHOUT

The Invitation Refused: Reply by McGeorge Bundy to the Invitation of April 10

April 16, 1965

Dear Mr. Buckhout:

It has taken me a few days to get to your letter of April 10.

I am sorry to say that I cannot accept your invitation for April

19 or 20. My schedule is so crowded that I have had to cancel an academic meeting on April 20, which was scheduled many months ago, and my prospective hosts would surely not understand it if I were suddenly to accept an invitation given on ten days' notice. Moreover, if I were to add another meeting to my schedule at another date, I should clearly owe precedence to those whom I have had to disappoint after an earlier acceptance.

I cannot honestly tell you that I think your letter reflects great credit on its authors, either as a piece of propaganda or as a serious effort to engage in discussion. Just as samples of the difficulties I find in it, let me cite the following:

1. I find strange your assumption that a public official is somehow especially accountable to the profession in which he worked before coming to the Government. I have supposed that Government officials were supposed to work for all of the American people, and that a businessman was not especially accountable to business circles, a man from labor to the unions, or a professor to university people. The premise from which you appear to be working is that of the corporative state, and I myself do not find Mussolini a sound guide to the principles of public service. There is no reason why I should be especially accountable to you, even on the uncertain assumption that you are truly representative of the academic community. It is true, of course, that I remain interested in university thinking and have spoken from time to time to academic audiences. I have spoken on the subject of our policy in Vietnam, in recent months, to such audiences at Georgetown University and Johns Hopkins University. I expect to speak again at other universities. I have also spoken recently on nationwide television. I therefore question whether you can fairly suggest that I have not joined in the general effort of the Government to give a public accounting of its policy.

2. As to your specific question who is the enemy, I direct your attention to the President's speech on April 7 [*1965, at Johns Hopkins University*], of which I enclose a copy. Your question is answered fully in that speech, which was on the record three days before you wrote.

3. You ask who are our allies and, in so doing, you quote an incomplete fragment of some remarks made by me eighteen months ago in the context of the difficulties faced, at that time, by the government of President Diem. I do not share your judgment that the problem of public support for the South Vietnamese Government is more severe now than then and I certainly do not believe that there is general popular support for the Vietcong in South

Vietnam. On the contrary, I think it plain, on the evidence of reliable observers from many countries, that the South Vietnamese as a people do not wish to be taken over by the Vietcong. . . .

4. I do not understand why a group of academic men, presumably careful students of the historical record, should frame a question about free elections on the premise that the men in Hanoi might permit such elections in North Vietnam. Whatever may have been the hopes of the signers of the Geneva agreements on this score, there is nothing in the record of the last ten years which suggests that this Communist regime is different from any other on this point. The center of the problem in South Vietnam is to ensure the right of the people *there* to peaceful self-determination and that is the purpose of the United States. That purpose is not advanced by the assumption that there is any serious prospect of genuinely free elections in the North, or any likelihood that Hanoi will offer such elections. Their position toward South Vietnam, in the memorable phrase of President Kennedy, is that "what's mine is mine and what's yours is negotiable"—except that they are not even willing to negotiate, so far.

There are other distortions in your letter, and other assumptions in its questions which are contrary to fact, but I may have written enough to suggest that if your letter came to me for grading as a professor of government, I would not be able to give it high marks.

McGeorge Bundy

McGeorge Bundy's
Bureaucratic Self-Righteousness

—HENRY DAVID AIKEN

Professor Aiken teaches philosophy at Brandeis University. This letter appeared in Time, May 21, 1965.

McGeorge Bundy's churlish reply deserves high marks, if he wants them, for its chilliness and scorn. However, these are not qualities that I, at least, greatly admire in a public official so fatefully close to the President of the United States. They are signs not of intellectual incisiveness or moral rigor but only of bureaucratic self-righteousness and too-prolonged insulation from the ever-growing anxieties that Mr. Bundy's ex-colleagues in universities everywhere feel toward the foreign policies that he has helped to shape in recent years. His mind is more rapid than accurate, more facile than profound; for if he did acknowledge a special accountability to the scholars where questions of fact and of truth are concerned, the result might be an improvement in the quality of communications emanating from the White House.

HENRY DAVID AIKEN

The Invitation Repeated

—ROBERT BUCKHOUT

April 22, 1965

My Dear Mr. Bundy:

In your recent letter you seemed to have misinterpreted certain of our statements and we would like, therefore, to clarify them and to repeat our invitation. We have an urgent interest in a direct debate on the basis of U.S. policy in Vietnam, as it is our conviction that many members of the academic community have not been impressed with the assumptions or reasons offered in support of that policy. The lack of candor about Government purpose makes it impossible to evaluate U.S. actions in this area, and the disparity between Government statements and the writings of responsible students of foreign policy and of journalists is a cause for concern and inevitably raises questions about the advice being given the Government on Vietnam policy.

As to the misinterpretations in your letter: Our position is, simply, that a scholar, in whatever capacity he may serve our society, has an obligation toward the principles of scholarship and that his transition from the academic community to Government service does not free him from this obligation. As the Surgeon General remains a physician, responsible to physicians generally for the ethics and principles demanded by his profession, so members of the academic community called into Government service *as* academicians continue to have a responsibility to the principles of scholarly discourse.

At the time when the anti-intellectualism of the Eisenhower period was replaced with what the nation hoped was a new era of willingness to apply the principles of scholarship to the basic re-examination of many of the tenets of our foreign policy, there were great hopes that this process would bear tangible fruit, which by now would have been visible. To our disappointment and, we believe, to the disappointment of the intellectual and academic community at large, those of its members who have joined in the policy-making process appear to have removed themselves from the system of discourse which has made their new position possible.

We need hardly point out again the most important principles of academic discourse: free and open debate, and exposition of the assumptions and principles which underlie decisions. It is not proper in a scholar to justify himself solely from the unassailable position of television addresses and ex-cathedra pronouncements. If we, or anyone else, are to evaluate that advice given to our Government which rests, at least in part, on academic validation, this advice must be tested by criticism and debate. We, therefore, reiterate our invitation to you to appear at this university or at any other place, at any time in the near future which is convenient, in order to debate with your colleagues your own position on the war in Vietnam.

You can take an important step toward winning back the confidence of your former academic colleagues and a greatly alienated world opinion if you accept this challenge.

ROBERT BUCKHOUT

A Plea to President Johnson

— ANATOL RAPOPORT

March 30, 1965

Dear Mr. President:

There is a plaque at the entrance to the Michigan Union on this campus which says:

Here, at 2:00 A.M. on October 14, 1960, John Fitzgerald Kennedy first defined the Peace Corps. He stood at the place marked by the medallion and was cheered by a large enthusiastic student audience for the hope and promise his idea gave to the world.

I hope to see the day when there will be a plaque on our Angell Hall, commemorating the First American Teach-in, March 24–25, 1965. . . .

It is important to understand why the sessions were held at night.

This was to call attention to the unusual role assumed by the spontaneously recruited faculty of what one of our invited speakers called the Free University of Michigan. Our purpose was twofold: to teach and to protest. In the teach-in, the professor appeared not only as a source of facts and a guide in analysis, but also as a voice of conscience. The teach-in was our way of discharging our responsibility to our students. We felt our students were being misinformed about the chain of events behind the present war in Vietnam, which has disgraced America in the eyes of the world. Therefore, we felt compelled to present the facts to our students. We felt that the meaning of the events in Southeast Asia were being obfuscated by "glossy generalities . . . and . . . deliberately obscure language," as Walter Lippmann put it. Therefore we were obliged to offer our students an opportunity for a thoughtful analysis with due regard for the complexity of our era. We felt that decisions involving, perhaps, the fate of humanity, were being made behind closed doors by people who thought only in terms of power, coercion, and terror. We exerted our efforts toward instigating a broad, unintimidated discussion, as befits a free people. Finally, we saw that America has become callous. We undertook to awaken the nation's conscience.

All of what I have just said can be documented. Suppression of facts is evident in the White Paper, an official pronouncement of our Government. Glib rationalizations and provincial self-righteousness pervade the pamphlet which the Department of State is disseminating in acknowledgment of letters written to the President. I am referring to *Challenge to Americans*, published by the Advertising Council. The Advertising Council tells us, presumably in the name of our Government, that we have an utterly evil, utterly ruthless enemy—Communism. Thus we are told exactly what the populations in the more backward of the Communist countries are told, with just one word, "Communism," substituted for "Capitalism." How callous the nation has become can be seen in the pictures of tortured prisoners published in the press with indifferent or approving captions; in the use of weapons designed to incinerate helpless civilians; in cynical explanations that the war is a good combat school (as one serviceman put it, "It's the only war we've got."); in the protestations that gases are being used only "experimentally." During the teach-in, we also saw a sample of sentiment aroused by the present undeclared war: a group of youngsters parading in a counterdemonstration, carrying a flag, beating a drum, and displaying two placards. One placard read "Bang the Cong"; the other, "Drop the Bomb."

We teachers are resolved to counteract misrepresentation of facts, oversimplification of issues, and the brutalization of people. We hope that our example will be followed and that the community of scholars, scientists, and teachers will do no less than what so many churches are already doing to call the nation back to sanity.

We hope, Mr. President, that you will be as responsive to world public opinion on the Vietnam issue as you were to the ground swell on civil rights.

ANATOL RAPOPORT, Secretary
The Inter-University Committee
for a Public Hearing on Vietnam

McGeorge Bundy Replies for the President

April 12, 1965

Dear Mr. Rapoport:

The President has asked me to acknowledge your letter, of March 30, explaining the point of view of those who engaged in the teach-in at the University of Michigan. I would be interested to know exactly where you get the documentation for your notion that decisions involving the fate of humanity are being made by people who think "exclusively in terms of power, coercion, and terror." This is only the most extreme of the comments in your letter, but it does not fill me with admiration for the academic quality of your thinking.

MCGEORGE BUNDY

Power, Coercion, and Terror: Replies to McGeorge Bundy from Anatol Rapoport

April 30, 1965

Dear Mr. Bundy:

In response to your latest invitation to document my statement about "power, coercion, and terror," I refer you to "U.S. Power in Vietnam," in *Time* magazine, April 23, 1965.

If your question is indeed serious, as you state, I suggest you read the article against the background of my assumptions, not yours, since it is I who have drawn the conclusion which you challenge. If you wish to challenge my *assumptions*, I am ready to discuss them on their own merits.

My assumptions are as follows. Ever since the close of World War II, the United States has been committed to a containment policy manifested successively as the Truman Doctrine, the policy of massive retaliation, etcetera. The essential idea of that policy has been the notion that any revolution interpreted by the United States as Communist controlled, influenced, or instigated is a threat to the security of the United States. This includes such events as anticolonial revolutions led by any forces which are not explicitly hostile to the U.S.S.R., China, or, now, Cuba.

Consistent with this policy, the United States refused to sign the Geneva agreement of 1954. Diem was installed in Saigon by the United States for the purpose of preventing the implementation of that agreement. The National Liberation Front was formed as a resistance movement against Diem's dictatorial regime. The present war is an attempt on the part of the United States to crush that movement.

Now, given this interpretation—which, please note, is shared by many thousands of very well-informed (some exceptionally well-informed) and perceptive people—the role of U.S. forces in Vietnam appears to be that of brutal suppression of a struggle against tyranny, not that of aid against aggression. Moreover, the sources of support to the National Liberation Front seem irrelevant in the light of the above interpretation, as do the acts of terror. Because of the tremendous military odds against them, resistance movements frequently resort to terror. Typically, resistance movements seek and often receive aid from the outside. We did when we fought for our independence; the anti-Castro forces did when they tried to overthrow Castro, whom they declared to be a puppet installed by a foreign power.

In short, the interpretation I have outlined, while it can no doubt be challenged, is by no means fantastic or bizarre. It is suggested by numerous historical analogies. It can be summarily dismissed only by someone who cannot, or will not, admit that the United States can ever play the part of an oppressor, a supporter of regimes whose only purpose is to protect privileges threatened by popular revolutions. Painful as it is, I must admit that the United States is playing precisely this part in Vietnam.

Therefore, the American Fighting Men, glorified in *Time* magazine, appear to be modern versions of the czarist cossacks. Their bloodthirstiness, frankly and gleefully spelled out, corroborates the parallel. If names and dates were suppressed, the leaders of these men could, from their comments, be easily mistaken for the SS. Some eyewitness descriptions of air-to-ground combat are close paraphrases of similar descriptions by Italian fliers in Abyssinia, in 1935.

A nation whose popular press nurtures the sentiments expressed by U.S. Marines, can be easily suspected to be guided by people whose primary commitments are to power, coercion, and terror. The personal qualities of these people, or even the bases of their policies in other contexts, are not relevant to the issue. I am concerned, at present, only with Vietnam, for the course of events there may well be crucially important in determining the fate of humanity.

This is the background of my conclusions to the effect that the fate of humanity is being decided by people concerned exclusively with power, coercion, and terror.

ANATOL RAPOPORT, PH.D.

May 4, 1965

Dear Mr. Bundy:

In view of the events of the past few days, do you still challenge my conclusion that the present U.S. foreign policy is based on power, coercion, and terror?

What other interpretation can be put on the intervention in the Dominican Republic in violation of solemn pledges? How can you explain the fact that while we tolerated the gangster and the instigator of assassinations Trujillo, we are determined to prevent a government led by Bosch, who has shown himself devoted to strictly constitutional rule? If the Government replies that Bosch's supporters have been "infiltrated by the Communists," why should I believe this, in view of deliberate falsehoods with which the Government has supported its coercive acts since the Bay of Pigs? Can I not conclude that these escalated falsehoods are part of the plan of every such operation? First we had the reassurance that the Marines have been sent to "evacuate Americans," then "to protect American property," then to "establish defensive positions only." Why should I not believe the Marine who replied to "Why are you here?" with "To clean out the rebels" and, to "Are the rebels Communists?" with "We don't know."?

Mr. Bundy, you are an educated man. Please explain to me where

President Johnson's attitude toward popular revolutions differs from that of Nicholas I, and where the role of American Marines differs from that of the cossacks. And, if you undertake to explain this to me, please remember that I, too, am an educated man.

ANATOL RAPOPORT, PH.D.

Final Reply from McGeorge Bundy

May 5, 1965

Dear Professor Rapoport:

I guess we are not getting anywhere. Your use of evidence and assumptions, inference and innuendo, are so foreign to my own standards that I doubt if we can gain much by pursuing our correspondence further.

MCGEORGE BUNDY

[*Handwritten addendum:*]

This comment applies also to yours of May 4, just received.

Concluding Letter by Anatol Rapoport

May 14, 1965

Dear Mr. Bundy:

We agree on one point, namely, that we are not getting anywhere. I wonder, however, if some thought should not be given to our failure to establish communication. I am able to communicate with thousands of my colleagues, presumably because we have similar standards of evidence, assumptions, and inference. If by innuendo you mean the connotative use of language, then we also use "innuendo" as an aid to communication. You have not told me what your standards of evidence, assumption, inference, and innuendo are, but I am sure there are many people in responsible positions who share them. Am I to infer from your last letter that important segments of America, each a source of considerable influence (although in different spheres), can no longer talk to each other? If so, do you not find this alarming?

Considering the background of our correspondence, I find this very alarming. Recall that your first letter to me was in the name of the President. I had transmitted to the President the grave concern of a large segment of the academic community with the present U.S. policy in Southeast Asia. You stated that the President asked you to reply to this letter, but the only content of your reply was an expression of disdain for the quality of my thinking. When I tried to explain how I arrived at some of my conclusions, you only impugned my standards of evaluation. At no time did you address yourself to any of the numerous issues I raised in my letter to the President or in my letters to you.

Does this summary dismissal and refusal to establish communication portend the way the U.S. Government will henceforth behave toward citizens concerned with the conduct of our foreign policy?

The innuendo in your letters to me indicates that you cannot communicate with someone whose standards are different from yours. If you and I, both reared and educated in the United States in similar institutions, cannot communicate, what can we expect in the way of establishing communications with others whose historical experience and standards of evaluation are altogether different from ours? Does your attitude toward me and thousands of Americans who think along similar lines portend the attitude to be assumed by the United States in negotiations with people who do not share *your* habits of evaluation? If so, we are in for serious trouble.

Please be informed that I am forwarding our entire correspondence to President Johnson. I also intend to make it public.

ANATOL RAPOPORT, PH.D.

4. THE NATIONAL TEACH-IN

The Original Proposal

Issued by the Inter-University Committee for a Public Hearing on Vietnam. The committee, organizer of the National Teach-In, was formed in April, 1965, at Ann Arbor, Michigan, to coordinate the activities of faculty-student groups on some 150 American campuses.

Dear Colleague:

The escalation of the Vietnam war has brought about a mobilization of public protest unprecedented in the history of the Cold War. In the academic community, a form of protest has appeared spontaneously and is spreading from campus to campus—the teach-in. These teach-ins are organized by local faculties and students. The usual format includes presentations by authorities on Southeast Asian affairs, intensive analyses of the events leading up to the present crisis, and explorations of alternatives to the present policy.

On May 15th, we propose to hold a national version of these local conferences, in Washington, D.C. The national conference will be essentially a confrontation between scholars and scientists, on the one hand, and, on the other, members of the Government and those former members of the academic community who are presently advising the Government on Vietnam policy. Members of the Government and their advisers will be invited to explain the rationale behind the present policy on Southeast Asia and to answer certain questions, for example:

1. Under what conditions would our Government agree to a cease-fire?

2. What sort of government would be acceptable to the United States in South Vietnam? Would the participation of the National Liberation Front be acceptable under any conditions?

3. Are the continued bombing attacks on North Vietnam likely to achieve the stated objectives?

4. What types of provisions have been made or are planned to ascertain the wishes of the Vietnamese people?

5. How does the war in Southeast Asia affect the relations between the United States and our allies?

6. What is the effect of the present war on other undeveloped nations?

7. How is the present war affecting Sino-Soviet relations?

8. What role should the United Nations play in resolving the present conflict?

9. Is the National Liberation Front primarily an indigenous resistance movement against an unpopular government? If so, should the United States be engaged in suppressing that movement?

In addition to directing these questions to the Government and its advisers, we shall invite senators and congressmen to participate in seminars on a variety of topics related to the Vietnam situation in all its ramifications. We shall bring together experts on the history, the economy, and the political structure of Southeast Asia; on guerrilla warfare; on relations between China and North Vietnam; on the National Liberation Front; SEATO; public opinion in South Vietnam; and related topics.

We are attempting to recruit a large, representative group of scholars and scientists to sponsor the National Teach-In. Sponsorship implies only a deep concern with the present situation in Southeast Asia and a conviction that questions related to peace and war should be open to responsible debate. Sponsorship does not entail the endorsement of any particular scheme for settling the situation in Vietnam. This is precisely what we are searching for.

You are invited to support this effort. . . .

Statement to the National Teach-In

— MC GEORGE BUNDY

This is Mr. Bundy's statement to the National Teach-In, May 15, 1965. For a discussion of the negotiations that led to Mr. Bundy's decision to accept an invitation to the teach-in, see "Dialogue or Monologue?" by Anatol Rapoport, in this chapter, Part 5.

I deeply regret that it is impossible for me to take part in the discussion, this afternoon, of our policy in Vietnam. I looked forward to this meeting and I hate to miss it. When I accepted your invitation I did so with a warning that I might be unable to attend because of other duties. It gives me no pleasure that this warning has come true. I regret my absence the more because I wholly disagree with those who have argued that it is inappropriate for a Government official to take part in a discussion of this kind.

It may be true, although I have no firsthand knowledge, that some of your meetings on Vietnam have failed to meet the standards appropriate to university and college discussion. It may also be true, and I have thought so once or twice myself, that a few of those who feel strongly about the situation in Vietnam have been more interested in pressure upon the Administration than in fair discussion with its representatives. But the preliminary arrangements for this particular meeting, so far as I have knowledge of them, have been fair to a fault. I am confident that the discussion this afternoon will be a model of its kind.

Members of the academic community and members of the Administration share a deep interest in the encouragement of such fair and open discussion. It has been argued that debate of this kind should be avoided because it can give encouragement to the adversaries of our country. There is some ground for this argument, since it is true that Communists have little understanding of the meaning of debate in a free society. The Chinese will continue to pretend, and perhaps in part believe, that American policy is weaker because 700 faculty members have made a protest against our policy in Vietnam. The American people, whatever their opinion, know better. They know that those who are protesting are only a minority, indeed a small minority of American teachers and students. They know, also, that even within that minority a great majority accept and respect the right and duty of the American Administration to meet its constitutional responsibilities for the conduct of our foreign affairs.

The American people know that the real day of danger will come when we are afraid of any popular minority or unwilling to reply to its voices. They understand what Communists cannot understand at all, that open discussion between our citizens and their government is the central nervous system of our free society. We cannot let the propaganda of such totalitarians divert us from our necessary arguments with one another any more than we can let them be misled by such debates if we can help it.

I will not take your time, in this brief message, for a rehearsal of the policy of this Administration on Vietnam. Let me take only a word to speak of our purpose there. That purpose is peace for the people of Vietnam, the people of Southeast Asia, and the people of the United States. We evidently differ on the choice of ways and means to peace in what we all must recognize to be a complex, ugly, and demanding situation. Those differences may go deep to the nature of the politics of Asia, to the legitimacy of force in the face of armed attack, and to the true prospects and purposes of the people of Vietnam themselves.

But my own assessment is that what divides us is less than what unites us. None of us wants the war to be enlarged. All of us want a decent settlement. None of us wants other men to be forced under a totalitarian political authority. All of us seek a solution in which American troops can be honorably withdrawn. None of us, I hope, believe that these are easy goals. All of us, I trust, are prepared to be steadfast in the pursuit of our purposes. I recognize the entire sincerity of the great majority of those who now disagree with our policy in Vietnam. I think many of these critics have been wrong in earlier moments of stress and danger and I think many of them misunderstood the hard realities of this dangerous world. But their good faith and good intent are not in question, and on other issues at other times their efforts have been of great service to the country.

Having said this much, perhaps I can ask in return that these critics recognize that the Administration which now bears the responsibility for the conduct of our foreign affairs does not admire force for its own sake or brinkmanship of any sort. The purpose of its foreign policy in Vietnam, as elsewhere, is that diplomacy and power and progress and hope shall be held together in the service of the freedom of us all. So I trust that the discussion this afternoon will not turn upon charge and countercharge against the motives of those with whom we disagree. Let it turn, instead, upon analysis of the situation as it is and of choices for the future which can serve the purposes we share. I repeat my apologies for my forced absence and I take comfort in the thought that I shall miss the meeting more than you will miss me.

Introduction to the National Teach-In

—ERIC WOLF

Professor Wolf was an organizer of the original teach-in at the University of Michigan, where he teaches anthropology. This is a transcript of his remarks at the opening session, Sheraton Park Hotel Ballroom, May 15, 1965.

It is my great privilege and honor to open the first session of an important event in the history of American democracy, an event in which a body of citizens has assembled in the nation's capital to seek from its elected Government and those who speak from it and for it a reasoned explanation for a course of action which it has undertaken abroad in the name of the American people. This National Teach-In is the culmination of many similar events held in universities and towns all over the nation. These events have been protests, in the true American tradition, against those who would foreclose and forestall debate, against an engineering of consent set in motion to make Americans placid followers rather than active participants in the democratic process. These protests have brought together men of very diverse opinions. Their common bond lies not in a unity of point of view but in their common desire to open discussion on a matter of vital national interest. Such active concern on the part of informed citizenry is the life blood of democracy. If it is cut off, democracy is threatened. That democracy is difficult, none of us wish to deny. But we are assembled in this public hearing to make this difficult undertaking possible. In honoring our invitation, the members of our Administration who will attend have also honored themselves and their country.

It is no accident, ladies and gentlemen, that this movement of protest, this seeking out of information and explanation, has come into being over Vietnam. An American people that has fought two major world wars and a bloody limited war in Korea is deeply involved in world affairs. American bases circle the globe. American personnel, civilian and military, have become acquainted with a wider world beyond America in ways not true of any previous generation. Americans today are both wiser in the ways of the world than their predecessors and more concerned about it. They have learned that the future of the United States no longer depends on the United States alone. That future is forged in relations with many nations in the wider arena of the world. Upon the nature of these relationships the fate of America depends. Therefore, an American people, informed and concerned as never before about the relations of America to the world, also demands to know the truth about its relations with other parts of the world. Deeply troubled about these relations, Americans only recently cast their votes against the very policies now being thrust upon us in Vietnam. We therefore want to know the truth about Vietnam because we are concerned about the place of America in a changing world.

This search for truth also enshrines a search for the principles, the premises, which guide our actions in the world. In our daily lives these principles are all too often obscured. They are obscured by the incessant stream of daily news. They are obscured by our empirical tendency to settle political disagreements by splitting the difference rather than by probing the reasons that underlie these differences. They are obscured, thirdly, by the tendency of men to take premises for granted and to act upon the demands of the day. In this, ends are forgotten and the means become the ends themselves. It is a function of democratic protest to recall men to a consideration of those ends and the principles and the aspirations which must guide the selection of means.

Protests are radical in the true sense of the word radical—they go to the roots. Protest and the call for more information, protest and the call for clarification, protest and the call for examination of basic principles are not, as some critics would have it, symptoms that a nation is sick and cowardly. It is the very essence of a healthy democracy that men must continually re-examine what they do and what they want. This is the function of an informed citizenry in a democratic society. Because many of us are teaching and doing research, we feel that it is our special responsibility to urge and initiate this task of democratic review.

We must be wary, in this debate, of accepting soft solutions and of oversimplification. We have been told by some that the issues involved in Vietnam and in the war in Vietnam are too complex to be understood by the average citizen; that we must trust our officials who, it is alleged, alone understand these issues in all their complexity. We dispute these claims, for we are convinced that as citizens we have a responsibility to make up our minds in terms of such information as we can obtain. We are here to seek the best information we can get. It is not clear that those who are supposed to have all the relevant information have always been right. It is not clear that they deserve our unqualified support. We have also been told that the issues are really very simple; that the world struggle is one between the forces of good and the forces of evil. We have been criticized for our inability to grasp these underlying simplicities. Again we say, this is no way to talk to American citizens. Those who do, assume that the people are fools, that they possess short memories. This generation has acquired a better memory through experience and through teaching than any generation of Americans in the past. We know that the ways of the world are not simple. We know that the United States has dealings with military dictatorships in Latin America and Spain, with Communist governments in Poland and Yugoslavia. We've heard the peoples of Germany and Japan described as devils in one set of circumstances and as valued friends and allies in another. We are aware of our own limitations. We are also aware, as never before, of the complex imperatives guiding the actions of others in the same world in which we live. As George Kennen has said: "When the ambivalence of one's virtue is recognized, the total iniquity of one's opponent is irreparably damaged." We are here to serve notice that American citizens are not children. We have long put away childish things. Those who advance simple stereotypes for persuasive purposes today become the captives of their creations tomorrow. They lose the capacity to learn from experience.

Political Folklore in Vietnam

—HANS J. MORGENTHAU

Professor Morgenthau is Albert A. Michelson Distinguished Service Professor of Political Science and Modern History at the University of Chicago and the author of Politics Among Nations. *This transcript of the first address at the National Teach-In is slightly abridged.*

I want, first, to take up the theme with which the chairman has introduced this extraordinary meeting. I refer to the extraordinary character of this meeting, for I doubt that in the history of any nation anything like this has ever happened: That out of the unorganized mass of a great people, there has arisen a spontaneous questioning of the policies of the Government, forcing the Government to justify itself in the eyes of the people. Perhaps in countries that are parliamentary democracies with an organized opposition such a popular movement is not called for. But, while we have a two-party system for the purpose of elections, we certainly do not have a two-party system in terms of alternative policy. So there is never an organized opposition which confronts the Government with criticism and with an alternative policy. In consequence, the Government can always try for what is euphemistically called consensus, which in truth means a kind of passive acceptance of whatever policy the Government pursues. The spontaneous teach-in movement performs, in a sense, the functions which in a parliamentary democracy an opposition party performs—that is to say, to question the Government, to probe into the foundations of its policies, and to suggest alternative policies.

The present Administration's reaction to this popular movement is significant and sheds an illuminating light upon the state of American democracy. It has reacted with scorn and with contempt. Leaders of the Administration, some of whom have been professors themselves, have referred to the "nonsense" the professors propound. One leading member of the Administration has scorned, in letters accessible to the mass media, the respected professors who have raised respectable questions requiring respectable answers. And I, as you know, have been accused, by one of the most fervent journalistic representatives of the Administration, of pompousness and ignorance, which is an impressive combination of negative attributes. Most interestingly, my appearance on this program on an equal basis with the main spokesman for the Administration has been categorically vetoed by that spokesman. [*Special Presidential Assistant McGeorge Bundy refused to accept Professor Morgenthau as his debating opponent at the National Teach-In. Regarding Professor Morgenthau's reference to the Administration official who expressed "scorn in letters," see "Dean Bundy and the Professors," Part 3 in this chapter. Professor Morgenthau's journalistic critic was Joseph Alsop.*] If the case that I and others have presented were so utterly weak as it has been made out to be, if we were really so pompously ignorant or ignorantly pompous and talked such nonsense, I would have thought that the chief spokesman for the Administration would have welcomed the opportunity to show us up for what we are.

I should also say . . . that I am as sensitive as the next man to an insult and I am sensitive to that one, too. I decided to come here only after a great deal of vacillation and heart-searching. My presence here is due to my devotion to this cause, to which I have subordinated my personal feelings. But let no one mistake my presence here for acquiescence in the tactics in which the chief spokesman for the Administration has engaged.

The case of the Administration is indeed weak, and if the attributes which have been applied to myself and others had any place in an intelligent debate at all—which they have not, because they are invectives and not arguments—they would apply to the case of the Administration rather than to that of the opposition. I shall not repeat here what I have put in print in recent years; I will only add two main points upon which, for the present at least, the case for the Administration seems to rest.

One point is that South Vietnam, a sovereign state, is subject to outside aggression; the second point is that we are in honor obligated, and in law committed, to aid this victim of aggression in its resistance to it. Both the arguments on the face of them . . . appeal to the moral emotions of the public at large to come to the aid of the poor victim of aggression and to honor one's commitments. Yet . . . both arguments are completely specious.

First of all, it is mere fiction to say that there are two sovereign states in the territory that is called Vietnam. There is one state populated by one population which, in 1954, was arbitrarily divided at the 17th parallel. . . . The Geneva agreement is emphatic in stating that the line of demarcation should not be regarded as a frontier dividing two states and that there are not two states, only two temporarily divided zones of administration, to be united after two years through general elections.

Furthermore, and most importantly, until the beginning of February (that is to say, until the moment at which we embarked upon a new military policy of bombing North Vietnam), it was the general opinion of the spokesmen of the Administration—as documented by hundreds of newspaper reports—that this was a civil war in South Vietnam, aided and abetted by the government in the north. It was only when our policy changed that facts had to be created to support our policy. We are here in the presence of a very interesting phenomenon concerning the relationship between intelligence and policy. Rationally, one would think that policy is to be based upon the facts provided by intelligence. But here, a fictitious world has been created in order to support a certain policy upon which the Government has embarked. It is, of course, true that the character of the war has changed in recent months . . . [as] the result of new steps taken by both sides. In the measure that we have extended the war into North Vietnam, North Vietnam has actively intervened in the war in South Vietnam. There is no doubt that, today, regular units of the North Vietnamese army are to be found in South Vietnam. But it is still a fact that the situation which has existed in South Vietnam for almost ten years is a result not of foreign aggression, in any sense in which this term can be used, but of an internal disintegration of which, of course, the Communists of the North have taken advantage.

I remember very vividly the long interview I had with President Diem, at the end of 1955, in which I told him that, if he continued in his oppressive policies, he would finally be left with the support of his family and a praetorian guard, while the people as a whole would be either indifferent or hostile to him, and that only the Communists could profit from that development. Mr. Diem was quite upset about this analysis, but if he had been less upset and more open to rational argument, he might still be alive and in power. So the roots of this disorder go far back into the internal history of South Vietnam, and it is a mere evasion of the actual facts to bomb, as it were, those roots out of existence by bombing imaginary bridges in the North. (I should say, in passing, that, if we are to believe the official reports about the bombing of bridges in North Vietnam, . . . North Vietnam must [have] more bridges than any [other country] in the world. But this is only one small aspect of the illusion which we have created in order to support a policy which cannot be supported by facts. . . .)

Now let me turn to the second main point on which the Administration bases its policy: the commitment, legal and moral, to the government of South Vietnam. There are three points that could be made about this argument, in ascending order of importance. First, the government of South Vietnam was installed by us. One of the members of the panel of this afternoon actually discovered President Diem in a monastery in the United States and presented him to the CIA. The CIA looked him over and thought he was a likely candidate. Then we put him into power and promised him our support. Thus, in actuality, we made an agreement with ourselves to support him. It is absurd to maintain that this kind of commitment to an agent we put into power ourselves, in order to take care of our interests in Southeast Asia, is the equivalent of an agreement with a sovereign government that has entered freely into a commitment. For, obviously, President Diem could never have become President of South Vietnam without the support of the United States. Without it, Diem's Government could not have survived for any length of time. [*The panel member referred to by Professor Morgenthau was Wesley R. Fishel, Professor of Political Science at*

Michigan State University and former head of that university's Advisory Group in Vietnam. See Robert Scheer, How the United States Got Involved in Vietnam (Report to the Center for the Study of Democratic Institutions), Santa Barbara, 1965.]

Second, the point has been made frequently that the South Vietnamese have asked us to come to their aid, that we have responded, and that it would be dishonorable of us if we now let them down. This is, again, a fiction which is pleasing to our political folklore but contradicted by the facts. For there is vast evidence to show how unpopular this war is among the people of South Vietnam, to what extent they regard this war as our war into which they have been dragged, . . . and that their real aim is to be done with that war, to get us out of South Vietnam, and to alleviate their terrible situation. . . .

The London *Economist,* certainly an impeccable source, and a pro-American one to boot, reported from Saigon, a few weeks ago, that two slogans are now heard quite often in Saigon and elsewhere: "Yank, go fight your war somewhere else" and, in army circles, "He who doesn't fight has no need to run away." In the *Washington Post* of May 2, we have a report about an article which appeared in the French newspaper *Le Figaro* (again a conservative paper of impeccable pro-American tendencies), written by a correspondent who had just come back from South Vietnam. He reports a conversation he had with an American captain attached to Vietnamese forces. "Every time," this captain told him, "I sent teams more than four or five miles away, we never heard from them again. I don't know what becomes of them. Every night, four men are placed there in the fort to handle two automatic weapons. The arms are chained to the wall, and the only door leading into the blockhouse is bolted on the outside. That way they can't turn their arms against us, and they have the choice of fighting or of letting themselves be killed like rats."

This is the noble war we are fighting, this is the commitment we are honoring. It is obvious . . . that this is, to a much greater extent, our war than it is the war of the South Vietnamese. I must give the Secretary of Defense credit for his frankness when he stated that we are in South Vietnam in order to contain Communism. This is, of course, the true reason, not the freedom of South Vietnam or the commitment we have entered into with South Vietnam. It is part and parcel of the policy of peripheral military containment of Chinese Communism, which we still—in spite of the President's speech of three days ago—in practice identify with

Asian Communism everywhere. This is the justification for the war in South Vietnam.

Now let me say a word on a higher level of principle about the problem of the commitment of one nation to another. We have a case in early American history which most beautifully illuminates the problem nations face when they embrace commitments to aid other nations. The President has said, time and again, that America honors its commitments and therefore we must honor this commitment to South Vietnam. In 1793, we had a commitment—as solemn, as clear as any commitment can be—to come to the aid of France if France were attacked. It was as simple a treaty of alliance as one could imagine, and indeed in contrast to the present situation, . . . the people at large would very much have liked to enter war on the side of France against the First Coalition of the European monarchies. There are reports to the effect that mobs roamed Philadelphia, . . . clamoring for the head of Washington, who refused to go to war. John Marshall, in his biography of George Washington, declared that if a motion of impeachment against the first President had not been tabled in Congress, it would have passed with an overwhelming majority. Washington refused to honor a clear and simple legal commitment [to go to war on the side of France] on the advice of Alexander Hamilton. Hamilton, in one of the Pacificus letters, . . . made, once and for all, the point that must govern sound policy on such commitments:

> There would be no proportion between the mischiefs and perils to which the United States would expose themselves, by embarking in the war, and the benefit which the nature of their stipulation aims at securing to France or that which it would be in their power actually to render her by becoming a party. This disproportion would be a valid reason for not executing the guaranty. All contracts are to receive a reasonable construction. Self-preservation is the first duty of a nation; and though in the performance of stipulations pertaining to war, good faith requires that its ordinary hazards should be fairly met, because they are directly contemplated by such stipulations, yet it does not require that extraordinary and extreme hazards should be run; especially where the object to be gained or secured is only a partial or particular interest of the ally, for whom they are to be encountered.

And Hamilton continues, quoting from Vattel, the great eighteenth-century authority on international law:

> We may learn from Vattel, one of the best writers on the laws of nations, that "if a state which has promised succors, finds itself un-

able to furnish them, its very inability is its exemption; and if
furnishing the succors would expose it to an evident danger, this also
is a lawful dispensation. The case would render the treaty pernicious
to the state, and therefore, not obligatory. But this applies to an
imminent danger threatening the safety of the state: the case of
such danger is tacitly and necessarily reserved in every treaty!"

And then Hamilton concludes:

If too, as no sensible and candid man will deny, the extent of the
present combination against France is in a degree to be ascribed to
imprudences on her part, the exemption to the United States is still
more manifest and complete. No country is bound to partake in
hazards of the most critical kind, which may have been produced or
promoted by the indiscretion and intemperance of another. This is
an obvious dictate of reason, with which the common sense and
common practice of mankind coincide.

This is the wisdom upon which this Republic was founded, and
the contrary opinions we hear today are the mere reflections of a
folklore that is pleasing to our sensibilities but that has no relation
to the actual problem or the actual issues with which nations are
confronted in their relations with each other. Let me say, in conclusion, that one could, of course, continue this critical discussion
about our policy, this confrontation of the assumptions of our policy with the actual facts, almost indefinitely in order to show how
we have embarked on a policy and how, after the fact, we set out
to create an imaginary world to fit the policy. But unfortunately—
or perhaps not so unfortunately—facts have their own logic, their
own dynamics, and they are not disregarded without terrible re-
venge; and in policy, domestic and international, one sees time and
again how such illusions lead to catastrophe if they are consistently
embarked upon. So it is, I think, a special virtue and a special
function of this meeting that it reminds all of us, and especially
those who govern us and would rather not be reminded, that our
policy is contradicted by the facts. If they do not have the wisdom
and the courage to adapt their policies to the facts, the facts will
overtake them and take vengeance on them for having been disregarded.

The Three Alternatives in Vietnam

—ARTHUR M. SCHLESINGER, JR.

Mr. Schlesinger, former Professor of American History at Harvard University and Special Assistant to President Kennedy, is Albert Schweitzer Professor of Humanities at the City University of New York. This transcript of the third speech of the morning is abridged.

I note that I am described in the program as speaking on the Government position on Vietnam. I will indeed speak on the Government position in Vietnam, but I would like to make it clear that I am speaking for myself. The Government is not responsible for anything I say, and I am not responsible for anything that representatives of the Government may say. Indeed, I come here with a certain feeling of detachment. I am surrounded on this platform by academicians on the one hand, and bureaucrats on the other. As an ex-academician and as an ex-bureaucrat, I am left somewhat in the situation of a displaced person.

Let me say first that, as one who has not taught in a university since the now almost forgotten days of the "silent generation" of undergraduates of the 1950's, I am impressed by this occasion. It is moving to see the deep national concern which has produced this meeting in Washington and so many other comparable meetings through the country this spring. Clearly no group has a greater right to express itself on questions of war and peace than those who, if war should come, must expect to bear the brunt of the fighting. . . .

As a displaced person, I feel free to deplore a certain self-righteousness which has crept into all sides of this debate. When one hears, for example, phrases about the "gullibility of educated men," and reflects on the White Paper on Vietnam, one is tempted to think about the gullibility of Secretaries of State. I doubt whether these are useful terms in which to approach a serious discussion. Equally, when my friends in the academic community act as if an intricate situation could easily yield to bright slogans and easy generalizations, one begins to feel that self-righteousness, like the rain, falls on the pure and the impure alike. As one who in the last

few years has had, from time to time, to undergo the painful task
of thinking about our problems in Vietnam, let me report my conclusion that there is plenty of room for honest perplexity and candid disagreement, and that there is no reason to suppose that one's
own side has a monopoly of wisdom or rectitude and that the other
side is animated by evil and wicked motives. I fear that emotion
has widened the scale of the debate and transformed marginal differences too much into absolutes. Forgive these procedural reflections, and let me now proceed to the subject of Vietnam.

Obviously, we are involved in a most grave and anguished situation. As a historian, I have often reflected on whether we had any
business getting into this situation at all—whether there were, in
1954, specific and vital U.S. national interests in Vietnam which
justified a U.S. commitment to protect the independence of South
Vietnam. . . .

I am willing to accept it as conceivable that our 1954 decision to
make a commitment to Vietnam was an expression of the illusion
of American omnipotence, rather than the result of hardheaded
and rational analysis of our specific national interests. But, I would
immediately add, this is a problem relevant to historians and not
to policy-makers. For, whether or not we had vital interests in
Vietnam in 1954, once we made that commitment we created a
vital interest. Whether or not we should have drawn the line where
we did, once we drew it and involved ourselves in sustaining it we
were stuck with it. This is the situation we face today. . . .

There are obviously three alternative courses in Vietnam.

The first is withdrawal. Some have argued for this course on
the grounds of realism. We are told that we must accept the inevitability of Communist domination, of Chinese domination of
Asia—at least of South Asia. We are told that it is irrational to
suppose that anything can block the spread of Chinese power. This
seems to me an unpersuasive argument. We have heard a good
deal before about supposed geopolitical imperatives. Back in 1940,
people used to tell me that there was absolutely no point in trying
to resist the inevitable German domination of Europe. In 1948,
friends of mine who were supporting Henry Wallace made the
same argument, except that, instead of the inevitability of German
domination of Europe, they talked about the inevitability of Russian domination of Europe. In retrospect, the notion that some
mystical necessity required either Germany or Russia to dominate
Europe looks very odd and silly today. I doubt whether there is any
greater inevitability about Chinese domination of Asia. Asia is a
very large continent. It has a diversity of cultures, traditions, states,

and so on. Nations like their independence in Asia just as much as they do in other parts of the world. To assume that some mystic inevitability has decreed that they are all to be swallowed up in the Chinese empire is not convincing. . . .

Instead of indulging in speculation about Chinese hegemony . . . let us consider concretely what the effect of precipitate American withdrawal from South Vietnam would be. Withdrawal under duress would, in the first place, gravely weaken the democratic position in Asia. It would be taken as evidence that the United States had lost both the interest and the capacity to meet its commitments. No Asian nation with any interest in survival could do anything, after American withdrawal from Vietnam, but go to Peking and make the best possible bargain for itself. Withdrawal could lead to the rise of anti-American, or at least neutralist, governments not only in Southeast Asia but in the Philippines and possibly Japan.

Is this the domino thesis? Well, it is not necessary to agree with Joe Alsop that the dominos have to fall all the way back to Malibu beach to recognize that our expulsion from South Vietnam will have its side effects. Take Laos, for example, where Prince Souvanna Phouma is trying to preserve his country as a genuinely neutralist state. Souvanna Phouma is strongly in favor of the present American policy in Vietnam, even the bombing. He knows that if the Americans are driven out of Vietnam, his hopes for a neutral Laos are doomed, and the Communists will take over. The socialist prime minister of Singapore, Lee Kuan Yew, recently told James Mossman of the *New Statesman:* "If Vietnam goes, the rest goes, including Malaysia." . . . It is idle to suppose that expulsion from Vietnam would be no worse than a bad cold. We may some day be forced out, but I see absolutely no advantage in anticipating what . . . would be a clear and profound disaster—less perhaps for the United States than for the presently independent states of South Asia.

A second reason why withdrawal should be rejected is surely that it would mean betrayal of those in South Vietnam who have been encouraged by our support to oppose the Communists. I hear moral arguments invoked on all sides of the Vietnam debate; and I tend not to believe it useful to think of foreign affairs in moralistic terms. But it does seem to me that, in this case, there is a moral argument well-founded in human reality. To [suggest abandoning] these people to slaughter, as if this would be an act of moral superiority, seems to be precisely equivalent to [the suggestion of] those abolitionists before the Civil War who wanted the slave states to leave the Union on the grounds that this would remove the weight of slavery from their own conscience, even though it might not improve the [condition] of the slave.

This willingness to yield the non-Communist people of South Vietnam to the Vietcong may perhaps stem in part from a misunderstanding about the Vietcong. Some may regard the Vietcong as a great idealistic movement. I doubt this. I do not believe that they are the Indochinese wing of the Populist Party. The Vietcong, so far as I can see, are a collection of very tough terrorists whose gains have come, in the main, not from the hope they have inspired but from the fear they have created.

Some people in this audience today perhaps feel that, if they were in South Vietnam, their sympathy would be with the Vietcong. I doubt this very much. The students and intellectuals in South Vietnam are not with the Vietcong. They are not with the government either. They have tended to be with the Buddhists, and it is around the Buddhists that the mainstream of Vietnamese idealism appears to have developed. The Buddhists have stood *not* for a Communist Vietnam—*not* for a Vietcong triumph—but for a neutral Vietnam; and it is notable that, in recent months, the Buddhists have been tending more and more to support the government. There have been no Buddhist demonstrations against the war or the United States since February. There has been an intimation that the Buddhists are coming to feel the best road to their objective of a neutralist Vietnam lies through support of the government rather than through the victory of the Vietcong. For this reason, too, it seems to me that we would be betraying people like ourselves in South Vietnam by a policy of withdrawal—a policy which would expose the intellectuals, professors, and students to the demonstrated lack of charity of the Vietcong.

A third reason why I oppose a policy of withdrawal is the impact such withdrawal would have on the fight within the Communist world between the Soviet Union and Communist China. The inescapable fact is that withdrawal under duress would be a triumphant vindication of the Chinese thesis as against the Soviet thesis in world affairs. If we were to withdraw now, it would prove to the Communist world that the Chinese are right in saying that militance pays. It would confirm the Chinese criticism of the Soviet attempt at coexistence. . . .

Moreover, such withdrawal would open up South Asia to Chinese expansion. I don't see how it is possible to suppose that the Soviet Union, with its interest in restraining Chinese expansion and in demonstrating the possibility of limited coexistence, would really prefer and desire a precipitate American withdrawal from South Vietnam. Withdrawal, in short, would reinforce the Chinese hard line. It would discredit and undermine the Soviet soft line. It would give the Chinese tremendous support in their struggle for leadership in the world Communist movement. . . .

The second possible policy is enlargement of the war. I hope I need spend no time here explaining why this seems to me the tragically mistaken course. I will save that lecture for the Air War College. Air power alone cannot win this war. Widening the war with the idea of somehow "winning" it would mean the extensive commitment of American ground forces—perhaps, as Hanson Baldwin has said, 1 million troops. It would require our forces to fight in terrain much more difficult than Korea, with much more vulnerable lines of communication and supply. It would very possibly provoke the entry of Communist China, with its inexhaustible reserves of ground forces. It would force the Soviet Union to declare itself within the Communist empire and give major assistance to Hanoi. It might even temporarily revive relations between Moscow and Peking. And behind all this would be the possibility that, as the warfare inevitably elevated in intensity, one side or the other might be tempted to nuclear war. For all these reasons, it seems to me the course of enlargement must be rejected.

This leaves the third course, and that is the policy of negotiation. This is the policy of the Administration. It is the policy I would defend today. . . .

I must frankly add that I do not agree with all the methods the Administration has taken to resolve the problem [of inducing Hanoi to negotiate]. It has thus far tended to see it primarily as a military problem. While this is better than not seeing it as a problem at all, it is not, in my judgment, the best way to solve it; nor do I think that air power is the appropriate kind of military force to apply. The reason why I am skeptical . . . is the experience of World War II, as exhaustively studied by the U.S. Strategic Bombing Survey. Air power, these studies show, generally has the effect of stiffening rather than weakening the will to resist. Moreover, guerrilla warfare does not offer a very productive target to air strikes. Finally, we risk Chinese reaction as our planes strike nearer the Chinese frontiers.

Air power, in short, seems to me an unseemly demonstration of the application of American force; nor do I think that Hanoi can be forced into negotiations by this kind of pressure. My view is that we should lay much less stress on the bombing and confine it . . . to very clear cases of interdiction of supplies moving into South

Vietnam. Instead, we should put much greater stress on a limited increase in our ground-force commitment in South Vietnam. . . .

If our object is to persuade North Vietnam that we are not going to withdraw, that object will be more effectively attained by ground-force commitments than by air strikes. Moreover, ground forces in South Vietnam offer less provocation to other countries and less risk of enlarging the war. Obviously, Chinese frontiers would not be threatened by ground forces in South Vietnam as they might be by air strikes in North Vietnam. And, most important, this fights the war where it must be fought—in South Vietnam. This last is especially significant, because there is mounting evidence that there will be no negotiations in South Vietnam until the Vietcong mount one major offensive, taking advantage of the monsoon season. If this is so, if the Vietcong will not negotiate until they can see if they can pull off their own Dien Bien Phu, it is important to those who believe in negotiations that this attempt be repulsed—and it is not going to be repulsed by air strikes.

Thus, it seems to me, a limited increase in the American ground-force commitment and a decreased emphasis on air power are indispensible to negotiations. Indeed, if we took the Marines now in the Dominican Republic and sent them to South Vietnam, we would be a good deal better off in both countries.

This, however, is only the military side of the problem, and . . . the problem is more than military. This point was well stated by Senator Robert Kennedy in [a recent] speech. He said:

> I believe, that our efforts for peace should continue with the same intensity as our efforts in the military field. I believe that we have erred for some time in regarding Vietnam as purely a military problem when, in its essential aspects, it is also a political and diplomatic problem. I would wish, for example, that the request for appropriations today had made provisions for programs to better the lives of the people of South Vietnam, so that success would depend not only on protecting the people from aggression but on giving them the hope of a better life.

For this reason, one welcomes President Johnson's speech of last Thursday, which showed, I think, a sensitive recognition of the problems as defined by Robert Kennedy.

I have no guarantee that a limited increase in the ground-force commitment, accompanied by suspension of the bombing, would induce any willingness to negotiate in Hanoi. And, if negotiations should come, obviously we will have to deal with more than Hanoi. This conflict began as a civil war, and Hanoi's resignation from it would only make it a civil war again. At some point we will have to confront the existence of the Vietcong and deal with them.

The road ahead is not clear. But, in my judgment, it is clearly better to try and move down this road than to assume the very sure and very terrible consequences of either enlargement or withdrawal. . . .

I think, too, that part of the problem of those who believe in negotiation and still condemn the Administration may simply stem from the ironies of timing. Attitudes were formed and demonstrations launched before President Johnson disclosed his negotiating purpose in the Johns Hopkins speech. The protest, once started, appears to have acquired a life and momentum of its own, regardless of the unfolding of Administration policy in the meantime. It may well be that the protest of the academic community had a role in producing these changes, though perhaps its effect was more on timing than on substance. But, whatever the issue before the Hopkins speech, I think no one can question today the fact that the Administration has negotiation at the forefront of its policy in Vietnam. This, therefore, calls on all who desire negotiation to view what the Administration is trying to do with sympathy and to offer their own notion as to how we can bring to the conference table adversaries who think they are about to win the war.

My own conclusion is that we must persevere in developing the combination of military, political, economic, and diplomatic action most likely to bring us closer to a negotiated settlement. This may not be very satisfactory. It doesn't promise a perfect solution. But life is not very satisfactory. [Applause.] I welcome this existentialist endorsement.

You must now consider this horribly complicated question through the day and the night. It may well be that what this country needs today more than anything else is a good night's sleep. But, as you pursue the discussion, let me say once again how important it is to remember that there are reasonable and decent men on all sides of this debate. The academic community has always been devoted to standards of rational discourse. Let not those on one side assume that their opponents are warmongers, or those on the other side that their opponents are cowards. Let us sustain the level of debate, assuming that there is an equality in purpose and virtue on both sides. Let us confine the debate to the real issues. I think the differences are narrower than the rhetoric on both sides suggests. Let us hope that, out of this session, there will emerge not only wiser policy but a freshened understanding and a deepened purpose.

The Syndrome of Oscillation

— STANLEY HOFFMANN

Professor Hoffmann teaches in the Government Department at Harvard University and is the author of The State of War. *The following statement, as printed in* The New Republic *(May 29, 1965), was excerpted from remarks he made during an evening panel on "The Making of American Foreign Policy," in which academic critics debated Administration supporters. Among the latter was W. W. Rostow, formerly Professor of Economic History at the Massachusetts Institute of Technology and, at the time of the debate, State Department Counselor and Chairman of the Policy Planning Council. A summary of Professor Rostow's panel remarks can be found in the same issue of* The New Republic.

The United States oscillates from periods in which it thinks that its task is to preserve its purity from the outside world to periods in which it thinks it has to purify the outside world altogether; from undercommitment to overcommitment. One might call it the Wilsonian syndrome. And another form of this dualism is a certain tendency to have a clear break between the realm of force, which very few of us would reject altogether, and the realm of friendship. We have a certain tendency, when faced with difficult problems, to jump on force as the cure. And on the other hand, we have a tendency to believe that our friends' assertions of total solidarity—for instance, talk about the Atlantic partnership—are really a solution for problems.

When we are faced with a difficult problem, our tendency is to cover the engineering operation, as if all that were involved were a choice of means rather than a definition of ends. We cover these operations with a reference to principles which are extremely noble, extremely generous, and very often quite irrelevant. Have we asked ourselves whether these principles we have brought with us from the 1930's are really applicable to the situation in Southeast Asia; or are they misplaced historical analogies? Is Vietnam the same thing as Korea? As what President Truman faced in 1947–48? As Munich? To have only the principles and only the engineering operations leaves us in trouble whenever we have to define a middle range of policy between the crisis of the moment and the ideal world of a very distant future. . . . The U.S. tends to believe it is entrusted with a universal mission. It asks our allies to share its burdens. It does not really ask its allies to share in the definition of the burdens.

Our approach to time is too much an engineer's approach. We are frantic each time a Russian appears in Guinea or a Chinese in Brazzaville. We see the future as the building of a house; we do not have a sufficiently evolutionary concept of international relations.

Finally, are we willing to believe that in this stage of international affairs force can be weeded out of politics? Are we really so convinced that revolutions are nothing but things exported aggressively from Moscow or Peking, and that we are going to see in every revolution in which a few Communists—or even many Communists—appear, something which requires our intervention? Will we declare that we have to prevent not only classical war and nuclear war, but revolutions altogether?

5. DISCUSSION OF THE NATIONAL TEACH-IN

Dialogue or Monologue? (Part 2)

—ANATOL RAPOPORT

Dr. Rapoport helped organize the National Teach-In. The first part of his article appears in Chapter I.

Many of us felt that the evil which had befallen American political life stemmed from the choking off of meaningful dialogue on foreign policy. The academic community, we thought, could contribute to a political awakening by mobilizing the knowledge and skills concentrated in that sector of society.

Others among us, however, saw the situation in a different light. To these, the teach-in movement (by now it was definitely a movement) was part of a swelling protest. The first teach-in was a demonstration, not a debate. To be sure, the meeting had the format of academic discourse, and, needless to say, the whole gamut of opinion found expression in the night-long discussions. But there was no question about the *basis* of the discussion. The point of departure was our conviction that the present U.S. policy in Southeast Asia was dangerous, ineffective, illegal, and immoral. No Government spokesman and no apologist for the Administration's policy appeared on the "faculty" of the "Free University of Michigan." Whatever opposition was voiced was directed at us from the floor, not from among us. To the critics of this procedure we replied that the Administration had its own channels of communication and its own apparatus of influence. Our task was to establish a counterforce to the engineering of consent. Many of us who thought of the teach-in movement in this way had conceived of the National Teach-In as the same sort of demonstration.

Here, then, a definitive choice had to be made. If the function of the National Teach-In was to demonstrate to the nation (possibly to the world) that a large segment of the academic community was determined in its opposition to U.S. policy in Vietnam (and, by implication, to the whole present course of U.S. foreign policy), then there was no need to include supporters of the policy on this program. If, however, the purpose was to kindle a "meaningful dialogue," then it was imperative to include spokesmen of the Administration.

The issue was both an ideological and a practical one. All of us felt that our Government had failed us. For some, however, the failure was in the way foreign policy was conceived (the overwhelming emphasis on the power struggle and on the role of the military in it); for others the failure was in the way foreign policy was *conducted* (the set course, the closed doors, the contemptuous dismissal of criticism). Undoubtedly, many (perhaps most) were dismayed by both failures in equal degree, but the decision had to be made where to place the emphasis. The decision had to be made fast.

The issue was decided in favor of the dialogue. The overweighing consideration was the prospect of confronting Administration spokesmen. Thus, the spectacle of intellectuals talking to themselves (while the power-holding officials were setting the country on a collision course) would presumably be avoided. The National Teach-In was to be a confrontation. A part of the enlightened public would have to be reckoned with, would demand information and a reasoned explanation of what was going on and why. Clearly, the crucial condition to be met, if this was indeed to be the nature of the affair, was the presence of a highly placed Government spokesman (not an academic supporter of the Administration's point of view) on the debate platform. Accordingly, a concerted effort was directed at getting such a spokesman to accept our invitation.

Mr. Bundy had declined the invitation from Washington University, accompanying his refusal with disparaging remarks about the professors who issued it [*See Part 3 of this chapter.*]

His reply to a similar invitation from Michigan, signed by nearly 400 faculty members, was more polite. To us he wrote, "I am sure you will agree that my job does not let me accept every invitation of this sort. I do want you to know, however, that I shall be glad to meet with a representative group of the signers of your letter if such a group wishes to come to Washington."

We construed this as a suggestion to initiate negotiations for a meeting in Washington, which we did. Mr. Bundy's first objection to our proposed format was based on the fact that we did not represent the whole spectrum of opinion in the academic community. In this he was undoubtedly right, although, to our way of thinking, this was irrelevant to what we thought the country needed—namely, a confrontation between the Administration and a responsible opposition. We felt that such an encounter was made necessary by the fact that a meaningful debate on foreign policy had been effectively prevented in Congress, where it should normally take place if the democratic process were not to become a dead letter. Whether we could make Mr. Bundy see this was beside the point. We were well aware that the final decision of whether Mr. Bundy, or any other spokesman for the Administration, would participate in the National Teach-In would be made unilaterally by the Administration in accordance with what *they* wanted the teach-in to represent. The only decision we faced was whether, on the strength of Mr. Bundy's refusal to face the opposition, we should go back to the protest format or attempt to work out a compromise.

Again the dialogue view prevailed. Negotiations proceeded to an agreement: The principal feature of the National Teach-In (the main bout, so to say) would be a debate between Mr. Bundy and an academic person to be selected; each side would be supported by a panel of four—all academics. In this way, the confrontation feature would still remain (contingent on Mr. Bundy's final acceptance), and the impression would be avoided—as Mr. Bundy insisted it should be—that the academic community was unanimously opposed to the present policy on Vietnam.

The next question arose in connection with Mr. Bundy's opponent. We proposed Hans J. Morgenthau, Professor of Political
Science at the University of Chicago. However, Professor Morgenthau was unacceptable to Mr. Bundy for, as he put it, personal
reasons. We next proposed Senator Wayne Morse (on the strength
of his distinguished academic background). He, too, was vetoed by
Mr. Bundy. Finally, Professor George M. Kahin, of Cornell, was
agreed upon. Mr. Bundy's final objection was to Professor Ernest
Nagel, whom we had selected as moderator. However, on this point
we stood firm. We simply could not bring ourselves to transmit
what we considered an insult to one of the most distinguished figures in American philosophy. Mr. Bundy yielded, and the rest of
the arrangements went smoothly. . . .

News about Mr. Bundy's acceptance was released, and headquarters of the Inter-University Committee for a Public Hearing
on Vietnam was set up in Ann Arbor. The nationwide character of
the meeting was ensured by a telephone network [tied in with
campus public address systems and radio stations, with 122 campuses participating] . . . The meeting was telecast live and complete by National Educational Television. The commercial networks carried half-hour and one-hour shows. The audience at the
morning session was about 3000; in the afternoon it swelled to
5000. About 1500 attended the final session from 11:00 P.M. to
12:30 A.M. Coverage in the principal newspapers was of the sort
accorded to national events of first magnitude. . . .

Our effort to bring the confrontation to the attention of the public was, therefore, a decisive success. But this only put the main
question into sharper focus: namely, what have we accomplished?

A primary goal of the National Teach-In, as it was finally conceived, was to convert the monologue of protest into a dialogue
of confrontation, specifically a dialogue between the Administration
and an enlightened opposition. This goal was attained only in the
evening seminars, in each of which an employee of the State Department participated. The goal was not attained at the main session, because the only Government spokesman scheduled to appear
at that session, Mr. Bundy, did not appear. . . . [*See "Statement
to the National Teach-In," Part 4 of this chapter.*]

Therefore, the first answer to the question "What have we accomplished?" can be given as follows. We did not succeed, this
first time, in effecting a genuine confrontation between the Administration and an opposition. We hope, however, that we made the
need for such confrontation apparent. To the extent that the na-

tion has become aware of this need, not only we of the opposition but also the American people as a whole have won.

The next question is a more difficult one. What do we hope to accomplish if and when we do effect a confrontation? Who will make the greater impact, the Administration on us, or we on the Administration? And, who will make the greater impact on public opinion?

As in every estimate of this sort, one must start by evaluating the strong and the weak points of both sides. With regard to intellectual prowess, the sides are probably equally matched. I will not venture to guess the number of scholars and experts of standing available to each side. These numbers are not important, because only two or three are needed to represent each side. With regard to access to information, it is hard to say which side has the advantage. The Administration probably has more sources of information available, but the academics probably have more time to digest it. The academics also have rather long memories and are in a position to confront the Administration with uncomfortable reminders. As to the advantage of having access to secret information, this is greatly reduced by the questionable reliability of such information. Secrecy inhibits independent checks. Some of the most crushing embarrassments suffered by our Government in recent episodes in Latin America have stemmed from precipitous actions taken on the basis of unreliable secret information. Moreover, the value of secret information as debate ammunition is highly questionable. The only way this information can be used in a debate is by allusion. However, frequent resorts to such allusion in support of implausible arguments makes the arguments only more suspect.

In one very important respect, the opponents are not evenly matched, the advantage being heavily on the side of the Administration. A position in an intellectually responsible debate derives its strength from the soundness of the assumptions on which it rests and from the quality of the reasoning which leads from the assumptions to the conclusions. However, the "soundness of assumptions" is not altogether an objective property of the assumptions. Underlying explicit assumptions may be other implicit ones of which we may be unaware, because they may reflect long-established habits of thinking. It is a formidably difficult task to pry people's thinking away from such internalized "self-evident truths."

The Administration enjoys the advantage of building its case on just such assumptions, which have drenched the very fabric of our public opinion during the twenty years of all-pervasive cold war propaganda. Moreover, the supporters of the Administration's position for the most part have acquired the same thinking habits and so enjoy a unanimity which cannot possibly be established among the critics of the accepted policy. To someone who has internalized the assumptions inherent in the official view (that is, to most Americans), the Administration's position appears simpler and, therefore, stronger than the critics'. When Secretary Rusk insisted that the situation in Southeast Asia was really "very simple," he was attempting to capitalize on just this advantage.

The assumptions from which the Administration proceeds are the following.

1. Communism—unless, perhaps, it is confined to the borders of the U.S.S.R. and her Eastern European satellites—is a menace to the security of the United States.

2. There is no limit, in terms of lives, treasure, or respect for international obligations, on the effort the United States must exert to prevent the expansion of Communism.

3. The establishment of any new regime anywhere in the world controlled by, or likely to become controlled by, Communists adds to the strength of the Communist bloc and therefore jeopardizes the security of the United States.

4. The United States is the sole judge of what constitutes the recruitment of a country into the Communist bloc.

Once these assumptions are granted, the Administration's case can be made to appear unassailable. As we have said, there is no lack of informed and intellectually agile defenders of the present policy. They enjoy the advantage of starting from assumptions that find ready popular acceptance by virtue both of making perplexing and disturbing events appear simple and of offering a clear target for hatred.

In short, the opposition cannot hope to demolish the Administration's case by impugning its logic. The logic can be made to appear plausible enough by the use of eloquence and by appeals to "realism." Therefore, the only promising strategy for the opposition is an attack upon the assumptions. As we have said, this constitutes a handicap for the opposition with respect to its ability to effect a change in public opinion, because the number of people who question the Administration's assumptions, although it is increasing, is still small.

There is also another difficulty involved in attacking the Administration's assumptions, and this is in the choice of target. In forensic strategy, it is not advantageous to attack all the assumptions at once. Also, the opposition may well include many who are sharply critical of specific manifestations of the Administration's policy—for example, the escalation of the Vietnam war or the occupation of the Dominican Republic—but who, nevertheless, accept the first assumption [above].

In choosing a target among the assumptions, one must choose between the vulnerability of the assumption and the payoff to be derived by attacking it. For example, the fourth assumption is probably the most vulnerable. But to concentrate fire upon it would mean to raise questions about who is and who is not a Communist, about how many Communists it takes to effect a "Communist take-over" or to threaten the likelihood of one, and so forth. Although in many instances the Administration's allegations about impending Communist take-overs can be easily refuted, preoccupation with these questions deflects from the central issues.

A challenge of the third assumption may lead into mazes of economic and strategic analysis. For example, a debate might ensue on the question of whether the inclusion of some African countries in the Chinese sphere of influence would actually strengthen the Communist bloc or, on the contrary, drain its resources. Indeed, a debate of this sort could be conducted on an extremely high level of technical competence. I suspect that this is just the kind of debate the Administration would like to see, if debate is inevitable; for such a debate would be instrumental in deflecting the attention of people away from central issues to peripheral ones.

An attack on the second assumption comes closer to the heart of the problem. This was essentially the course taken by Hans J. Morgenthau, one of our speakers in the morning session and a member of the afternoon panel at the National Teach-In.

Professor Morgenthau argued (as I understand him) that concern for national interest requires also a realistic appraisal of political and military realities. He pointed out that an attempt to resist China's political and cultural expansion by *military* means would lead to a war with China and that such a war cannot be construed as serving America's national interests in any way, regardless of its final outcome, if any. Professor Morgenthau suggested that failure to see this could stem only from self-hypnosis, imposed on our decision-makers by the delusion of omnipotence and by indulgence in self-righteousness.

Professor Morgenthau's arguments do get at the central issue. Nevertheless, it is important to note that these arguments do not challenge the classical view of international relations, the view that the "realities" of such relations are (and, by implication, must for a long time remain) a struggle for power among sovereign states.

"Rationality" in this struggle is the rationality of strategic calculation. One does not undertake impossible tasks and one does not jeopardize one's position in the power struggle by embarking upon hazardous adventures. However, national interest itself is defined, in this view, in terms of concepts handed down from Clausewitz and Bismarck, and so a challenge to these concepts is not brought into play [*in arguments such as Professor Morgenthau's*].

There remains the first assumption, the keystone of the Cold War. An attack on this assumption is tantamount to an attack on all of them. It is here that the dialogue-monologue dilemma becomes central. For, in order to attack the "menace of Communism" dogma, one must invoke concepts foreign to what is widely accepted as "intellectually responsible dialogue." One must abandon the conventional language of political science, economics, and military strategy, because one must assail the *relevance* of these frameworks of thought to some fundamental realities of life, as these realities are felt by ordinary people who are not political scientists, economists, or diplo-military strategists. . . .

If issues of humanity and morality are to be raised in a confrontation with the Administration (which is what an attack on the first assumption must involve), the opposition's task will prove more difficult. For the issue is not the lack of humanity in the decision-makers as people, but the irrelevance of their humanity to the conduct of diplo-military policy. The supreme tragedy of our time is the circumstance that it is no longer necessary to be evil in order to do evil. This is what military technology has brought about. A man has to be indeed evil, or at least blinded by rage, to kill a human being with a knife. It takes less savagery to shoot a human being with a rifle; still less to blast invisible targets with artillery. But *anyone* can sit in a comfortable control room and move levers in response to flashing lights. Any one can check off "eliminated" cities on a score board.

Nor is the automation of genocide the only symptom of *de facto* dehumanization, which many of the opposition view as an inevitable by-product of the Cold War conducted in the nuclear age. Old fashioned savagery has been revived in the gloating accounts in the right-wing press (see, for example, *Time*, April 23, 1965) of the bloodthirstiness of the American fighting man. Also, whatever notions have lingered concerning America's leadership in strengthening the rule of law rather than of force in international relations have been submerged under the avalanche of American unilateralism. Toughness, self-righteousness, and tribal loyalty are so easily linked in the American mass mind that it has been easy to strangle the new ideas of international cooperation, which made their short-lived appearance in the Roosevelt era.

This is not to say that these matters cannot eventually be brought out in a continued dialogue. But it is a long, long way from the question of what to do about Vietnam to a really fundamental re-examination of America's role in world affairs, including a long, thoughtful look at what the role of the world's policeman has done to the quality of life in the United States. To do this, it is necessary to sweep away the whole demonology with which the assumptions underlying U.S. foreign policy have been pervaded; this, in turn, demands an examination of matters not ordinarily included on the agenda of intellectually responsible debate (as implicitly defined by the Administration and, I am afraid, by a large part of the academic community). In order to bring these matters into the dialogue, it is necessary to convince the Administration that the connections between national interest (as the Administration views it) and the interests of the American people (let alone the human race) are not self-evident. It is necessary to convince the Administration that not only political scientists and strategists but also psychologists, philosophers, and men of letters have something important to contribute to the analysis of current chronic and acute crises. We are still very far away from this sort of confrontation. For example, there was not a single psychologist, philosopher, or theologian among the nine participants in the main session at the National Teach-In.

Therefore, it appears that, so far, matters related to the quality of life and the nature of the human condition are themes of a monologue, not a dialogue, because they are phrased in a language which the Administration does not understand, or refuses to understand, or declares to be unsuited for intellectually responsible dialogue. What the proponents of the monologue among us are saying is that questions relevant to human (not just political) realities must be raised. Since they cannot at this time be raised in a dialogue, the monologue must also continue. In fact, the monologue must be directed downward toward ordinary people rather than upward toward the decision-makers.

What have we accomplished? The nation listened. Judging by comments in the responsible press, a part of the nation even applauded. The most gratifying aspect of this applause was that it was by no means confined to an expression of self-congratulation ("It was a good, clean fight; let's do it again some day"). Indeed, we felt that our voices were joined with those already raised in the press expressing sharp misgivings . . . about the high-handed way in which the Administration has been brushing off cogent criticism. Dare we hope that we have effectively stepped in to discharge the responsibility so ignominiously abrogated by Congress, that is, to resist a *gleichschaltung* of the discussion of foreign policy? Dare we hope that a break-through finally has been made in the mass media, that television is about to become a vast nationwide forum, thus solving the problem of preserving a genuine democracy in a super-state?

After the Washington Teach-In

— MEG GREENFIELD

Meg Greenfield is Washington editor of The Reporter, *in which this article appeared, June 3, 1965.*

While Washington has experienced just about every other conceivable kind of protest in the past, it was clear to those in charge of the Government side that the new technique required new and rather elaborate responses. Accordingly, the Government's spokesmen were chosen with great care for their academic credentials. Many of them attended strategy sessions in the office of William Jorden, who among other duties runs a sort of State Department speakers' bureau. The bureau attempts to counter the charge of governmental unwillingness to discuss Vietnam by sending Government representatives to campuses around the country, where they are then denounced as "truth squads" and "propagandists." Between them, the State Department and the White House are said to have requested (and been granted) more than three hundred tickets out of the several thousand available for the [National Teach-In], and reporters did believe they discerned a pronounced and atypical enthusiasm for the Government's position in the first four rows of the cavernous hall. The department had also rented the hotel's Franklin Room for the day, in the privacy of which a number of edgy-looking persons stood about waiting to meet any research emergencies.

The arrangers for the other side—chiefly teachers from the University of Michigan—were spread through a suite of stencil-littered rooms elsewhere in the hotel. There, by midweek before the Saturday event, a reporter could wander pretty much at will and observe them making such snap decisions as whether or not to continue a crucial telephone conversation with a television representative at the risk of failing to meet the plane of the Sovietologist Isaac Deutscher, who was flying in from London for the occasion. Unlike the Government side, the teach-in leadership had taken its support where it could find it and, whether by reason of an excess of democracy or as a result of other pressures, it had done little or no coordinating or even previewing of its speeches. Thus, there was considerable surprise in the hall when Deutscher rose at the opening meeting and delivered a classical attack from the Left on Stalin for failure of revolutionary zeal. Press accounts of this remarkable episode tended to dwell upon Deutscher's physical appearance—his gestures, his beard, his resemblance to Lenin. And while such observations may have been superficial, it is nonetheless true that within minutes of embarking on his Trotskyite discourse, Deutscher had so utterly transformed the ballroom into some remoter hall in time and space and had worked such tricks upon the imagination that one expected him to be interrupted in midsentence by a bearded figure rushing onto the stage with an ax.

For all its more careful planning, the Government side is said to have undergone a few surprises of its own, among them the speech of Arthur Schlesinger, who in turn seemed somewhat taken aback by the crowd's reaction to him. In establishing his independence of the Administration, he dealt what many considered to be a superabundance of blows at Dean Rusk, the White Paper, the Dominican action, and the decision to become involved in Vietnam after the signing of the Geneva accords. Not that any of this seemed to make more palatable to the audience his arguments against a U.S. withdrawal from Vietnam or his declaration that the intellectuals of South Vietnam were not allied with the Vietcong and that withdrawal would mean "betraying people like ourselves" there. When Schlesinger had finished his remarks, members of the audience, bursting with impatience, lined up six deep at various microphones to present him with their many-parted questions of rebuttal. "When I hear questions like that, I begin to wonder whether Mac Bundy might not be right," he growled at one point to a full accompaniment of boos and hisses. "What kind of audience is this?" he murmured when he came down off the stage.

The audience, of course, was preponderantly academic, both in profession and in style. Everyone on both sides seemed to have a favorite historical analogy at the ready; excessively courteous titles were dispensed ("Mr. Ho Chi Minh"); the grim and sidewise joke, particularly as it was offered up by Morgenthau ("the noble war we are fighting," the "poor victim of aggression"), rarely failed to get a laugh. And, not surprisingly, people who had traveled hundreds and even thousands of miles to register a protest were overwhelmingly inclined to the view that (1) the Government was acting out of unexampled malignity and (2) it had caused us to be hated with renewed fervor around the world. . . .

Among the sponsors and supporters of the teach-in were veterans of the peace movement, which has primarily concerned itself with disarmament in the past decade and which has focused rather suddenly and late on the problem of Vietnam—A. J. Muste, Seymour Melman, Arthur Waskow, Kenneth Boulding, Herbert Kelman, Staughton Lynd. Some—such as the economist Paul Sweezy, who, in 1949, was arguing the perniciousness and futility of the Marshall Plan at the Waldorf-Astoria world peace conference—have been making their dire predictions at these conventions for almost twenty years. Others who were present in large numbers probably weren't twenty years old—students from high schools and universities in the Washington area. The meeting was notable for the dearth of big names from the world of arts and letters and even more notable for its heavy weighting of sociologists, physical scientists, and, above all, psychologists. There were, for instance, 181 professors of psychology as compared with seventy-eight political scientists in the roster of teach-in sponsors.

Despite the emphasis that the teach-in's leaders placed on facts and expertise, it remained essentially an apolitical—or even an anti-political—affair. Speaker after speaker professed not to understand why, if the Government was engaged in negotiations, it could not tell the people all about them. Much of the argument seemed to be based on a psychiatric explanation of the behavior of Communist countries coupled with a kind of mote-and-beam moral logic by which the United States was disqualified from making even the simplest political judgments. As one of the organizers of the teach-in, Professor Anatol Rapoport, put it in the course of an interview, "Is it up to us to say who is a Communist and who is not?" The world whose outline had emerged by the end of the day's discussions was one without people or politics but only the reality of "social and economic forces." One of the heartiest laughs the audience enjoyed, in fact, was at the expense of a pro-Administration panelist who went so far as to suggest that revolutions were fomented by revolutionaries. Revolutions, the counterargument ran, were fomented by "forces," which were regularly exacerbated by us. "Terror on our side," said Professor Stanley Millet of Briar-cliff, "accounts for all that has happened in Vietnam."

On the occasions when speakers for the Government side at-tempted to question the moral character of some of the protesters' positions, however, the protesters took shelter in a sudden hard-headed practicality. To the observation of Professor Wesley Fishel, of Michigan State University, that he could not see why they were so eager to hand sixteen million people over to Communism, [George M.] Kahin quickly replied that no one was "eager" to do that, but one had to be "realistic." Professor Mary Wright, of Yale, even found evidence of some sort of superior life adjustment on the part of the Government's critics, who were "more able" than the Government spokesmen "to accept the fact" of Communism's inroads. As the day wore into night and a kind of combined ex-haustion and stupefaction overtook the assemblage, the statements seemed to become ever more extreme and improbable, ending with a postsymposium outpouring from the floor. "We in the West are irrelevant," one man sternly announced. And a young woman as-sociated with the American Friends Service Committee related the impression that she and Seymour Melman had gained after a re-cent interview with Secretary of Defense McNamara. There was "no question in our minds," she said, "that the President is advised by men of unparalleled arrogance, stupidity, and incompetence." There was applause.

In an appeal for public support, the organizers of the National Teach-In were at pains to point out that sponsorship of their effort implied "only a deep concern with the present situation in South-east Asia and a conviction that questions related to peace and war should be open to responsible debate." The description could prob-ably fit the position of any number of Government supporters and it surely was broad enough to include almost all the participants in the teach-in—from those at one end who seemed genuinely curious and troubled to those at the other who were raising money for medical supplies for the victims of "U.S. aggression." One of the built-in problems of the new movement, however, seems to be its indiscriminate generosity in granting critics of every persuasion of the Government's activities in Vietnam a home within its ample tent. The dangers of the practice—diffusiveness, pointlessness, and the final lack of any coherent and identifiable argument—all seemed to be realized at the end of fifteen hours at the Sheraton Park. Nor did the combination of protest and analysis develop as a particularly happy one. The sleepless, marathon aspects of the meeting only served to blur any hoped-for sharpness of argument; selectivity and purpose were sacrificed to a public display of endurance. To whom were the participants addressing their arguments? The public? The Administration? Each other? Was the teach-in a protest or was it, as announced, a chance for a great and informative debate? The question is nowhere resolved in the literature of the movement, and the participants spent a good amount of their time extolling the event as a major contribution to the process of debate in a free society. Still, it appeared unlikely that many of the teachers-in had come to Washington with a view to being taught anything at all. When I asked Dr. Rapoport, on the eve of the meeting, whether he entertained the possibility of changing— even ever so slightly—any of his opinions as a result of the pending exchange, he replied: "I do not feel the Government has any case whatsoever."

Within the huge audience, and even among the teach-in leadership, there was a fairly wide range of attitudes toward the function —particularly the future function—of the teach-in. And such differences of opinion and of degree of militancy as existed in the group seemed to be reflected in their different responses to the sudden cancellation of Bundy's appearance. Shortly after 10:00 on Saturday morning, Richard Mann and Professor Ernest Nagel, of Columbia, had been called out of a meeting in the hotel and told that Jorden would take them to the White House, where Bromley Smith, of Bundy's office, wished to see them. Word of the cancellation started to spread around the hotel shortly after noon; and it soon was evident that there was anything but unanimity on the part of the leadership on what it meant and how to deal with it. Mann, who accepted the legitimacy of the explanation, attempted to soften the attacks Bundy's absence quite naturally provoked. A professor from Hofstra explained it all as evidence that Bundy had felt "personally threatened" by the criticism of his former colleagues. Arthur Waskow, in an impromptu press conference, averred that he had been told by a State Department official that Bundy's action was intended as an insult. "I suggest that individual press conferences take place somewhere else," another teach-in leader remarked when he came upon Waskow and the reporters outside the press lounge. Waskow finally drafted the telegram of challenge to Bundy that the group dispatched the next day, and it was somewhat milder in tone than a "minority report" version that was voted down in a sponsors' meeting that Sunday morning.

What by then had come to be known as "the question of Bundy" consumed almost as much time as the group's efforts to arrive at a conclusion on how to organize itself for political action in the future. But a good deal of time and argument was devoted to the latter problem. There were some who wanted to work through existing peace and political organizations. Others wanted to institutionalize the loose teach-in organization that had been set up. There were motions and motions to reconsider motions to set up a variety of guiding boards and committees. There were short tempers also. "I have never seen a more self-destructive act in my life," said Barry Commoner, a Washington University botanist, when a Michigan woman moved to reconsider some motion or other. How could Commoner say that, another man rose to ask, at a meeting on *Vietnam* policy of all places?

Little was settled as to future plans before the group dispersed and went back to their campuses. But it was clear that they had some decisions to make on how to bring their influence to bear on Washington and that their problem was not unlike some of Washington's own—particularly the one the group had theoretically assembled to consider. "The Administration won't talk to us," as one professor solemnly warned his colleagues, "unless we have some strength."

Pseudo-Debate in The Teach-In:
Criticism Contained

— WILLIAM APPLEMAN WILLIAMS

Professor Williams' address at the University of Wisconsin Teach-In appears in Chapter II. This article is from The York Gazette and Daily (York, Pennsylvania), *June 19, 1965.*

The recent National Teach-In held in Washington revealed as much about domestic affairs as about policy in Vietnam.

White House proxy McGeorge Bundy missed class because he was on an unsuccessful field trip to correct ancient mistakes in foreign policy. But the important thing is that a significant number of Americans were less disturbed by his absence than many of the professors.

That portion of the public followed the proceedings with an attention and involvement that revealed their deep uneasiness about present policy. Many of them had never before heard a serious discussion of foreign policy.

As for the columnists, many of them seemed not to have listened, for they filled their space with remarks that reflected their existing attitudes about the state of the nation.

In truth, the teach-in was an occasionally dramatic event which can easily mislead the participants as well as the public. The first and crucial thing to understand is that the students largely supplied the initiative and power behind the entire movement.

They won early and useful support and leadership from some professors on every campus, and from some nonacademics in those communities. But the students were the ones who infused the activity with a deep concern and a fundamental moral commitment.

The commentators who emphasize the presence of the beatniks, or the students who think they are nihilists or Communists, are missing the main point. To use the language of the day, a kind of sophisticated square is emerging from this new generation. This does not mean that they are merely sexually liberated Puritans or more efficient New Dealers.

They are young men and women who are intelligent and perceptive enough to learn from their elders without making all the same mistakes. They have had enough of hipsterism as well as of the jet-set, and of the Old Left as well as of the Establishment. And they are aware that emancipation involves men as well as women, and that it concerns something beyond changing patterns of sexual behavior and beyond the freedom and the opportunity to hustle their wares in the marketplace.

They are morally committed to the proposition that the American system must treat people as people, and that the system must be changed if that is necessary to achieve that objective. They are deeply angry about the double standard of morality they constantly experience.

It was these students, supported by the adults who share and respond to their concern and courage, who sparked the general criticism of American domestic and foreign policy and who forced the Government to agree to the teach-in.

The Administration's response to this opposition was regrettably effective. It first delayed accepting the challenge until the school year was almost over. That blocked an early return engagement, and so thwarted the possibility of a continuing dialogue.

It next exploited the desire of the critics for a direct confrontation by refusing a series of man-to-man encounters. It made its participation conditional upon the panel approach. It also exerted pressure against specific critics.

Finally, just before the event, President Johnson used his shrewd sense of timing to create the impression that the Government was modifying its policy.

The official strategy was largely successful. On the one hand, it diffused the criticism. On the other hand, it served in the main to contain the criticism within the assumptions of official policy. These results can be seen in what happened to the excellent performances by professors Kahin, Morgenthau, and Deutscher.

Deutscher's assault on the assumptions of American policy, and Morgenthau's laying bare the dangerous unreality of officialdom's so-called realism, were blunted by being interlarded with the high-cholesterol rhetoric of Arthur Schlesinger, Jr. And, in a similar way, the impact of Kahin's quiet, mannered, ruthless destruction of the official argument was gradually lost in the subsequent pseudo-debate between too many people who were given too little time.

The teach-in movement began as a technique of protesting and countering the incomplete and misleading official rationalization of a poor and dangerous policy. The Washington affair carried it unfortunately far toward being institutionalized as a glorified faculty meeting of the Establishment.

The teach-in, if it is to avoid that unhappy success, must return to its roots in student and associated protest, and establish a strong liaison with the civil rights movement. It might even consider becoming the foreign policy forum of the Freedom Democratic Party.

Otherwise, it will soon become a periodic seminar oriented toward the far less important task of finding even better ways of doing what we are already doing too well.

The Teach-In: A National Movement or the End of An Affair?

— JOAN WALLACH SCOTT

Mrs. Scott is a graduate student in history at the University of Wisconsin. The following article is from Studies on the Left, V, No. 3 (1965).

Those who expected the National Teach-In, held in Washington on May 15, to embody and enlarge upon the efforts made on individual campuses left Washington disillusioned. The National Teach-In did not re-enact the excitement and spontaneity of the campus events; it did not mobilize the academic community around an intense and penetrating critique of the basic assumptions of American policy in Vietnam and of the Government's attitude toward its critics. If a national movement is to come of the teach-ins, it will come from a different kind of effort, from a very different body, with assumptions very different from those held by the organizers of the Washington "affair." The last word is used advisedly; from the first press release announcing that "the people involved in the National Teach-In have a deep love affair with American democracy, they are going to Washington to find out if she still loves them," to the wind-up meeting on Sunday morning, the organizers conducted themselves as suitors; they directed most of their efforts to winning a rather coy, if not uninterested, Administration. Confused about whether they loved the existing system or the enduring principle of American democracy, the professors were bound to be disappointed. Anything said about the success of the Washington effort cannot overlook this aspect of it.

This is not to say that the effort itself was wasted. Certainly, the fact that so many professors took a public stand, that so many prominent academics came as critics of American policy, was important and significant. The widespread publicity, the hours of time on national radio and television networks exposed a vast audience to the debate on American foreign policy. As a one-shot affair, the Washington hearing was important and praiseworthy, conceivably, as one correspondent put it, "historic." But its members' attempt to initiate a long-term relationship with the Establishment could prove disastrous. When news reporters like Max Frankel and James Reston hailed the debate as a new American institution, and welcomed the professors into the Administration dialogue, they defined the limitations of the movement. The teach-ins began as protests against the war in Vietnam. They were not designed as debates; most participants felt that the other side was adequately represented by national news media. By adopting the debate format, the Washington Teach-In abandoned the idea of a protest, the very thing that the principle of democracy, and a love of it, made necessary. And, by adopting the debate format, the professors, in effect, ceased to represent their constituencies. Rather than the representatives of a large and angry movement of students and faculty members, they represented only themselves. The professors came as experts in their particular fields and they came to demonstrate a greater dexterity to Administration officials who had misused their expertise. . . .

On the stage, remote and apart from the audience, sat the professors, some critical of American policy, an equal number acting as spokesmen for the Administration point of view. The reason for this format—McGeorge Bundy—was absent. . . . When Bundy did not appear, the show lost its star. And it was inevitable that some of the glamor and, more important, some of the impact of the day was lost. For it had been billed as a confrontation with the Administration. . . . And the refusal of the professors to protest Bundy's absence, if only by leaving an empty chair on the stage, made matters worse. No other official was sent in Bundy's place. Rather, a professor stood-in for him. The meaning was clear—there were more important things than the professors. Intellectual exchange could be left to intellectuals, while officials attended to the more important business of making policy. The inherent implication was a complete denial of political meaning for the teach-in—for, while the critics were talking, the Administration was not listening, but continuing its actions. Your talk, Bundy's statement as much as said, is academic and irrelevant; we make policy apart from it. . . .

Perhaps the most disturbing aspect of the debate was the confusion it engendered. For, in arguing with the Administration, most of the dissenters spoke within the existing context of foreign policy. Thus, both Professors Kahin and Scalapino, though they differed on the interpretation of Vietnam, argued within the context of the Cold War. The speakers who urged the adoption of an entirely different foreign policy were few and did not set the tone of the day. If you had not already made up your mind, you could only have been confused by the day. And, when the TV spectators turned off their sets, most probably turned their thoughts back to personal preoccupations and left the "complexities" to the experts. In this sense, especially, the Washington Teach-in was a boon to the Administration. For it established a case for the experts. Only those who knew specifically about Vietnam or foreign policy participated, and none of those who had spoken at campus teach-ins for the right of dissent or for acting on a moral conviction appeared.

The crux of the problem lay in the underlying assumptions of the group. This became most evident in the evaluation and planning meeting held on Sunday, where the word most used to characterize the group was that of a "Loyal Opposition."

All the overtones of the term were implicit, in one form or another, in the organizing professors' approach. The specific sense of a parliamentary opposition was definitely intended. Given the absence of real divergence in Congress, this group saw itself as providing another side. Not, however, as representatives of a constituency or of particular interests in the society but as special consultants to the State Department. Some labored under the illusion that they had more information about Vietnam than the Government advisers; others seemed to feel better equipped to interpret the facts. Most held the illusion of power that the term Loyal Opposition implies, but they felt they had power not because they had voters behind them but because of their positions of intellectual expertise. They did not acknowledge that the primary reason the professors were in Washington, the primary reason the Administration had agreed to hear them all, was not for what they had to say or who they were as individuals but precisely because of the constituency they did represent.

Behind those professors were students. The impact of the thousands of students at the March on Washington and, even more important, at the campus teach-ins had been felt. The Administration recognized the radical potential and scope of the student protest when it sent "truth-teams" to campuses and when it agreed to participate in the Washington Teach-In. By constituting themselves as "consulting engineers" rather than as representatives of the university community, the professors deprived themselves of their real source of power and weakened their position. Instead of presenting themselves in their role as social and political critics, the professors tried to compete with policy-makers. They were bound to lose; for, in the context of expertise, a policy-maker's words automatically carry greater authority than an intellectual's ideas.

The real strength of the teach-in movement as it was manifested in local campus activity lay in its assertion that war in Vietnam was morally indefensible and that intellectuals, as the upholders of humanitarian ideals and as perpetuators of human values, could, on those grounds, criticize American foreign policy. The importance of the teach-in lay not in proposing specific alternatives for a particular course of action but in establishing the validity of a moral basis for dissent. The National Teach-In did not implement this potential.

The National Teach-In neglected students. None had any role in the proceedings; few, if any, seemed to have shared in the planning. At the final meeting on Sunday, the discussion of future possibilities omitted students. . . . No one suggested developing the idea of the teach-in, of institutionalizing it, or expanding it to include greater numbers of students and teachers. Rather, they spoke vaguely of clergymen, lawyers—fellow professionals and other members of "the community."

In directing most of their attention to the question of future dealings with power, the professors in charge presumed they had a powerful position from which to speak. Instead of attending to the real question of how to consolidate and build the as yet potential power of their own community—which is, after all, the university and not the Department of State—the professors spent most of their meeting discussing the advisability of giving Bundy a make-up exam. Having been once rejected, the suitors decided to pursue the courtship again.

The National Teach-In was like a faculty meeting and, as such, represented only half the picture of the local manifestations. Hopefully, the professors learned of their inadequacy as lovers and of their potential power as critics. But they could not learn this without their students. For, if the radical potential of campus teach-ins is to be realized, discussion, decision, and action cannot take place at faculty meetings, but must take place in the classrooms, where the teach-in began.

The Teach-In Could Become a Useful Tool

— J A M E S   R E S T O N

From The New York Times, *May 17, 1965.*

Something new and enterprising happened in the national capital last weekend. The political and intellectual communities of the nation came together and engaged in a serious and responsible debate on the policy of the United States in Vietnam.

President Johnson was originally against this erudite confrontation. He took the opposition on the campuses of the country to his Vietnam policy as another act of highbrow hostility to him, personally. Finally, he agreed to let his principal White House adviser on foreign policy, W. McGeorge Bundy, former Dean of the Harvard Faculty, address the visiting professors and students, but in the end, Bundy didn't show up.

Nevertheless, despite Bundy's regrettable absence, the exchange of ideas in the meeting was useful and may have set an important precedent for the future.

This was not merely a protest by students and professors about what is happening there—though their previous protests brought it about—but an inquiry, an honest search for answers to the moral, political, and military dilemmas that confront the country in Southeast Asia.

Most important, it was a model of what can be accomplished in a vast democratic continental society when modern instruments of communication are used to discuss fundamental questions of public policy.

It was not only that hundreds of students and professors gathered here to express their concern about the Johnson Administration's policy in Vietnam, or that representatives of the Administration explained at last what the Government was doing there, but that the whole discussion was carried by radio to university communities in thirty-five states and this enabled the students to continue the discussion in the coming days and weeks.

This is something quite new and different from the struggles between governments and universities in other countries. The energy and zeal of university students elsewhere are usually directed either against the government, as in many Latin American countries, or as an instrument of government propaganda in many Communist and newly developed countries.

But the interuniversity meeting here in Washington last weekend provided an opportunity to find the truth between the policies of the Government and the conflicting views of its critics.

Nothing was really resolved in the process, but an important technique of serious discussion was discovered.

Presidential talks in the past have not produced objective national discussion of political realities. The press and radio and television have merely dramatized the differences of opinion over policy. The political debates in Congress have only encouraged partisan and subjective conclusions about how to proceed. And, until this past weekend, the demonstrations on the American campuses have provoked more heat than light.

The debate here in Washington, however, was more balanced and realistic. The Administration, which at first was aloof, full of resentment and self-pity, finally participated in the discussion and helped itself and its critics to deal with realities in the process.

Even so, this debate between the intellectual and political communities of the country is still unsatisfactory. It is still dealing primarily with the effects of the disorder of the world and not with the causes. Vietnam, which was the main subject of the weekend's discussion, is not a cause but merely one effect of the problem.

The cause is the poverty, misery, and resentment of most of the human race and the exploitation of these things by the cunning techniques of Communist subversion.

Another cause is the failure of the Western world to devise effective means of dealing with these facts.

China is now the central problem. It has a grievance, an atomic bomb, a religious ideology, and a staggering surplus of people. In Asia, it is the arsenal of rebellion, and the problem is how to deal with this astounding fact.

The most dangerous thing in the world today is that the West has found no means to deal with this rising problem and the university professors and students are quite right in recognizing that no government has come up with the answer.

The importance of the weekend's debate is that at least a means has been found to discuss these realities, to move from protests against the effects of world disorder to analysis of causes and a choice of hard options.

The Inter-University Committee, which was responsible for the Washington teach-in, should be continued and supported financially. It started at the University of Michigan as a protesting movement against the Government's Vietnam policy, threatening an academic strike, and has now developed into a forum of national debate which could be of fundamental importance to the nation.

Genesis of the Confuse-In

—RUSSELL BAKER

From The New York Times, *May 20, 1965.*

The untold story of American foreign policy this spring is the triumph of the pop diplomatic device which insiders here call the "confuse-in."

The idea of the confuse-in was born last winter at a secret high-level meeting attended by four men. For security reasons, they can be identified only by their nicknames, which are Bob, Mac, Dean, and The Chief.

At that time, the Government faced the necessity of evolving a policy on Vietnam. One of the men, whose identity cannot be revealed, said, "The trouble with our policy is that everybody knows what it is—hope and prayer.

"Now when I was running the Senate," he went on, "I found the best way to get results was to keep everybody confused about what I was going to do next. While everybody was running around like a Purd'nalis prairie dog looking for his supper, I could quietly build away on the Great Society."

With that, the speaker outlined his plans for the first confuse-in. "First off," he said, "we'll have to bomb North Vietnam, and I'll say we want no wider war, and then we'll really start bombing until everybody is confused about whether we want a wider war or not."

"That will upset a lot of senators," said Bob, "and they will start demanding a lull in the bombing."

"Right up confusion alley," Mac said. "We'll say that senators who want a lull in the bombing are enemies of peace because we are only bombing for peaceful purposes."

"Right," said Dean, "and then, when we've silenced all the senators, we'll halt the bombing ourselves. That will confuse them."

"We will say we stopped the bombing in order to promote peace," Bob said. "That will create a lot of confusion because after we stop bombing in order to promote peace we'll start bombing again and pass the word that we're only bombing to promote peace."

"That will create some really ripping confusion," Dean said.

"It won't confuse them enough, though," said the Presiding Officer. "When they get a little bit confused, a lot of professors are going to start asking what our policy is. That's when I want you to come in, Dean, and declare that professors who question the policy are a bunch of knuckleheads."

"Excellent, Chief," Mac said. "And after Dean denounces the professors, I'll come in and say that professors who question the policy are doing a great service to democracy."

"Not only that," said the Chief. "You'll even arrange to go to a big meeting of professors and discuss the policy with them."

"And then, for a switcheroo," Bob said, "after Mac has agreed to go to the meeting, he doesn't show up."

"What bothers me," said Dean, "is that there isn't enough confusion inherent in Vietnam to keep the picture muddled very long."

"Don't worry about it," said the Presiding Officer. "There's always a revolution brewing in the Caribbean. When one blows, we'll send in the Marines and announce that they are there only to protect Americans. Then, next day, I'll come out and say the Marines are there to prevent a Communist take-over."

"Chief," said Bob, "that's what I call confusion."

"And then what we can do," said Mac, "is form a couple of competing juntas, and first back one junta, and then back the other junta, and just when everybody thinks we're junta lovers, we switch our support to the rebels."

"I don't know," said Dean, "it's going to confuse the public pretty badly, not to mention the Communists."

"The beauty part!" said the Presiding Officer. "We'll paralyze them with confusion. While they are trying to make sense of what we're doing, we'll have breathing space to figure it out ourselves."

6. CONFRONTATION ON TV

Dean Bundy Meets Professor Morgenthau

On June 21, 1965, under the auspices of CBS-News, the confrontation between McGeorge Bundy and his academic critics that had failed to materialize at the National Teach-In in Washington took place. Supporting Mr. Bundy were professors Z. K. Brzezinski and G. J. Pauker; opposing them were professors H. J. Morgenthau, J. D. Donoghue, and O. E. Clubb. Excerpted here are exchanges between Mr. Bundy and Professor Morgenthau. It should be recalled that organizers of the National Teach-In had chosen Professor Morgenthau to debate Mr. Bundy and that Mr. Bundy had rejected the proposal (see Anatol Rapoport's discussion in Part 5 of this chapter). From CBS-News Special Report—Vietnam Dialog: Mr. Bundy and the Professors.

MR. BUNDY. Well, I am here partly because I failed to keep an earlier engagement, partly because I deeply believe in the process of fair and open discussion. Most of all, because I believe with all my heart that the policy which the United States is now following is the best policy in a difficult and dangerous situation and the one which best serves our interests and the interests of the world, the interest of peace.

MR. MORGENTHAU. I am opposed to our present policy in Vietnam on moral, military, political, and general intellectual grounds. I am convinced that this policy cannot achieve the desired results and that, quite to the contrary, it will create problems much more serious than those which we have faced in the recent past.

MR. SEVAREID [Moderator]. Well, gentlemen and members of this audience, we thought we would try to divide this discussion to follow into four rather large, encompassing questions or aspects of the whole Vietnam problem. And the first question is why—what are the legal and moral and political reasons or justifications for the American presence in Vietnam—why are we there?

Let's begin with Mr. Bundy.

Mr. Bundy. Well, Mr. Sevareid, I think the best way, the shortest and the most accurate way, for me to state the reasons for our presence in Vietnam is to take just a moment to read from the President's speech of April 7, at Johns Hopkins in Baltimore, because there is no more authoritative statement of our position.

"We are there," he said, "because we have a promise to keep. Since 1954, every American President has offered support to the people of South Vietnam. We have helped to build and we have helped to defend. Thus, over many years, we have made a national pledge to help South Vietnam defend its independence. To dishonor that pledge, to abandon this small and brave nation to its enemy and to the terror that must follow would be an unforgivable wrong." So the first point is that we have a commitment, matured through time, made for good reasons, and sustained for the same reasons.

We are also there, the President went on, "to strengthen world order. Around the globe, from Berlin to Thailand, are people whose well-being rests, in part, on the belief they can count on us if they are attacked. To leave Vietnam to its fate would shake the confidence of all these people in the value of American commitment. The result would be increased unrest and instability or even war."

And the President went on to set the stakes in terms of the problem in Asia itself. "We are also there," he said, "because there are great stakes in the balance. Let no one think that retreat from Vietnam would bring an end to conflict. The battle would be renewed in one country and then another. The central lesson of our time is that the appetite of aggression is never satisfied. To withdraw from one battlefield means only to prepare for the next."

Our objective, he said—and this is perhaps, in the end, the defining point immediately of the contest—"our objective is the independence of South Vietnam and its freedom from attack. We want nothing for ourselves—only that the people of South Vietnam be allowed to guide their own country in their own way."

Mr. Morgenthau. Well, I would offer two political arguments against the official position that we are in Vietnam in order to honor a commitment and that we are there in order to defend the freedom of South Vietnam, that we cannot let South Vietnam down.

First of all, one should not overlook the fact that it was we who installed the first government in Saigon, the Diem Government. In other words, the state of South Vietnam is, in a sense, our own creation—for without our support, the regime in Saigon could not have lasted for any length of time.

So when we say we must keep a promise, we have really made a promise to our own agents. In a sense, we have contracted with ourselves, and I do not regard this as a valid foundation for our presence in South Vietnam.

Furthermore, even if it were otherwise, I refer you to the statement which Alexander Hamilton made on the occasion of the Neutrality Proclamation of Washington, in 1793, when the United States had an obvious and undoubted treaty agreement to the effect that it must come to the aid of France if France were engaged in a war in Europe. And Hamilton, in a definitive fashion, laid down the principle that no nation is obligated to endanger its own interests, let alone its own existence, in order to come to the aid of another nation.

Second, it is obvious from the facts of the situation . . . that we are quite unwelcome in South Vietnam. There is an abundance of reports to the effect that what most of the South Vietnamese want is to be left alone, that they would be delighted to see us depart.

A month ago, for instance, the Vietnamese correspondent of *The Economist*, a very respectable periodical of Great Britain, reported that the slogan which makes the rounds in Saigon is "Yanks, fight your wars elsewhere."

Mr. Sevareid. I would like to go to the second question that we discussed before, and this is a little more specific.

What is the fundamental nature of this war? Is it aggression from North Vietnam or is it, basically, a civil war between the peoples of South Vietnam?

Let's start with Dr. Morgenthau.

Mr. Morgenthau. I would say, it was also the official position until February of this year, that the major problem was a political problem in South Vietnam. And I remember very well, at the end of 1955, when I had a long discussion with President Diem, that I pointed to the likelihood that his policies would lead to the breakdown of his regime and to a general alienation of the population with the Communists profiting therefrom. So, what we had at the beginning—and it is obvious when you look at the development of the civil war in South Vietnam—[was] a revolt, especially of the peasants against the Diem regime and, from 1959 or 1960 onward, the North Vietnamese Government, to an ever-increasing extent, aided and abetted this revolt. So, I find it rather farfetched, up to recent months—of course, in recent months, our extension of the war in the North [has changed] the Vietnam situation—to speak of aggression [from] the North. What you had was a revolt in the South aided and abetted from the North.

MR. BUNDY. I would like to make two points on what Professor Morgenthau said.

First, he implied that the U.S. Government has changed its tune on this point within the last few months, which is, in my judgment, simply wrong.

I would like to read just two short quotations as samples. Here is an example from a news conference of Secretary Rusk, in November, 1961. "The determined and ruthless campaign of propaganda, infiltration, and subversion by the Communist regime in North Vietnam to destroy the Republic of South Vietnam and subjugate its peoples is a threat to the peace."

There couldn't be a clearer statement of a position which has been repeated a number of times.

I could go right through a whole series of statements which President Johnson and, before him, President Kennedy, have made on this. But more compelling evidence, in a way, is what the Communists themselves say about it.

In 1959, Ho Chi Minh announced, in an article in the Belgian Communist organ: "We are building socialism in Vietnam, but we are building it in only one part of the country while in the other part we still have to direct and bring to a close the middle-class democratic and anti-imperialist revolution," and again, in 1963, the North Vietnamese Communist Party organ stated quite simply: "The authorities in South Vietnam," it was speaking of, "are well aware that North Vietnam is the firm base for the southern revolution and the point on which it leans and that our party is the steady and experienced vanguard unit of the working class and people and is the brain and factor that decides all victories of the revolution."

We really shouldn't argue about this point because the evidence is overwhelming.

MR. SEVAREID. Gentlemen, I would like to turn to our third topic or question and this is a large one.

What are the implications of this Vietnam struggle in terms of the whole rise, and future, of Communism in Asia as a whole, particularly in terms of Communist China's power and aims and future actions?

Who would like to start on this? Professor Morgenthau?

MR. MORGENTHAU. It is, of course, correct to say that one cannot look at the Vietnamese situation in isolation from our over-all policy in Asia and in isolation from the over-all policy in Asia of our enemies. And here [we] come back to what we have discussed before. We are really in Vietnam not because we must honor a commitment or because we want to help the people of South Vietnam who rely on us. We are there because we want to contain Communism. And I have no quotation to read from, but I have a very good memory.   [Laughter.]

I remember well that, for instance, the Secretary of Defense has said, and I think quite correctly, that we are in South Vietnam in order to stop Communism and if we don't stop it there we will have to stop it elsewhere, and some people have gone so far as to say if we don't fight in Vietnam we [will] have to fight in Hawaii or, perhaps, in California.

Now, we are really in Vietnam as part—yes—part and parcel of the containment policy, military containment policy, which was eminently successful in Europe against the Soviet Union and, in my view, is bound to fail in Asia against China. For the situation in China—pardon me—the situation in Asia is fundamentally different from the situation in Europe.

In Europe, you could draw a line across a map and tell the Soviet Union, "Until here and not farther." And behind that line, on our side, you had viable social, political, economic, and military units. Nothing of the kind exists in Asia. Second, and most important, the Russian threat was primarily a military threat and against this threat the policy of military containment was indeed adequate and successful.

The threat of China is primarily a political threat and nothing we do in South Vietnam or don't do in South Vietnam is going to make any difference with regard to the potency of such threat in the rest of the world. We may hold South Vietnam. We may win a victory in South Vietnam. This means nothing with regard to whether or not Indonesia will go Communist, or an area in Africa will go Communist, or Colombia will go Communist.

In other words, we have the success of our policy of military containment in Europe and [it] has led us into the fallacy of applying the same instruments to a situation which is entirely different and where such instruments cannot succeed.

MR. BUNDY. I think the point to be made—and it is one which really takes us to the question of what Professor Morgenthau's real position is—is that, as he states it, no particular point is worth defending. I think also, that he gravely misstates the policy of the United States in Vietnam when he asserts, I think on quite incomplete [grounds] and as far as I know, with no citation, that our policy is merely to contain Communism everywhere and that we do not have a specific interest, sustained and important, in victory in South Vietnam. I can suggest to him the importance I think of this point by remarking simply that it seems as [clear as] a pikestaff to me that if we are successful there the effects will be constructive and helpful all around Southeast Asia and on [an] even wider framework.

Mr. Sevareid. I think we might very usefully spend the rest of this hour on the fourth and final question we had on our minds before we began and that is the question of alternatives to our present policy in Vietnam.

What are these alternatives? Let me start with Mr. Bundy.

Mr. Bundy. Well, there are a number of alternatives.

Let me begin by pointing out that the alternative which is more important than the one presented by these gentlemen, in terms of real choices and in terms of levels of support by the United States and in terms of the level of our interest there—and it has been rejected by the Administration—is the general and less restrained carrying of the war ever further northward, without regard to cities or population or boundaries or to what country you are choosing to attack [and with] the view that air power will somehow settle this thing, that there is no issue in South Vietnam. That is not the policy of the Administration. That policy was proposed in certain quarters, in 1964. It was rejected; it is still rejected. There is a very interesting and important issue—a more important one in terms of the sentiment of the American people—in the general proposal moving toward withdrawal which I take to be (although they were stated for themselves) the position of the gentlemen opposite. Within the framework of the choices available to us, we can move without restraint against those who have engaged in this aggression from the North. We can move toward withdrawal without regard to our obligations to those in South Vietnam or to the political consequences in other countries.

We can stay roughly where we are in essentially the passive role or we can carefully, and with a choice of specific ways and means, move to sustain our part—and it can only be our part—of a contest which is of as great importance to us as it is to the people of Vietnam.

It is not for me, on this occasion, to discuss specifically what steps may come in the future. I think it is fair to say that the position of the Administration, and I think the position of a solid and very strong majority of Congress and of the people, is that we should stay there, that we should do our part as may become necessary, . . . bear in mind that the center of the contest is in South Vietnam—though there is more aggression from the North—and seek constantly, as we have for months and months, to find a way to get this dangerous and difficult business to the conference room.

Mr. Sevareid. Mr. Bundy, has the Administration changed its views about negotiating at any level, at any time, with the Vietcong?

Mr. Bundy. The Administration's position is that we will negotiate with governments. Now, there is no barrier to serious negotiations in this question of the Vietcong. The Vietcong have traveled for years on North Vietnamese passports. It is not a difficulty, from their point of view, if they are ready to see a negotiation, to pass the signal to friends, supporters, and, I say, directors and controllers. It is not the question of who sits for the Communists that stands in the way of a conference.

Mr. Sevareid. I want to get clear that we would negotiate with the Vietcong as long as they are legitimately established . . .

Mr. Bundy. That is not a question which stands in the way of a conference. We propose to discuss this matter with governments.

Mr. Morgenthau. There are, I think, theoretically speaking five alternatives which are before us.

We can get out, without further ado.

Second, we can—we don't need to oppose moves (which, in the past, have been made by the government in Saigon) to come to an understanding with the Vietcong which would lead to our departure on their invitation and the invitation of the government in Saigon.

Third, we can greatly increase the air attacks, going farther and farther north.

Fourth, we can greatly increase our commitment on land by sending a couple of hundred thousand, or as Mr. Hanson Baldwin [Military Editor of The New York Times] suggested, 1 million men to Vietnam. Or we can, as Senator Fulbright recently suggested, try to hold a few strong points on the coast of Vietnam, proving to the Vietcong that they cannot win a military victory, and on that basis try to negotiate with them in the fall.

Now, my personal position, which must come as a surprise to some listeners here, is that Mr. Fulbright's position is by far the most acceptable.

I think our aim must be to get out of Vietnam, but to get out of it with honor. I have, indeed, always believed that it is impossible for a great power which must take care of its prestige to admit, in so many words, that its policy has been mistaken during the last ten years and leave the theater of operation. But there are all kinds of face-saving devices by which a nation or a government which has made a series of mistakes can rectify the situation, and I think

President de Gaulle has shown how to go about this, with regard to Algeria. And, if you look at the prestige of France today, it is certainly higher than it was when France fought in Indochina.

If I may just say one sentence about the previous discussion about the facts. It is of course obvious, and it has been obvious to me all along, that the Government lives in a different factual world from the factual world in which its critics live. It is an open question who is psychotic in this respect, who has created a kind of a quasi-world in which he lives.

But I would call the attention to the fact that my view of the facts is certainly supported by all of those observers from neutral or friendly countries who have been in Vietnam, who have lived with the Vietcong. I remind you of the articles in *L'Express* by Mr. Chauffard; I remind you of the articles in the *Figaro* by its correspondent. I remind you of the articles in the *Economist*. They all support my general view of what the factual situation in Vietnam is.

And I should also say that the factual situation, the deterioration of the military situation, is infinitely graver than we have been made to believe on the basis of official and unofficial reports.

You see, for instance, the desertion rate of the Vietnamese Army in recent months has been enormous. Generally, it has been said that the recruits desert at the rate of 30 per cent. But around Da Nang, in the war zone, 40 per cent of the combatant units have, in recent weeks, defected.

Mr. Bundy. I simply have to break in, if I may, Mr. Sevareid, and say that I think that Professor Morgenthau was wrong on his facts as to the desertion rate, wrong in his summary of the Chauffard and *Express* articles, wrong in his view of what the *Economist* says, and, I am sorry to say, giving vent to his congenital pessimism with respect to these matters. And I want to take a moment to give you direct quotations to show what I mean.

In 1956, Professor Morgenthau wrote of Western Europe, "Communism is far from defeated in Western Europe, and the Marshall Plan is partly to blame for that failure. The dangers to the stability and strength of Western Europe have grown in the past and the defects of that structure have continued to grow, because those defects were not repaired. The Marshall Plan almost completely lost sight of those roots of instability and unrest which antedated the emergency and were bound to operate after it was over."

And it is only nine years later that he tells us that "the Marshall Plan was eminently successful in Europe" and that, to the west of that boundary, there lay an ancient civilization which was but temporarily in disarray and which proved itself capable of containing Communist subversion.

And, closer to home, just four years ago, Professor Morgenthau wrote about Laos two things which are interesting.

"As these lines are being written, early June, the Communist domination of Laos is virtually a foregone conclusion." And, reading the mind of the Administration, he went on to say, "The Administration has reconciled itself to the loss of Laos."

Now, neither of those things is true, neither of them has happened, neither of them corresponds to the reality of the political situation in Southeast Asia.

Mr. Morgenthau. I may have been dead wrong on Laos, but it doesn't prove that I am dead wrong on Vietnam.

Mr. Sevareid. Since this has become something of a personal confrontation I think Professor Morgenthau should have a small chance at least to answer Mr. Bundy.

Mr. Morgenthau. I admire the efficiency of Mr. Bundy's office . . .

Mr. Bundy. I do my own [work].

Mr. Morgenthau. Oh, well, I am honored by the selected quotations from my writings.

As I have said before—privately, have said this—nobody who deals with foreign policy professionally can be always right. Obviously, one makes mistakes. And I probably was too pessimistic about Laos. But not terribly more pessimistic than the situation warranted.

I should also say, to quote a great man, that I have not always been wrong. And especially when it comes to Vietnam, Mr. Bundy might have quoted certain things I wrote in 1961 and 1962 or quoted what I wrote at the end of 1955, after my interview with President Diem, about what the future of South Vietnam might be.

So, I think no useful purpose is served by pointing to one mistake, and I admit freely that I have made mistakes, I have made many more than Mr. Bundy has found—but I have not always been wrong. And in any case, it is no argument to say this man has been wrong about Laos, how can he be right on Vietnam.

Mr. Bundy. Actually, what Mr. Morgenthau said about Vietnam in 1956—this is the one I happen to have here—was that a miracle had been wrought under President Diem.

The TV Debate

—STANLEY DIAMOND

Dr. Diamond is Professor of Anthropology at Syracuse University. These remarks appeared in Bi-Weekly Information Action Report (BIAR, a newsletter published by the teach-in movement at Ann Arbor, Michigan), July 2, 1965.

After viewing the program . . . I am forced to conclude that we pursued McGeorge Bundy until he caught us. Had he appeared . . . at the National Teach-In, I believe that we would have dealt his credibility a severe public blow. But this second round was waged on grounds more familiar to him and in a milieu that dictated accommodation on our part. Since I was a member of the team that negotiated the program in Washington, I think it proper that the course of events be discussed, at least as they appeared to me, so that we can learn more precisely what happened.

Our initial proposal was that a two-hour program be televised consisting of three people on each side, presenting both prepared statements and spontaneous cross-arguments within a format sufficiently structured to permit adequate formulation of our positions. We visualized such a structure as keeping irrelevancies and pseudo-responses to a minimum. We were well aware that the Administration has the initial advantage in any such confrontation because of (1) *noblesse oblige,* (2) a certain amount of charisma, (3) mass political inertia, and (4) the privileged access to, and presentation of, quasi-facts. But these factors would weigh in inverse proportion to the increasing length of the program. We had no interest in putting on an "entertainment," that is to say, a "show" which could have been staged in the absence of the teach-in movement. (Indeed, at one point, CBS quietly mentioned that, should we withdraw from the show, they might go ahead with it anyway, rounding up their own critics.)

We arrived in Washington with no particular preconceptions of the auspices of the event, but with the general sense that it was *our* business and that *we* would negotiate with the networks, perhaps following the pattern of the National Teach-In. However, we learned at once that Bundy had already been in touch with CBS and had, in effect, given them the "show," although there is some indication that we could have gone to another network. What was completely clear was that Bundy was not going to speak at an event staged by us and covered by the networks at will. . . .

In giving CBS responsibility for the program and in declining a second hour, either live or video-taped, Bundy assured himself all the initial advantages that we had tried to neutralize by our proposal for two hours. He was thus, in effect, choosing the time, place, and context of his appearance. We tried to mitigate this by presenting CBS with four substantive questions which divided the time, but the format was, in principle, theirs. As a mass communications medium, CBS was naturally interested in giving the impression that it was *their* show and they were also concerned with such matters as liveliness, holding the audience, etcetera. Theoretically, we would have been at least equally as concerned with reaching a smaller audience more heavily saturated with, let us say, teachers on the local level. And several of us were as concerned with the possibilities of distributing the video-tape through National Educational Television as we were with the initial impact. CBS appreciated the argument, but hot news on the spot, not history, is, of course, the lifeblood of the mass media. This is not to say that CBS was unsympathetic. They were sympathetic, and we seemed to have gained the affections of Eric Sevareid. But we have the obligation not to be sentimental about the personal aspect of these affairs. We are a movement and . . . our *structural* integrity is the only defense we have against the overwhelming experience of the establishment.

There was no controversy about our selection of speakers. We could have presented just about anyone we pleased. In the end, the four of us . . . explicitly entrusted with the negotiations agreed; but we did have rather lengthy discussions about whether it was wiser to present a person directly experienced in village Vietnam or a representative of the non-Communist left, which is a significant part of our movement. Unfortunately, we couldn't find a single person combining both virtues.

Since CBS flatly rejected a fourth man, despite the fact that he would have been substitutive rather than additive, so far as allotment of time was concerned, we finally decided against the non-Communist leftist, hoping that he might be added during the proposed (by Fred Friendly) video-taped hour. In any case [we hoped] the position could be absorbed by the three speakers selected. In my judgment, this did not happen; that is, the notion that the United States must come to terms with revolutionary nationalisms among the Afro-Asian peoples was noted superficially, and only in passing. This permitted the other side to capitalize on a falsely sharp distinction between national and social revolutions in these areas. National revolutions in the emerging areas sooner or later are directed against both native elites *and* foreign domination. The demand that this makes upon our foreign policy and the implications that it has for our domestic social commitments is on a level of analysis that I believe we must pursue as fully as possible in the future.

Returning now to the problem we had to resolve, in the first instance, about putting on the program, we decided to go ahead with it on the basis that some exposure of some of the views of . . . our side was better than nothing at all. But it would be disastrous to view the program that actually occurred as anything more than an episode in a developing and deepening series of events created by *us*. The Bundy issue is now dead, certainly from his point of view. At one stroke, he glided off the hook and at least stalemated the professors. And, assuredly, the Administration views the program as a kind of feeble consummation of our efforts of the past several months. . . .

We should cultivate the academic resources that we have in depth; that is, we should not depend on a small circle of more or less popularly known spokesmen. The danger, here, is that pride of position generally, and adherence to or departure from a particular set of opinions in which one has a public investment, may cloud the immediate issues that are under consideration. Summing up the value of the program, I believe that we wasted more time and energy than it deserved, but that we will not have lost anything if future events reduce it to its proper proportions.

V

The Teach-Ins and Academic Freedom

Editors' Introduction

The sharp criticism of U.S. foreign policy in academic circles led some Americans to view the dissent as prima-facie evidence of disloyalty. In contrast, Senator J. William Fulbright and Professor Henry Steele Commager eloquently state the legal, moral, pragmatic, and historical imperatives for open and unlimited debate. Both deplore the tendency to equate dissent with disloyalty. Such an equation, they suggest, demands a uniformity of thought contrary to this country's most creative traditions. In the address containing his now famous warning against the "fatal arrogance of power" in American attitudes, Senator Fulbright draws a different equation, one positing the equivalence of criticism and a "higher patriotism."

A special kind of controversy produced by teach-in dissent developed around what came to be known as the Genovese case. No single teach-in, even in this movement born and nourished by controversy, could match the furor created by the Rutgers University Teach-In of April 23, 1965. On that night, Dr. Eugene D. Genovese, a young "obscure historian," as the press customarily (but mistakenly) described him, delivered an address that inadvertently thrust him into the center of New Jersey politics and brought national attention upon that state's 1965 gubernatorial campaign.

"I do not fear or regret the impending Vietcong victory in Vietnam," stated Professor Genovese, "I welcome it." This remark was isolated from a long address and used by State Senator and Republican gubernatorial candidate Wayne Dumont to mount a campaign demanding that Governor Richard Hughes, the Democratic incumbent and candidate, force the ouster of Professor Genovese from the Rutgers faculty. Dumont was backed by former Vice-President Richard Nixon, who entered the campaign on his behalf; in a letter to *The New York Times*, Nixon, although defending academic freedom in principle, drew the line at a scholar's advocating victory for the enemy in wartime. New Jersey voters apparently were not affected by the arguments of Nixon and Senator Dumont; Governor Hughes, who agreed with the university's decision not to fire Professor Genovese, was elected by an overwhelming majority. (This apparent victory for academic freedom should be footnoted by mention of an incident, related to the Genovese case, that ended somewhat differently. James G. Mellen, an Instructor of Political Science at Drew University, made some controversial remarks at another teach-in at Rutgers, September 30, 1965. He was subsequently dropped from the Drew faculty, although university authorities claimed the decision had been made prior to the teach-in.)

The teach-ins, in general, and the Genovese case, in particular, gave new emphasis to perennial questions relating to academic freedom. What are its ground rules? What, if any, are its limits? Does an instructor, particularly one employed by a state university, have the right to favor the victory of an opponent in time of war? Other, perhaps more important, general issues regarding academic freedom were highlighted as well. Can an instructor who embraces a specific world view, such as Marxism, teach objectively and critically? In what ways do his political values bias his classroom presentation? Is such bias, openly proclaimed, necessarily harmful? These and other acute questions are taken up by Arnold Beichman's review of the Genovese case.

1. TWO VIEWS ON DISSENT AND DISLOYALTY

The Higher Patriotism

— J. WILLIAM FULBRIGHT

Senator Fulbright's academic credentials are impressive: He has been a Rhodes Scholar, an Instructor in Law at George Washington University, and President of the University of Arkansas. This is the abridged text of the first of Senator Fulbright's Christian A. Herter Lectures at Johns Hopkins University; from the Congressional Record, *April 25, 1966.*

To criticize one's country is to do it a service and pay it a compliment. It is a service because it may spur the country to do better than it is doing; it is a compliment because it evidences a belief that the country can do better than it is doing. "This," said Albert Camus, in one of his "Letters to a German Friend," "is what separated us from you; we made demands. You were satisfied to serve the power of your nation and we dreamed of giving ours her truth."

In a democracy, dissent is an act of faith. Like medicine, the test of its value is not its taste but its effects, not how it makes people feel at the moment but how it inspires them to act thereafter. Criticism may embarrass the country's leaders in the short run but strengthen their hand in the long run; it may destroy a consensus on policy while expressing a consensus of values. Woodrow Wilson once said that there was "such a thing as being too proud to fight"; there is also, or ought to be, such a thing as being too confident to conform, too strong to be silent in the face of apparent error. Criticism, in short, is more than a right; it is an act of patriotism, a higher form of patriotism, I believe, than the familiar rituals of national adulation.

In the three lectures which we begin tonight, I am going to criticize America—I hope not unfairly, and always with the hope of rendering a service and with the confidence of paying a compliment. It is not a pejorative but a tribute to say that America is worthy of criticism. If, nonetheless, one is charged with a lack of patriotism, I would reply with Camus: "No, I didn't love my country, if pointing out what is unjust in what we love amounts to not loving, if insisting that what we love should measure up to the finest image we have of her amounts to not loving." . . .

My question is whether America can overcome the fatal arrogance of power. My hope and my belief are that it can, that it has the human resources to accomplish what few, if any, great nations have ever accomplished before: to be confident, but also tolerant; to be rich, but also generous; to be willing to teach, but also willing to learn; to be powerful, but also wise. I believe that America is capable of all of these things; I also believe it is falling short of them. Gradually, but unmistakably, we are succumbing to the arrogance of power. In so doing, we are not living up to our capacity and promise; the measure of our falling short is the measure of the patriot's duty of dissent. . . .

The universities—and especially institutions like the [Johns Hopkins] School of Advanced International Studies—have a special obligation to train potential public servants in rigorously independent thinking and to acquaint them, as well, with the need for reconciling loyalty to an organization with personal integrity. It is an extremely important service for the universities to perform, because the most valuable public servant, like the true patriot, is one who gives a higher loyalty to his country's ideals than to its current policy and who, therefore, is willing to criticize as well as to comply.

We must learn to treat our freedom as a source of strength, as an asset to be shown to the world with confidence and pride. No one challenges the value and importance of national consensus, but consensus can be understood in two ways. If it is interpreted to mean unquestioning support of existing policies, its effects can only be pernicious and undemocratic, serving to suppress differences rather than to reconcile them. If, on the other hand, consensus is understood to mean a general agreement on goals and values but not necessarily on the best means of realizing them, then, and only then, does it become a lasting basis of national strength. It is consensus in this sense which has made America strong in the past. Indeed, much of our national success in combining change with continuity can be attributed to the vigorous competition of men and ideas within a context of shared values and generally accepted institutions. It is only through this kind of vigorous competition of ideas that a consensus of values can sometimes be translated into a true consensus of policy. Or, as Mark Twain plainly put it: "It were not best that we should all think alike; it is difference of opinion that makes horseraces."

Freedom of thought and discussion gives a democracy two concrete advantages over a dictatorship in the making of foreign policy: It diminishes the danger of an irretrievable mistake, and it introduces ideas and opportunities that otherwise would not come to light.

The correction of errors in a nation's foreign policy is greatly assisted by the timely raising of voices of criticism within the nation. When the British launched their disastrous attack on Egypt, the Labour Party raised a collective voice of indignation while the military operation was still under way; refusing to be deterred by calls for national unity in a crisis, Labour began the long, painful process of recovering Great Britain's good name at the very moment when the damage was still being done. Similarly, the French intellectuals who protested France's colonial wars in Indochina and Algeria not only upheld the values of French democracy but helped pave the way for the enlightened policies of the Fifth Republic, which have made France the most respected Western nation in the [eyes of the] underdeveloped world. It was in the hope of performing a similar service for America on a very modest scale that I criticized American intervention in the Dominican Republic, in a speech in the Senate last year. [*See "The Situation in the Dominican Republic,"* Congressional Record, *III*, No. *170,* (*September 15, 1965*), 22998–23005.]

The second great advantage of free discussion for democratic policymakers is its bringing to light of new ideas and its supplanting of old myths with new realities. We Americans are much in need of this benefit, because we are severely, if not uniquely, afflicted with a habit of policy-making by analogy: North Vietnam's involvement in South Vietnam, for example, is equated with Hitler's invasion of Poland, and a parley with the Vietcong would represent another Munich. The treatment of slight and superficial resemblances as if they were full-blooded analogies—as instances, as it were, of history repeating itself—is a substitute for thinking and a misuse of history. The value of history is not what it seems to prohibit or to prescribe but its general indications as to the kinds of policies that are likely to succeed and the kinds that are likely to fail or, as one historian has suggested, its hints as to what is likely not to happen. . . .

In addition to its usefulness for redeeming error and introducing new ideas, free and open criticism has a third, more abstract, but

no less important, function in a democracy. It is therapy and catharsis for those who are troubled or dismayed by something their
country is doing; it helps to reassert traditional values, to clear the
air when it is full of tension and mistrust. There are times, in public life as in private life, when one must protest, not solely or even
primarily because one's protest will be politic or materially productive but because one's sense of decency is offended, because one
is fed up with political craft and public images, or simply because
something goes against the grain. The catharsis thus provided may
indeed be the most valuable of freedom's uses.

While not unprecedented, protests against a war in the middle
of the war are a rare experience for Americans. I see it as a mark
of strength and maturity that an articulate minority have raised
their voices against the Vietnamese war and that the majority of
Americans are enduring this dissent, not without anxiety, to be
sure, but with better grace and understanding than has been the
case in any other war of the twentieth century.

It is by no means certain that the relatively healthy atmosphere
in which the debate is now taking place will not give way to a new
era of McCarthyism. The longer the Vietnamese war goes on without prospect of victory or negotiated peace, the [higher] war fever
will rise; hopes will give way to fears, and tolerance and freedom
of discussion will give way to a false and strident patriotism. In
Mark Twain's novel *The Mysterious Stranger,* a benevolent and
clairvoyant Satan said the following about war and its effects:

There has never been a just one, never an honorable one—on the
part of the instigator of the war. I can see a million years ahead,
and this rule will never change in so many as half a dozen instances.
The loud little handful—as usual—will shout for the war. The pulpit
will—warily and cautiously—object—at first; the great, big, dull bulk
of the nation will rub its sleepy eyes and try to make out why there
should be a war, and will say, earnestly and indignantly, "It is unjust and dishonorable and there is no necessity for it." Then the
handful will shout louder. A few fair men on the other side will
argue and reason against the war with speech and pen, and at first
will have a hearing and be applauded; but it will not last long;
those others will outshout them, and presently the antiwar audiences
will thin out and lose popularity. Before long you will see this
curious thing: the speakers stoned from the platform, and free
speech strangled by hordes of furious men who in their secret hearts
are still at one with those stoned speakers—as earlier—but do not
dare to say so. And now the whole nation—pulpit and all—will take
up the war cry, and shout itself hoarse, and mob an honest man who
ventures to open his mouth; and presently such mouths will cease

to open. Next the statesmen will invent cheap lies putting the blame upon the nation that is attacked, and every man will be glad of those conscience-soothing falsities, and will diligently study them and refuse to examine any refutations of them; and thus he will by and by convince himself that the war is just, and will thank God for the better sleep he enjoys after this process of grotesque self-deception.

Past experience provides little basis for confidence that reason can prevail in an atmosphere of mounting war fever. In a contest between a hawk and dove, the hawk has a great advantage, not because it is a better bird, but because it is a bigger bird with lethal talons and a highly developed will to use them. Without illusions as to the prospect of success, we must try, nonetheless, to bring reason and restraint into the emotionally charged atmosphere in which the Vietnamese war is now being discussed. Instead of trading epithets about the legitimacy of debate and about who is and is not giving "aid and comfort" to the enemy, we would do well to focus calmly and deliberately on the issue itself, recognizing that all of us make mistakes and that mistakes can only be corrected if they are acknowledged and discussed, and recognizing, further, that war is not its own justification, that it can and must be discussed unless we are prepared to sacrifice our traditional democratic processes to a false image of national unanimity.

In fact, the protesters against the Vietnamese war are in good historical company. On January 12, 1848, Abraham Lincoln rose in the U.S. House of Representatives and made a speech about the Mexican War worthy of Senator [Wayne] Morse. Lincoln's speech was an explanation of a vote he had recently cast in support of a resolution declaring that the war had been unnecessary and unconstitutionally begun by President Polk. "I admit," he said, "that such a vote should not be given in mere wantonness, and that the one given is justly censurable if it have no other, or better foundation. I am one of those who joined in that vote; and I did so under my best impression of the truth of the case."

That is exactly what the students and professors and politicians who oppose the Vietnam war have been doing: They have been acting on their "best impression of the truth of the case." Some of our superpatriots assume that any war the United States fights is a just war, if not, indeed, a holy crusade, but history does not sustain their view. No reputable historian would deny that the United States has fought some wars which were unjust, unnecessary, or both—I would suggest the War of 1812, the Civil War, and the Spanish-American War as examples. In a historical frame of reference, it seems to me logical and proper to question the wisdom of our present military involvement in Asia.

The wisdom and productivity of the protest movement of students, professors, clergy, and others may well be questioned, but their courage, decency, and patriotism cannot be doubted. At the very least, the student protest movement of the 1960's is a moral and intellectual improvement on the panty raids of the 1950's. In fact, it is a great deal more: It is an expression of the national conscience and a manifestation of traditional American idealism. I agree with the editorial comment of last October's very interesting issue of the *Johns Hopkins Magazine*, in which it was suggested that the "new radical" movement "is not shallow and sophomoric, it is not based on the traditional formula of generational defiance, and it is not the result of an infusion of foreign ideologies. It is based instead on personal disenchantment and the feeling of these radicals that they must repudiate a corrupted vision of society and replace it with a purer one."

Protesters against the Vietnamese war have been held up to scorn on the ground that they wish to "select their wars," by which it is apparently meant that it is hypocritical to object to this particular war while not objecting to war in general. I fail to understand what is reprehensible about trying to make moral distinctions between one war and another, between, for example, resistance to Hitler and intervention in Vietnam. From the time of Grotius to the drafting of the United Nations Charter, international lawyers have tried to distinguish between "just wars" and "unjust wars." It is a difficult problem of law and an even more difficult problem of morality, but it is certainly a valid problem and, far from warranting contempt, those who try to solve it deserve our sympathy and respect.

There can be no solution to a problem until it is first acknowledged that there is a problem. When [*former Presidential Press Secretary*] Moyers reported, with respect to the Vietnam protests, the President's "surprise that any one citizen would feel toward his country in a way that is not consistent with the national interest," he was denying the existence of the problem as to where, in fact, the national interest lies. The answer, one must concede, is elusive, but there is indeed a question and it is a sign of the good health of this nation that the question is being widely and clearly posed. . . .

The good order and democracy of our society, therefore, depend on the keeping open of these channels. As long as every tendency of opinion among our people can get a full and respectful hearing from the elected representatives of the people, the teach-ins and the draft-card burnings and the demonstrations are unlikely to become the principal forms of dissent in America. It is only when Congress fails to challenge the executive, when the opposition fails to oppose, when politicians join in a spurious consensus behind controversial policies, that the campuses and streets and public squares of America are likely to become the forums of a direct and disorderly democracy.

It is the joint responsibility of politicians and opinion leaders in the universities and elsewhere to keep open the channels of communication between the people and their Government. . . .

The Senate as a whole, I think, should undertake to revive and strengthen the deliberative function which it has permitted to atrophy in the course of twenty-five years of crisis. Acting on the premise that dissent is not disloyalty, that a true consensus is shaped by airing our differences rather than suppressing them, the Senate should again become, as it used to be, an institution in which the great issues of American politics are contested with thoroughness, energy, and candor. Nor should the Senate allow itself to be too easily swayed by executive pleas for urgency and unanimity, or by allegations of aid and comfort to the enemies of the United States made by officials whose concern may be heightened by a distaste for criticism directed at themselves.

In recent months, the Senate Committee on Foreign Relations has engaged in an experiment in public education. The committee has made itself available as a forum for the meeting of politicians and professors and, more broadly, as a forum through which recognized experts and scholars could help increase congressional and public understanding of the problems associated with our involvement in Vietnam and our relations with Communist China. It is my hope that this experiment will not only contribute to public education but will help to restore the Senate to its proper role as adviser to the President on the great issues of foreign policy. . . . [*See Chapter VIII.*]

In conclusion, I reiterate the theme . . . that, as a nation extraordinarily endowed with human and material resources, as a nation which is a synthesis of many nations, America has the possibility of escaping that fatal arrogance which so often in the past has been the legacy of great power; that it has the possibility, instead of seeking to remake the world in its own image, of helping to bring about some reconciliation, perhaps even some synthesis, of the rival ideologies of our time.

None of us—student, professor, politician, or private citizen— can advance this aim by uncritical support of the policies of the moment. All of us have the responsibility to act upon higher patriotism, which is to love our country less for what it is than for what we would like it to be.

The Problem of Dissent

— HENRY STEELE COMMAGER

A noted American historian and author, Professor Commager has long been concerned with the problem of dissent in a democratic society. His Majority Rule and Minority Rights *(1943) and* Freedom, Loyalty, Dissent *(1954) are considered classic works on the subject. The following article appeared in* The Saturday Review, December 18, 1965.

It is barely two months now since Pope Paul VI made his historic plea to the United Nations and to the peoples of the world for an end to war and a restoration of brotherhood. "No more war. War never again," he said, and the whole nation applauded his noble plea. But when young men and women from our colleges and universities take the papal plea in good faith, and demonstrate against the war in Vietnam, they are overwhelmed with a torrent of recrimination and obloquy that is almost hysterical. Even students catch the contagion. "We're sick and tired of peaceniks" shriek the students of the Catholic Manhattan College. Are they sick and tired of Pope Paul, who said, "It is peace that must guide the destinies of mankind"?

Surely it is time to bring a little clarity and common sense to the discussion of this matter of student protests and demonstrations.

First, as Attorney General Katzenbach has reminded us, there is no question about the right of students—or of others—to agitate, to demonstrate, to protest in any nonviolent manner against policies they consider misguided. That is, after all, not only a right but a necessity if our democracy is to function. People who ought to know better—Senator Dodd of Connecticut, for example—have loosely identified agitation with "treason." [*See Senator Dodd's evaluation of the teach-ins, Chapter VII.*] Treason is the one crime defined in the Constitution, and the Senator would do well to read that document before he flings loose charges of treason about. Students have the same right to agitate and demonstrate against what they think unsound policies—even military policies—as have businessmen to agitate against the TVA or doctors against Medicare. . . . Businessmen and doctors and lawyers, to be sure, funnel their protests through respectable organizations like chambers of commerce, or the American Medical Association, or the American, and state, bar associations, or resort to well-paid lobbyists to express their discontent; students have no such effective organizations, nor can they support lobbying. To penalize them for their weakness and their poverty is to repeat the error of the Cleveland Administration in arresting Coxey's army for walking on the grass, or of the Hoover Administration in sending soldiers to destroy the pitiful Bonus Army. The rich and respectable have always had their ways of making their discontent heard; the poor and the unorganized must resort to protests and marches and demonstrations. Such methods have not customarily been considered un-American.

Second, we are not yet legally at war with Vietnam, though what is going on there has, to be sure, the character of war. Nor are we acting in Vietnam under the authority or the auspices of the United Nations, as we did in the Korean crisis. We are in Vietnam as a result of executive decision and executive action, and it is not yet traitorous or unpatriotic to criticize executive action. In so far as they were consulted on the matter, the American people voted, in 1964, for the candidate who appeared to promise them peace in Vietnam and against the candidate who advocated war. It was not thought unpatriotic for President Johnson to demonstrate against war in Vietnam in 1964; what has changed in the past year is not the law or the principle, but Presidential policy, and it is not unpatriotic to fail to change when the President changes his policy.

But, it is said, whatever the legal situation, war is a fact. We do have 165,000 men in Vietnam; we do send our bombers out every day to rain destruction on our "enemies" there. The time for discussion, therefore, has passed; we must close ranks behind our Government.

What is the principle behind this line of reasoning? What but that it is right and proper to protest an error—or what seemed even to President Johnson to be an error, as long as it was a modest one, but that it is unpatriotic to protest an error when it is immense. If this is sound logic, the moral for men in high position is clear. If any policy upon which you are embarked excites criticism, expand it, enlarge it, pledge all of your resources to it; then criticism will be unpatriotic and critics will be silenced. A little error is fair game for critics, but a gigantic error, an error that might plunge us into a world war, is exempt from criticism. . . .

Third, there is the now popular argument that whatever the logic of protests, they are intolerable because they might give comfort to the enemy. Whatever may be said for the sentiment behind this argument, it can be said with certainty that it runs counter not only to logic but to history and tradition as well. When George III resolved on war against rebellious colonies, nineteen lords signed a solemn protest against the war; the Commander-in-Chief of the Army, Lord Jeffery Amherst, refused to serve; the highest commanding naval officer, Admiral Keppel, refused to serve; Lieutenant General Frederick Cavendish resigned his commission. We do not think poorly of them today for refusing to fight in what they thought an unjust war, and Amherst College is not about to change its name to Lord North. . . .

But, it will be said, as it is always said, that this war is different. Whether history will judge this war to be different or not, we cannot say. But this we can say with certainty: A government and a society that silences those who dissent is one that has lost its way. This we can say: What is essential in a free society is that there should be an atmosphere where those who wish to dissent and even to demonstrate can do so without fear of recrimination or vilification.

What is the alternative? What is implicit in the demand, now, that agitation be silenced, that demonstrators be punished? What is implicit in the insistence that we "pull up by the roots and rend to pieces" the protests from students—it is Senator Stennis we are quoting here. What is implicit in the charge that those who demonstrate against the war are somehow guilty of treason?

It is, of course, this: that, once our Government has embarked upon a policy, there is to be no more criticism, protest, or dissent. All must close ranks and unite behind the Government.

Now we have had a good deal of experience, first and last, with this view of the duty of the citizen to his government and it behooves us to recall that experience before we go too far astray.

We ourselves had experience with this philosophy in the antebellum South. The dominant forces of Southern life were, by the 1840's, convinced that slavery was a positive good, a blessing alike for slaves and for masters; they were just as sure of the righteousness of the "peculiar institution" as is Senator Dodd of the righteousness of the war in Vietnam. And they adopted a policy that so many Senators now want to impose upon us: that of silencing criticism and intimidating critics. Teachers who attacked slavery were deprived of their posts—just what Mr. Nixon now advises as the sovereign cure for what ails our universities! Editors who raised their voices in criticism of slavery lost their papers. Clergymen who did not realize that slavery was enjoined by the Bible were forced out of their pulpits. Books that criticized slavery were burned. In the end, the dominant forces of the South got their way: Critics were silenced. The South closed its ranks against critics and closed its mind; it closed, too, every avenue of solution to the slavery problem except that of violence.

Nazi Germany provides us with an even more sobering spectacle. There, too, under Hitler, opposition to government was equated with treason. Those who dared question the inferiority of Jews, or the justice of the conquest of inferior peoples like the Poles, were effectually silenced by exile or by the gas chamber. With criticism and dissent eliminated, Hitler and his followers were able to lead their nation, and the world, down the path to destruction.

There is, alas, a tragic example of this attitude toward criticism before our eyes and in a people who inherit, if they do not cherish, our traditions of law and liberty. Like the slavocracy of the Old South, the dominant leaders of South Africa today are convinced that whites are superior to Negroes, and that Negroes must not be allowed to enjoy the freedoms available to whites. To maintain this policy and to silence criticism—criticism coming from the academic community and from the press—they have dispensed with the traditions of due process and of fair trial, violated academic freedom, and are in process of destroying centuries of constitutional guarantees. And with criticism silenced, they are able to delude themselves that what they do is just and right.

Now, it would be absurd and iniquitous to equate our current policies toward Vietnam with the defense of slavery, or with Nazi or Afrikaner policies. But the point is not whether these policies have anything in common. The point is that when a nation silences criticism and dissent, it deprives itself of the power to correct its errors. The process of silencing need not be as savage as in Nazi Germany, or in South Africa today; it is enough that an atmosphere be created where men prefer silence to protest. As has been observed of book-burning, it is not necessary to burn books; it is enough to discourage men from writing them.

It cannot be too often repeated that the justification and the purpose of freedom of speech is not to indulge those who want to speak their minds. It is to prevent error and discover truth. There may be other ways of detecting error and discovering truth than that of free discussion, but so far we have not found them.

There is one final argument for silencing criticism that is reasonable and even persuasive. It is this: that critics of our Vietnam policy are, in fact, defeating their own ends. For by protesting and agitating, they may persuade the Vietcong, or the North Vietnamese, or the Chinese, that the American people are really deeply divided and that, if they but hold out long enough, the Americans will tire of the war and throw in the sponge. As there is, in fact, no likelihood of this, the critics are merely prolonging the agony of war.

These predictions about the effect of criticism in other countries are of course purely speculative. One thing that is not mere speculation is that American opinion is, in fact, divided; that's what all the excitement is about. We do not know how the Vietcong or the Chinese will react to the sounds of argument coming across the waters. Perhaps they will interpret criticism as a sign of American weakness. But perhaps they will interpret it as an indication of our reasonableness. And, assuredly, they will, if they have any understanding of these matters at all, interpret it as a sign of the strength of our democracy—that it can tolerate differences of opinion.

But there are two considerations here that invite our attention. First, if critics of our Vietnamese war are right, then some modification of our policy is clearly desirable; and those who call for such modification serve a necessary purpose. We do not know whether they are right or not. We will not find out by silencing them. Second, if government, or those in positions of power and authority, can silence criticism by the argument that such criticism might be misunderstood somewhere, then there is an end to all criticism, and perhaps an end to our kind of political system. For, men in authority will always think that criticism of their policies is dangerous. They will always equate their policies with patriotism and find criticism subversive. The Federalists found criticism of President Adams so subversive that they legislated to expel critics from the country. Southerners found criticism of slavery so subversive that they drove critics out of the South. Attorney General Palmer thought criticism of our Siberian misadventure—now remembered only with embarrassment—so subversive that he hounded the critics into prison for twenty-year terms. McCarthy found almost all teachers and writers so subversive that he was ready to burn down the libraries and close the universities. Experience should harden us against the argument that dissent and criticism are so dangerous that they must always give way to consensus.

And as for the argument that criticism may give aid and comfort to some enemy, that is a form of blackmail unworthy of those who profess it. If it is accepted, we have an end to genuine discussion of foreign policies, for it will inevitably be invoked to stop debate and criticism whenever that debate gets acrimonious or the criticism cuts too close to the bone. And, to the fevered mind of the FBI, the CIA, and some Senators, criticism always gives aid and comfort to the enemy or cuts too close to the bone.

"The only thing we have to fear," said Franklin Roosevelt, "is fear itself." That is as true in the intellectual and the moral realm as in the political and the economic. We do not need to fear ideas, but the censorship of ideas. We do not need to fear criticism but the silencing of criticism. We do not need to fear excitement or agitation in the academic community, but timidity and apathy. We do not need to fear resistance to political leaders, but unquestioning acquiescence in whatever policies those leaders adopt. We do not even need to fear those who take too literally the anguished pleas of a Pope Paul VI or the moral lessons of the Sermon on the Mount, but those who reject the notion that morality has any place in politics. For that, indeed, is to stumble and sin in the dark.

2. THE "GENOVESE CASE"

American Imperialism Confronts a Revolutionary World

— EUGENE D. GENOVESE

Professor Genovese, who teaches history at Rutgers University, delivered these remarks at that university's teach-in on April 23, 1965; slightly abridged.

Unlike some of my colleagues, I do not normally have the opportunity to discuss international politics with you as a natural and proper part of my classroom work. Since it is my own interest and inclination that has kept me from studying recent history, I have no complaint. I do, nevertheless, feel the loss and welcome this opportunity to present to you, this morning, what will be a frankly political assessment of the struggle for the underdeveloped world of which the war in Vietnam forms a part. As I understand the teach-in, it is not in any sense an enlarged classroom, but a place where professors and students can speak their minds on vital questions in a manner not ordinarily proper in class.

This freedom carries responsibility. I ought to make my framework clear at the outset and, in any case, I have no wish to hide any of my private intellectual or political commitments. But let me emphasize that in telling you where I stand on certain fundamental questions, it is, first, to put you on guard against my prejudices as you should be on guard against everyone's, especially your own, and second, to suggest that no matter how deep the ideological and political divisions among us, it is vital to our country's survival that we find a common basis on which to defend the peace. Those of you who know me know that I am a Marxist and a socialist. Therefore, unlike most of my distinguished colleagues here this morning, I do not fear or regret the impending Vietcong victory in Vietnam. I welcome it. Unlike most liberal and conservative opponents of the war, I do not believe that American foreign policy is stupid or irrational. I believe it to be intelligent, if crude, rational and predatory.

"We're defending freedom . . ." We're defending freedom by supporting Chiang Kai-shek, Tshombe, Franco, Salazar, whichever general is fronting in Saigon. Everyone, I think, will now recognize that this is nonsense. But perhaps we are defending our freedom and the freedom of some others by supporting these thugs. The implication here, I suppose, is that it is better to have a pro-American thug than an anti-American one and, by definition, all anti-Americans are thugs, so there we are.

I shall make no moral case against this argument, although it clearly reduces to ashes everything in the American sensibility that once made our country an inspiration for the world. Rather, let me focus on the immanent contradiction on which it breaks. If we support these men because there is no one better, what do we do when the opposition appears? Politically, economically, and morally, we are bound to help crush all opposition. All the more so since there will always be left-wing and Communist elements among these rebels. This contradiction has always been pointed out, not only in relation to countries ruled by dictators, but in relation to those ruled by exploitative upper classes, such as exist throughout much of Latin America. Our policy-makers are not stupid. They support corrupt and exploited regimes in Thailand, the Philippines, Iran, and everywhere, because those regimes meet two essential tests. Two, not one. They are willing to subvert their national economies to the exploitation of foreign capital and they are determined to hold the line against socialism at home and abroad.

These are, I suppose, solid virtues, but only from the point of view of those who would benefit from the exploitation of others and, of course, [from the point of view of] their ideologues. They have nothing to do with the freedom or welfare of the people of the United States, much less the freedom or welfare of the people of the Congo, or Iran, or Brazil. Notwithstanding the vast sums of American taxpayers' money that have been poured into colonial and neocolonial areas, I am at a loss to think of a single underdeveloped country that has been industrialized under American or other foreign capitalist auspices during our century. I am at a loss to think of one such country to match the achievements of the socialist countries, all of which were economically backward until recent decades. Despite wars and revolutions, despite the deformation of Stalinist bureaucratism, despite the most painful curtailment of civil liberties, these countries have avoided economic strangulation and have avoided the worst and most telling features of foreign domination—although, unfortunately, no small country can be truly and completely independent, especially in foreign policy, so long as the Cold War continues.

The aims of American foreign policy may be evaluated in relation to two cases. Our policy of fomenting the invasion of Cuba is defended on the grounds that Cuba is a potential military threat as a Russian base, and that Cuba is supporting revolutionary movements in Latin America. Let us forget that the United States, by President Kennedy's own admission, sponsored an invasion of Cuba and continues to support subversion there. Would the United States accept the Castro regime if firm guarantees against foreign military presence in Cuba were provided? And if Castro agreed to adequate verification techniques to prevent the shipment of arms and guerrillas abroad? Would the U.S. Government then enforce its own laws against harboring those who are actively engaged in trying to overthrow another country?

The threat from Cuba [lies in] its example and its ideology. Here is a small country rebuilding its distorted economy on a socialist basis, evicting foreign capital, and suggesting to others that they, too, are entitled to be masters in their own house.

But it is in relation to Vietnam that American policy stands completely naked. We were morally obligated, in 1954, to permit free elections in South and North Vietnam. We refused. We decided to defend freedom by putting the Diem regime in power. And you'll remember Diem. The American Government and *The New York Times*, which is almost as pure as the American Government, told us that Diem was a Christian, a democrat, a defender of the Free World. He was the first of a long line of those things in Saigon. Since then, we have defended freedom in South Vietnam by applying napalm to a people that every honest reporter admits would still overwhelmingly elect Ho Chi Minh. And so much for the defense of freedom.

The United States, some say, cannot permit Chinese expansion across Asia, cannot permit Chinese military domination of the Far East. I do not believe that China is expansionist or a threat to its neighbors, but let us grant the fear and deal with it. If the fear is genuine, then American policy ought to be willing to support any regime, capitalist or Communist, which would maintain Vietnamese independence against Chinese encroachment. European opinion, measured by the press, repeatedly makes an unanswerable point that the only force in all Vietnam willing and able to maintain the independence of the country is the Communist Party under the leadership of Ho Chi Minh. That is, if Chinese military expansion were our real fear, as apparently it is De Gaulle's real fear, we could deal with it firmly, if roughly, in the following manner: . . . A complete withdrawal and agreement to unification under Communist or other viable auspices—and I think, in this case, it will have to be Communist—on the condition that Vietnamese troops under no circumstances cross [Vietnam's] borders and on the condition that absolutely no foreign military bases be permitted in Vietnamese territory. I cannot be sure, but I think that we could swing that deal in two hours.

Now, the question is, what would guarantee it? What would guarantee that Ho Chi Minh and Mao Tse-tung would keep their part of the bargain? What guarantees Turkey against a Russian attack? Certainly not an American air base. What guarantees Turkey, and would guarantee the peace in Vietnam, is the simple assertion by the United States, under conditions which [would leave no] doubt about our seriousness, that a violation of the treaty would mean all out war with the parties involved and those who support them. The Russians do not doubt our commitment to Berlin or Turkey. We did not doubt their commitment to the Communist regime in Hungary. That clarity of purpose is all the guarantee that either side ever needs. Consider, too, that the Vietcong have fought at least since World War II—first as the Vietminh against the French, and now against the United States and its puppet regime. And for what? Can anyone seriously believe that the Vietnamese Communists, including Ho Chi Minh and his political and military leaders, have lived in caves, starved themselves, risked their lives, shed their blood in order to make foreigners the masters of their country? These men have fought for national independence and socialist reconstruction. They mean to have both.

What, then, is the Pentagon trying to do there? May I suggest that Washington would like nothing better than to reduce Ho Chi Minh to the status of a Chinese puppet. They will not succeed, I think, as much because of China as because of North Vietnam, but we may leave that aside. If we can demonstrate to all the underdeveloped countries that choose a revolutionary socialist path, that they will have to face napalm, mass extermination, the most brutal oppression, perhaps we can slow down the process of socialist revolution and convince many to abandon the attempt. This is a rational and sophisticated policy. It is also a policy that completely fails to understand the origins of these movements and that completely underestimates the quality of the opposition. It is a policy that will end in a debacle. But not before it slaughters millions, unless the American people call a halt.

Our policy in Vietnam is a policy of exacting a murderous price from the Vietnamese and, if possible, of provoking the Chinese so as to provide an excuse to punish Chinese cities and atomic installations. But remember that the Chinese Communists fought a twenty-year war for power, from caves, literally, and under every possible deprivation; I think only fools think that they are going to be cowed or bluffed. They are not 10 feet tall and they are not supermen, but they are men, and they are determined to defend what they want; it would be the gravest of miscalculations to think otherwise. Then, I suppose, the question of the H-Bomb will have to be faced. The end of that road is the end of our own country as well as of much of the world. This policy is rational, but it is the rational desperation of men defending a social order that cannot be defended. Lyndon Johnson is not an evil man. I have to say that; I do believe it, but I have to say it if only for the reason I voted for the man—and what else can I say? You will recall that we voted for him last November because we didn't want the war in Vietnam escalated.

Today on our campus there are placards agitating for an accelerated war effort in Vietnam. Now this puzzles me a little bit. During the 1930's, many left-wingers and middle-class Democrats of all sorts advocated war against fascism in general and Franco in particular. They advocated war as an instrument of policy. They carried out their convictions. They went to Spain, they bled, and they died. Now, is it too much to ask that when our drum beaters advocate war, they stand by their convictions with similar resolve? We could respect their position if they held it sincerely. But the test of their sincerity is just this: He who believes in this war, if he is physically able, ought to fight it.

The test of patriotism is the defense of our national honor. Our country once stood for freedom, for national independence, for the right of self-determination, and those values still pertain. The duty of all Americans is to expose and defeat those who are making our country the most hated country on earth. America's war in Vietnam is a war of aggression. It is aimed at containing a rival social and economic system and punishing those who move toward it. In opposing that war, we defend the best of our own heritage. We defend the honor and the image of our people and our nation. Patriotism today demands firm and unswerving opposition to our Government's policy, neither more, nor less.

The American people shall, I hope, force a just and decent settlement in Vietnam, one that will restore the country to the Vietnamese while guaranteeing the legitimate interests of all powers. But then what? If we are to have done with Vietnam, we shall have to do a good deal more and the American people will have to do it. I mean we will have to uproot this social order and replace it with one that has no need to throttle anybody and, when we do so, then and only then will America have realized its promise of civilization and civilized values. For a socialist America—that is to say [an America] combining a socialist economy and social structure with that priceless heritage of Anglo-Saxon liberty to which it is heir—will then, without sham, be able to lead the world, the whole world, to the era of peace and accomplishment we all seek.

Report on the "Genovese Case"

—ASSEMBLYMEN WILLIAM V. MUSTO
AND DOUGLAS E. GIMSON

> *These are extracts from a report (June 28, 1965) prepared for the General Assembly of the State of New Jersey after Professor Genovese had come under attack by various individuals, political figures, and organizations in New Jersey. Assemblymen Musto and Gimson met with President Mason Gross of Rutgers to review the law and university regulations pertinent to the case.*

On April 23, 1965, a "Vietnam Teach-In" was conducted on the New Brunswick campus of Rutgers–The State University under the sponsorship of the Rutgers chapter of Students for a Democratic Society. It should be noted at this point that this "Vietnam Sit-In" [sic] was not a novel occurrence; similar discussions have been conducted at numerous colleges and universities and off-campus in recent months. President Lyndon B. Johnson and congressional leaders of both political parties have stated that such political discussions, even though highly critical of our foreign policies, should not be discouraged. Officials of our State Department have participated in such "sit-ins," and they have been broadcast and televised on national networks.

The primary concern expressed to the General Assembly was directed at certain statements which, it was reported, were made by Professor Eugene D. Genovese during the course of the "teach-in."

It is true that Professor Genovese stated that "Those of you who know me know that I am a Marxist and a socialist. Therefore, unlike most of my distinguished colleagues here this morning, I do not fear or regret the impending Vietcong victory in Vietnam. I welcome it. . . ." It is this statement of Professor Genovese that was primarily responsible for the expressions of concern and the requests for legislative inquiry addressed to the General Assembly and not his highly critical analysis and judgment of our foreign policies in Asia, Latin America, Africa, and, particularly, in Vietnam.

Professor Genovese offered [a] frank and forthright characterization of his personal political orientation and convictions at the "teach-in" apparently, in part at least, to explain his understanding of "teach-in" and his role in the "teach-in."

The Rutgers administration reports that Professor Genovese is regarded by historians outside Rutgers as an able and provocative historian and scholar.

The senior members of the History Department at Rutgers, the administration reports, regard Professor Genovese's work as "very good"; his colleagues consider him "superior to outstanding" in teaching effectiveness, research, scholarship, professional activities, and general usefulness. The administration reports that the comments of his students are "very favorable." . . .

The University regulations dealing with "academic freedom" provide that:

§3.91. The faculty are members of a great and honored profession; their conduct should be in accordance with standards dictated by law, professional ethics, and good morals, especially as members of the student body may be influenced by their example and the opinion of the public, with respect to the University, may depend in considerable measure on their acts and utterances.

§3.92. Since the very nature of a university and its value to society depend upon the free pursuit and dissemination of knowledge, every member of the faculty of this University is entitled, in the classroom and in research and in publication, freely to discuss subjects with which he is competent to deal, to pursue inquiry therein, and to present and endeavor to maintain his opinion and conclusions relevant thereto. While free to express those ideas which seem to him justified by the facts, he is expected to maintain standards of sound scholarship and competent teaching.

§3.93. Outside the fields of instruction, research, and publication, which are the subject of Section 3.92, the faculty member shall be free from institutional discipline unless his actions or utterances are both reprehensible and detrimental to the University.

The clause "to discuss subjects with which he is competent to deal," in Section 3.92, is interpreted by the administration, in regard to a professor's classroom activities at least, to mean those subjects which he is employed to teach. Inferentially, the professor's freedom "to present his opinion and conclusions" in the classroom does not extend to areas outside those he is employed to teach.

Conclusions and Recommendations

1. The inquiry of the undersigned disclosed no violation of the laws of this State nor any infraction of the university regulations. The administration reports its assurance that Professor Genovese

has not expressed his personal convictions and opinions in the classroom on subjects other than those with which he is competent to deal.

2. The undersigned disagree completely with Professor Genovese's views on the Vietnam situation and reject the Marxist and socialist objectives he professes to accept. They believe that the teacher has the privilege of freedom to search out and teach the truth and that he should be protected by the University and the State in the exercise of that freedom. Nor do they question the right to hold unorthodox views. Heterodoxy is essential to freedom and our way of life. Full and frank discussion of current issues and the presentation of all legitimate points of view are to be encouraged. There is no question of professional competence. The primary question, the undersigned believe, concerns the faculty members' obligations—statutory and extrastatutory—upon which his freedom rests.

3. Professor Genovese has been quoted as saying, "To be quite frank, I'm not certain what the commotion is all about" and that his political views "are my own business." (*The Sunday Home News*, New Brunswick, May 30, 1965.) The undersigned find it difficult to believe that a person of Professor Genovese's experience would not anticipate adverse reactions by a considerable segment of our citizens to his public avowal, as a faculty member of a state university, that he is a "Marxist and socialist" and that he welcomes "the impending Vietcong victory in Vietnam." Whether or not he was free to express those beliefs in the circumstances in which he expressed them, the undersigned believe—as many of our citizens do—that he should have foreseen the many expressions of concern and requests for formal administrative and legislative inquiry that did follow. To be anticipated also were the many questions, reflecting all shades of political belief, directed at the state legislature and calling for clear, explicit, and detailed definitions of academic freedom.

Nor can the undersigned accept the conclusion that a state university professor's political beliefs are his own business and no one else's. No freedom is unqualified. Academic freedom at our state university and colleges has at least one statutory limitation: He may not believe in, or advocate, unconstitutional means to change our government. The university regulations do not permit him to express his personal views in the classroom on subjects outside the subject areas with which he is competent to deal.

Furthermore, beyond any statutory and regulatory limitations, the undersigned believe there are others that necessarily flow from his membership in an honored profession and [from his position] as a faculty member at a state university, and from his role in the teacher-student relationship. This belief was incorporated in Section 3.92 of the university regulations prior to recent amendment:

> The teacher is a citizen, a member of a learned profession, and a representative of this university. Since the public may, because of his position, give special attention or credence to his utterances and tend to judge his profession or this university by his conduct, his position imposes on him the following special obligations: (1) that he bear these possibilities constantly in mind and seek at all times to conduct himself appropriately. . . .

Professor Genovese spoke at the "Vietnam Teach-In" as a citizen. But he was introduced as Professor Eugene Genovese. His audience included university students. The "teach-in" was held on the university campus. It was sponsored by a student organization approved and sanctioned by the university. To many reasonable citizens, the differences between such a "teach-in" and a classroom, and the differences in the limitations to express one's personal views in these two situations, are not clear. This indicates a need for a reappraisal of the pertinent university regulations. The undersigned, therefore, recommend to the General Assembly that it request the Board of Governors and the administration of Rutgers–The State University to reappraise at this time (1) the university regulations pertaining to academic freedom and the proper and reasonable limitations thereon, which should be defined and (2) their employment practices and procedures in this regard. The concern of our citizens is real and legitimate and should not be ignored.

Professor Genovese and Academic Freedom

— RICHARD M. NIXON

Letter to The New York Times, *October 27, 1965. For an expansion of the former Vice-President's views on the limits of academic freedom, see his remarks to the graduating class of the University of Rochester, June 5, 1966, reprinted in* The Saturday Review, *August 27, 1966.*

October 25, 1966

In accordance with the great tradition of *The Times* for complete and objective coverage of the news, you might want to carry

statements I made on the Genovese case which were omitted in
The Times news story of October 25.

Every American is for free speech and academic freedom. The
question is, how do we preserve that freedom?

We do so by recognizing and protecting the right of individuals
to freedom of speech.

We do so by defending the system of government which guarantees freedom of speech to individuals.

Unfortunately, there are occasions—particularly in wartime—
when the individual's rights and the nation's security come in conflict.

Justice Learned Hand summarized it best when he said, "A society in which men recognize no check on their freedom soon becomes a society in which freedom is the possession of only the
savage few."

In his recent speeches in New Jersey, Robert Kennedy, by contending, in effect, that the right to freedom of speech is absolute
and unrestricted, confused the fundamental issue involved in the
Genovese case.

He charged that Senator Dumont's demand for Professor Genovese's dismissal was the same as Governor Barnett's demand that
professors at the University of Mississippi who advocated integration should be discharged.

He completely missed the fundamental distinction between the
two cases. No one has questioned the right of Professor Genovese
or anyone else to advocate any controversial issue in peacetime.

The question in the Genovese case is whether a professor, employed by a state university, should have the right to use the prestige
and forum of the university for advocating victory for an enemy of
the United States in wartime.

The victory for the Vietcong which Professor Genovese "welcomes" would mean, ultimately, the destruction of freedom of
speech for all men for all time, not only in Asia but in the United
States as well.

The question at issue, therefore, becomes: Does the principle of
freedom of speech require that the state subsidize those who would
destroy the system of government which protects freedom of
speech?

We are confronted in the Genovese case with this choice:

The responsibility of the state to protect the right of freedom
of speech for an individual.

The responsibilty of the state to defend itself against enemies
whose victory would deny freedom of speech to all.

America's twentieth-century war Presidents, Woodrow Wilson and Franklin D. Roosevelt, were forced to make this cruel choice and, in both instances, they properly concluded that, in wartime, preservation of freedom for all the people must take precedence over the rights of an individual to exercise freedom of speech when it would serve the enemies of freedom.

Reports from Hanoi and Peking conclusively indicate that the demonstrations against our policy in Vietnam encourage the enemy, prolong the war and result in the deaths of American fighting men.

Our recognition of this unhappy truth does not mean that we suppress the views of all those who may oppose the war in Vietnam for ideological reasons. But there is a point at which a line must be drawn.

I say, as long as the demonstrators and those participating in teach-ins are acting in an individual and private capacity, no action should be taken to curtail their activities. But any individual employed by the state should not be allowed to use his position for the purpose of giving aid and comfort to the enemies of the state. Where the choice confronting us is between the lives of American men fighting to preserve the system which guarantees freedom of speech for all and the right of an individual to abuse that freedom, the lives of American fighting men must come first.

We must never forget that if the war in Vietnam is lost and the victory for the Communists, which Professor Genovese says he "welcomes," becomes inevitable, the right of free speech will be extinguished throughout the world.

RICHARD M. NIXON

Study in Academic Freedom

—ARNOLD BEICHMAN

Mr. Beichman is a free-lance writer specializing in political issues. This article, here abridged, appeared in The New York Times Magazine, *December 19, 1965.*

Thirteen years ago, Rutgers University forced the dismissal of two professors who had claimed protection of the Fifth Amendment in appearances before the Senate Internal Security Subcommittee. Questioned under oath about past or continuing membership in the Communist Party, the two men—[one] a Professor in the College of Pharmacy for twenty-seven years and [the other] a teacher of classics for four years—declined to answer and cited their constitutional guarantees against self-incrimination.

A Faculty Committee of Review recommended "no further action be taken" against the professors following their refusal to testify. Nevertheless, on December 12, 1952, the Rutgers Board of Trustees, supported by the then university president, concluded a two-and-a-half-month debate by voting, 39–12, that, unless the two men testified before the Senate subcommittee by the end of the year, their teaching appointments would be terminated. The professors ignored the ultimatum and, on December 31, they lost their jobs.

On Election Day last month, another battle over academic freedom at Rutgers came to a different ending. The Republican nominee for Governor of New Jersey, State Senator Wayne Dumont, had conducted a bitter campaign ostensibly against an expelled Communist Party member, now a professed "Marxist and socialist," teaching and enjoying tenure at Rutgers. Actually, Dumont's real target was incumbent Gov. Richard Hughes, for having refused to pressure the university into firing historian Eugene D. Genovese, a 35-year-old associate professor who had declared at a campus teach-in, on April 23:

"I do not fear or regret the impending Vietcong victory in Vietnam. I welcome it."

If public concern can be measured by election results, New Jersey voters were unmoved by Dumont's campaign outcries. Hughes won by 354,000 votes, a record margin in the state. Even Republican leaders who made pilgrimages to New Jersey to extol Dumont's other virtues—the pilgrims included Dwight D. Eisenhower and governors George Romney of Michigan, William Scranton of Pennsylvania, and John Chafee of Rhode Island—carefully steered clear of the Genovese issue. Only Richard M. Nixon echoed Dumont's protests over *l'affaire* Genovese. Such leading New Jersey Republicans as U.S. Senator Clifford Case and C. Douglas Dillon were openly critical of Dumont's tactics.

The general dismay over the character of Dumont's campaign revealed the remarkable change in attitudes toward academic freedom since the expulsions at Rutgers thirteen years ago. This time, demands for capitulation by the university were solidly opposed by the university's administration and its lay governing boards. More predictably, in a letter to Rutgers' President Mason Gross, Genovese's colleagues in the History Department expressed their support in this fashion:

> Some may assert that because he has described his intellectual position as Marxist, Professor Genovese cannot therefore perform acceptably as a scholar. The test here, we believe, would be the professional evaluation of the articles that he has published and the books that will appear within the next few months. Members of our department hold widely varying beliefs in religion, in ethics, and in social and political philosophy, but we do feel strongly that none of these beliefs in itself disqualifies a man as a teacher or a scholar.

The most important outside backing, of course, came from Governor Hughes. He refused to interfere, he said, on the assurance by Rutgers that Genovese "had observed the [university's] prohibition against using the classroom to mention his personal political viewpoint [and] that his position at the university is based not upon his political opinions but upon his reputation as a scholar."

In its most significant aspects, the Genovese case raised the problem of locating the outer limits of academic freedom more sharply than they had been for years. The limits change with the times, and the times are changing.

It has been quite obvious, for example, that with the gradual weakening of the Communist Party on the American campus, Communist membership alone is no longer regarded—as it once was by many people—as evidence of scholarly incapacity and, therefore, grounds for refusing academic tenure.

One debate nowadays is whether "Marxists, socialists" and others who do not belong to any "subversive" apparatus should enjoy the protections of academic freedom. Or, to consider the issue from the opposite political perspective, does a university have the right to fire a professor with tenure for praying that the Ku Klux Klan will win in the South? Though some liberals would squirm at the notion of defending a racist, the principles of academic freedom demand protection for professorial free speech.

Hughes's statement on Genovese defined the conventional bounds of academic freedom: A professor can speak on an off-campus soapbox as long as his classroom does not become a propaganda forum for his "personal political viewpoint." But the soapbox and the classroom are often indistinguishable as far as the public is concerned; in fact, it is being argued that, in his role as teacher, the professor is entitled to use his classroom as a soapbox and can hardly avoid doing so.

Such questions demonstrate the difficulty of specifically defining academic freedom. (Can any freedom ever be inclusively defined?) To complicate the issue, the professor not only enjoys rights as a teacher; he is a scholar and citizen, too, and each of his three roles involves problems of academic freedom that provoke overlapping controversies.

The academician who stirred the latest debate is a specialist in Southern history and the institution of slavery and the author of a recently published book, *The Political Economy of Slavery.* . . . While at Brooklyn College, at 17, he became an open Communist Party member and organizer for the Communist-front youth organization American Youth for Democracy. But because of disagreements on Communist Party tactics, he was expelled three years later, he says, charged with being "anti-Semitic, anti-Negro, and a Browderite right-wing deviationist."

"The real reason for my expulsion," Genovese explains, "was I zigged when I was supposed to zag. Actually, I should have been expelled because I was violating party discipline." . . .

After ten months [in the Army], he was discharged for having been a Communist Party member, a fact he had not concealed from the authorities. Attending Columbia University graduate school, he received his Ph.D. in 1959, with a dissertation entitled "The Agricultural Reform Movement in the Slave South." His first teaching job was at Brooklyn Polytechnic Institute, in 1960, and, in 1963, having complied with the New Jersey loyalty oath prohibition against membership in "subversive" organizations, he was appointed an assistant professor at Rutgers. Last spring he was promoted to associate professor with full tenure. . . .

The basic academic freedom issue raised by the Genovese case concerned the right of an academician, as a citizen, to discuss anything he wants, whether he is an expert in the subject or not. This thesis was recently summarized by Professor Robert A. Nisbet, of the University of California at Riverside, who wrote in the current issue of *The Public Interest*:

> It is, today at least, the very essence of academic freedom that a faculty member's views on matters outside his stated professional competence—however shocking these views may be, however suggestive prima facie of want of ordinary intelligence or moral responsibility—shall not be held against him when he is being considered for retention or promotion. Academic freedom, so conceived, justifies itself not by what it grants the individual but what it does for the university. We have learned that it is absolutely necessary to the search for, and the communication of, knowledge. It is an essential attribute of the university; not a special privilege of the individual.

A somewhat different viewpoint was expressed by Dr. Grayson Kirk, President of Columbia University. In an essay adapted from his last commencement-day address and published in the *Columbia University Forum*, he declared:

Academic freedom for a professor means that his career may not be jeopardized by the expression of his views to his students or to the public. But, however much a professor may assert his rights as a citizen to speak out on any topic, he ought to think twice before he makes a ringing public declaration on a controversial subject, particularly if it is far removed from his own field of scholarly competence. He should hesitate before doing so simply because, no matter how loud or sincere his disclaimers, he can never entirely shed his scholar's gown.

It may well be that when he seeks to take off his academic gown he will have beneath it only the emperor's clothes, but he cannot escape a certain popular presumption of intellectual authority—and he has the responsibility not to abuse it. A scholar has an implied professional commitment to approach all issues in the spirit of a judge rather than as an advocate. . . . When a scholar fails to keep this admonition in mind, in the long run he puts in danger the public acceptance of the essential integrity of the university.

Professor Richard Hofstadter, Columbia's Pulitzer Prize-winning historian and co-author of *The Development of Academic Freedom in the United States*, believes that professional competence is no longer the test. "Now the question is, basically, the rights of a professor as a citizen," he said in an interview. [He went on to say]

Today the model for academic freedom should be civil liberties.

Perhaps it should be one's moral imperative to think twice before speaking. Yet most voters make decisions without much information and, of course, the experts can be wrong. It's up to the public to know that the professor of mathematics is wrong about the Dominican Republic but the professor of mathematics isn't thereby obliged to shut up.

Usually, I should add, these warnings against half-baked opinions are made when the opinions are heterodox. One rarely hears such warnings if the professor agrees with public policy, however stupid that policy may be.

Professor Walter P. Metzger of Columbia is co-author with Hofstadter of *The Development of Academic Freedom in the United States*. For ten years he has been a member of the potent Committee A of the American Association of University Professors, which investigates issues of academic freedom and tenure. Metzger feels strongly that a professor should not use his lectern as a pulpit and should avoid irrelevant discussion. He cites the AAUP principle on academic freedom: "The teacher is entitled to freedom in the classroom in discussing his subject, but he should be careful not to introduce into his teaching controversial matter which has no relation to his subject." Yet, concedes Professor Metzger, this caveat is "unenforceable, because the classroom is as private as the confessional."

The academic profession seems agreed that a professor is entitled, as a scholar, to argue any position within his area of expertise even though that position may represent a minority of one. The test is the quality of his scholarship and research.

Much more controversy surrounds the professor's role as teacher in the classroom and as citizen in the public forum. Rutgers University regulations on academic freedom provide that "outside the fields of instruction, research, and publication . . . the faculty member shall be free from institutional discipline unless his actions or utterances are both reprehensible and detrimental to the university."

Is the teacher free to press his political opinions in the classroom? Theoreticians of academic freedom offer no clear answer, but in practice it seems that more militant professors have seized the right and university administrations have been more or less compelled to back them up. The alliance is based on two factors: the greater bargaining power of the individual professor in a society that has elevated education to new eminence, and the increased politicalization of the American campus.

"The academic market place has changed greatly," explains Professor Richard P. McCormick, acting-Chairman of the Rutgers History Department and the official university historian.

In the old days, a man expected to remain an assistant professor for six years before he got tenure. Today, this is out the window. If you've published one book, you're an associate professor—with tenure. The old slogan "publish or perish" doesn't apply any more. Today it's "publish and prosper."

At the same time, something is happening in the academic profession. It is becoming more politically committed and concerned. Therefore, the academic community must clarify its responsibility and its understanding of that responsibility in dealing with a political problem on the campus and in the classroom. Some professors believe a man's political views should be pushed in the classroom; not only should he have a commitment, they say, but he should also preach it.

Professor Genovese believes that, as a teacher, not only does he have a right to discuss his political beliefs in the classroom, but the subject he teaches makes such discussion inevitable.

I teach Southern history and Negro history up to the present day, and I must discuss civil rights. Whatever I say in my analysis of the civil rights battle is affected by my politics. You can't avoid these issues.

On the other hand, I don't believe in digressions, because they're an insult to the students. A man has a professional responsibility to teach his material. Yet the material often overlaps between past and present. The history of abolitionism, for example, shows how the dynamics of a small, unpopular group in America affected politics through the radicalism of its stance. It can be related to present problems and the students can draw their own conclusions.

It happens that I don't teach abolitionism this way because I'm distrustful of historical analogies and I don't push them too far. But, if I wanted to direct this comparison between the abolitionists and contemporary extremist groups, I would regard that as o.k. as long as there was no proselytizing.

As for propagandizing in the classroom, everybody does it and I do it, minimally. I regard propagandizing in the classroom as distasteful because it's a captive audience. A professor who isn't teaching his subject will acquire a reputation accordingly and suffer professionally. But if he's skillful in relating his political views to his material, that's a strong prima-facie case that he's a good teacher.

Of course, the classroom lends itself to all kinds of abuses. If you're going to have maximum freedom of inquiry, you have to suffer windbags, fools, and people with axes to grind. The question is whether the university is strong enough and self-confident enough to absorb these abuses in order to do the job it has to do. If it isn't, then you can't have universities.

Professor Daniel Bell, Chairman of Columbia's Sociology Department, believes a professor invariably brings his intellectual prejudices into the classroom. Yet, as long as they are openly labeled as prejudices, not "true knowledge," then the professor has a right to do so.

"A man is hired to teach a subject," said Bell. "As long as he does not conceal contrary evidence, he has a right to his beliefs. For example, he may be a great admirer of the Soviet Union. But if he denies the existence of famines under Stalin, if he denies the facts about the Soviet Union, then that's another matter. In any case, other faculty members are free to combat him."

Professor Bell's chief objection to the Dumont campaign in New

Jersey was the Republican candidate's statement that academic freedom "does not give to a teacher in a state university, supported by taxpayers' money, the right to advocate victory of an enemy in war, in which some of his own students may very well lay down their lives in the cause of freedom."

"This is really a most threatening statement," said Bell. "The taxpayers' money supports the one person out of seven who today earns a living by working for some branch of government or a government agency. But, according to Dumont, somehow, if you're working for the federal, state or city government, your free-speech rights are restricted, unlike the rights of citizens in private employment. This is setting up a double standard."

The greater liberality of faculty members, college administrations, and the general public toward academic freedom is unquestionably due to the tremendous importance of higher education in the country today. This change in atmosphere is recent. Professor Hofstadter, in his book *Anti-Intellectualism in American Life,* has noted that while "anti-intellectualism in various forms continues to pervade American life . . . at the same time intellect has taken on a new and more positive meaning and intellectuals have come to enjoy more acceptance and, in some ways, a more satisfactory position."

Thus, Rutgers President Mason Gross warned that "the consequences for Rutgers would be disastrous" if the university deviated from the principles of academic freedom in the Genovese case. Gross said he feared "censure and probable loss of accreditation. This, in turn, would result in loss of faculty and great difficulty in recruiting new faculty." Loss of accreditation could also mean difficulty for Rutgers students who apply to graduate schools.

In short, the college teacher today lives in a seller's market. If he is halfway good and productive, he can pick his employer and expect rapid promotion. And in a seller's market, the academician has the kind of power over his terms of employment that he lacked in previous generations.

Flexing its muscles, the academic profession has now begun to discuss the need to examine hiring policies by university administrations. Since dismissals on ideological grounds can be masked, especially if the faculty member lacks tenure, full disclosure of hiring policies would make it tougher for officials subsequently to fire a professor on some pretext that would not arouse the suspicions of the AAUP's vigilant Committee A.

Committee A veteran Walter Metzger says:

In America, academic dismissals on any ground are infrequent; academic dismissals based on utterances are still more infrequent. In the major institutions, intramural relationships have a benign, if not a halcyon, appearance. What is significant about the extreme example, the case that seldom occurs, is the illumination it throws on morbid tendencies that lie beneath the smiling surface and often escape our view.

In this double meaning, the Genovese case revealed its share of morbidity and hope. It may also have provided a glimpse into the future.

In an era of the antihero, the antitheater, the antinovel and anti-art, will the professor seeking self-realization subvert himself into becoming the anti-academician?

VI

The Teach-In and the Intellectual

Editors' Introduction

The declaration, in 1960, by leading French intellectuals refusing to support their government's colonial war in Algeria, was the most notable act of conscience over patriotism in recent European history. In the American experience, too, there have been clashes of moral sensibility and patriotic acquiescence, and American armed involvement abroad has generally evoked a certain amount of open criticism from our intellectuals; sometimes it has taken the form of civil disobedience and political action. Henry David Thoreau preferred jail to paying taxes while his country warred on Mexico, in 1846; Edward Atkinson organized opposition to hostilities with Spain, in 1898; Randolph Bourne excoriated American intellectuals for keeping silent when the United States decided to enter World War I. Nevertheless, although many other examples might be cited, they cannot be said to comprise a sustained tradition of American academic or intellectual dissent. It is this generation of professors and students that may be creating one.

The extent to which "the craft of the intellect" should allow political engagement is the general theme of this chapter. It opens with Professor Germaine Brée's University of Wisconsin Teach-In address on commitment in the experience of two famous French intellectuals. The issues brought into focus by Professor Brée's interpretation of the Sartre-Camus debates are as relevant to present-day American teachers, students, artists, and authors as they were to French intellectuals in the decade immediately following World War II.

Much of the opposition to academic protest has centered on the argument that many of the dissident professors are in fields unrelated to foreign affairs; hence, the argument goes, they are poorly equipped to criticize American policy abroad. One analyst, for example, demonstrates that the antiwar academics tend to be in fields where "no training, experience, knowledge, or perspective on foreign policy, Communism, or Vietnam is either required or assumed" and, conversely, that "recognized U.S. scholars" in these fields are supporters rather than critics of existing foreign policy. (Rodger Swearingen, "The Vietnam Critics in Perspective," *Communist Affairs*, IV, No. 3 [May–June, 1966]; see also Thomas Conlon's remarks in Chapter IV.)

One might object that the Vietnam war offers poor soil for such arguments. Supposed Government expertise, comprised in part of the advice of "recognized U.S. scholars" in the field of foreign policy, has thus far proven to be badly shortsighted in the basic assumptions, predictions, and policies governing the commitment of increasing numbers of American troops to combat. Further, the whole notion of relying on the authority of "experts" is open to question—and sometimes sharply condemned, as by drama critic Eric Bentley. Mr. Bentley's article is, in itself, proof that nonspecialists are capable of perceptive and critical scrutiny of official rhetoric.

An opposing view, voiced by Professor Russell Kirk, is that, although the scholar has a right to be as concerned with public policy as any other citizen, his primary commitment should be to scholarship. Professor Kirk's fear is that the scholar's political commitment will lead to "action ungoverned by reflection," which in turn will hurt both honest scholarship and practical politics. The motives that move scholars to overt commitment are examined by Professor David Krech. Dr. Krech is typical of those academics who find Russell Kirk's admonition unconvincing. Not only should intellectuals challenge what they believe to be incorrect, Dr. Krech argues, but they should protest loudly and clearly, "with the hot conviction of a man whose passion has been aroused." For Dr. Krech, the slaughter in Vietnam indicates that the time for "reasoned discussion" has passed.

Sartre and Camus:
Two Concepts of Commitment

—GERMAINE BRÉE

Germaine Brée, the noted literary critic and editor of the writings of Albert Camus, is a member of the Institute for Research in Humanities at the University of Wisconsin. Reprinted here is the concluding section of the Phi Beta Kappa Address and the third Kathleen Morris Scruggs Memorial Lecture, delivered by Professor Brée at Randolph-Macon Woman's College, Lynchburg, Virginia, April 14, 1966, and published by the college in the fall of 1966. The lecture was originally delivered at the University of Wisconsin Teach-In of April 1, 1965.

From the very start, the two men had set out on different paths. Philosopher that he was, Sartre, having rejected the intellectual and moral ordering of the world that he had inherited, had given himself the task of examining the structures of his own consciousness in order to reach a true, or a least a dependable, understanding of his relation to the world around him and by means of a method of thought so basic that it could apply to all men. He proceeded along the lines of traditional philosophical speculation, adapting to his own ends the methods of German phenomenology then current. His ultimate purpose was to restructure his own view of human reality so that he could more correctly understand himself and act with integrity in function of that understanding. His fundamental commitment was intellectual, his mode of approach speculative and rhetorical. Its point of departure was a reaction "against." He thinks, he said, "against himself." He also thinks against others. Hence, his natural leaning toward the Hegelian dialectic. The initial theses from which Sartre starts are generally given; he moves naturally from given statement to contradiction, to synthesis, and on again, without pause. The form of his rhetoric transmits a sense less of conviction than of the will to convince. Behind it one often senses the belief that thought is, in principle, a perpetual irresolution that can never achieve an end, nor renounce the seeking of it. The quest that never comes to its resolution becomes a measure of success.

Camus's quest was affective and immediately concrete in kind. It was an effort to realize a way of life that would give man's creative possibilities, his capacity for love and happiness, their maximum chance. His mode of approach was dual—practical and esthetic. In his writing, he formulated his point of view, preferably, through myth, symbol, and image. Where Sartre sought to shock and persuade by argument, Camus sought to elucidate and communicate, developing points of view rather than, as Sartre, a system. At the source of his questioning, there was a double recognition and acceptance rather than a refusal: the recognition that a certain harmony exists between man and his cosmos and is manifest in man's sense of the natural beauty of the world; and a sense of deep compassion for all forms of human suffering, a sense of solidarity with all men. The dispute that later separated the two men was, thus, almost inevitable. But, in the 1930's, each was engaged in forming for himself an image of man that would satisfy his need for coherence and integrity. Neither adhered to the Christian faith and both felt that the humanistic values on which the ethics and institutions of Western society rested had become empty rituals— when they were not mere window dressing. As young men, consequently, both had felt an urgent and admirable need to lay bare the roots of their beliefs and commitments so that they could confront themselves and their lives with integrity. Both belonged, politically, to the French Jacobin tradition and, intellectually, to a general philosophic trend of Western thought. The first years of the 1940's brought a drastic change in their situation. They were confronted dramatically with the problems of history, of history as the "evil that is bound up not with man's condition but with his behavior toward others."

The German occupation of France, the Resistance, and the liberation fashioned the collective experience of the French in a particularly dramatic way. Sartre's and Camus's first works can be read without reference to the historical situation, but not the rest of their writing. Sartre was drafted, taken prisoner, and, after a few months, sent back to France; he taught philosophy in Paris, sporadically wrote for clandestine Resistance sheets, and finally joined an intellectual association of Resistance writers. Camus was rejected by the army for reasons of health; after some months of anxious dissatisfaction, he joined an active Resistance group ("Combat") and was engaged in its clandestine activities under various pseudonyms. It was in those years that both men rose to literary prominence, emerging, in 1944–45, as the two most influential figures in French, and possibly European, intellectual circles.

At the time of his manifesto, therefore, Sartre was no longer an obscure writer. He was the recognized, though sometimes reluctant, leader of a school of writing and thought. His play *The Flies* had made available to a nonspecialized public the thought that had inspired his vast ontology *Being and Nothingness* and that was shaping the course of his grimly committed new periodical *Les Temps modernes*. Sartre's arguments concerning commitment for the writer lose some of their pertinency when taken out of the context of his thinking. I shall, here, briefly recall the basic pattern of his thinking, dangerous as this may be, to establish the framework of our discussion.

In *Being and Nothingness*, published in 1943, Sartre had posited as the two irreducibles in the human situation, *being* (that is to say, as Mary Warrock summarizes it, "those patterns that are built into our situation and are beyond our control"—the physical world, social institutions, our own situation in the world) and *consciousness* (the human factor that is *not* all the rest—hence, the use of the term "nothingness"). Consciousness, for Sartre, is the factor that wrenches us from what is and thus becomes the agent of our freedom. Our freedom is, therefore, our human ability to create phenomena that would otherwise not exist, and our acts acquire value inasmuch as they create the history for which we are responsible. By definition, the values by which we live cannot be, without examination, those "given" us on authority. We are, as Sartre put it, condemned to be free and the failure to face that fact leads to the sin without remission, bad faith. Although Sartre's description of human reality is given as objective, in fact, as Eugenia Zimmerman has shown, the imagery that accompanies it is highly subjective and carries with it a valorization. Being is felt as weight, stone, mask, statue—alien, in Sartre's terms, and dangerous. Consciousness is light, mobile, transparent, fluid, something felt as desirable. However the content of these categories may change, the images hold true; so that there is, in Sartre's imagery, a rather disturbing and psychologically revealing self-containment, particularly when it is set to work within his dialectic. It suggests, almost automatically, certain moral values for positions whose significance in moral terms remains logically unproved. Since he was thinking within the progressive-optimistic tradition that dominated the nineteenth century, it was not too difficult for him to equate ethical choice in the socio-political domain with the doctrines of socialism.

In the great surge of optimism that came with the liberation, Sartre carried through into political affairs the patterns of choice and responsibility which he had evolved under the occupation. He judged his former detached intellectual righteousness harshly. He had been satisfied to take intellectual positions and let concrete events take their course. He had, in his terms, indulged in "magical conduct"—the type of human behavior that structures reality according to human desire and not according to objective fact. He now became deeply concerned with the collective reality subsumed in the word History, with the image of man as a historical being, and, consequently, with the philosophies of history. It was at this point that his preoccupation with Marxism began to develop; he saw Marxism as a method of analysis and a coherent philosophy, as a springboard for efficacious action. He was not concerned with its sectarian and schematic versions.

There were points of contact between his brand of existentialism and Marxism: Sartre's somewhat sentimental and nostalgic feeling for the working classes and his built-in optimism could tally with the Marxist view of the over-all movement of History. There was one major difference—Sartre's definition of man as "freedom." Sartre's *What Is Literature?* had done away with literature as an absolute; and another absolute had appeared: the mandatory exercise of Sartrian freedom—that is, commitment. It offered no guarantees. "With regard to one's acts, one does what one can," he wrote in 1946. In the years that followed, he became more and more concerned with the immediate political situation. It was the period of the Cold War, of the increasing tension between the two blocs—the Soviet-dominated and the American-dominated—that culminated in the Korean War. Sartre began to define the choices and commitments of the writer in political terms and political obligations. History, in these years, became for him a kind of absolute, a first and drastic reduction of his system. In his deep concern not to founder once again into ineffectual idealism, not to let history "steal his future" as it had once succeeded in doing, he plunged into political action and attempted to found a socialist, non-Stalinist, Marxian party. He failed. To be consistent with himself, he was forced to make a final reduction. To act effectively—that is, consciously and voluntarily—upon the course of history, within the structures he had defined as a French bourgeois intellectual in the post-World War II situation, only one path was open to him: to act within the framework of the French Communist Party. It was a hard conclusion and it was characterized by a tremendous deployment of rhetorical argumentation. Creativity, that is to say freedom, would be effective only insofar as it worked on the "right" side of history: in favor of the proletariat and against the *bourgeoisie*; in favor of the new nations as opposed to the imperialists; in favor of

Russia as opposed to the United States. Sartre's "commitments" were now all laid out. The "radical conversion" of which Mary Warrock speaks and which Sartre himself mentions in *The Words* is vividly dramatized in the last pages of *Saint Genet*, a book that was written before his *The Devil and the Good Lord*, although it was published later.

At the end of his psychoanalytic biography of Genet, Sartre appended a chapter on the "proper use" society might make of Genet. He saw Genet, somewhat sentimentally, as the product and the scapegoat of the bourgeois world, the incarnation of our bourgeois impotence and sophisms. The chapter swings into a moment of intensified rhetoric: "The future is here, more present than the present. We feel that we are being judged by the masked men who will succeed us; our age will be an object for their future eyes. And a guilty object." We are in the realm of what Mircea Eliade called "the terror of History." The free and open Sartrian future had now become petrified under the gaze of a grim tribunal, "the masked men" of the future, the implacable judges of future History, a Sartrian myth. Sartre had come to see human beings as definable solely in historical terms; freedom consisted in being voluntarily and consciously so defined. He tolerated no other point of view.

Camus, in the meantime, had been engaged in a different kind of assessment. He was concerned with another kind of problem related to Marxism. Is it justifiable to accept the sufferings and annihilation of millions of human beings on the grounds that their situation places them in the way of History? His effort to give shape and a valid expression to the violent experience of the war was inspiring what he called the Promethean cycle of his work. It involved him in a critique of Stalinist neo-Marxism and of the perspective that established man as an entirely historical being. That perspective, according to which (as was the case for many doctrinaire Marxists) the patterns of History were seen as mechanically predetermined and "good" and "bad" attitudes dogmatically defined, led, he felt, to a nihilistic indifference to human aspirations and suffering, an indifference as monstrous as any of the forms of bourgeois complacency. What Camus questioned was the sacrosanct dialectic, the idea that conflict and violence were a necessary phase in the creation of social developments that could be rationalized in historical terms of right and wrong. Inevitable perhaps in human affairs, violence, he felt, when justified in moral terms as an inevitable step toward a better future, could signify merely the complacent acceptance of a ferocious human drive. Too many of his contemporaries, obsessed with a messianic view of history, were, he thought, being swung into action by just such a drive. What he attacked was the sanctifying of murder and terror by such a label as historical necessity and future progress. What he wished to bring to light were the deeper commitments, lying below the level of historical patterns, and transcending historical necessity, which tell us something about the human exigencies that move human beings to throw their weight behind certain movements, to make their history. Hence, the symbol he chose for his novel *The Plague*. What marks the limits of the plague's dehumanizing power is not the fight against the plague, necessary and relentless though it .be; it is the inner flame of comradeship in the service of human survival. There is only one answer, in this novel, to the great plumes of smoke that rise from the funeral pyres of the victims of the plague: the warmth of friendship; the open dialogue; the searching meditation of the few men, so different in point of view, who come together to fight the plague; the sense of trust and respect that they maintain throughout the weary, unglamorous struggle. There is no dogma here; rather, there is the sense of a relationship between men that can be destroyed in equal measure by the plague and the fight against the plague.

Sartre, involved in the extension of his dialectic to the historical scene, saw the creative future as more and more bounded, first in terms of the Marxist projection of history, then in terms of the Communist Party itself. Camus had broken away from what he called the gigantic myth of History. In *The Rebel*, he was speaking of political action, but he was not speaking in terms of the existentialist Marxist dialectic; he was questioning it.

"The first choice an artist makes," Camus wrote, is "to be an artist, and if he chooses to be an artist it is in consideration of what he is himself and because he has a certain concept of art." The first responsibility of the artist to his art is that he should meet his responsibility as a man, so that he may preserve an inner integrity without which his creative work is impaired. Art, for Camus, was the contrary of dogma, which imposes silence. It was a communication, an invitation to dialogue, and, therefore, a call to freedom: "The writer's function is not without its arduous duties," he said in his Nobel Prize acceptance speech. "By definition, he cannot serve today those who make history; he must serve those who are subject to it." For Camus, the writer can be only on the side of freedom against tyranny, never in the service of an ideology or dogma. For Sartre, the bourgeois writer in France today, if he is to be politically effective, can follow only one road: He must denounce the "mystifications" of bourgeois society and so prepare the way to a proletarian revolution.

The different sensitivity involved is evident in two plays that followed close upon each other: Camus's *The Just*, in December, 1949; Sartre's *The Devil and the Good Lord*, in June, 1951. Both plays belong to the theater of "boundary" situations whereby the French dramatists clarified and debated broad issues of interest to their countrymen in metaphoric terms. An austere play, *The Just* borrows its cast and external design from the real history of a small terrorist socialist group in Russia who, in 1905, assassinated the Grand Duke Sergei, Governor-General of Moscow. This was a group "committed" if ever there was one. Camus does not raise the problem of commitment itself. He never has, since *The Stranger*. All his characters are in some way embarked, "committed." He kept the essential historical facts of the incident: One of the terrorists, a young and idealistic poet Yanek Kaliayev, had been given the task of throwing the bomb as the Grand Duke's carriage passed on its way to the opera. In the carriage he saw, beside the Grand Duke, two children. He refrained. Two days later, the Grand Duke passed, alone in his carriage; Kaliayev threw the bomb, killed the man, was captured and hung. Camus unified the action by concentrating the play on the tragic awareness of two idealistic central figures: the poet and scrupulous thrower of the bomb, Kaliayev; and Dora, who works with the group. Kaliayev and Dora are in love. Begun in a climate of eager heroism, the play ends in a disturbing atmosphere of doubt. Camus was raising many questions: the relation of the means to the end; the discrepancy between the act imagined and the act carried through; the price paid; the seriousness of "commitment" when seen in the perspective of life and death. In the play, a first conflict arises between the doctrinaire Stepan and Kaliayev, a revolutionary out of generosity toward other men. "I have no stomach for such silliness," Stepan says as the two men confront each other after the first, abortive attempt. "Not until the time when we stop sentimentalizing about children will the revolution triumph." Dora answers, "Even in destruction there's a right way and a wrong way and there are limits." And Stepan replies, "There are no limits." Here, the opposition arises between what Camus called the scrupulous murderer and the doctrinaire, the complacent murderer, comfortably installed in his theories of righteousness. For Stepan, the legitimate aspiration toward justice, in a society where institutions work against justice, has become perverted; it has turned into a justification for a machinery of violence that brooks no opposition, a catastrophic dialectic. For Kaliayev, violence is a desperate resort and he is ready to pay for it with his life. It is a poor substitute for the constructive action made impossible by the political circumstances.

The real core of the discussion takes place between Kaliayev and Dora after the first attempt, when he begins clearly to see what his action involves. "Today," he says, "I know something I did not know before. . . . You were right Dora. It isn't as simple as it seems. I thought it was quite easy to kill provided one has courage and is buoyed up by an ideal. But now I've lost my wings. I've realized that hatred brings no happiness. I can see the vileness in myself and in others too. Murderous instincts, cowardice, injustice . . ." Yet love, their kind of love for humanity, consists in sacrificing everything to their cause. "There are times," Dora answers, "when I wonder if love isn't something else; something more than a lonely voice, a monologue, and if there isn't an answer. And then a picture appears before my eyes. The sun is shining, pride dies from the heart, and every barrier is down. Summer, Yanek, can you remember what that is like, a real summer's day?" Later, his act accomplished, isolated in his cell and awaiting his death, Kaliayev, who loved life, can see only "a world of tears and blood." A world of tears and blood—a real summer's day. Camus's play has no thesis. What he is pointing to is the desperate plight of society in which two basic human needs—a measure of justice and a measure of happiness—have become incompatible, so that the better individuals, a Kaliayev, a Dora, are torn, destroyed, forced to the kind of violence Stepan has chosen as a way of life. There are no just in this quandary, only desperate human beings. The play is a warning and a comment on the blindness of a whole society to intolerable conditions that leave no issue but violence for their redress. Kaliayev and Dora will die and the Stepans will impose on their fellowmen an inhuman, abstract dictatorship. "We live in terror," Camus wrote, "because persuasion is no longer possible, because men have become enslaved to History and cannot turn to that part of themselves which is as valid as their historical selves"; that self has its source in the feeling of harmony with the natural world and in the love each individual feels for a few human beings. Camus was clearly committed to the path of uncertainty and questioning, to the open mind and dialogue, to the fight against the social conditions that breed injustice and doctrinaire fanaticism.

Sartre's play is quite different in structure and intent. It is set in sixteenth-century Germany at the time of the Reformation and the peasant's war, a clear analogy with our own time of disorder and violence. The central character is Goetz, a bastard and the leader of a mercenary band. At the beginning of the play, he is pre-occupied only with his own anarchistic image as rebel, a rebel against all men, a rebel against the order of creation embodied in God. In Sartrian terms, he is acting in bad faith, perversely conforming to the image of himself that society holds up to him. All he does, as one of the characters points out to him, is to create a "useless uproar." Goetz himself realizes the pointless monotony of his stance. "Torture and hanging. Hanging and torture. The boring part of Evil is that one gets used to it. One needs genius to invent."

When a tormented priest, Heinrich, points out to him that Evil is the easiest thing to do, Goetz decides, on a throw of the dice in which he cheats, that he will exemplify absolute good. He causes disaster. The perfect peaceful peasant community he had organized is overrun and the peasants killed to the last man. In the last scene of the play, having lost everything, Goetz appears at the camp of the peasant leader Nasti, who is losing his fight on behalf of the peasants. Goetz's play-acting is over. The following dialogue takes place.

Goetz: I want to be a man among men.

Nasti: Only that.

Goetz: I know: it's the most difficult of all things. That's why I must begin at the beginning.

Nasti: What is the beginning?

Goetz: Crime. Men of the present day are born criminal. I must demand a share of their crimes if I want a share of their love and virtue . . .

Nasti now asks Goetz to take command of the troops. At first, he refuses. "I am resigned to kill. I shall let myself be killed if I must, but I shall never send another man to his death." Persuaded by Nasti to take the command, Goetz is confronted by the rebellious captains. "Nasti has named me chief and leader; will you obey my orders?" he asks. "I'd rather die" is the answer. "Then die, brother" answers Goetz and stabs him. "As for you others," he continues, "listen to me! I take up the command against my will, but I shall be relentless. . . . There is a war to fight, and I will fight it."

Goetz, in Sartrian terms, has achieved a new ethical awareness. He has deliberately chosen to put his strength and capacity for violence at the service of the peasants. His decision is made in relation to a concrete situation. He has found fulfillment in a historical future rationally projected, not in random action. Sartre's new absolute, at the turn of the mid-century, is clearly stated here. The play is written in a clearly Marxian perspective. But the conclusion of the play, in contrast with *The Just*, sounds, humanly, pretty hollow. Stepan is not far away. Nonetheless, both Sartre and Camus are deeply concerned with the same question, the question of social injustice and violence in situations that call for redress.

The parallel I have presented is simplified, too neatly antithetical. But the issues have not vanished nor are they merely theoretical. We are confronting them today at every turn. They are the issues that the Vietnamese, fighting with or against us, face more or less consciously, that our Negro citizens in the United States have also raised. As Camus said, we are "embarked" and events themselves have put a question to each of us: What commitment have we accepted? We can participate in the "useless uproar," whether of violence for the sake of violence, or debate for the sake of debate; we can choose the path of the doctrinaire and perpetuate the cycle of violence and repression, throwing the Doras and Kaliayevs of our time among the forces that oppose us. Or we can, like the Sartre of the 1930's, let events steal upon us from behind and rob us of our future. In this perspective, I think that the questions raised by Sartre and Camus, two men of exceptional stature and integrity, however schematically I have stated them, can tell us something about what is at stake for us at the present moment and, however obliquely, throw light on the challenges we face as individuals and as a community.

The Treason of the Experts

— ERIC BENTLEY

Mr. Bentley is Brander Matthews Professor of Dramatic Literature at Columbia University and a noted authority on the life and works of German poet and playwright Bertolt Brecht. This article is from The Nation, *December 13, 1965.*

Last spring, the president of a leading American university said that teachers should think twice before giving students advice in areas where they have no special expertise. How many times should university presidents think before giving teachers advice in areas where they have no more expertise than their faculty? And what is all this about "expertise" anyway? When is expertise ever required of people except when they are already judged to be wrongheaded? Are professors who support highly patriotic wars asked to have expertise in warfare or even in patriotism? Are they not—so far as their presidents are concerned—merely praised for their high sense of duty? Similarly, students who protest against a war are asked to have expertise, while those who support it are allowed to be ignoramuses—undoubtedly, their ignorance is a big help. Similarly, too, McGeorge Bundy and his friends try to disqualify criticism on the plea that their critics don't have access to essential information: If we all had access to the data Mr. Bundy has access to, we would all reach his conclusions. Since we don't, we must trust him.

We are hearing a lot about trust these days. And the man we are, above all, to trust is Lyndon Johnson. Which is too bad, as he is not an unusually trustworthy person. I voted for him at the last election because I considered that he had virtues not shared by his opponent. An unusual degree of trustworthiness was not, however, one of these. People used to ask of Richard Nixon: Would you buy a used car from this man? Well, which of us wouldn't prefer buying a used car from Barry Goldwater to buying one from Lyndon Johnson? The very quality for which Johnson is most admired —political dexterity—carries with it the defect of trickiness. He strikes me, also, as a man lacking in all conviction. That seems to be the source of his strength: He is without prejudice. He could at one time talk and act like a segregationist, but he *really* didn't mean it: He doesn't *really* mean anything. He is like a lawyer: totally willing to take his client's side, and give his all to it, with every outward sign of sincerity and felt fervor. When his client is the public, this makes him a very democratic figure, and when his client is only part of the public, he will show great skill in (a) wooing other parts, and (b) pretending that he has already wooed and won all parts. However, from time to time, the unforeseen happens, and someone actually speaks *against* Johnson or even acts against him. It doesn't seem right, but it happens. And right now in the United States that is the one fly in the political ointment. Everything is under control. All would be well. We would have the best of both worlds—all the comfortable advantage of peace and welfare added to the heroic afflatus of a just war—if it were not for this impudent indocility, this active . . . mistrust. Even the Bible, though warning us not to put our trust in princes, says nothing against Presidents.

Trust the President. Trust Mr. Bundy. Both Mr. Bundys. Also Mr. Rusk. And, until recently, there was the supremely trustworthy Adlai Stevenson. Yet Adlai Stevenson was caught lying in the U.N. when he denied that the United States had anything to do with the Bay of Pigs invasion. We have all lied in our time, but maybe not in such a big way. Besides we don't all ask everyone to take us on trust. Then again, some lies make for practical problems. Let me again cite the Bay of Pigs. In connection with that adventure, a Government spokesman defended lying. It might be a patriotic duty, he said. Maybe so, but we would like to know when our leaders are *not* lying, so we can talk over the truth—the actual facts—with them. When Mr. Bundy implies that, if we knew the inside story about Vietnam, we would approve of each stand our Government has taken, including, no doubt, stands that contradict one another, is he patriotically lying? Is Johnson's explanation of what he did in the Dominican Republic a tissue of lies?

Consider one admitted lie. Debating on TV with John F. Kennedy on October 22, 1960, the Vice-President of the United States let the people know that, so far as his Government was concerned, U.S. support for an anti-Castro invasion was out of the question. Kennedy's plea for such support he called "the most shockingly reckless proposal ever made in our history by a Presidential candidate during a campaign." Nearly four years later, *The New York Times* announced: "Mr. Nixon subsequently explained, in his book *Six Crises*, that he believed Mr. Kennedy had been endangering the security of the invasion plan . . . and therefore felt obliged to attack a plan he privately supported." It follows from this that when the intelligent citizen hears one of his trustworthy pastors and masters attacking a plan, any plan, he should ask himself whether, maybe, the said pastor and master isn't privately supporting that plan. Perhaps these trustworthy folk could actually be trusted if one made a habit of reversing all their statements? Could one trust them to support a thing privately *if* they are publicly attacking it? I wouldn't count on it. What we *can* probably count on is that, at the moment when we are confronted with any crisis, we shall not be placed in possession of the facts that govern the outcome. . . .

Since being elected, Johnson's main point about the Vietnamese has been that he keeps asking them all to negotiate, but they won't. Another provable, if patriotic, lie is involved. Hanoi is now known, even in the United States, to have also offered to negotiate. Arthur Miller brought this up recently, and a Johnsonian magazine that reported the matter tried to refute Miller with the observation that the terms offered by Hanoi were unacceptable. So: "refusal to negotiate" means "refusal to agree to our terms." Besides which, there might be something to say of the tactic of *bombing* an antagonist, ostensibly as a way of forcing him to negotiate but actually as a way of forcing your terms on him. Only to a public-relations man is that any different from plain old war. But we are ruled by public-relations men. Which is another reason why, much as we may admire the flexibility of the gentlemen, we cannot reasonably be asked to give them our trust. . . .

A corollary of that university president's remarks would seem to be that professors who *are* experts do have the right to hand out advice. One question would be: Expert in what? History? Geography? Political theory, and Communism in particular? Southeast Asia, and Vietnam in particular? Then again, aren't experts purchasable? Can't anyone have the experts he can afford? And can't anyone hire experts to defend any position he likes to take? Above all, will not the entrenched positions, in the nature of things, be well-defended? Won't Soviet experts *on* capitalism be experts *against* capitalism? And isn't just the converse true of American experts on this subject? Even if I am wrong here, do the experts ever agree on anything? And, if they don't, which ones should we be guided by? Are there experts on choosing-among-experts and, if so, do *these* experts agree?

A moment's thought about such difficulties can only cause us to wonder why there is so much talk of expertise all of a sudden. Isn't the main commitment of democracy, for better or for worse, to the nonexpert, that is, people at large? For America, the country with the strongest populist tradition in the world, it is certainly strange doctrine that we should all be dissuaded from independent thinking and individualistic action.

The argument behind the "patriotic" line of college presidents and other Establishment figures is this: America is not a Communist country, and therefore we need not believe Communist experts; it is an anti-Communist country, and therefore we should follow the advice of the anti-Communist experts. One can respect this logic to the extent of admitting that, in a war, there are only two sides and thus, if one took a side, but not Johnson's side, in the Vietnam war, one would be fighting against the Army of the United States and alongside many Communists. But then, unless one *is* a Communist, one is not taking a side, not advocating fighting for Hanoi, but a cessation of fighting by all parties. President Johnson has been urging recently that the Vietnam demonstrations are against the national interest. Of course, they are against the national interest if his policy is *in* the national interest, but that is precisely the question. Antiwar talk is *always* against the interest of a Government at war. Does that mean that antiwar talk is to be permitted only when there is no war [against which] to be anti? That such talk brings comfort to "the enemy" may well be true. In a given case, the enemy may deserve comfort, and, in any case, such talk has to be heard, surely, before it can be assessed. . . .

At this point, the Establishment will ask if, then, I am proposing to *appease* the Communists? And some will add that people like me (or is it people like *them?*) appeased Hitler in the 1930's. How about Walter Lippmann, for instance? Wasn't he some kind of "appeaser" in the 1930's? And, if he was, doesn't that explain his advocacy of "appeasement" now? And entitle us to disregard him? This was strongly implied, in a recent article in *The New York Times Magazine*, "A Professor Votes *for* Mr. Johnson," by John P. Roche, and surely Mr. Roche does not stand alone. The cold warriors, self-styled and otherwise, all bank very heavily indeed on a historical analogy which they seldom expose to full view, between the present and the 1930's, and, specifically, between the present-day Communist powers and the Nazi-Fascist powers of a generation ago. To me, it seems that these people are so determined to play Churchill that they would feel badly let down if the Soviets refused [to play] their assigned role as Hitler Germany. Yet, wouldn't it make sense—from the Communist viewpoint, I mean, of course—for the Soviets to do just that? In that case, some people are determined to play Churchill against an *imaginary* Hitler Germany.

I think Professor Roche's other arguments can be answered, too. But he is an expert and had better be answered by experts: I confidently hand him over to those he has shrugged off with quips. What I have a vivid sense of, after reading his piece, is his style. A quotation may bring it to mind:

> Even our bombing pattern in the North has followed a careful etiquette of "controlled response": we have observed what Herman Kahn would call the "city threshold" and only went after a few of the SAM missile launchers when they began to broaden their protective mission beyond Hanoi-Haiphong. We are, in short, fighting a carefully limited war in the effort to attain a perfectly reasonable objective. . . .

It must be nice to feel that such a thing as bombing can be neatly combined with perfect reasonableness, but some of us find this coolly babbling prose unconvincing, if not corrupt. And I think I shall start praying at night—God save me from Professor

Roche's careful etiquette! Someone lives in a dream world, he or I; for, let me admit that I am one of those who cannot think of the American action in Vietnam otherwise than in terms of outrage. It is true that history is one outrage after another, and that the Communists have perpetrated some gigantic outrages in their time. But is America to be excused its atrocities on the ground that others commit them too? Is it even to lead the way in outrage now, because others have led the way at some other date? Or, if it is a matter of evening-up the score, wasn't a tremendous step toward that made at Hiroshima? And are not further steps taken almost monthly in the deep South? I miss, in Professor Roche's exegesis, the note of concern. If he does not understand my indignation, I do not understand his nonchalance. . . .

It takes all sorts to make—or remake—a world. It may even be that it is best for the intellectual to represent something other than the viewpoint that is, or even is going to be, dominant, and that one should ask of him how much he modifies the existing state of things, rather than what he would do if he were in power. However this may be, it seems likely that what most menaces the world today is neither Communism nor imperialism as such but the possession of so much power by so few men, be they "Communists" in Moscow or Peking, or "imperialists" in Washington, especially since the official view of each side is that it has a monopoly of civic virtue.

In this situation, the critical act, the intellectual's act, can have historic importance—whether it be Yevtushenko criticizing Soviet anti-Semitism or Robert Lowell refusing an invitation from Lyndon Johnson. In such ways is the claim to a monopoly of virtue challenged. Which, in turn, means that the regime concerned will be that much less ready to *act* in the name of virtue. Such protests are against "the national interest" not only in encouraging the enemy abroad but also—which the authorities are naturally not so apt to mention—in discouraging the trigger-happy friends of power at home. For the world's danger is what the *Strangelove* movie said it was. Not literally, of course. It was quite beside the point for the experts to refute Terry Southern, *et al.*, with solemn proof that the bomb cannot be exploded by a single "kook" in the War Department. The point was, rather, that our whole world is, in all too real a sense, crazy; anything is possible, and the worst really can happen.

In this situation, the classic function of the intellectual—to be the voice of reason amid the clamor of the world's irrationality—attains a peculiar urgency. The intellectuals can hope, must hope, to discourage the generals and the politicians from blowing up the world in one of their fits of patriotic (or proletarian) virtue. *Discouragement* is of the essence, and it was good to note that Lowell *had* discouraged even the ebullient Texan who is our Commander-in-Chief.

Intellectuals of the world unite! To a degree, they have already done just that. Living behind the Iron Curtain, I was surprised by the extent to which the intelligentsia there has the same gripes—and hopes—as ourselves. And they have to fight off the same facile accusation of disloyalty with the same entirely sincere answer: No, they don't wish to "defect" to the "other side," they wish to re-make their side or, if that is not immediately practical, to restrain it from practicing what it preaches, to prevent it from having the courage of its professed convictions, to *discourage* it.

Discouragement, deflation—this is the negative side. There is much negative work to do, and the talents of an intelligentsia, from a Terry Southern to a Dwight Macdonald, may be specially apt for this work. But the intention, naturally, is positive, and there is a corresponding body of positive labor before us. It is the work of conciliation. Here the pioneers have been Martin Luther King and Pope John XXIII. Whether or not one can envisage the world acting on the lines laid down in *Pacem in Terris*, one can surely believe that the spirit the encyclical embodies might influence the world. If one cannot believe this, one's view of politics is wholly cynical. Not to give up politics in that way is to bear witness to a degree of faith in human possibility. But this faith intellectuals must possess, if only to justify their own existence as the carriers of intellect.

So, when I am asked if I think our students are entitled to protest, I must not limit my answer to a patronizing yes, but must go on to congratulate the younger generation on boldly bearing witness at a time when so many of their elders were pussyfooting around discussing *whether* witness should be borne. This is not to say that all forms of protest are proper—or even shrewd. Some are obviously idiotic; some feeble; some morally ambiguous; some morally wrong. But the discontent itself is more than justified; it is necessary. For, aside from its political effects, it is helping, in an age of phony virtue and real murder, to keep alive both the body and the spirit.

The Scholar Is Not a Lion or a Fox

—RUSSELL KIRK

Professor Kirk is the author of Academic Freedom.
The following is from The New York Times Magazine, *May 1, 1966.*

In 1966, more than ever before, American public opinion needs
responsible leadership in the understanding of foreign affairs. American foreign policy requires close criticism in this time of upheaval
and thrust. Of a sudden, many gentlemen in the academy volun-
teer their services as molders of public opinion and as critics of the
State Department and the Pentagon: challenge and response.

But, are all these "committed" scholars really endowed with a
mastery of statecraft? Senator J. William Fulbright thinks that our
professors may be trusted to guide foreign policy aright. At the
height of the hearings of the Senate Committee on Foreign Relations concerning the struggle in Vietnam, Mr. Fulbright declared
that the men of the academy ought to become even more active
in current foreign affairs controversies. He seemed confident that,
in such concerns, the opinions of the professors would coincide
with his own. [*See Chapter* V.]

Conceivably, Senator Fulbright is troubled by a few subsequent
misgivings, now that the scholars' Vietnam testimony before the
Foreign Relations Committee has been concluded. For, some of
the professors upon whom Mr. Fulbright presumably relied for
reinforcement of his own views must have been disappointing to
him . . .

However that may be, the general question which Senator Fulbright raised deserves attention. Should the scholar give primacy
to our present discontents? Should he issue manifestoes and fulminations on the principle issues of foreign affairs, protest and
demonstrate, league himself with party and faction, offer a confident prescription for the woes of all the world?

Or should he stick to his folios, most of the time? Should he take
meditation and research and the teaching of his discipline for his
fundamental duties? Is he competent—collectively speaking—to
ride the diplomatic whirlwind and direct the international storm?

"He that lives in a college, after his mind is sufficiently stocked with learning," wrote the young Edmund Burke, "is like a man who, having built and rigged and victualed a ship, should lock her up in a drydock." Though Burke was far from despising learned professors of arts and sciences, he meant that the man who aspires to alter public affairs should enter upon public life and not linger within college walls. The politician must live the politician's existence, and the scholar, the scholar's.

Yet, not a few professors today demand the best of both worlds. Their exemplar is Dr. Staughton Lynd, leading marches on Washington, speechifying in Hanoi, joining the Du Bois Clubs as a gesture. They would relish mightily the role of Mr. Nelson Algren or Mr. Norman Mailer, discoursing in public of the infamy of American foreign policy—even if the discourses are blemished by remarkable exhibitions of ignorance. They aspire to enjoy simultaneously the prestige (and security) of the academy, and the excitement of the soapbox.

Thus we observe afresh many of the attitudes of a group of professors in the 1930's. Consider the virtual adulation, in certain quarters, of Dr. Herbert Aptheker, a dogmatic Communist, one of the dullest speakers ever to try the patience of college audiences— who, Bourbonlike, has learned nothing and forgotten nothing since the days of popular fronts. Professors are eminent among the men of the left who hope to secure a seat in Congress for Dr. Aptheker. More, Dr. Aptheker was named to give a major address to the Organization of American Historians (formerly the Mississippi Valley Historical Association) this past week, on the day after a testimonial dinner in Manhattan meant to launch him on the sea of practical politics. When certain professors of history—themselves sufficiently liberal—objected to this part of the OAH program, they were informed that Dr. Aptheker had been chosen to speak because he had "suffered persecution."

Such muddy sentimentality, and such notions of "no enemies to the left," recently have been so conspicuous among a number of scholars that Mr. Joseph Alsop and other commentators have mused mordantly upon a possible widespread revival, among American intellectuals, of the illusions of a generation gone. For my part, I do not believe that our community of scholars, or any large part of it, will worship anew the God That Failed. Yet a scattering of individuals may blight their own intellectual promise, and bring disrepute upon the academy, by pontificating on foreign and domestic policies of which they know next to nothing.

I should point out that, although for the past two generations the ideological pressures within the American academy have come mainly from the left, one may conceive of circumstances in which scholars of the right might be equally imprudent and intemperate. The lonely figure of Professor Revilo Oliver, at the University of Illinois—an admirable scholar in Greek and Latin, but an ideologue of the Birch Society when he ventures into the murky waters of foreign policy—may be sufficient illustration. Or professors with Government subsidies may become the servants, rather than the architects, of quasi-conservative state policies: Consider the social scientists of Michigan State University, recently accused of having been undercover operatives of the CIA in South Vietnam, for good or ill. ("Most of these grand Washington schemes for sending a covey of professors overseas," a well-known sociologist remarked to me, "involve either Harvard or Michigan State. When the people in Washington wish a project to succeed, they turn to Harvard. When they mean a project to fail, they contract with Michigan State.")

It would seem worthwhile, then, to draw a line of demarcation between the scholar and the ideologue. A scholar has, of course, the right and the duty to be as much concerned with the common good as is any other citizen. But, by definition, he must give most of his time and his mind to learning.

By contrast, the ideologue—a political dogmatist hotly seeking his particular Utopia—has little to do with the speculative pursuit of truth; he already knows all the answers to everything, for they are contained in his simple social formula; for him, research is but a means to his political end, and writing ought to be propaganda. No man may be at once a genuine scholar and a convinced ideologue.

Do not mistake me: I do not suggest that every scholar who publicly expresses his political convictions is an ideologue, or that a scholar may not have knowledge of high value in the conduct of foreign affairs—this latter depending, often, upon his particular scholarly discipline. Distinctions must be made.

Consider the teach-ins about the Vietnam war. Most of the professors and instructors who have taken an active part in these gatherings have given off more heat than light; and it has been remarked that the more remote their scholarly specialty seems from diplomatic and military affairs in southeast Asia, the more such gentlemen behave as if omniscient. They are converting themselves into ideologues.

Between the mere enthusiast with a recent Ph.D., however, and the learned man who criticizes policy in Vietnam on the basis of much study, a gulf is fixed. On the one hand, we see the young instructor in philosophy (perhaps bored by his own logical positivism) who reveals in the teach-ins a burning certitude about foreign affairs which he never professes in his lectures on metaphysics or ethics; he mistakes a university post for a political prophetic afflatus. On the other hand, we find that similar practical conclusions are drawn by scholars like Dr. Hans Morgenthau, who—whether or not one agrees with him—at least speaks with some authority about the theory and the practice of diplomacy. The former professor is in process of becoming what the Greeks called a "philodoxer," a lover of private opinion and the winds of doctrine. The latter professor disdains ideology, remaining a realist; his judgments, whether sound or erroneous, are prudential, rather than ideological.

In essence, my argument is this: If the scholar deserts his realm of scholarly competence for the agora, he is liable to attain neither wisdom nor the public good. The man who has been an able professor may become an able politician. Congress has, in both parties, a fair number of useful members with such a background, and others are in the "executive force." Very few persons, nevertheless, can be competent simultaneously in quite different vocations. For better or worse, the scholar turned politician must give up pure scholarship. If one has a taste for the hustings, one ought to abandon the pose of speaking authoritatively from a chaste, impartial love of pure learning.

When, however, scholarship and political passion are embroiled in a confusion worse confounded, both honest learning and practical politics suffer. Let me suggest, first, the dangers to learning which result from this admixture.

When professors and men of letters let themselves be frozen into ideological rigidity, the community of scholars is disrupted. College faculties are bitterly divided by ideological passions, so that appointment and promotion are determined, too often, by conformity to the prevalent doctrine of the hour. The classroom becomes a center for political indoctrination of the students, at the expense of free discussion and exploration. Humane and scientific studies are subordinated to political or economic prejudices. A sour, fanatic temper infects both senior scholars and students. Literature sinks into sloganizing, special pleading and the baser sort of polemics. Before scholarship at last recovers from the merciless grip of ideology, whole generations may suffer.

This baneful academic phenomenon has been described perceptively by two scholars who both know Europe and America: Mr. Raymond Aron, in *The Opium of the Intellectuals*, and Dr. Thomas

Molnar, in *The Decline of the Intellectual.* However much ideological infatuation and prejudice may have touched the American intellectual community from time to time, we may be thankful that, ordinarily, we have escaped the severer consequences of bundling scholarship and political dogmatism together in one extramarital bed. Contrary to the assumption of many Americans, there may be less ideological prejudice at a typical American university than at Oxford, say, or at Cambridge. . . .

In the academy, the scholar turned ideologue does mischief to his colleagues, his students, and the search for wisdom. And if the scholar-ideologue contrives to inflict his abstractions upon the affairs of nations, more harm is worked. The academy simply is not the best place to acquire an apprehension of the complexity of public affairs, or an acquaintance with the skills and limits of diplomacy. Politics being the art of the possible, a broad knowledge of the world, the flesh, and the devil ought to be possessed by the architect of foreign policy. In the politician, prudence is the chief virtue. But the ideologue, sheltered by academic tenure and campus immunities, demands that we work, instanter, a radical reformation of man and society; and he knows not prudence. Fancy Dr. Staughton Lynd, or a professor of the Birchite persuasion, as Secretary of State!

I readily acknowledge that scholars (as distinguished from ideologues) may become statesmen. In this century, Presidents Wilson and Hoover were men of real scholarship in their own fields, and also practical—if not wholly successful—politicians. In general, though, the scholar does well to cling to his original calling. Robert Taft . . . said once that businessmen should stick to business, leaving politics to the politicians. This is no less true of scholars and scholarship. Quite as *some* men of business can become competent political leaders and administrators, so can *some* scholars; yet we retain a legitimate presumption that talents for making money or for writing dissertations do not, per se, qualify well-intentioned folk to administer justice and defend the national interest.

It is easy enough to understand the frustrations and aspirations which impel some scholars—particularly members of our "academic proletariat" of overworked, underpaid, and mass-campus–harassed young instructors and graduate assistants—to leap from the dull "survey" course to the advocacy of some political cause—nay, *any* political cause. At least a teach-in audience pays attention, unlike the typical classroom of undergraduates; and it would be so very pleasant if, through direct political action, somehow one might transform Behemoth State University, or Dismal Swamp A. & M., or all America, or all the world, into a domain of sweetness and light. It seems infinitely difficult to leaven the lump of campus smugness. But it seems so delicious to declaim about the sinfulness of war—and to be applauded.

Have scholars, then, nothing to do with public affairs? My belief is quite the contrary: The professor, in whatever discipline, does and should exercise a profound influence upon the civil social order. But that power is exerted through study, teaching, and contemplation. In the comparative leisure of the academy, the minds of the rising generation are molded; and the arts and sciences alter, enduringly if imperceptibly, the world without. Reinhold Niebuhr or T. S. Eliot, say, will influence the commonwealth and the conscience long after the names of Hubert Humphrey and John Tower (with all respect to those former professors) have become names only.

Six decades ago, Irving Babbitt wrote, in *Literature and the American College*: "Of action we shall have plenty in any case; but it is only by a more humane reflection that we can escape the penalties sure to be exacted from any country that tries to dispense, in its national life, with the principle of leisure." Babbitt meant the leisure, the meditation, the seminal quietude, of the academy. Perhaps true scholarship will not produce philosopher-kings; yet, it works upon mind and heart to give us a better republic.

Senator Fulbright wants to beckon the scholar into political action, now. But action ungoverned by reflection is uncontrollable and unpredictable; while "activist" professors and students have a tricky way, abruptly, of taking up other causes and commencing new actions unpalatable to the gentlemen who persuaded them to shut their books.

By his nature, the scholar is not calculated for direct action, nor is the professor endowed with the talents of either lion or fox. "In politics, the professor always plays the comic role," says Nietzsche.

Yet the professor need feel no shame at this. Practical politics is not the whole of life, nor the most important aspect of life. Socrates took the measure of the demagogue Cleon and the oligarch Critias, and found both wanting. Would Socrates have done well to have thrust himself into one of the seats of the mighty? Had he done anything of the sort, he would mean no more to us today than do Cleon and Critias. He fulfilled his duty to the state, spear in hand; but he knew that the lover of wisdom must not drink deep from the cup of power.

Order and justice and freedom cannot be secured by professorial haranguing of crowds. The scholar truly committed is the man of learning who works honestly and tirelessly at his high duty of elevating mind and conscience.

Passion in Clear Reason

— D A V I D   K R E C H

Dr. Krech is Professor of Psychology at the University of California and the author (with Richard S. Crutchfield) of Elements of Social Psychology. *This article appeared in* The Nation, *March 28, 1966.*

My text comes from a story, no doubt apocryphal, that had its origin on the Vassar campus. The tale is told of Professor Lanier, who explained why, after ten years, he thought the time had come for him to leave Vassar—lest he lose completely his identity as a man. It seems the professor's office overlooked a part of the campus that is a favorite sunning spot for the Vassar girls and, thus, out of bounds to whatever men happen to stray onto the grounds. One day, while the girls were lying around in their sun suits, he heard a mildly hysterical call from one of them: "Professor Lanier, oh Professor Lanier, come down quickly—there's a man here!"

As I have listened to the many university- and faculty-sponsored Vietnam meetings, the teach-ins and study-ins and forums and position papers and critiques, and as I have read the half-page and full-page ads paid for by Harvard professors and Berkeley professors and Stanford professors, I have come to the conclusion that apparently the professors themselves agree with the Vassar girls' judgment. Very rarely do we hear from the professor as *Man*. Almost never does he lash out against America's Vietnam war with the hot conviction of a man whose passion has been aroused, who has come to hate in full and bitter measure the cruelties and deceptions and obscenities that are being committed by his Government. We professors have been trying too hard to play the role of the glandless eminence who is all gray cortex and has within him none of the energizing secretions of the thyroid, the driving fluids of adrenalin, the vitalizing mysteries of the androgens. We have trapped ourselves into believing that "reasoned discussion" is what we professors should hold fast to in this time of confusion and bitterness and frustration, and that reasoned discussion means the discussion only of diplomatic documents, historical precedents, and international policy; the discussion only of elections held and elections not held, of political expediency and legal authority; of the virtues of open debate and the recognition or nonrecognition of this or that body; the discussion only of domino theories and paper tigers and enclave strategies. Never, never, must reasoned discussion have recourse to what are pejoratively called the emotional arguments—to blood and death, anguish and fear.

But this, surely, is an absurd caricature of reasoned discussion. To believe that reasoning man is, can be, or even should be uninfluenced by his fears, angers, hates, aspirations, and hopes is bad physiology and very bad psychology.

It is bad physiology because it seems to assume that the brain of an academe—professor or student—floats suspended in sterile space, unbathed by those vulgar, hot vital fluids which nourish and condition the brains of the lesser citizenry. And it is bad psychology because it is bad physiology: Quite simply, no man born of woman does reason in this manner.

Those who refuse to weigh and consider emotional arguments in a reasonable discussion only *seem* to do so. They are really no less guided by emotions than those whom they castigate. The difference lies only in this: The so-called unemotional reasoners are guided by private, unexpressed, and unadmitted hates, fears, anxieties, and desires. I am not saying that we are all doomed to be creatures of unreasoning emotional urges and surges. Blind feelings and mindless emotions are good for nothing at all and we need not succumb to that mindless outrage which serves neither the heart nor the brain. But as any psychologist knows, and as Karl Jaspers has put it so clearly, "Without passion in clear reason, no human truth is possible." When a man considers, in clear reason, a course of action that may bring about his death, or make him a hired killer, certainly he cannot arrive at any meaningful or significant truth on the question without passion. And to arrive at a truth which he can hold passionately, a man must consider all of his passions and determine whether they support or negate that truth. What evil nonsense it is to argue that, when a man debates whether he should do this and probably live, or that and probably die (especially when a young man so debates), his passionate desire to live is irrelevant—an "emotional argument."

But I am afraid that many of us—most academes—behave as though we believe just that. In our public discussions we seem to have defined "reasoned discussion" as "emotionless mind." Therefore, we have failed to reason with our students and we have shied away both from discussion with them and from *encouraging them to discuss*, those very passions which must be acknowledged with clear reason if human truths are to be found. And I am not speaking here of subtle and esoteric matters, but of the most simple and the most compelling.

When the student comes to our forums and teach-ins for guidance, do we talk to him about the decisions *he* must make; about the possibilities of his own annihilation? No, we behave as though such matters were irrelevant and talk, instead, about the decisions *Johnson* must make, and the possibilities of the annihilation of *America's* containment policy. What a bizarre logic it is that makes the latter relevant and the former irrelevant. And the student leaves our forums with a belief, perhaps, that the domino theory is questionable, that Congress should be allowed to discuss foreign policy, and that professors Able and Baker have made interesting and telling points which President Johnson ought to consider. But he wonders—and not for very long—if that is reason enough for him to make a spectacle of himself and march in protest parades—or refuse to serve his country when duty calls. He may admit to himself that he would rather finish out his schooling and his career, and all of his many yet unformed plans in his own fashion, rather than be shot off to Vietnam; and he may even admit to himself that he wants to live and fears he will not. But he thinks all these things with silent passion, for that seems to be *his* problem. Just maybe he is a coward after all, and the important thing really is foreign policy. Thus, the student leaves our forums without any new truth or insight; more often than not, he plans to take no action. He takes no effective sides and makes no effective commitment, precisely because we haven't *reasoned* with him. Too many of the relevant considerations we have ruled out as tainted by passion, "unfit for reasonable consumption by students and professors."

Because I hope that we professors may serve our students better, I propose the following: Let us, in our forums, talk as reasonable men, but as passionately reasonable men looking for human truths, not afraid to take out and examine any relevant consideration. Let us express and examine values, morals, fears, and angers, no less than statistics, documents, and maps. Let us say to our students something after this fashion:

"When you think about what to do; when you decide how much, if anything, you are ready to do for peace in Vietnam— whether to march in demonstrations or to refuse to serve as an American expeditionary soldier; when you make these decisions, remember that on them may depend *the uses of your life*. And here *you* are the expert. Here *you* must talk and think. Here you cannot assume that *they* know something you don't know. You are being asked to go and act the killer. You are being asked to jeopardize your own life in that enterprise. To examine the meaning of such requests is not the sign of a coward or of an emotional fool. It is the way of a man who reasons and considers and acts in terms of all that is relevant.

"Perhaps you *are* prepared to kill and be killed in order to gain a greater good. Some of us, in past wars, have thought and done just that and some of us still believe that what we did was right. But think, then, what is the greater good, this time, for which you are being asked to play the executioner and the victim? And for whom is this the greater good? Read all the arguments and reasoning and position papers, and ponder over this and that informed opinion and assessment. And then place all that you have learned against your wish to live—and let live. For the question to which all of this is addressed is meaningless except in the context of your readiness to shoot and kill and die. And when you have done all this—then decide on your course of action. And, once you have decided what to do, go then and do those things with all your might and with all your soul, for remember, in the scale may be all of your unspent and untasted years."

If we spoke thus and reasoned thus in our forums and teach-ins and in our conversations, we would be serving our students better, and our cause as well—for we do have a cause and we are committed to it.

We profess to be of help to our own colleagues as well as to our students. But when our colleagues seek further understanding and guidance, do we discuss openly and cleanly—like complete men— those concerns of anguish and fear which disrupt our nights and our days; the dread realization that our sons are no longer exempt from threat; that as the war escalates, student deferments are revoked and everybody is called to war? I'm afraid that we don't. Almost obscenely, we play out the roles assigned to us by the Vassar girls—"balanced gray men of cortex pure." We tell one another how complicated the problem is; we tell one another that congressmen are now debating; and we adjourn the meeting, believing that, indeed, the matter is complicated and hoping that congressmen will continue to debate—hoping, even, that the President might eavesdrop. But we do not go away from these almost irrelevant discussions strengthened by the knowledge of a shared fear—and with that strength, determined to do what needs to be done.

And there is much that we can do. I would say to my colleagues: Read, think, examine—and then go and do with vigor what you think is best to do. But don't refrain from this or that program of action because it seems not to be the best of all possible programs —and thus refrain from doing anything. Think of what grasps you when you remember your son, or your brother's son, or your neighbor's son. Join, demonstrate, write, contribute money—but don't do nothing, lest you find yourself one day with a Government telegram in hand, and begin the eternal agony of telling yourself: "Perhaps, perhaps . . . if only I *had* done more, if only I had done this —or that—perhaps . . . who knows?"

VII

What Do the Teach-Ins Mean?

Editors' Introduction

Among participants, the teach-ins generated almost as much debate about their significance as they did about foreign policy. Scholars are, of course, an unusually articulate and contentious group, but there are further reasons for this debate. Any avowedly political movement must subject itself to constant assessment of goals, strategies, and tactics from within, as well as undergo critical assaults from the outside. Thus, the interpretations presented here cannot boast objective finality or certainty—although some may merit more attention than others; rather, they are frankly politically motivated attempts to analyze a movement still in motion.

Senator Thomas Dodd, for example, sees teach-ins as a movement infiltrated by Communists. He judges critics not by their arguments but by their ability to prove that they screen Communists from their ranks and "Communist influences" from their beliefs and actions. The real political or ideological affiliations (if any) of the protesters, as well as the validity of the protest itself, is easily clouded by the simple assertion that this or that Communist group, here or abroad, expressed support for the teach-ins. Such a technique goes far toward discrediting the movement among certain sections of the American public.

The rest of this chapter contains evaluations of the teach-ins by leading members and organizers of the movement. Again, the reader's attention is called to the tension between those who see the teach-in as a form of dialogue aimed at influencing policy-makers and those who see it as a form of protest leading to further political action by dissenters. The assumption of the latter group is that policy-makers are hopelessly insulated against the pleas of critics;

any number of direct and indirect "dialogues" and "confrontations" have taken place between members of the Administration and members of the movement during the first two years of teach-ins, yet official policy seems not to have deviated by one iota from the logic of escalation. In this view, confrontation is meaningless unless it springs from a base of political power to which the Administration must respond.

In this chapter, Kenneth E. Boulding, Richard Flacks, and Arnold S. Kaufman represent those who welcome the creation of a dialogue, in line with Professor Boulding's contention that "there is an educational task ahead rather than a task of pure protest." The other group is represented by Christopher Lasch and Peter Lathrop. They challenge Professor Kaufman's view that "the Administration should realize that it has a genuine interest not only in cooperating with, but in promoting, the teach-in movement." "No amount of persuasion," Professor Lasch argues, "will change the central fact of American politics" that no opposition party exists. Professor Lasch calls not for the furthering of a dialogue with those in power but for the building of a radical-Left opposition pledged to achieving genuine change. Cast in this light, the teach-ins are important insofar as they further a movement that might force a reassessment of fundamental assumptions guiding the bipartisan Cold War policy of global anti-Communism. Isaac Deutscher stresses the same theme in the concluding article, examining the teach-in movement in the perspective of a European familiar with the dynamics of political "thaw," both East and West.

The Anti-Vietnam Agitation and the Teach-In Movement

—THOMAS J. DODD

Excerpts from Senator Dodd's introduction to a staff study prepared for the Internal Security Subcommittee of the Senate Committee on the Judiciary (Washington, D.C., 1965).

The current surge of criticism about Administration policy in Vietnam may be divided into four broad categories:

1. The honest criticism of loyal Americans who oppose Com-

munism but believe that the method we are using to fight it in Vietnam is wrong and urge a different method.

2. The honest criticism of those who believe Communism is evolving into something less than a real threat, or who believe that Vietnam is outside our sphere of influence and that we are pursuing a course of folly in committing ground troops to a war in that area.

3. The honest criticism of convinced pacifists who believe that force is wrong in any and all circumstances.

4. The dishonest criticism of those who support the general aims of Communism; who look upon America as the villain and regard Moscow or Peiping as the new Utopia; who hold that Western democracy is, in fact, a capitalist dictatorship, while Communist totalitarianism is synonymous with people's democracy; who are all for so-called wars of national liberation, but who tell us that the free world sins when it uses force to defend itself against Communist aggression.

The position of those in the first three categories commands respect, and their voices must be heard, no matter how much any of us may disagree with them, if the processes of democracy are not to be stultified.

It is unfortunate that, in the clamor and chaos of the anti-Vietnam agitation, the voices of many thousands of loyal Americans in the first three categories have become confused and blended with the voices of those pseudo-Americans in the fourth category.

It is, however, easy to discover who the true pacifists are, and the fact that many, and perhaps most, of the demonstrators are not genuine pacifists can be established from a simple scratching of the surface. Those, for example, who openly urge support for the Vietcong, denying documented facts and figures of murder, kidnaping, and assassination by the Vietcong, are, almost without exception, partisans of Communism; their criticism of our policy is rooted in nothing better than the commitment to the interests of Communist expansion.

Condemning the growth of such groups on the left, an eminent liberal, Professor John Roche, of Brandeis University, a former national chairman of Americans for Democratic Action, said this:

What particularly disturbs me is the growth of part-time pacifism, or liberal isolationism. Fine liberals, who would storm Congress to aid a beleaguered Israel, suddenly shift gears when Asia is involved and start talking about "the inevitability of Chinese domination" and the "immorality" of bombing North Vietnam. Let me make it perfectly clear that a pacifist can, on principle, argue that the use of force in international affairs is immoral. Though I do not hold this position, I recognize its principled foundation. But a pacifist is, thus, forbidden by his moral imperatives from having any favorite wars. (*The New Leader*, April 26, 1965.)

When playwright Arthur Miller refused to attend the signing of the new Arts and Humanities Act, in protest against the Government policy in Vietnam, he stated that "when the guns go boom-boom, the arts die." But Mr. Miller did not get away that easily. David Merrick, one of Broadway's busiest producers, pointed out that:

> This is not what he said when he was all for the guns going boom-boom, a few years ago, against Nazi aggression. I find it puzzling that he doesn't want the guns to go boom to stop the Red Chinese aggression. (*New York Herald Tribune*, September, 28, 1965.)

The fact is clear that many of the most vociferous of the Government's critics do not oppose the use of force. They simply oppose the use of force against Communists.

The publicity that has been accorded the anti-Vietnam agitation has created a greatly exaggerated impression, both in this country and abroad, of the dimensions of the intellectual opposition to the Administration's Vietnam policy. This point was made emphatically by Max Lerner, distinguished liberal, professor, and author of *The History of American Civilization*. [*Senator Dodd is apparently referring to* America as a Civilization.] Said Mr. Lerner:

> I have taken no poll but I have traveled on many campuses . . . and I find the scholars close to Asian studies support the President, because they know what would happen in Asia if America were to withdraw. The men in the political studies also . . . support him, because they know something about the ways of Communist expansionism. The men in the military studies support him, because they know this is a minor war compared to what we would have to wage if it failed. . . . If I am right, then my guess is that there is an inverse relation between militancy or hostility to the President's policy and closeness to the subject matter. (*New York Post*, April 30, 1965.)

But, while Mr. Lerner's findings may be statistically correct, this in no way gainsays the fact that, by dint of sheer noise and persistence and clever propaganda, the sponsors of the anti-Vietnam movement have succeeded in creating the impression that they speak for the better part of the American academic community.

Writing in *The Militant*, organ of the Trotskyist Communists,

Harry Ring sums up the Communist view of what is currently occurring:

> Opposition to Washington's aggression in Vietnam . . . is deeper and more widespread than generally realized. . . . The opposition has found expression, so far, primarily among college students and professors. But, this campus sentiment does not run counter to a contrary one in the general community. . . . The campus protest has already produced three widespread important actions: (1) The April 17 march on Washington to end the war in Vietnam, which drew 20,000 participants; (2) the May 15 National Teach-In, in Washington, which attracted 5,000 direct participants; (3) the May 21 Vietnam Day at Berkeley where 15,000 students protested U.S. aggression. . . . It was a hard jolt for President Johnson when the distinguished literary figure, Lewis Mumford, chose the annual meeting of the ultrastaid Institute of Arts and Letters to cry out against the Administration's criminal aggression against the Vietnamese. . . . In every sense, the present opposition to U.S. war policies is deeply significant. It is the most extensive organized opposition to war that has ever been manifest while a war was going on. There were antiwar movements in this country prior to World War I and World War II, but they collapsed the day the shooting started. . . . Every fighter for peace has reason to be heartened by the present trend of developments. . . . (*The Militant*, June 14, 1965.)

Nor can there be any denying the fact that the Communist apparatus has been able to exploit this situation with remarkable success for propaganda purposes.

That the Communists have every reason to be satisfied is a point that must be conceded.

Writing in *The New York Times,* in June, 1965, Mr. C. L. Sulzberger, dean of the . . . *Times* foreign correspondents, made this statement:

> The remarkable Communist propaganda apparatus seeks to undermine the resolve of Governments in Saigon and Washington. . . . Many American intellectuals display a strange lemming instinct and refuse to see the struggle in its true meaning as advertised quite openly by the Communists themselves: a showdown with global implications. . . . Our adversary finds it possible to use democratic processes of free speech to harass distant vulnerable spots.

It is no part of the purpose of this study to suggest that all of those who disagree with the Administration's policy on Vietnam, or who participate in demonstrations against this policy, are Communists or Communist dupes. There are, indeed, many men with impeccable records of anti-Communism who have expressed disagreement with the Administration's policy, in whole or in part.

It is, rather, the purpose of the study contained in the following pages to try to establish whether the Communist Party and its various affiliates have succeeded in infiltrating and manipulating and exploiting the so-called teach-in movement and the anti-Vietnam agitation in general and, if so, to what extent and in what manner.

I hope that the facts here set forth will, among other things, assist loyal critics of Administration policy to purge their ranks of the Communists and crypto-Communists, so that the national debate on Vietnam policy can be carried forward as a discussion between honest men, unencumbered by the participation of the Communists, who have been seeking to subvert the entire process of free debate, as they seek to subvert our society. . . .

In reality, the great majority of the teach-ins (there were a few notable exceptions to this rule) have had absolutely nothing in common with the procedures of fair debate or the process of education. In practice, they were a combination of an indoctrination session, a political protest demonstration, an endurance contest, and a variety show.

At most of the teach-ins, the Administration's point of view was given only token representation. The great majority of the speakers, by deliberate design, were critics of the Administration.

At many of the teach-ins, spokesmen for the Administration's policy were subjected to booing and hissing and catcalling, so that it was impossible for them to make a coherent presentation of their case.

Communist propaganda films were frequently shown. Communist literature was frequently distributed.

People of known Communist background were frequently involved.

And at virtually every teach-in, the anti-Administration speakers vied with each other in their extremist denunciations of Administration policy. . . .

Communist Exploitation of the Anti-Vietnam Teach-Ins and the Anti-Vietnam Movement

Whatever the intent of those who originated the teach-in movement, the fact is clear beyond challenge that the Communist propaganda apparatus has been able to exploit the teach-in movement and the anti-Vietnam agitation, in general, for purely Communist purposes.

Even if the teach-ins had drawn a firm line against Communist participation, Moscow and Peiping would have found some means of exploiting them. But the exploitation has been made so much easier by the fact that, so far, none of the leading luminaries of the teach-in movement have considered it necessary to draw such a firm line—with the result that a substantial Communist infiltration is demonstrable, that a much more substantial infiltration is probable, and that there has been a tragic blurring of the distinction between the position of those who oppose our involvement in Vietnam on pacifist or idealist or strategic or other grounds, and those who oppose our involvement in the war because they are Communists or pro-Communists. . . .

Summary of Conclusions

1. The great majority of those who have participated in anti-Vietnam demonstrations and in teach-ins are loyal Americans who differ with Administration policy in Vietnam for a variety of reasons, ranging from purely strategic considerations to pacifism.

2. The Communists have traditionally sought to infiltrate and exploit all organizations dedicated to peace; and a reading of the official Communist press and of confidential directives to party members makes it clear that the CPUSA and its affiliates have given all-out support of the anti-Vietnam demonstrations and teach-ins, have directed their members to participate in them, and have sought to influence them in the interests of Communist expansion.

3. While leaders of other pacifist organizations, like the National Committee for a Sane Nuclear Policy, have sought to protect themselves by demarcating their own position from that of the Communists and by establishing certain criteria and certain controls to protect their organization against Communist infiltration, there is nothing in the public record to suggest that the leaders of the anti-Vietnam agitation and of the teach-in movement have similarly sought to demarcate their position on Vietnam from the Communist position on Vietnam or to repudiate Communist support or to establish criteria and controls designed to prevent Communist infiltration and exploitation of their movement.

4. In the absence of any such effort by the non-Communist leaders of the movement to prevent or limit Communist infiltration or participation, a significant number of people of known Communist background or with long records of association with Communist

fronts have been able to play a prominent role in the movement.

5. The control of the anti-Vietnam movement has clearly passed from the hands of the moderate elements who may have controlled it at one time, into the hands of Communists and extremist elements who are openly sympathetic to the Vietcong and openly hostile to the United States and who call for massive civil disobedience, including the burning of draft cards and the stopping of troop trains. This is particularly true of the national Vietnam protest movement scheduled for October 15–16 [1965].

6. The great majority of the teach-ins have had absolutely nothing in common with procedures of fair debate or the process of education. In practice, they were a combination of an indoctrination session, a political protest demonstration, an endurance contest, and a variety show. The proceedings were characterized by extremist statements and the open distribution of Communist literature.

7. The National Teach-In, in Washington on May 15, was characterized by a plausible effort at impartiality during the morning and afternoon sessions, but, in the summary session that evening, all pretense at impartiality was abandoned in favor of a totalitarian one-sidedness, with panelist after panelist and speaker after speaker excoriating the Administration and calling for the mobilization of a national movement of protest.

The National Teach-In sessions, of May 15, 1965, received complete support from the Communist and pro-Communist publications in the United States like *The Worker*, the *People's World*, *The National Guardian*, and *The Militant*.

The National Teach-In, of May 15, 1965, was arranged in a manner that left an impression condemnatory of U.S. policy in Vietnam.

Writing in the *Washington Daily News* of May 17, 1965, Bruce Biossat confirmed the general impression of other observers when he declared:

> The participants, in overwhelming majority, made it plain they came seeking confirmation of their pre-Washington judgments that Administration policy in Vietnam is almost wholly wrong. Contrary arguments, no matter how seemingly well-buttressed with fact, were generally greeted with skepticism, scorn, or derision. . . .
>
> In the whole fifteen and a half hours, I did not hear from the lips of any critic a single approving word about U.S. policy in Vietnam or anywhere else. The Government was portrayed as stupid, ignorant, arrogant, secretive, and persistently wrongheaded.

8. The evidence is overwhelming that the world Communist apparatus—in the United States, in Moscow, in Peiping, in Hanoi, in Havana, and elsewhere—has been able to exploit the anti-Vietnam agitation and the teach-in movement for the purpose of confusing their own people, for the purpose of fostering the impression that the majority of the American people are opposed to the Administration's policy in Vietnam, and for the purpose of attacking the morale of American servicemen in Vietnam.

9. It is also clear, from numerous statements by Communist spokesmen, that many of them believe their own propaganda and that they are convinced that American public opinion will compel the Johnson Administration to pull out of Vietnam and leave the field to Communism.

10. What all this adds up to is a global effort, on the part of the Communist apparatus, to force the withdrawal of American troops from Vietnam by means of a massive psychological warfare attack. In this effort, the Communists are exploiting all the idealism of honest critics to bolster their position, just as they used Communist-front groups to bolster their position in various crisis situations in the 1930's and 1940's. In many cases, the personnel is the same. The only thing which has changed is the cause—and even this is the same if we consider that the greater cause of all Communist activity in America is to bolster the international gains of world Communism by urging Americans that what occurs in Vietnam, or Korea, or Berlin, or Greece, or Turkey, is essentially none of our business.

Reflections on Protest

—KENNETH E. BOULDING

Dr. Boulding is Professor of Economics at the University of Michigan and was a participant in the first teach-in. This article is from Bulletin of the Atomic Scientists, *October, 1965.*

In a way, the forerunner of [the teach-in] movement was the remarkable mobilization of faculty members on university campuses against Goldwater, which represented political arousal on a scale which has rarely, if ever, been seen before in these supposedly cloistered circles. The teach-in movement is clearly a response to Johnson's behaving like Goldwater and so, in a way, is part of this same arousal.

Nobody, unfortunately, is much concerned to study the effects of all this, some of which may be quite different from what the people who are aroused by the arousal intend. I am constantly impressed by the ironies of social systems, where action often produces quite the reverse of the consequences which are intended. On the other hand, presumably, the better our knowledge of social systems, the more likely are we to avoid any unintentional consequences. It is important, therefore, for protesters to have some theory of protest and to be sensitive to those circumstances in which protest is effective in achieving its intended consequences, and those circumstances in which it is not. . . .

Unlike the civil rights movement which had fulfilled almost all the conditions for successful protest, the peace movement only fulfills some of them. The condition which it fulfills is that related to the long-run payoff. There is no doubt that the payoffs of a stable peace are enormous. The $120 billion a year that the world spends on the war industry is an appalling waste, which may well set back the achievement of world development by even hundreds of years and might even prevent it altogether. The probability of long-run change toward a system of stable peace is therefore high, and the peace movement fulfills this one essential requirement for the success of a movement for social change. On the other hand, it fulfills practically none of the other conditions. Its objectives, in terms of specific institutional and behavioral change, are not clear. We still do not really know how to get stable peace and what particular forms of behavior lead us toward, rather than away from, this goal. There is, furthermore, a great diversity of view as to immediate objectives within the peace movement.

It is clear, also, that American society at least is not supersaturated in regard to social change toward stable peace. In a sense, the task of the peace movement is fundamentally education, rather than protest. Most of the communications which are received by Americans, whether in the formal educational system or in the informal contacts of face to face conversation, tend to create an image of the world in which war is a recurrent necessity and in which, furthermore, for the United States, war has paid off pretty well. We tend to associate war with easy victories, like the war against Mexico or Spain, or with periods of economic prosperity and recovery from depression, as in World War II. We are not, and never have been, a peace-loving nation; we are not only ruth-less and bloody but we feel no shame about it. There is nothing in our Constitution; in our national heroes, many of whom are gen-erals; in our national origin, which came out of a war; in our great-est single national experience, which was the Civil War; or in any-thing contributing to our national image that makes war illegiti-mate in the way racial discrimination is felt to be illegitimate and inconsistent with our national ideals. In the case of war, we have very little hypocrisy, and change is very difficult. The peace move-ment is not simply trying to mobilize an already existing mass feel-ing or sentiment; it is trying to create a radical change in the na-tional image, against which all the forces of ordinary legitimacy seem to be arrayed. In the case of the peace movement, therefore, protest arouses counterprotest with great ease. The hawks in our society far outnumber the doves, and those who flutter the dove-cotes stand in danger of arousing clouds of hawks from their in-numerable nests. It will take an extensive process of education and, perhaps, even the grim teacher of national disaster before we learn that the prevailing national image is incompatible with our well-being or even with our survival; we have yet to learn that we are only one people among many, that we are not the rulers of the world, that power cannot be exercised without legitimacy, and that the costs of stable peace, significant and important as they are, are far less than the benefits.

The teach-in movement represents, perhaps, a partly subcon-scious recognition of the validity of some of the above principles. It began as a movement of pure protest and outrage. The motiva-tions which inspired it were no doubt various. They included a genuine fear of escalation into nuclear warfare; they included also a sense of moral outrage at the use of such things as napalm and the "lazy dog," and the appalling sufferings which we are imposing on the Vietnamese in the supposed name of freedom and democracy. Coupled with this, unquestionably, were some people on the left who were politically sympathetic with the objectives of the Viet-cong, though in the original movement there were few if any of these. I am inclined to think that the largest motivating factor was a sense of simple human sympathy with the sufferings of the Viet-namese, a sense of outrage at the utterly inhuman weapons of the American air force, and a sense of outrage, also, that we were using Vietnamese as the guinea pigs in weapon experimentation. The method of protest first suggested by the original group at the Uni-versity of Michigan was a work moratorium and a one-day suspen-sion of classes. This violated a good many of the above principles.

It is a form of protest which is not related to the object of protest; it immediately aroused a large counterprotest over the means, as well as over the object of protest, and it was very strongly on the protest side of the spectrum and away from education. The teach-in, which was adopted as a substitute, was much more successful. It at least edged toward the education end of the spectrum, even though it still retained a good many of the qualities of protest, and it was appropriate to the situation. The teach-in movement, furthermore, seems to be developing more and more in the direction of dialogue rather than pure protest, and this itself reflects the fact that there is an educational task ahead rather than a task of pure protest. The basic problem here is change in the national image itself, and this is something which protest is singularly unable to do, for protest has to take the image for granted and call attention to certain inconsistencies and incompatibilities. It assumes a given national image and says, in effect, to the policy-maker, "be consistent with it."

Under these circumstances, what is likely to be the best strategy for those of us who are interested in producing social change toward stable peace? The answer seems fairly clear. It should be a strategy of limited protest and extensive education. We should not, I think, abandon protest altogether, for there are many points even now at which, for instance, the conduct of the war in Vietnam violates a widespread national image of the United States as a reasonably decent and compassionate country. Protest, I suspect, should be directed mainly at the air force; it should be directed at the use of specific weapons which certainly fall under the heading of "cruel and unusual punishments," the moral feeling against which is securely enshrined in our Constitution and history. We have paid enough lip service to the United Nations also, to render protests on this score viable. The contrast between the shred of legitimacy which the United Nations gave us in Korea and the total absence of legitimacy in Vietnam is very striking, and protest could well be concentrated on this. We also have, in our national image, a high value on negotiation and a willingness to negotiate, and our present interpretation of negotiation as the abject surrender of the other side can be protested fiercely and effectively. Beyond this, I suspect, protest will be ineffective, with one possible exception. Our deepest trouble in Vietnam arises out of the total failure of our China policy. At this point, it may well be that the country is ripe for change, and that . . . protest will shake the tree. There is real danger lest, in our obsession with Vietnam, we forget the larger issue and we forget that the solution to Vietnam lies in our relationship with Peking.

Beyond this, social change toward stable peace can only come through education and research. The educational task is to convince people that stable peace is possible. Here we need to point to the many examples in which it has already been achieved. In the educational process, unlike the process of protest, we want to tie in, as far as possible, with existing legitimacy, existing images, and familiar history. We need to play up how we got a security community with the British and the Canadians. We need to play up historical examples of peaceful coexistence, such as was achieved between Protestants and Catholics in the Treaty of Westphalia in 1648. We need to emphasize the continuing dynamic that goes on in socialist countries as well as in our own, and to emphasize the learning process and our role as a teacher. We need to emphasize, also, the possible role of the United States not as a great power or as a world dominator but as a leader in a world movement for stable peace. All these things can easily be fitted into existing images and existing legitimacies. Then, at some point, a protest movement may be necessary to crystallize the image as a peace-leader. This may be some time off, but we should be ready for it when it comes.

Some Social Implications of the Teach-Ins

— RICHARD FLACKS

Dr. Flacks is Assistant Professor of Sociology at the Unversity of Chicago. This article appeared in Bulletin of the Atomic Scientists, *October, 1965.*

The teach-in movement discussed by Kenneth Boulding [above] symbolizes the possibility of a restructuring of the foreign policy apparatus. For the teach-ins suggest that a substantial segment of the academic community has become a self-conscious public, both willing and able to hold the decision-makers to account. Such publics are an essential element in the achievement of a democratically responsible foreign policy. If our constitutional system were functioning properly, such publics would be represented in Congress and would be addressed by the mass media. Since this is not the prevailing situation, the emerging academic public has had to create its own forums, assemblies, and communication networks with the instruments and resources at hand. The teach-in was the first such invention; since then, the techniques of expression have expanded to unofficial congressional hearings, international fact-finding teams, international radio networks, etc.

This emerging public is so far located almost entirely on the campus. It is appropriate that its nucleus should be found there, because academic people tend to have two qualities which are of particular importance in this situation—competence in finding and using new sources of information, and value-commitments which extend beyond the boundaries of the nation-state. But the possibility of democratizing foreign policy cannot be achieved if the foreign policy public remains largely academic. The longer-run promise of the teach-in, then, rests in the possibility that professors will redefine their role to include the task of creating an expanding public, competent and willing to confront decision-makers with the demand for responsibility. That task can be performed in the classroom—and, indeed many students are eager for such an experience —but it also requires an active and direct relationship with the larger community.

Thus, in addition to the problems of "education" and "protest" raised by Kenneth Boulding, academic men have, all unknowingly, presented themselves with a fundamental problem of self-definition. Can we provide—for our students and for people generally— a viable model of the free and active citizen? The sense that such redefinition was occurring was a source of exhilaration during the long nights of the teach-in.

There are, of course, some critical pressures operating against such a redefinition. In the first place, there is the press of day to day commitments which prevent many from serious engagement with concerns that are not clearly professional. Second, one would have to admit to the continuing presence of habits of timidity and rationalization acquired by many during the decade of the 1950's. Third, there is continuing worry about the appropriateness of partisanship in the academy—a concern often taken up by members of the Administration and directed at their critics rather than their supporters.

Counterposed to such pressures, it seems to me, is the argument that the development of democratic publics is a legitimate and relevant component of the academic role. Moreover, the fact that the participants in the teach-in movement are now loosely, but effectively, organized on a national scale offers hope that the longer-run promise of the movement (a promise which extends beyond the potential effect on Vietnam policy) will be sustained.

If it can be sustained, then we can hope for the development of new mechanisms for gathering and disseminating information for public education, for building an international community, for strategic protest, for critical analysis and research, which are independent of the foreign policy apparatus but politically substantial enough to move it in responsible and responsive directions. And, it should be added, if the new image of the academy as a center of citizenry initiative does take hold, a significant by-product is likely to be the renovation of the educational system itself.

Teach-Ins: New Force for the Times

—ARNOLD S. KAUFMAN

Dr. Kaufman, who teaches philosophy, helped organize the first teach-in, at the University of Michigan. His article is reprinted from The Nation, *June 21, 1965.*

Perhaps we are witnessing the death throes of McCarthyism. The man has been dead for almost ten years, but his spirit continues to frighten people and contaminate intelligence. Now, the main custodians of human intellect and its works in a society such as ours—the scholars and the teachers—are counterattacking. The teach-in movement is part of their effort to strengthen institutions without which freedom of inquiry and integrity of commitment cannot be preserved.

To suppose that the teach-ins are no more than a specific expression of opposition to Administration foreign policy would be a fundamental error. The National Teach-In at Washington was a step—perhaps a giant step—in the attempt to build a society which is free because its citizens are thoughtful and informed. A dream, perhaps; but a dream that is not alien to the traditions of this nation. McGeorge Bundy, in the statement announcing that he could not attend the teach-in, put it as well as anyone:

The American people know that the real danger will come when we are afraid of any unpopular minority or unwilling to reply to its voices. They understand what Communists cannot understand at all —that open discussion between our citizens and their Government is the central nervous system of our free society.

But Mr. Bundy has not kept himself informed about *the* American people. It is precisely because too many Americans, some of them in high places, do not understand what Bundy credits them with understanding that academic communities are in motion. The main disagreement between Bundy and his critics is about the present and urgent need to repair and reinvigorate the "central nervous system" of American democracy. The basic conflict is between those who respect truth and understand the processes by which informed public policy must be pursued, and those who do not.

The issue has been joined over the Vietnamese disorder precisely because Administration spokesmen have propagated a myth. Walter Lippmann makes the point with typical precision: "The essential fact about these disorders is that they are, at bottom, indigenous to the countries where the social order is broken down [and] not originally, not essentially, conspiracies engineered from the centers of Communist power." Lippmann concludes, "Surely it is time to grow up." (*Newsweek,* May 24.)

Most people know that more than fifty teach-ins have occurred around the country and that the surge of activity culminated in Washington on May 15. Few realize just how deeply the teach-ins are reaching into campus life. Trouble is brewing in the most unlikely places.

Arizona was the only state in the Union outside the Deep South that gave Goldwater a plurality. Today, both of Arizona's state universities are in ferment, and the pronouncements being made would have been inconceivable a short time ago. Purists who insist on the distinction between protest and debate should bear in mind that when that which cannot be discussed *is* discussed, the debate is, by its very content, a protest. It is not surprising, then, that when, at the recent Arizona University Teach-In, a member of the faculty remarked that the United States might be unable to prevent Asia from going Communist, political tempers shot up like rockets. The [Arizona] Senate Appropriations Committee and the State Institutions Committee summoned both university presidents and their respective governing bodies to the legislature for an accounting. The outcome is still in doubt.

And what more unlikely place for acts of political courage than the University of California branch at San Diego? Right-wing extremism flourishes in the area. When twenty-three students and teachers protested against intervention in the Dominican Republic, the *San Diego Union* [announced] . . . that if the regents do not put a stop to political shenanigans, "this newspaper will do everything possible to see that the state legislature does." The response? The faculty and students are organizing a teach-in; and the chancellor of the university, John S. Galbraith, has pressed the point home by reaffirming the university's commitment "to the great traditions of free inquiry and free expression. . . ." This is heady stuff for San Diego.

Indeed, freedom is a heady business. No one understands this better than college administrators. As long as genuine freedom is celebrated by rhetoric rather than by public exercise, campuses remain quietly comfortable. But it appears that the peace that frustrates understanding is no more. The rhetoric of free expression is being translated into *action relevant to power*. It's enough to make the stomach of even the doughtiest administrator rumble. If the inevitable pressures to conform are resisted by those who run our universities, this society will have passed a milestone on the road to genuine democracy.

What has set into motion so many of those Americans who cherish the skills of the mind? There are many causes, and the precipitating one was clearly the Administration's decision, contrary to all assurances given before the election, to enlarge the war in Vietnam. The opposition of those already opposed to U.S. policy was intensified; many others who had been teetering haplessly on the edge of indecision fell into opposition. And, because they felt duped and manipulated, their reactions were correspondingly intense. The intensity of the reaction is very important. Dissent from official policy will not propel men into the sorts of actions that have been taken unless they feel *intensely* opposed.

Opposition to [U.S.] Vietnamese policy has been, in large part, inspired by general dissatisfaction with the main lines of American foreign policy. Many of us who endorsed the Marshall Plan and the Truman Doctrine, who supported U.S. action in Berlin, Korea, and Cuba, are simply unwilling any longer to accept as valid the assumption that the threat Communism poses is either monolithic or predominantly military. Nor are we willing any longer to credit the claim that all revolutionary disturbances are essentially conspiracies, engineered from the centers of Communist power. We do not propose abdication of responsibility. We are not isolationist, neo-isolationist or crypto-isolationist. And we will not be detracted by such vapid criticism.

Nor will we any longer accept the simple-minded litany about the fight between tyranny and freedom—between the forces of darkness and the forces of light. Far from being unwilling to acknowledge the existence of evil in the world, we realistically insist that these tendencies are as likely to be buried in the breast of the publisher of some Western news magazine as in the breast of the editor of *Pravda*. . . . Those who have inspired the teach-in movement believe that revolutionary movements must not be suppressed. Instead, this nation must learn to respect revolutionary energies that are consistent with a genuine concern for liberty and social justice. In some places, they may take the form of social democracy. In other places, the situation may require an accommodation with Communist power. For, once we stop viewing Communism as monolithic, we are free to *consider the possibility* that accommodation may be preferable to endorsement of some equally, or more, oppressive regime which lacks even the degree of popular support that indigenous Communist movements enjoy. In any event, we are determined that *de facto* support of non-Communist tyrants shall not be concealed by the rhetoric of the American credo. What seems especially clear to us is that our policy-makers have been neither resourceful nor always committed to the values of liberty and social justice in the making of American foreign policy.

And it becomes increasingly clear that they do not even pursue our vital national interests effectively. The wide range of criticisms has brought together strange bedfellows. Any protest movement that contains both A. J. Muste [*a leading pacifist*] and Hans Morgenthau must have a broad base of support—to put it mildly. But widespread criticism of American policy does not alone account for the spectacular spread of the teach-in movement.

Nothing has aroused more irritation among thoughtful men than the Administration's huckster approach to the problem of "selling" its policies to the American public. Nowhere is the aversion to being manipulated into consensus felt more strongly than on campuses. But academicians are not alone in this: one great ally has been the working press. Not long ago, a few of us, active in organizing the National Teach-In, were interviewed by a reporter in behalf of a prominent magazine. After the article on which he worked had appeared, he wrote an apologetic note to me: "Unbelievable," he called it. "Almost a classic example of the old gag line: 'My mind is made up—don't bother me with facts.'" The working press is sick of the deception and distortion that so many publishers and officials force it to accept. It is disgusted with news management that undermines respect for both the reporter and his craft. Newsmen are fed-up with a process that converts honest work into a product indistinguishable in its fidelity to truth from the wares of the *Daily Worker*. The tacit support from members of the working press has made it possible for the teach-in movement to become effective.

Another motivation has been discontent with the functioning of our political institutions. In his book *The Public Philosophy*, Walter Lippmann complained about the intrusion by the legislature into what were properly the functions of the executive branch of government. This difficulty he termed a "derangement of powers." One of the ironies of the present mess is that Lippmann has become one of the strongest critics of a policy the defects of which are due in no small measure to Congressional abdication of constitutional responsibilities to the executive. President Johnson seems bent on reducing Congressional opposition to ineffective jabbering by portraying critics as mavericks and kooks. . . .

The teach-in movement is partly an effort to fill the resulting organizational vacuum. Democracy requires dissent. Dissent requires an effective and courageous opposition to Government policy. It is a reflection of the weakness of the American system that effective opposition has not been adequately voiced in our legislative assemblies. It is a reflection of the basic strength and adaptability of the system that substitutes for this lack are being provided by members of the academic community.

Many active in the Vietnam protest have been stalwarts in the civil rights movement and have participated in its impressive victories. The way in which "hard realities" have yielded to civil rights pressure has, along with President Kennedy's deliberate efforts to engage academic people in public life, lessened the intellectual's traditional sense of powerlessness. There is nothing like a good dose of fulfillment to strengthen a person's will to believe that possibilities can be converted into policy change. And few things will as effectively transform quiescence into activism as a strong will to believe. These background circumstances also partly account for the sturdy links between the civil rights movement and the Vietnam protest. The political implications of this relationship are explosive.

Finally, but perhaps most important in explaining the teach-in movement, is the condition of discontent and ferment that exists on our campuses themselves. . . . The reactions [to the first teach-in] that meant most to me were those of students who, afterward, claimed that the teach-in was the most meaningful *educational* experience they had ever had. For the first time, they realized what a university might be. The letter I most cherish was one from four students which began: "We are encouraged and deeply moved by your participation in the recent demonstrations on Vietnam—because it indicates that you have seriously dealt with the question of responsibility and commitment." . . .

The other relevant condition of our campuses is less spiritual, but not less important. Teachers are simply more secure than most people. Good educators get tenure quickly and are in a powerful bargaining position. No major university, no state legislature, can afford to act oppressively toward any portion of their faculty, for to do so might result in the alienation and prompt departure of many besides the main "offenders." It is easier to be outspoken in behalf of convictions when doing so does not place one's job in jeopardy.

With certain exceptions, the National Teach-In has received a remarkably sympathetic hearing from press and public. All things considered, there has not been much red-baiting. Most of the criticism has consisted of the charge that we acted "irresponsibly" and "unpatriotically." The main argument leveled against our activity is that we are giving aid and comfort to the Communists, postponing the day when they will be willing to begin negotiations and thereby jeopardizing American lives committed to battle. . . . Very briefly, the validity of the argument rests on the assumption that present Government policy will bring those who can stop the conflict to the bargaining table. But, as that is one of the very points at issue, the criticism reduces to the claim that those who do not accept the Administration reasoning are unpatriotic. A point of view more irresponsible, more subversive of genuine democratic commitment, can hardly be imagined.

Besides this bit of circular reasoning, we have been subjected to little more than *Time*'s predictable adjectives ("cattiness and caterwauling"), and the normal sorts of misdescription that creep into reports of any complex event. The truly responsible press has described what went on at the National Teach-In with remarkable fidelity to fact and with sympathy and respect. In an editorial, *The New York Times* commented, "the academicians on both sides conducted themselves with a dignity and respect for fact that contrasted favorably with the emotionalism that too often passes for discussion in foreign affairs." James Reston credited us with having "developed into a forum of national debate which could be of fundamental importance to the nation." [*See Chapter IV.*] How have we managed to avoid most of the more contemptible forms of criticism? How have we managed to earn as much respect and sympathy as we have?

It would be nice to think that it is all due to the fact that our virtue shines through. It is undoubtedly true that we have managed to convince some reporters that we mean what we said, that we are not being disingenuous when we claim to have a concern for the quality of the democratic process. It is also true that the National Teach-In received an immense, and unexpected, TV coverage. Millions of Americans could see for themselves that "cattiness and caterwauling" were hair-raising distortions of the reality of the event that took place in Washington. Moreover, our sponsors include men of unimpeachable integrity and commitment to scholarly inquiry. . . .

But the prestige of one's sponsors is a thin reed on which to rest one's claim to legitimacy. Besides the latent sympathy of those newsmen who have been subjected to the same forms of manipulation and constraint that we have caviled against, there are other conditions. There is great public distrust of the Administration's Vietnam policy. The latest Gallup poll (*New York Herald Tribune*, May 16) indicates that 48 per cent of the population has yet to be convinced that the Government is handling affairs in Vietnam as well as one might expect. This does not mean that 48 per cent of the population opposes present policy, but it does mean that anyone who develops reasoned criticism serves a very general need for greater understanding. Moreover, among those who support present policy and think the Administration has done as well as can be expected, there are many who realize that they might be mistaken. They must, if they are sane, be fearful of potential miscalculation. They, too, must appreciate reasoned discussion and debate, if only because it reinforces their conviction that the Administration's fateful decisions are correct.

Moreover, it is obvious to those who have even the most casual acquaintance with the teach-in movement that we do not hew to a "line." Our opinions vary from those who demand instant withdrawal to those who believe only that the decision to enlarge the war was wrong—and everything in between. What we have in common is a conviction that the Administration has not leveled with the American people, and a determination to bring the disciplines of careful thought and scholarly inquiry to bear on the momentous issues of peace and war.

Another factor that has contributed to our good public image is that academic communities are, from the point of sheer size, a very significant part of the total population. More than three million students combine with approximately half a million faculty; and these are linked in an indefinitely large number of ways to people in business, the professions, and public and political life. From a purely political point of view, it is not a group that can be ignored.

Our connection with people in public life is the keystone in the arch. Had McGeorge Bundy not accepted our invitation, we could hardly have attracted the attention we did attract. He is reported to have told friends, "These are my people; I must talk to them." Moreover, there is, in his statement of regret, a sentence that may yet prove to be of enormous importance. "I wholly disagree," he said, "with those who have argued that it is inappropriate for a Government official to take part in a discussion of this kind." This is an astonishing acknowledgment of the legitimacy of the National Teach-In enterprise. We are not going to sit around, holding our breath, waiting to see whether Bundy really means what he says, or whether, in saying it, he speaks for the Administration. But we are not, on the other hand, going to play the cynic in order to avert the charge of naïveté. We shall see. Ours are not the only credentials that must be certified by events.

It is also the case that thousands of academics who are presently aligned against the President's policy were politically active in the last campaign. For example, among the sponsors of the Michigan Teach-In were the past chairman of our local Citizens for Johnson-Humphrey Committee (he received four different invitations to the Inaugural Ball and profuse thanks for his efforts); the only Democratic mayor Ann Arbor has had in more than three decades; one of the principal campaign managers for our successful Democratic candidate for Congress; and countless people active in the precincts. Moreover, the local Democratic Party recently passed, by a vote of more than 2 to 1, a resolution condemning the Administration's enlargement of the Vietnam conflict.

Finally, our relative immunity from vilification is, in large part, due to the fact that the public has a rather schizophrenic attitude toward colleges and universities. On the one hand, they typically view institutions of higher education as places to which children must go in order to acquire earning power and social status. On the other hand, they think of commitment to the life of scholarly inquiry as somehow sacred. And they regard members of academic communities as still predominantly committed to the search for truth and understanding. Most people respect these pursuits as long as they do not encroach too severely on the conventional wisdom. Critical examination, self-examination, is acceptable as long as it does not penetrate beyond limits prescribed by genteel morality. The point is, the public is ambivalent. Respect for members of the academic community coexists with a crassly instrumental conception of the uses of universities; and both are hedged round by a fear of, and a contempt rooted in envy for, the disciplines of intellect.

One illusion prevalent in every society is that those who possess power necessarily exercise it responsibly. Until and unless this claim is put to the test of criticism, it is so much superstition.

After the clamor of war has died, what was achieved on May 15 will stand as a monument in the continuing effort to forge institutions that subject power to the test of reason in full view of the public. That such an event occurred at all will stand as a tribute to the resilience and adaptability of our institutions. It could not have occurred, nor probably can it occur again, without the cooperation of those in Government who understand the conditions which permit "the central nervous system" of a free society to function.

An Administration self-confident enough to permit such a process of confrontation to develop can go down in history as having made a fundamental contribution to the evolution of the democratic process. An Administration wise enough to encourage this confrontation will go down in history as having shaped the democratic process in profoundly creative ways.

We have glimpsed only the potentialities. In a column in *The New York Times,* Jack Gould described the TV coverage of the National Teach-In as an "important landmark in the evolution of communications." Whether or not this is a judicious estimate of our achievement, it is undoubtedly true that TV coverage has given us a glimpse of the way in which the medium can be used to inspire, rather than stultify, the intelligence and spirit of the people. The ability to grasp the opportunities that are available, to exploit in creative ways what has been achieved, depends to a very large extent on the response of the Government.

The Administration should realize that it has a genuine interest not only in cooperating with but also in promoting the teach-in movement. Apparently, the one criticism that makes those responsible for our foreign policy shoot off like firecrackers is the charge that they are Strangelove types. Assuming that they are not inflexibly committed to military action wherever and whenever trouble brews, they should greet with relief and enthusiasm any movement that opens to public inspection the full range of available policy alternatives. And they should respond in this way even if the attempt to explore alternatives comes in the garb of protest and debate. That is, perhaps, more than one can normally expect of human beings. But why shouldn't our policy makers be better than normal? Why shouldn't they even be statesmen?

For too long certain reasonable alternative policies have been irresponsibly ruled out of contention because of purely domestic political considerations. The issue of recognizing Communist China
is a case in point. . . . More important, unfettered discussion of
reasons for and against alternative policies has been restricted to
inner sanctums of one form or another—the inner sanctum of the
academies or the inner sanctums of the White House and the Pentagon. The American people have been treated like children, and it
is time to bring an end to manipulative paternalism in the conduct
of foreign policy. Why shouldn't the American people be exposed
to the thinking of Trotskyites as well as the thinking of Birchites?
Why shouldn't we, as a nation, move closer to that theoretical ideal
that has inspired so many of the builders of Western civilization—
a true market place of ideas? Only remember, ideas are not there to
be bought and sold like commodities. Ideas are there to be assimilated, rejected, treated seriously and with the respect due the premier productions of human organisms.

If a revolution in our national habits of public discussion could
be brought about along the lines envisioned above, it would—far
from inhibiting the making of American foreign policy—for the
first time liberate it and permit it to conform to reason.

Teach-Ins: New Force or Isolated Phenomenon?

— PETER LATHROP

*Peter Lathrop is the pseudonym of a philosophy in-
structor at a Midwestern university. This article is
from* Studies on the Left, V, No. 4 (1965).

Men committed to developing economic, social, and political institutions in which truth and reason can function as the principal
tests of power are always threatened with extinction. Their number dwindles alarmingly when the needs of all men become increasingly incompatible with the interests of the minority group
which monopolizes wealth and power. By uneven degrees, truth
and reason yield to myth and irrationality; as the Cold War wears
on, the tempo of America's drift into irrationality quickens. At
home, American power clumsily begins to translate the vulgar image of "The Great Society" into reality. By militarizing the econ-

omy and by extending narcotic handouts to dispossessed Americans through intervention and regulation, the Government attempts to guarantee continuous growth of corporate profits, some of which trickle down to middle-income groups. While indulging his own people, President Johnson—like Jehovah in His primitive Old Testament form—slays external enemies by pursuing a policy of escalated murder to systematically eliminate the "enemies of freedom" in other lands. Today, they are the guerrillas in Vietnam; tomorrow, there will be new adversaries.

The frightening consistency between a foreign policy of aggression and a domestic program of pacification displays itself, on a human level, in countless ways. The manipulated individual, well-adjusted to an increasingly irrational whole, turns into an ideal type. In a recent interview, a U.S. Marine captain in Vietnam offered the following explanation of a "shallow hole surrounded by blackened grass." "Another mine," he said. "Hit by a local ice-cream man on his bicycle. *He's still in orbit somewhere.*" And we, like helpless spectators, stare at the horror film in which killer and killed alike become the human casualties of power unbridled by reason.

In this nightmarish social context, individuals, such as Professor Arnold Kaufman [*above*], who seek to reinstate reason and human welfare deserve our admiration and attention. Though a temporarily insignificant minority, men devoted to building a rational society also merit one another's sympathetic, candid criticism. Although in general agreement with Kaufman's discussion of the origins of the teach-ins and his excellent description of their democratic form, I find little evidence to substantiate the general contention that the May 15 [National] Teach-In provides a microcosm of a new democratic institution or "force," which will extend from the university ponds to the wider, thoroughly parched areas of American society.

Kaufman argues that "The National Teach-In at Washington was a step—perhaps a giant step—in the attempt to build a society which is free because its citizens are informed. A dream, perhaps; but a dream that is not alien to the traditions of this nation." A force designed to "repair and reinvigorate the 'central nervous system' of American democracy," the teach-in, Kaufman maintains, transforms the "rhetoric of free expression" into "action relevant to power."

The teach-in *does* venture beyond the acceptable perimeter of American academic social criticism. Although cautiously condoning free discussion of all issues from all points of view, the multiversity unfailingly breaks the circuit of social criticism by separating man as thinker from man as actor. Under such circumstances, reason remains subservient to power. By institutionalizing rational debate of contemporary issues affecting power, the teach-in provides a democratic forum through which individuals and groups can formulate their own answers to the largest dilemmas of the society and then attempt to act, or to endorse action, consistent with analysis. Combining theory with practice, objective analysis with passionate commitment, this fresh model of democratic social criticism constitutes a symbolic threat to those whose power rests on an irrational base. The present American Establishment, therefore, must remain basically antagonistic to *any* form of comprehensive social criticism which, if united with action, might cause a majority to discover the generator of irrationality—and possibly a cure as well.

To be successful, to reinvigorate the "central nervous system" of democracy, the teach-in must coalesce with other democratic forms and spread from the campus to virtually every other sector of American life. Until then, reason cannot become the criterion of power. Any assessment of the actual and potential social significance of this new form must follow from a careful consideration of the extent to which the teach-in can become powerful enough to affect the formation of major political decisions.

1. Of the alternative patterns of development which teach-ins may assume, three seem worth considering. The first possibility, for which Kaufman argues, is that the teach-in may represent a giant step in the gradual, if frequently interrupted, development of democracy within the present American socio-economic system. Such an optimistic projection, of course, presupposes that those who defend the status quo can, either willingly or because of an aroused and informed public, yield to the gentle persuasive powers of reason. Thus far, however, Kaufman's explanatory model of the teach-in as a means of forging a rational, democratic society has failed to fit the realities of the spring and summer. Any "force" which the teach-in may have exerted certainly cannot be measured in objective results. Since May 15, our foreign policy has remained inflexible, in Vietnam and elsewhere. The war in Asia has been gradually escalated within the Johnson Administration's framework of rationality: In these few months, we have doubled the American commitment in Vietnam, indiscriminately bombed suspected Vietcong strongholds, burned village huts with cigarette lighters, exploded Lazy Dog missiles, and measured the success of every operation by the number slaughtered.

The "rationality" of such a course can only be derived by comparing present American strategy with such proposed tactics as bombing Hanoi. Kaufman seems slightly encouraged by the Administration's sense of restraint and responsibility. So am I. But ever so slightly. But why should the game theorists risk a long pass on first down? In 1964, we elected the partially debilitated in preference to the totally insane. Hence, we should not expect American irrationality to assume raving, hysterical forms. Ours is the calm, arithmetic, antiseptic insanity of Herman Kahn, not the flamboyant madness of Strangelove. In addition to generous paychecks, RAND men, it should be noted, quite regularly draw logical inferences from arbitrary assumptions which express minority wishes, not objective realities.

Even such limited rationality (which, of course, bears an inverse relation to the search for reason) has in no way been encouraged by the teach-ins. The explanation, I think, is far simpler. McGeorge Bundy's partial rationality results from an interest in the survival and preservation of the American corporate class. Bundy surely does not need the academics to brief him on the nature of the interests he serves. There is, then, no reason to infer that the teach-ins have influenced the thought or action of the highest level of American policy-makers. Washington may import "intellectuals," but it cannot purchase reason at the same economy prices.

What has been the impact of the teach-ins on the content and form of public opinion (excluding the campus)? Consider Vietnam, the most immediate issue. A full-scale, open discussion of the general and specific features of American foreign policy probably should have increased dissent markedly. Yet, in a mid-July poll on Vietnam conducted by the American Institute of Public Opinion (Princeton, New Jersey), 48 per cent approved Johnson's policy in Asia, 28 per cent disapproved, and an astonishing 24 per cent *expressed no opinion whatsoever!* Analysis of the specific reasons for disapproval yields even more depressing results. Of the 28 per cent who disapproved, only about half endorsed less aggressive alternatives. Thus, in July, a mere 10–15 per cent of the American public rejected the present intensification of the war. And one can only speculate about the number within this tiny minority who regard Vietnam as a temporary aberration in an essentially sound foreign policy. Furthermore, a sizable percentage of these dissenters undoubtedly exist at the source of the teach-ins—the American campus. Since May, then, the teach-ins have failed to enlarge their base of operation.

The exercise of power has neither been affected nor tested by reason. Kaufman argues that the teach-in represents the intellectual community's "counterattack" against the cynical "manipulation" of public opinion. But the public has not even acknowledged the skirmish. *For the most discouraging statistic in the poll is that only 1 out of every 100 adults* stated that "the country should be *told* more of what is going on." The form of the question reveals the depth of our antidemocratic ideology of foreign policy formulation: Even if the individual should be *told* about high-level decisions, he should certainly not consciously shape the courses of action. Foreign policy has been redefined as a technical, sensitive subject accessible only to highly intelligent, qualified (and, not so incidentally, state-subsidized) experts.

If the teach-ins have, thus far, failed to penetrate large sectors of American society, they have, as Kaufman suggests, quite obviously affected the quality of intellectual life on many campuses. Isaac Deutscher remarked that the teach-in represents "the awakening of the critical spirit in America." On large campuses as well as in remote, conservative areas, one can observe and document what Kaufman aptly terms an "aversion to being manipulated into consensus." After having actively participated in teach-ins, nearly 100 Stanford professors picketed President Johnson's U.N. speech in San Francisco. Although they had had no previous marching experience, the professors decided that the absence of sufficient organizational means of conveying their reasoned opposition to the Administration's Vietnam policy necessitated a public act. Discussion and criticism within the framework of the teach-in led to action. And as the Administration's basic myths about foreign policy require more potent doses of complexity and cynicism, we can expect the reaction of an even larger minority of students and faculty to intensify, thus enlarging the scope of the teach-ins.

The initial success of the teach-ins on American campuses is as undeniable as their total failure to influence high-level decision-making directly or through public opinion. But what about the future? To become an effective force, the teach-in must expand in two directions: on the campus and in the society at large. Kaufman assumes that the scale models of democratic process will aid in developing a thoughtful and informed citizenry by a more or less simple process of reproduction. Concentrating on the logical possibilities for growth, however, he does not adequately discuss the severe social and political limitations on democratic institutions. There is, of course, every reason to believe that the scope and influence of the teach-in can be somewhat enlarged. Yet, at the same time, there are definite boundaries beyond which, it seems to me, this new institution cannot proceed.

First, the search for reason in an increasingly irrational social context simply does not pay off. And the overwhelming majority of students and faculty know this only too well. They are indifferent or hostile to the idea of commitment to any cause, especially an unpopular one. Having been nurtured by American culture of the Cold War period, most inhabitants of the American campus quite understandably arrive and depart with a cool, aloof attitude concerning issues beyond their immediate reality of self, career, and family. For them, college constitutes a necessary—and often unpleasant—obstacle on the trail to a handsome salary and social prestige. . . . As a counterforce, the teach-in will attract only a few of these hopelessly uncommitted.

Furthermore, freedom is not only a "heady business," it is also an unwise, and occasionally dangerous, business. Though somewhat removed from the conformist world of the government bureau and the corporation, the American university, nevertheless, mirrors the larger society of which it is an integral part. In the process of becoming financially dependent upon the corporations and the Government, the university has been more or less refashioned in the image of the institutions which it serves. Hubert Humphrey's recent, fatherly advice to new congressmen conveys the spirit of caution which pervades campuses as well as other dominant American structures: "If you feel an urge to stand up and make a speech attacking Vietnam policy, don't make it. After you've been here a few years you can afford to be independent. But if you want to come back in 1967, don't do it now." (Quoted in *Life*, July 30, 1965.)

In addition to the fairly obvious limitations on the quantitative growth of democratic institutions on campuses, there are even more formidable obstacles to a qualitative leap from the university to the society at large. Kaufman suggests several potential links between the teach-in and the public: "One great ally of the teach-ins has been the working press." After citing one or two isolated examples of reasonably objective coverage—*The New York Times* and Walter Lippmann's column—Kaufman concludes that "with certain exceptions, the National Teach-In has received a remarkably sympathetic hearing from press and public." The inference is astonishing: Kaufman too easily dismisses the "predictable adjectives" of *Time* (whose readership exceeds three million) and simply fails to mention the almost unanimous sarcasm and hostility to the teach-ins expressed in the mass media.

A handful of newsmen and the "truly responsible press" hardly comprise an effective antidote to the enormous cultural apparatus which operates full time to suppress reason. A few expendable in-dividuals cannot influence—let alone alter—the principal means of information and entertainment, which are so generously financed by those unable to survive a *sustained* rational examination of for-eign and domestic issues affecting the entire social system. And without a massive transformation of the present patterns of opinion formation, the possibility of a public participating in democratic decision-making evaporates. Kaufman may regard a good word from Walter Lippmann or an occasional television special as hopeful break-throughs for reason. However, it is the simple addition of exceptions that fosters Kaufman's illusion about the potential force of the teach-in. In the total context of the mass media in America, such illuminating moments have little effect on public opinion.

2. To provide substance to his dream of a democratic society, Kaufman must project his reproductive model of the teach-in onto an imaginary social landscape devoid of interacting forces. Only by assuming the possibility of a more or less free-floating institution can one overlook the complex economic, social, and political forces which confine democratic thought and action to margins of the American scene. Furthermore, Kaufman's model prevents him from characterizing at least two other shapes into which the teach-in may be molded by larger social pressures: it may be isolated as a social disease or incorporated as a status quo institution. Both apparently conflicting estimates have characterized the numerous criticisms of the teach-ins which the mass media have generously amplified and transmitted to the public.

First, by providing the means for a continuing rational critique of foreign and domestic policy, the teach-in may come to be re-garded as a social disease to be quarantined on the campus. Thus far, it has been discredited primarily by verbal techniques. There are enough tired stereotypes and half accurate cliches about the university teacher and student to convince almost every group in America (including, of course, most of the academics themselves) that this "new force for the times" should be ignored or avoided.

The crudest charge, of course, is that the teach-ins are Commu-nist inspired or influenced. Kaufman notes that "All things consid-ered, there has not been much red-baiting." Perhaps not at the University of Michigan or in *The New York Times*. But the re-marks of Senator Dodd probably appeal to greater numbers of the vigilant—as well as of the politically incurious—than Kaufman ad-mits. [*See Senator Dodd's evaluation of the teach-ins, in this chap-ter.*] True, red-baiting as a national technique of divorcing criticism from action has been overused. Like so many other rhetorical fads, it has lost much of its hypnotic effectiveness, especially among the sophisticated. Yet, while exposing the naive who still cling to old cults, the urbane simultaneously create more subtle forms of ostracism.

Most partial explanations which have the intent—or at least the effect—of transforming the teach-in into an irrelevant, or even an unpatriotic, institution are rooted in the ancient ivory tower image of the university. Being comfortably removed from the real world of commerce and power politics, university professors are supposed to be idealistic men who cannot deal with hard realities. . . . Grayson Kirk, President of Columbia University, recently stated that, among members of the university community, "there must be self-imposed restraints as well as asserted and recognized rights." (From *The New York Times*, June 6, 1965.) Invoking the traditional ascetic dictum, Dr. Kirk cautioned the scholar to approach controversies "more in the spirit of a judge than that of an advocate." Thought and action must part company at the entrance to the campus. Yet, the professor of engineering who designs a missile for Lockheed remains a "scholar," whereas the political scientist who combines his criticism with action against, say, war profits, becomes an "advocate," thereby losing the exalted title.

The catalogue of moral and psychological explanations of student behavior is endless. Dr. Kirk, for example, states that the university is "filled with young people whose natural idealism is at yet untempered by the patience and tolerance of maturity. . . ." Immaturity, alienation, a youthful inclination to hell-raising are some of the familiar rationalizations which allow observers to dismiss the teach-in and other forms of campus protest. The evaluations implicit in these diagnoses range from the righteous indignation of the taxpayer who cannot understand why he should support heretics to the more tolerant intellectual who views the teach-in, in psychological perspective, as part of the maturation process.

According to tolerant opponents, the university, as "continuing critic of society," is the institution through which youthful criticism should be discharged. Social criticism of, say, funeral directors and labor racketeers is celebrated as the spice of democracy. But, when criticism threatens to unite with action against the present social structure, the majority of the intellectual community, Government officials, the mass media (and consequently the American public) overreact—as they did to the teach-ins. Of course, many of the psychological and moral diagnoses are valid, if not particularly profound. By pointing out that "youthful idealism" led many to object to the Administration's war on Vietnam, one is merely attempting to determine *why* the proposition occurs to a certain group (and, perhaps, at the same time, not to others). But the validity of the proposition itself must be argued on other grounds. In most cases, an unsophisticated psychological observation which evokes stereotypes and prejudices firmly implanted in the national consciousness blunts further investigation. Whatever the merits of these partial misleading explanations, their effect is (1) to prevent analysis of, and interest in, the teach-in as a potentially influential democratic institution; and, therefore, (2) to distort it into a tiny social phenomenon, increasingly radical, shrill, activist, uncritical and, subsequently, impotent.

3. Distortion by isolation reveals the obsessive fears of those who wish to avert genuine democratic discussion and action. Since this tactic represents a wish concerning the future of the teach-in—not a present reality—it may backfire. For, as Kaufman observes, many of the participants, such as B. F. Skinner, Jonas Salk, and Max Born, are highly respected professors and scholars. These men cannot be expected to abandon the new institution on the basis of false charges.

Distortion can also be achieved through expropriation: The teach-in can be converted into a paramultiversity, into still another inactive and, therefore, essentially harmless market place of ideas. Kaufman states that "the Administration should realize that it has a genuine interest not only in cooperating with but in promoting the teach-in movement." Objectively, Kaufman's remark is perhaps more accurate than he realizes. When not reacting out of fear and anger, Administration officials have unenthusiastically endorsed the teach-ins. Subjective fear and objective interest, then, form the basis for the ambivalent attitudes of, say, McGeorge Bundy. Underlying both basic responses, however, is the need to stunt the growth of a powerful institution for democratic thought and action.

An emasculated teach-in would augment the emasculated university. And the search for reason would be transformed into a contest to rationalize existing configurations of power—a far different, but socially acceptable, task. Furthermore, this market place of ideas could provide a source of intellectual raw material which the state might exploit to rationalize various parts of the system. In this way, the whole, the gigantic, central irrationality of a militarized economy might be preserved or, at least, extended. Of course, brain-picking is now common practice in industry as well as in government. Somewhat ingeniously revealing his attitude toward reason and the life of the mind, President Johnson recently directed his associates to listen to the ideas of "kooks," of "longhairs who can't find their way along the sidewalk without getting hit by a car." The image is flawless: In the world of Mr. Johnson, reason must be tailored to the demands of power.

The teach-in cannot sustain an overly friendly assault by representatives of the status quo. Courting "persons in public life," as Kaufman suggests, guarantees an early death by incorporation. For, inevitably, those who must rationalize power will inhibit fundamental criticism and, if necessary, will crush action based upon a truly rational critique of their interests. The powerful and their representatives cannot be expected to submit themselves to the test of reason. That truism explains precisely why "Administration spokesmen have propagated a myth." Having perceived the fiction, Kaufman cannot confront its social causes.

Moreover, he seems willing to pay the Administration's fee for bestowing respectability—that the teach-in function as a loyal opposition, a debating circle devoted to formulating foreign and domestic policy "alternatives" consistent with the preservation of the present American social structure. To ensure Administration participation, Kaufman uncritically assumes (1) that reason can be approximated within the existing socio-economic structure and (2) that all rational men are anti-Communist. On a world scale, these are the ultimate questions which a full discussion of specific issues such as Vietnam should evoke.

By focusing on the logical possibilities for growth, instead of on the hostile social conditions under which the teach-in must attempt to survive, Kaufman exaggerates both past achievements and prospects for the immediate future. After ignoring the ultimate boundaries of the teach-in (or of any other democratic institution in American society), Kaufman fails to discuss the impending dangers of distortion by isolation or by incorporation as a status quo institution. Neither the desperate need for democratic institutions nor the equally desperate hope of those committed to forging a more rational society should cause us to avoid a thorough assessment of the immense difficulties confronting the teach-in. An awareness of the obstacles is a precondition to transcending them.

Kaufman argues that the "intellectual's traditional sense of powerlessness" has diminished in the 1960's. "There is," he adds, "nothing like a good dose of fulfillment to strengthen a person's will to believe that possibilities can be converted into policy change." At the same time, there is nothing more fatal than an overdose of *apparent* fulfillment. For without comprehending the conditions under which possibilities can become policies, the intellectual quickly reverts to his ancient fantasy of power. What began as "the awakening of the critical spirit in America" ends prematurely in a self-imposed delusion. The implication of the teach-in is not that the intellectual is powerless. Nor is he suddenly potent after all these centuries. The central lesson transcends the intellectual's preoccupation with his image. The teach-ins dramatically demonstrate that, at present, no group or coalition in American society can combine the capacity and the willingness to instate reason as the test of power. That harsh lesson defines our task.

New Curriculum for the Teach-Ins

— CHRISTOPHER LASCH

Professor Lasch, author of The New Radicalism in America, 1889–1963, *teaches American history at the University of Iowa. The following is from* The Nation, *October 18, 1965.*

. . . The assumption of the teach-ins seems to be that the Government must be persuaded, by a combination of argument and orderly demonstration, to end the war. It must be made to see that other alternatives exist, that it is possible to negotiate a settlement, that the North Vietnamese and the National Liberation Front are ready to negotiate. But what if the Government chooses to remain deaf to such appeals? We have been told that at least one approach from North Vietnam was rejected by the Johnson Administration because it came during the Goldwater campaign and Johnson was afraid to appear before the voters as an "appeaser." I did not hear a single reference, during the entire conference in Ann Arbor [*on Alternative Perspectives on Vietnam; see Chapter VIII*], to the domestic political implications of a settlement in Vietnam. I heard many references to the fact that France had been able to withdraw from Algeria without losing its international prestige, but no one pointed out the obvious differences between the French case and the American.

France was able to remove itself from Algeria because a national hero coupled withdrawal with an appeal to glory; and even then, De Gaulle found it necessary to suppress the opposition by force and to impose on the country a regime of repression which has not been lifted yet. Johnson is not a national hero, nor is he in a position to suppress the Republican Party; and his political vulnerability—the vulnerability of any Democratic President on Cold War issues—opens up the prospect that we may have to wait for a Republican President, another Eisenhower, to put an end to the war in Vietnam. (By that time, there will be nothing left of Vietnam.) Appalling as this prospect is, it is one that critics of President Johnson would do well to take into account.

Those critics would do well, in short, to consider the possibility that no amount of persuasion will change the central fact of American politics—the fact that there is no opposition party, no political opposition at all to the rhetorical but enormously effective demand that we stand up to the Communists, resist "aggression," avoid another Munich. Until the political complexion of the country is radically changed, the political liabilities of liquidating the Cold War will continue to outweigh its advantages. As long as the appeal to anti-Communism brings automatic and unfailing success, we shall continue to be faced with the phenomenon, superficially so hard to explain, of "liberal" Presidents who execute the policies of their most outspoken critics on the far Right. Things would be different if the American Left had not long ago committed itself to outdo the Right in its anti-Communist zeal; but, once the Left itself accepted anti-Communism as the *sine qua non* of political respectability, it became the prisoner of its own immediate success, surviving the postwar hysteria only to find that hysteria had become a permanent feature of the political scene.

These facts, so notably absent from the discussions at the University of Michigan, so indispensable to any consideration of American policy in Vietnam or anywhere else, explain why it is futile to reason with the present Administration or, indeed, with any administration. The Administration cannot be persuaded; it has to be forced to change the direction of American policy. The real question, which critics ought to be considering, is what kind of force promises the earliest success.

There would seem to be two possibilities, not necessarily incompatible but difficult to pursue at the same time. One is mass civil disobedience, the weapon of the civil rights movement, and it is interesting, in this connection, that Robert Parris and a few other leaders of the civil rights movement were present in Ann Arbor. One of them, Carlton Goodlett, editor of the San Francisco *Sun-Reporter*, cited the free-speech movement at Berkeley as an example of the possibilities of civil disobedience; and one could recall many such examples—beginning with the Montgomery bus boycott

—from the civil rights struggle in the South. Whatever the moral implications of civil disobedience, whatever the importance of making a "witness" against arbitrary power, the essence of civil disobedience, as Goodlett tried to show, is coercion. By bringing the normal processes of government to a halt (as, for instance, when more arrests have to be made than the normal agencies of law enforcement can possibly handle), masses of demonstrators can sometimes force authority to yield on a given point. And mass civil disobedience is a tactic that conceivably might be used in the peace movement as well.

So far, civil disobedience in the peace movement has figured only in the form of isolated acts of conscience, possibly educative but hardly coercive. If civil disobedience were to be really effective, the movement would have to become much larger than it presently is. That is one of the difficulties [that stands] in the way of using civil disobedience as an instrument of agitation against American foreign policy. The other difficulty is that the situations in which civil disobedience has been successful are not precisely analogous to the foreign policy crisis. In the case of Montgomery and Berkeley, civil disobedience was effective because it could be used against local authorities who were fully implicated in the policies under dispute. Those policies—racial discrimination, free speech—were issues of national importance which, nevertheless, had a local dimension and a local impact. Questions of foreign policy, however, rarely present themselves as local issues; and even when they do, as in the case of the opening or closing of military installations which have local significance, so much of the ultimate power of decision lies in Washington that it is hard to bring nonviolent coercion to bear. . . .

The other alternative, the other means of forcing a change in American policy, is to build an effective opposition along traditional lines—a body of opinion, translatable into votes, which will be resistant to Cold War cliches and skeptical of anti-Communist crusades. Communism has too long been an obsession of American politics; it is time some drastic therapy laid it to rest. I do not propose a direct assault on the radical Right or even on the Center. It is the anti-Communist Left which most needs to be purged of its obsession with the menace; for it was the failure of the Left, its failure to function as an opposition, which, in the 1940's and 1950's, made possible the emergence of the "bipartisan" foreign policy from which we still suffer. Even now, the political climate is beginning to change, for a new generation is emerging for whom the trauma of Stalinism is a dead issue. But older liberals, with their tremendous emotional investment in the disappointments of the past, assume toward the new generation an irritating condescension and assure them that they will live to suffer the same disappointments and learn the same bitter lessons about the incompatibility of freedom and revolution. The new Left, in reply, denounces the old as "irrelevant"—the fate of all middle-aged people in America. The generational split on the Left thus mirrors a deeper sickness of American life—the absolute discontinuity between youth and age; and to attack the problem at the political level might suggest the possibility of attacking it at other levels as well.

The importance of the generational issue is what made the device of the teach-in initially so suggestive as a technique of agitation. Teach-ins represent precisely the mingling of age groups which has to occur before an effective Left can take shape—for the students alone do not constitute an opposition, whatever some of them may say about the irrelevance of their elders. Unfortunately, the very political crisis which created the teach-ins—the war in Southeast Asia—prevents them from becoming an effective instrument either of opposition or of education; the leaders of the movement have subordinated everything to the effort to stop the war in Vietnam. Quite apart from everything else, stopping the war in Vietnam is not a subject worth "teaching." It has very little intellectual content; a certain number of points can be made, and the subject is quickly exhausted. The real subject that needs to be "taught" is the history of the Cold War and of the relation of the American Left to Communism. The Left needs to reconsider its own history, as a patient therapeutically reconstructs his past. It needs to reconsider the origins of the Cold War; it needs to reconsider what it means to have "chosen" the West; it needs to reconsider Stalinism itself—was it an aberration or a historical necessity?—in order to get some perspective on the history of the twentieth-century revolution.

These are subjects—as distinguished from "alternatives" in Vietnam—worth teaching. Until the teach-ins begin to teach, they will be politically useless and intellectually boring. It will be interesting to see whether the failures of higher education—the confusion of education with expertise, the idea that students are a needless obstacle to "research"—will now repeat themselves in the political agitation to which teachers find themselves so unexpectedly committed.

The Teach-Ins and the American "Thaw"

—ISAAC DEUTSCHER

*Mr. Deutscher, who resides in London, is the re-
nowned biographer of Leon Trotsky and a political
analyst specializing in Soviet affairs. On May 15,
1965, he addressed the morning session of the National Teach-In; speaking frankly as a Marxist, he
presented a critique of the basic anti-Communist
premises of American foreign policy. Later, he flew
to California, where he spoke at the mass Berkeley
Teach-In. This is an abridged version of a longer article that appeared originally in* The Statesman
(Calcutta), June 9 and 10, 1965.

The United States is living through a great political thaw which
brings the promise of a profound change in its political climate.
After the long and dreary period of Cold War conformism—after
nearly two decades, during which successive administrations were
free to carry out the major acts of their foreign policy without meeting with any domestic opposition—a loud cry of protest against
President Johnson's armed interventions in Vietnam and Latin
America is at last resounding from coast to coast. The cry comes
from the vigorous throat of the young American generation, from
almost every university in the country. Several thousand professors
and hundreds of thousands of students participate in the protest
movement. . . .

What is the significance of this movement and what are its prospects? I must admit that I am skeptical about the chance the
present protests may have to alter official policy. President Johnson
is not going to yield to the cry for an American withdrawal from
Southeast Asia. He will continue to pour troops and bombers into
South Vietnam. But he no longer has the freedom of maneuver he
and his predecessors enjoyed when the American public was completely silent and acquiescent. A brake has been put on the American escalator; and, even if the forces driving the escalator upward
are far more powerful, the brake may have some effect.

However, the main significance of this intellectual and political
ferment lies in its probable long-term effects. This reawakening of

a critical political spirit in the United States is, in my view, second in importance only to the Russian de-Stalinization of the 1950's; and, in some respects, it is akin to it. What we are witnessing is the birth of a new American Left. The old Left has been almost dead for more than a decade; it had been morally crippled in the course of many decades. Several major traumatic shocks nearly destroyed it. In the 1930's and early 1940's, it debased itself by its identification or flirtations with Stalinism. Instead of acting as American radicals—reformers or revolutionaries—the men of the old Left had allowed themselves to be turned into the dupes, and even agents, of a foreign power. The shock of de-Stalinization deprived them of even the shaky moral ground they still felt under their feet. Then came the hammer blows of McCarthyism. The old Left succumbed to them because it had been morally corroded within. The American intellectuals who entered political life in the 1940's, 1950's, and even in the early 1960's, reacted to this debacle of the Left with hostility and disgust. Anti-Communism and anti-Marxism was the dominant, the almost exclusive, ideology of these intellectuals.

But now a new generation is entering politics, one which has not suffered from any of these shocks, has not been degraded by Stalinism, has not been shell-shocked by de-Stalinization, and has not been intimidated by McCarthyism. It enters the political stage without guilty conscience or paralyzing misgivings. It behaves with a beautiful and innocent courage. It reacts vigorously against the anti-Communist cliches and the anti-Marxist certitudes of its elders. It is sick of Cold War indoctrination. It is disgusted with the self-righteousness and complacency of the American Establishment, so boastful of its prosperity and might. It is acutely aware of the miseries of that prosperity, of the vast, persistent "pockets of poverty" in American society, of the new structural unemployment appearing amid booms, and of the oppression of the Negroes. It is deeply ashamed of the use to which America's power is being put in Southeast Asia and Latin America.

Reacting against official indoctrination, the young intellectual feels that Marxism is not at all the villain of our age, and that its ideas may yet prove relevant to the problems of contemporary society, including American society. Having learned from the sad experience of the old Left, the new radicals do not look for revelations either to Moscow or to Peking. They want to use and refine the tools of Marxism independently for their own analysis of American society and their own solutions to its problems. How they will cope with these tasks remains to be seen. But I have no doubt that

Marxism is emerging (or re-emerging) in the United States as a major intellectual and moral force, far more attractive than it has ever been there.

The weakness of the new Left lies in its lack of contact with the American working class, which, in its mass, remains apathetic and passive. But it should not be forgotten that, in the States, the universities are not quite the ivory towers they are in Europe. U.S. academic communities are proportionately much larger; they are also a much more active factor in the nation's industrial and social life.

Nor is this new Left completely confined to its campuses. The original impulse to the protests against the Administration's foreign policy derived from the Negroes' fight against racial oppression and from the freedom marches in the South. Men and women who organized that fight and those marches are prominent in the campaign against the war in Vietnam. The Negroes, it turns out, have broken the magic spell of white American conformism. They have taught the young educated white Americans an unforgettable lesson. They have set an example of resistance and struggle. And the mass of the young radicals is increasingly aware of the connection between Washington's reactionary foreign policy and the essentially undemocratic condition of American society. At the same time, they are drawing moral nourishment from America's democratic tradition, which remains alive despite all the long and frantic orgies of American reaction.

The teach-ins are only one phase in the emergence of a new and active social consciousness in the States. It is difficult to predict what the next phase is going to be. As I was leaving the States, the organizers of the teach-ins were discussing among themselves how to widen the base of the movement and how to assure its continuity. The movement is almost certain to have its ups and downs. Yet, whatever its ultimate fate, it is already transforming the moral and political climate of the country.

Henceforth, non-Americans should be aware that the voice of official Washington is not the only one with which America speaks. The voice of American youth and intelligence is already contradicting it; and it will go on contradicting.

VIII

Escalation of the Teach-Ins

Editors' Introduction

Perhaps the clearest indication of the teach-in's viability has been its ready employment by groups not concerned primarily with Vietnam and American foreign policy. As a form of educational discourse in which opinions can be aired freely, the teach-in is a natural device for generating enthusiastic criticism and debate over a whole range of issues. For instance, social workers used a teach-in to examine critically the Administration's "war on poverty." The organizers invited representatives of the Federal Government to confront both academic critics and independent organizers of the poor, many of whom were also highly skeptical about Administration policy. As the program indicates, the Poverty Teach-In pitted Tom Hayden, organizer of the radical Newark Community Union Project, against William Haddad, who had been Inspector-General of the Office of Economic Opportunity.

The dynamic fashion in which the teach-in can engender critical assessment has brought lively debate to areas generally regarded as noncontroversial. *The Times Educational Supplement* (London; October 8, 1965) reported that a "teach-in [at Stevenage, Hertfordshire] on secondary school reorganization got off to an encouraging, if exhausting, start . . . with a withering five-and-a-half-hour bombardment from an impressive array of experts." Debate covered such topics as the means of "apportioning children to local grammar schools" and the amount of government expenditure to education.

The teach-in idea has been so successful that it has been adopted by intellectuals in other lands. Included in this chapter are reports and evaluations of teach-ins held in Puerto Rico, London,

Toronto, Japan, and Paris. (For speeches delivered by Frank N. Trager and Donald G. Brennan at the Oslo Teach-In, April 16, 1966, see Chapter II.) Of these events, the most unusual was the Toronto Teach-In. Providing neutral ground for an international forum, the Toronto affair drew representatives from both industrialized and underdeveloped nations to debate the problems of a world in revolution. For example, former Assistant Secretary of State A. A. Berle, Jr. clashed with the former Premier of British Guiana, Dr. Cheddi Jagan, over U.S. response to revolution in Latin America. In another session, Professor Zbigniew Brzezinski, of Columbia University, debated V. N. Nekrasov, chief foreign editor of *Pravda*. The success of this teach-in led to a second International Teach-In at the University of Toronto (October, 1966), in which China was the central subject. (Texts of the major addresses delivered at the International Teach-In are available in *Revolution and Response*, edited by Charles Hanly, Toronto, 1966.) Serious reservations about the impact of the International Teach-In are expressed by Arthur Pape. In line with the concern of many in the American teach-in movement who noted that the excessive formalism of the National Teach-In muffled protest and restricted student-faculty exchanges, Mr. Pape warns that institutionalizing the teach-in may mean throttling it as well.

Out of the teach-in movement grew many new forms of action and confrontation. The Michigan Conference on Alternative Perspectives on Vietnam, organized primarily by the Inter-University Committee for Debate on Foreign Policy (the original teach-in sponsoring group), invited scholars from throughout the world to formulate viable alternatives to U.S. policy in Vietnam. The same committee also organized a national week of first anniversary teach-ins in 1966, as well as programs of direct political and community action. Community action, as the next task of the teach-in, was particularly stressed by I. F. Stone and Tom Hayden, among others.

On another front, eighty-five professors conducted a two-day academic lobby on Vietnam. In visiting congressmen and senators in Washington, they assumed, as Dr. Everett Bovard reports, that professors, "because of their influence on students . . . have status with members of Congress."

The teach-ins also inspired a group of artists and writers to express dissent from the Administration's policies by organizing a series of "Read-Ins for Peace in Vietnam." Borrowing a page from the teach-ins, they read from works conveying their dismay and anger at the war. A moving statement, made at the first read-in by literary critic Susan Sontag, closes this chapter.

Perhaps the most persuasive confirmation of the teach-in as a catalyst for criticism of U.S. foreign policy came from its extension into Congress. The televised hearings on Vietnam, conducted by the Senate Committee on Foreign Relations in February, 1966, were aptly dubbed "Fulbright's Teach-In." The hearings represented the first serious postwar debate in Congress on the assumptions underlying American foreign policy. Senator Fulbright himself remarked that if such an inquiry had been held earlier, "the teach-ins on the university campuses would not have been so necessary."

1. ANOTHER SUBJECT FOR THE TEACH-INS

The Teach-In on the War on Poverty

—FRED NEWDOM

Mr. Newdom, a member of the Poverty Teach-In's coordinating committee, prepared this statement for the editors.

The idea arose out of informal discussion among several students of community organization at the Columbia University School of Social Work. We felt that the "war on poverty" was a totally inadequate means of attacking poverty in the country and, beyond that, was a ruse intended to buy off discontent among the poor. These feelings, plus the belief that social work students should be concerned with the bases of a program in which many will find future employment, led us to organize the teach-in.

Our first step was to call together a group of social work students from the schools around New York City—we eventually had representatives from Hunter, New York University, Yeshiva, and Columbia on the coordinating committee. These students represented varying shades of political conviction and varying degrees of doubt about the point of view the teach-in should take, if any.

PROGRAM: TEACH-IN ON THE WAR ON POVERTY
December 5, 1965, at the Society for Ethical Culture,
New York City

1:30—*Welcome and Introductory Statement:* Leonard Mandelbaum (Leader, N.Y. Ethical Culture Society); Tom Karp (Sponsoring Committee).

2:00—*Background:* Joseph L. Vigilante (Dean, Adelphi School of Social Work); Richard H. P. Mendes (Department of Sociology, Brooklyn College); Tom Karp (Columbia University), moderator.

3:00—*Community Action Phase of the War on Poverty:* William Haddad (former Inspector-General, Office of Economic Opportunity); Tom Hayden (organizer, Newark Community Union Project and founder, Students for a Democratic Society); Fred Newdom (Columbia University), moderator.

4:00—*Government and the Elimination of Poverty:* Philip Sokol (Deputy Commissioner of Welfare, New York City); Charles Grosser (New York University School of Social Work and, formerly, Mobilization for Youth); Tom Levin (former Director, Mississippi Project Headstart); Irving Weisberg (Hunter College), moderator.

5:00—*Who Controls the Antipoverty Program? A Case Study:* Ted Velez (East Harlem Tenants Council); Ed Daniels (Executive Director, Massive Economic Neighborhood Development); Mel Kleiman (New York University), moderator.

6:00—*Dinner break.*

7:00—*Assessment of the Antipoverty Program:* Samuel Proctor (Northeast Regional Director, Office of Economic Opportunity); Richard A. Cloward (Columbia University School of Social Work and Mobilization for Youth); Leo Hirsch (Adelphi College), moderator.

8:00—*Specific Aspects of the Antipoverty Program:* Hyman Lumer (author, *Poverty, Its Roots and Its Future*); Esther Lentschner (Yeshiva School of Social Work); Gil Gordon (Yeshiva University), moderator.

9:00—*New Directions and Alternatives:* Mark Tarail (New York University); Warren Haggstrom (Director, Community Action Training Center, Syracuse University); Stanley Aronowitz (Editor, *Studies on the Left* and member, Committee for Independent Political Action).

[*Each speaker was allotted fifteen minutes; audience participation followed each set of presentations.*]

2. AN AMERICAN EXPORT: THE TEACH-IN ABROAD

International Teach-In on Revolution and Great Power Response

Program
October 8–10, 1965, at the University of Toronto

SESSION 1 (October 8, 8:30 P.M.)—*Revolution and Ideological Conflict.* Representatives of the great powers will discuss their approach to revolutionary political changes in less developed countries. In particular, they will define the conditions under which they believe that intervention is proper and the form such intervention should take. *Participants:* Professor Z. K. Brzezinski (Director of the Research Institute on Communist Affairs, Columbia University); V. N. Nekrasov (Chief Foreign Editor, *Pravda*).

SESSION 2 (October 9, 9:30 A.M.)—*Latin America: Revolution and Intervention.* There will be a confrontation of conflicting views from Latin America and the United States concerning problems of revolution and intervention in that area. An important area for exploration will be the Alliance for Progress and the question of whether this is a suitable means of bridging the gap between great powers and underdeveloped countries. *Participants:* Andres Lockward (Executive Committee of the Social Christian Party, Dominican Republic); Dr. Cheddi Jagan (former Premier of British Guiana); Dr. A. A. Berle, Jr. (former Assistant Secretary of State for Latin American Affairs).

SESSION 3 (October 9, 2:30 P.M.)—*Vietnam: Revolution and Intervention. Participants:* Patrick Gordon Walker (former British Foreign Secretary and Labour MP); Phuong Margain (Secretary General of the Cambodian Cabinet); Nguyen Thu Duc (Ministerial Adviser to the South Vietnamese Representative to the U.N.); Professor R. A. Scalapino (University of California, Berkeley).

SESSION 4 (October 10, 10 A.M.)—*Revolution and the Right to*

Self-Determination. Participants: Ali Mazrui (political scientist from Uganda); Roger Garaudy (teacher and member of the French Communist Party); Max Freedman (American newsman and political analyst).

SESSION 5 (October 10, 2:30 P.M.)—*Revolution and the Citizen's Moral Responsibility. Participants:* Professor Staughton Lynd (Yale University, head of the Congress of Unrepresented People, proponent of radical action in obtaining minority rights); Lord Fenner Brockway (former left-wing British Labour MP); Professor George Grant (philosophy teacher, expert on theology, author of the Canadian best-seller, *Lament for a Nation*).

Teach-In as Institution

— ARTHUR PAPE

Arthur Pape is a member of the Student Union for Peace Action Vietnam Project in Montreal. The following is from The Canadian Forum, *November, 1965.*

The original teach-ins stemmed from a belief that the U.S. war effort in Vietnam was partially supported by American academics—faculty and students—who carried on business-as-usual within the university; public silence was seen as equivalent to consent. The teach-in was intended to break that silence, thereby reaffirming the university's commitment to help solve society's problems and bridging the chasm between knowledge and personal action. Moreover, although the events took place within the university, they were radically different from normal courses or seminars; thus, they were a commentary on the situation in which the discussants found themselves as well as on the issues discussed. The process, as well as the content, of the teach-ins made them worldly, forthrightly political, and spirited.

The International Teach-In, held in Toronto, was radically different. It attempted to treat the subject matter as separate from the situations encountered in creating the meeting and it tended to minimize intellectual debate and personal moral choice. As above, this is shown by the process as well as the content of the affair.

The Toronto [organizing] committee hoped to create a forum

where significant ideas and policies concerned with revolution and response would engage in dialogue. Numerous difficulties of a political and social nature foiled the committee's efforts; they chose to see those difficulties as separate from the subject under discussion and, thus, created an international conference rather than a teach-in.

Originally, it was hoped governments would represent themselves. After months of negotiations, only Cambodia was willing to appear officially. This refusal by governments of all ideological types to defend their policies in a public academic forum should have been a subject of discussion, but was not. Similarly, the Canadian Government seemed unlikely to issue visas to representatives of the National Liberation Front unless the Saigon Government was also invited to speak. Yet, although this forced the committee to alter their plans and may have contributed to the ultimate non-participation of the NLF, at no time before or during the teach-in was this Government interference discussed or protested publicly. When Robert Scalapino refused to share a platform with Mike Myerson, a Berkeley graduate student who was to explain the Hanoi Government's policy, the committee acted behind the scenes to repress the whole matter. [*Professor Scalapino had also refused to participate in the Berkeley Teach-In, May, 1965; see Chapter I.*] In fact, the incident provided an ideal opportunity to bring into the open prejudices and traditions now well-established in the United States, which severely limit basic political debate and thus influence American responses to revolutions. (Scalapino refused to debate Myerson because in so doing he would add to the prestige and legitimacy of an American supporting the view of a Communist nation.)

There was, then, much concrete evidence of ways in which intellectual endeavor is severely limited by the nation-state system, in general, and by wartime, in particular. Wealthy nations' responses to revolution are largely made and sustained by conditions like these, apparently far from the crisis area; the Vietnam war is based as much in the suburbs and schools and power structure of the United States (and Canada) as it is in the rice paddies or power struggles of Southeast Asia. By not making these unpleasant but very real elements central to the discussion of the weekend, the International Teach-In tended to, in essence, retreat into the ivory tower from which the original teach-ins tried to escape.

The format of the Toronto affair was such as to insulate non-speakers from many of the verbal challenges provided during the weekend. There were only two scheduled occasions for small group

discussions, and both these were brief. They were treated as peripheral, rather than central, to the weekend and were poorly attended.
The mass meetings were, by nature, impersonal; nonspeakers were
spectators rather than participants. Although the committee's members said, several times, that the weekend should be a beginning of
action and not an end in itself, in fact, the structure of the weekend gave the opposite message, because lengthy and perhaps even
discomforting personal discussions were not an integral part of the
program.

Thus, in its internal structure, the ITI paralleled the university.
Its program was predetermined, not developed by or with those
who came to learn. People were talked *to* about personal issues, not
talked *with*—thus, the brilliant and moving speeches, in the final
session by Lynd and Grant were much like existentialist texts as
treated in a *lecture* series on ethics!

The pressure to appear objective was very heavy on the organizers of the Toronto affair; public relations, the support of the university, development of a broad committee, and financial requirements all seemed involved in that. Thus, many leading members of
the committee who had participated in the vigil protesting the
University of Toronto's honorary degree to Adlai Stevenson, last
spring, felt unable to reassert their views in a way which would not
jeopardize the planned ITI. When we remember that it was exactly
this kind of consideration and mood—which seemed to make it
dangerous and ineffective to publicly state unpopular views—that
gave rise to the *original* teach-ins, it is alarming to see how full
circle things have come in a short time.

None of the above statements should be construed as meaning
the International Teach-In was not worth while. The parochial
worlds of Toronto and its university—and to a lesser extent other
centers in North America—were exposed to people and moods and
ideas not much seen in these parts; that could only be to the good.
And, without a doubt, many individuals learned a great deal because of the weekend of meetings.

The fact of these valuable accomplishments should not decrease
our concern to examine the basic nature of the affair. It seems likely
that the teach-in, like so many innovations, is becoming institutionalized; and it is being transformed in that process of cooption.
It is certainly not a radical departure in education or politics, as it
has developed. In fact, the Toronto affair likely provides a clue to
modifications in store for large Canadian universities. It seems to
meet the requirements of those now running the universities: it can
service mass audiences; it is exciting and glamorous while still sub-

ject to the discipline of a predetermined curriculum; the subject matter is related to issues concerning many students; and yet, what is perhaps ultimately most important—the format—is such as to insulate the student from the impact of the subject matter, leaving him relatively untarnished for a society which requires his conformity and his skills, but not his personality.

Puerto Rican Teach-In Marked by Violence

—DIMAS PLANAS

From The San Juan Star, *October 14, 1965.*

Hundreds of *independentista* and statehood sympathizers hurled insults, tomatoes, and rocks at each other across Avenida Ponce de Léon yesterday as violence climaxed a teach-in protest over U.S. actions in Vietnam.

While scores of missiles were hurled back and forth across the street bordering the University of Puerto Rico, no one was injured among either the Federation of University Students for Independence (FUPI) or the Association of University Students for Statehood (AUPE). Nor was anyone arrested by the dozen policemen on hand, although at least one fight broke out between sympathizers of the two factions.

Nearby the teach-in went on peacefully—and loudly.

The teachers set up loudspeakers on ladders just outside the campus walls—and broadcast their message to about 500 people sitting inside the wall on the university grounds.

The teach-in went on for four hours, with teach-in leaders pleading with their listeners not to get involved in the nearby rioting.

The rioting began at 2:30 P.M.—a half-hour after the teach-in began—and continued intermittently until about 5 P.M. The missile-throwing lasted for about one hour.

The teach-in was being held outside the main gate [of the University of Puerto Rico] because university authorities had refused to authorize the use of campus facilities for it.

[*The story continues with details of the riot.*]

Stateside professors Richard Levins, Charles Lewis, and Georg Fromm, and their Puerto Rican counterparts Jose Emilio Gonzalez, Manuel Aponte, and Iris Zavala, spoke to an orderly crowd, in marked contrast to the rowdy, near violent scene a short distance away.

Main points brought out in the teach-in were: All information coming out of Vietnam is "managed" by U.S. authorities; the National Liberation Front (Vietcong) is waging a war for the "liberation" of the Vietnamese people; U.S. forces in South Vietnam have supported the South Vietnamese Government in not honoring the Geneva agreement to unite all of Vietnam after free elections.

Fromm drew a parallel between "Puerto Rico's struggle for liberation and that of the Vietnamese people."

Teaching-In in Tokyo

— CARL OGLESBY

Carl Oglesby is past president of Students for a Democratic Society. This report appeared in the Bi-Weekly Information Action Report (BIAR), No. 4 (Fall, 1965).

The Tokyo Teach-In happened all over town on August 14 and 15—August 15, 1965 being the twentieth anniversary of Japan's World War II surrender. The single largest assembly—about 2,000 —came together, on the afternoon of August 15, in a large Tokyo theater, and that was where I gave a brief speech about our peace movement. The crowd was extremely warm throughout, but their most emotional response came when I said: "We Americans against the Vietnam war are grateful for the chance to work with the people of Japan—with the people of all other countries. But we know, at the same time, that if peace is to be saved, it must be saved in America; and, if war is to be stopped, it must be Americans who stop it. The burden is mainly ours."

By then, the central part of the teach-in was history; the all-night meeting in the ballroom of the Akasaka-Prince Hotel lasted from 10:30 Saturday night to 6:00 Sunday morning, and all but the last two hours were televised nationally by TBS. For an idea of how many watched: The basic political program in Japan has an index rating of 0.5; basic entertainment fare rates 1.0; between midnight and 2:00 A.M., the teach-in had a rating of 3.0

It was during those hours that I was made a national political figure for the Japanese. Here's what happened.

The first part of the all-nighter was a panel discussion between eleven intellectuals and eleven politicians, a rather lonely two of whom supported the U.S. action in Vietnam (both were members of the ruling Liberal Democratic Party). This ratio does not, by any means, represent the power balance in the Sato Government, but it· may not be too far from representing actual Japanese opinion.

After about two hours of panel discussion, the floor was opened. As arranged with Oda and Tsurumi—the chief organizers of the teach-in—I was introduced first and invited to say a few American words, my translator, Muto, beside me. I had, earlier, asked Oda what kind of speech I should make. "Strong," he said.

Easy to do. One Liberal Democrat, Yasuhiro Nakasone—I'm told he's head of the Diet's Foreign Affairs Committee—had remarked that Americans are very good-natured at bottom, and so was their Vietnam policy. The other Liberal Democrat, Kiichi Miyazawa—a "friend of Mr. Rusk's"—had argued that the Saigon Government was, after all, "legal"; that it had "legally" requested U.S. military aid; and that that was all there was to it.

I said what most of us would say about these ideas, and the applause lasted a solid minute (about 1000 were present).

I started to go on. But a shout rang out, then another. Nakasone and Miyazawa were mad about something. Answering shouts came quickly from the floor. More shouts from the two Liberal Democrats: "Who is he?" "Is this a trick? A new cult of the foreigner?" Others on the panel were soon demanding loudly that I be allowed to speak, and, in a few moments, the whole audience was on its feet in my behalf. Cameras zoomed, flashbulbs popped, there was jubilant, angry chaos. My "strong" speech had become an "incident." The next day, taxi-drivers, ticket-takers, immigration officers, and bank clerks greeted me by name and gave me their thanks.

Finally, I had to sit down, without finishing. But it seemed, right away, that a good thing had happened; and, indeed, I was soon passed a note from Oda (who was on the panel) saying, "Your mission has been fulfilled!" The Japanese had seen, by the millions, how liberal and democratic the Liberal Democrats were; and, for the first time, they had heard an American criticize American foreign policy.

Much later that long night, when the politicians had all gone home to bed, I was asked to read to the assembly—still all there at

6:00 A.M.—my messages from the American teach-in and Students for a Democratic Society. The ovation seemed endless. That ovation was for what we are trying to do here. I saw how important we are to them. It made me take a long, deep breath.

London Teach-In Castigates United States

—CLYDE H. FARNSWORTH

Clyde Farnsworth is a reporter for The New York Times, *where this news story appeared on June 12, 1965.*

The speaker, a stocky assistant professor of political science, gestured toward the audience of 1,000 students jammed into a cafeteria at University College, London.

"The guerrillas on the banks of the Mekong," he said in a resonant voice, "these are my people—the people I support."

Applause broke out and a bespectacled Chinese student sitting on a table clapped longer than the rest.

It was the fifth hour of Britain's first teach-in on Vietnam, and during the earlier and later hours the tenor of the comments was much the same.

The United States was termed the aggressor, the oppressor of the Vietnamese people. Vietnam was viewed as another Ethiopia, another Guernica of the Spanish Civil War, another Algeria.

The British Labour Government was considered a grave disappointment because of its tacit support of the United States.

Isaac Deutscher, an author, authority on Soviet affairs, and participant in last month's Washington teach-in, said that everywhere he went in the United States he was asked: "Why does your Labour Government betray us?"

He characterized President Johnson as the gendarme of world counterrevolution and Prime Minister Wilson as the assistant gendarme.

Of more than twenty speakers, only three—by the sixth hour of the teach-in—offered support for the United States. These were an unflappable retired brigadier general, an intense young man sent by the Conservative central office, and a columnist, with Conservative leanings, for the *Sunday Telegraph*.

They were roundly heckled during their speeches but managed to finish and, for the most part, held the attention of the group. The teach-in was, at all times, orderly.

The U.S. Embassy had been expected to send two men—a political officer and the press attaché. The South Vietnamese Embassy was to have sent its first secretary.

However, at the last minute, the Americans and South Vietnamese bowed out—to the dismay of the teach-in organizers, a group of students striving to present a balanced analysis of the Vietnamese situation.

Alan Freeman, chairman of the organizing committee, said James Pettus, the press attaché, had told him the Americans had accepted on the basis that it would be an internal academic seminar, not a large-scale public debate.

The U.S. Embassy sent a film that was shown during a half-hour break. It dealt with a speech by President Johnson in which he called for world cooperation to raise the living standards of the Vietnamese people and spoke of American efforts to fight disease and raise agricultural output in South Vietnam.

Teach-In, Paris Style

— JOSEPH BARRY

Joseph Barry is a syndicated columnist and political analyst. The following article appeared in The Village Voice, *June 2, 1966.*

The left bank Salle de la Mutualité is a favorite meeting place of protest for Frenchmen ranging from Pierre Poujade to Pierre Mendes-France. It has also been the favorite spot for at least one foreign correspondent to exercise a kind of vicarious moralism, for nothing is easier than to be moral about other peoples' dirty wars. And during the Algerian War, I freely exercised it. How could the French people continue to permit it, how could they witness the demoralization of a generation of drafted youth without doing something about it?

The other night, the shoe was on the other foot. And it hurt. The dirty war was one's own country's and several thousand came to the Mutualité to condemn it. "Six Hours for Vietnam," it was titled. Familiar names, such as Sartre, Ricoeur, Schwartz, Vidal Naquet, were appended to the call. And it was organized by the keepers of the French conscience: French teachers and students.

There was some comfort in the presence of American professors —from Princeton, Boston, and Berkeley. Indeed Professor Smale, of the University of California, got almost as big a hand as Monsieur Vanh Bo of North Vietnam. Such is the sentimentality of the left. Even the chant that followed Smale's speech—"U.S. go home! U.S. go home!"—was obviously a left-handed tribute.

The same sentimentality followed us into the seminar devoted to American opposition to the Vietnamese war. (There were three other seminars; the whole program was modeled, in a rather free fashion, after the American teach-in.) In fact, the Frenchmen on the panel, as well as the American professors, painted such a picture of a tidal wave of protest from the American left that your correspondent felt obliged to point out that there was also an American right. Also, that President Johnson, confronted by the few critics who manage to reach him, habitually pulled out the latest Gallup poll (from the pockets of his pyjamas, according to Reston's story, in that morning's *New York Times*, of the latest such incident) to prove the majority supported him.

Simplism of the more elementary Marxist sort—common among French students—accompanied the sentimentality. Passionately, one of them scolded the American left for being pacifist. That was no way, he said, to make a revolution; only an international of the proletariat fighting for peace would end war. Told that American labor leaders, not necessarily disavowed by the rank and file, were generally for Johnson, he thought it the product of the "conditioning" of the working class by the capitalist government, characteristic of America. Reminded that the French working class, largely led by the Communist Party, had never struck for peace in Algeria, he may have begun to understand what a real teach-in might be: the examination of assumptions—even one's own.

(Sartre himself, in disenchantment with the French proletariat and its party, once sourly concluded that the Algerian affair was finally resolved by only three players: the FLN (Algerian army), the French army, and De Gaulle. Though he signed the appeal for the night's meeting, he was not present on the platform.)

In another seminar, on "Imperialism in Southeast Asia," according to a French friend, there was a similar challenge to simplistic assumptions. Professor Ruhlmann, a French expert on the Far East, remarked (to jeers) that "other" powers are, or have been, imperialist in that part of the world—China, for a thousand years, among them. And, among his listeners and fellow panelists was Monsieur Vanh Bo of Hanoi, not one of the least fascinated.

The last few hours of the "six for Vietnam" brought everybody back to the main hall for more speeches, a Joris Ivens film, "A Cry for Peace," and Hugues Aufray. And, again, there was some comfort, in a long night's criticism of America, in the final notes of American influence. Hugues Aufray's immense popularity is based, primarily, on Bob Dylan's songs, which he belts out with astonishing conviction. Dylan, who just passed through Paris for a one-day stand, confused practically all his French fans by declaring the Vietnam affair didn't concern him. Aufray, before singing Dylan's songs, half-apologized, half-confessed his own confusion. (The very political French do not understand the politics of America's apolitical, or is it I who am confused?) And he ended one song with "May God give us peace—if he's on our side."

3. BEYOND THE TEACH-IN

Alternative Perspectives on Vietnam

The Inter-University Committee for Debate on Foreign Policy was originally formed in Ann Arbor, Michigan, soon after the first teach-in. In July, 1965, the committee, together with clergymen, laymen, and other student and faculty groups, issued the following statement and call. See Christopher Lasch's discussion of the Conference on Alternative Perspectives on Vietnam in Chapter VII.

A Statement of Assumptions

Deep concern about the war in Vietnam continues, now that the U.S. Administration is increasing its military involvement there and committing massive numbers of combat troops. American intellectuals—both within and outside of the universities—have become increasingly articulate, during the past few months, in expressing their concern about the Vietnam situation and calling for a thorough reanalysis and re-evaluation of American policy in that part of the world. The most dramatic expression of this concern has been the teach-in movement, which has captured the imagination of intellectuals not only in the United States but also in many other countries.

The teach-ins and discussions, so far, have been extremely effective in raising fundamental issues and in analyzing the weaknesses and dangers of current policy; they have been less effective, however, in identifying alternatives to current policy. It is to the search for alternatives that we must now devote our primary attention. This, in turn, requires us to develop new perspectives on the problem, out of which alternative solutions are more likely to emerge.

Much of the debate on Vietnam, so far—even when it has taken place—has been carried out within an excessively narrow framework. The analytic perspective that is typically brought to bear on the issue is rooted in the assumptions of the Cold War; the evaluative perspective is provided by considerations of national interest and national power. These perspectives govern the approach not only of the United States but also of the Soviet Union and of China; not only toward Vietnam but also toward the Dominican Republic and other foreign policy issues. Our concern for the moment, however, is primarily with U.S. policy toward Vietnam.

Regardless of the degree to which one accepts or rejects the assumptions of the Cold War and of the doctrine of national interest, it seems clear that these perspectives have led us into a dead end on the issue of Vietnam. The problems of Vietnam have proven incapable of any acceptable resolution within the terms of the Cold War and of power politics. Yet, our policy makers seem to be trapped by these pervasive assumptions and helplessly pulled by them into actions that are both futile and dangerous. What is desperately needed is a way out of this trap, a way that would cut through the assumptions of the Cold War and permit us to define the problem in terms less refractory to solution. In other words, we need to bring radically new analytic and evaluative perspectives to bear on the issue in the hope that these will point to policy alternatives that could not emerge out of the closed system of the Cold War philosophy.

The search for alternatives must begin with the raising of certain basic value questions: Toward what ends ought our Vietnam policy to strive, and what are the means appropriate to the achievement of these ends? By approaching these questions from the moral perspectives of all great religions and philosophical systems, we may find solutions that are more consistent with fundamental human value than current American policy in Vietnam has turned out to be.

These value questions, however, must not be asked in the abstract, but in conjunction with new analytic perspectives on the conflict in Vietnam. Such perspectives can be derived from a combination of two major sources: from various social-theoretical formulations yielding general propositions that can be applied to the special case of Vietnam; and from concrete knowledge of the social, economic, and political conditions within Vietnam and within the larger region of which it forms a part.

The development of new perspectives and the consequent broadening of the range of policy alternatives represent a major challenge to the intellectual community of the world. This challenge must be met by the combined efforts of humanists and religious thinkers, of social theorists and social philosophers, of students of Southeast Asia and of the developing world. American intellectuals must take the primary responsibility for meeting this challenge, for it is the policy of our Government that is creating a moral crisis. In this effort, however, we must have the participation of intellectuals from all over the world, not only because the intellectual community, by its very nature, transcends national boundaries, but also because— coming from outside of American society—they are in a unique position to approach American policy from fundamentally different perspectives.

A Call for An International Conference on Alternative Perspectives on Vietnam

A group consisting of faculty members and students from the University of Michigan, of clergymen, and of other citizens of Ann Arbor, Michigan, has come together for the purpose of organizing an international conference on Alternative Perspectives on Vietnam. The conference is designed as an initial effort to meet the challenge described in our Statement of Assumptions.

The conference will be held under the sponsorship of a national group, the Inter-University Committee for Debate on Foreign Policy, and of two local groups—the University of Michigan's Office of Religious Affairs and the Faculty-Student Committee to Stop the War in Vietnam—and with the cooperation of the Universities Committee on Problems of Peace and War. It will take place on the campus of the University of Michigan, September 14–18, 1965.

In line with one of our basic assumptions about the nature of the task before us, the conference is being planned as an international cooperative venture. It is very appropriate for this initial effort to take place during International Cooperation Year, which is designed to step up the level of international cooperation in all areas of human endeavor. It would be a very fitting contribution to the purposes of International Cooperation Year if the September conference could begin to establish patterns of international cooperation among intellectuals in the systematic exploration of questions so central to human survival and to fundamental human values. . . .

The purpose of the conference is to combine three functions that are integrally related: *analysis, communication,* and *action.* To fulfill these functions, the conference will be divided into three parts:

1. International study groups (September 14–16): About thirty humanists, religious thinkers, social theorists, and area and development specialists will meet in small groups, each set up to examine the problem of Vietnam from a particular new perspective, differing from that provided by power politics within the Cold War framework, and to derive some concrete alternatives to current American policy from that perspective.

2. Open sessions (September 17): Members of the university community and of the wider Ann Arbor community, and individuals from other campuses and communities throughout the country, will hear reports from the study groups and addresses by study-group members from different parts of the world; they will then participate in a series of seminars concerned with alternative perspectives on Vietnam, in which study-group members will also play a major role.

3. Action workshops (September 18): Individuals and groups from various parts of the United States and from other parts of the world will report on their various activities and plans; participants, in accord with their various interests, will then divide themselves into a number of workshops designed to map out specific action projects of a local, regional, national, or international nature.

It is hoped that the international study groups will have a number of useful effects: that they will generate new ideas on which the participants will be able to draw in their subsequent activities; that they will contribute to the development of international networks of intellectuals; that they will make possible the drafting of a joint statement of principles; and that they may yield some documents suitable for wide distribution.

There is a further value, however, in embedding these study

groups in a larger conference that also includes open sessions and action workshops. This format makes it possible for the study groups to contribute directly to the activities of the teach-in movement. Ideas generated in the study groups can be fed into the subsequent seminar discussions, and these, in turn, can feed into the next day's action workshops. It is our hope, in short, that the momentum built up in the study groups will help to stimulate new thinking and new action on Vietnam not only at the University of Michigan but on other campuses as well; not only on the campus but also in the community.

Professors Lobby on Vietnam

— EVERETT W. BOVARD

Dr. Bovard teaches anatomy at the Albert Einstein College of Medicine in New York. This memorandum, issued on April 13, 1965, was prepared for the staff and students of the college.

Probably the most important event of this two-day lobby [*April 8–9, 1965*] by eighty-five professors and scientists was a forty-minute conference, on Friday, of twelve professors—each representing a different state—with Paul Bailey, Chairman of the Democratic National Committee. He promised to take back to the President the following points:

1. That the present military policy in Vietnam has led to serious disaffection among those members of the academic community who had previously supported and worked for President Johnson, and that, in the absence of any change in this policy, support from the academic community for the Democratic Party, in 1966, is unlikely. Mr. Bailey indicated 1966 would be a tough election.

2. That, in his policy in Vietnam, President Johnson has had bad advice from Messrs. Bundy and McNamara and that he should seek a wider range of advice from those with direct knowledge and experience in Southeast Asia.

3. That the bombing of military and nonmilitary targets in North Vietnam should be halted, at least for a few weeks, to prepare the ground for negotiations. It was pointed out that massive bombing of Britain and Germany in the last war merely united the

population behind their respective governments and did not adversely affect morale.

The discussion with Mr. Bailey was frank and friendly, in a "family argument" atmosphere. He himself suggested that many people had voted for Johnson last fall because they were against Goldwater's war policies. The group pointed out that these policies were now being carried out by President Johnson himself.

Both in this conference and in others with Senator Javits and Kennedy [*of New York*] and with the staff of Senator Yarborough [*of Texas*], it was apparent that the decision center for events in Vietnam was the White House. In particular, a member of Yarborough's staff said that Lyndon Johnson would "listen to the votes" as represented by teach-ins, newspaper ads, block-by-block campaigning, and lobbying activity. It was generally agreed that President Johnson's speech last week [*at Johns Hopkins University*] represented a change in policy brought about largely through opposition by a few members of Congress.

All this suggests the conclusion that the White House policy on Vietnam can be directly affected by activity within the normal political framework. This military policy is political in origin and direction and is particularly susceptible to political pressure.

It became apparent from these and other conferences that the President lacks a consensus on Vietnam, though he has not yet had a great deal of opposition from Congress in this matter.

It further became apparent that professors, because of their influence on students from many [congressional] districts, have status with members of Congress. Members of the lobby were treated with deference and respect and were encouraged by Senator Javits and many others to put this sort of university lobbying on a regular and organized basis. Judging from their reaction, a good many members of Congress personally were glad to see us in Washington. It would seem possible that the academic community can have a direct effect on the course of events in Washington, once the techniques of political action have been learned.

These can only be learned on the job, so to speak. Many of us, without previous experience, were soon pulling representatives and even some senators off the floor for conferences, with and without prior appointments. The conclusion I would suggest is that it would be fully within the power of the academic community of this country to modify military policy on Vietnam through such political action as lobbying, teach-ins, participation in campaigns, and use of advertisements and demonstrations to influence the climate of opinion. Just as the clergy may have been the decisive influence on civil rights, so professors and scientists may conceivably be the decisive influence on Vietnam.

What Should the Peace Movement Do?

—I. F. STONE

I. F. Stone is the author of The Haunted Fifties *and publisher of the Washington newsletter* I. F. Stone's Weekly *in which this piece appeared, June 28, 1965.*

We hope the student movement will not be led astray by stunt-mongers and suicide tactics. We believe the teach-ins have made extraordinary progress. The Washington teach-in was too diffuse, the TV discussion with Bundy was too concerned with abstractions. But debate has been opened up. The Administration has been put on the defensive. The polls show that, while the majority is prepared to support Johnson wherever he leads—in the sheeplike way that human herds always move toward war—the educated minority question his course. Our job is, by the widening of debate, to increase their number. Add their dissent to a general anxiety and we have leverage for peace. It is reflected in the Senate, where Robert F. Kennedy—in the spirit of his brother's American University speech—was calling, at press time, for a fresh effort to bring China into talks to end the proliferation of nuclear weapons. It was reflected in the unusually wide response that speech stirred from more than a dozen worried Senators on the floor. If the teach-ins can be taken from the campuses to the communities, if we can have teach-ins in every town or city, we can build up formidable pressure for peace.

But this demands a real effort to reach and teach, to speak in a tone not of desperation but of faith in the power to touch the hearts and minds of our fellow Americans. The wonderful students I have seen at various teach-ins, from Washington to Berkeley, have achieved more than any one dreamed was possible a few months ago. They must widen their efforts. Their task is not to express alienation, or to bring about estrangement, but to make free institutions work in foreign policy. Their duty is to help humanity by furthering the reconciliaton and consciousness on which our survival depends: reconciliation with our Communist rivals abroad; reconciliation, in equality, between white and black men at home; the consciousness of common heritage and of common danger as human beings; the consciousness of the urgent necessity of brotherhood. Religious faith and revolutionary zeal could make a contribution if they joined in this healing task.

A Protest Against the Draft and Death of Intellect

—TOM HAYDEN

Mr. Hayden is a community organizer and a founder of Students for a Democratic Society. The following is from Viet-Report, June–July, 1966.

Until recently, the Johnson Administration has pursued a "soft" line toward those in the universities who express dissent about the war. The President claims to welcome debate and protest, and even has sent his representatives to our teach-ins. But this public tolerance is more than offset by the gradual tightening of the Selective Service measures, which now touch every student in the country. Those who protest, those who worry in silence, and those who assent to our country's Vietnam policy now are made to face, together, this question: Will they take a Selective Service test to determine who will study at home and who will risk death overseas?

Long before the invention of these tests, of course, the draft affected the lives of young people. The young poor, especially black but also white, go to places like Vietnam when they lack the money to put them into college. Other young people who seek careers outside of the draft-exempt university—those, for instance, who would rather die registering voters in Mississippi than live to shoot those who want to vote in Danang—are threatened or drafted by their local boards. And now, with the current tests, the more privileged young people are being drawn nearer the war machinery themselves. Some will be taken away, the victims of their fellow students' higher aptitude for answering questions on a test. Others will be using their pencils to avoid using the gun; they will consciously rededicate themselves, in time of war, to avoid the draft and let others go. Students who already are out of touch with the world's bitter poverty will believe more firmly that they are "chosen" to be the nation's educated elite, deserving of exemption. The values of primitive capitalism reappear: The "fittest" are preserved because the "unfit" defend them.

These issues appear before the academic community as a whole, not simply the students. University administrations choose to become part of the Selective Service system itself by setting aside places for the testing and by notifying students of their opportunity to escape the draft. Teachers who give grades are becoming part of a system which determines who will die. The university as a whole, already dependent in numerous ways on the military and industrial power centers, by this process falls further from its ideal of independence. . . .

Students and intellectuals are being insulted by the Johnson Administration, however soft the insults have been. Like the rest of the American people, we have never been consulted adequately about this war. We helped to elect a President pledged not to "go North" in Vietnam. Three months after his election, in a situation which was not an emergency, without public debate in the country, without a congressional declaration of war or a United Nations' sanction, the President did what he said he would not do. This war has been opposed by men of international stature in the fields of history and political science, philosophy and law, the arts, science, and medicine; by thousands of scholars and religious men; by thousands of graduate, undergraduate, and high-school students. Despite this outpouring of protest, unprecedented during wartime in our national history, the war grinds on and on, widening gradually but consistently, as if it were too much for our Administration to reveal, at once, the military future that has been chosen for us.

The reason the Government does not take our protest seriously enough to end the war is that it is assumed, not only in the White House but throughout the country, that we will only protest intellectually and be satisfied with maintaining a constant dialogue with the Administration while the war escalates. This the Administration can tolerate, even subtly turn to its own uses, since the debate "proves" the democratic nature of our society. To break this image of passivity, we can enter politics and demonstrations as we have done. But, unless we fully emerge from the protective cover of the ivory tower, and unless we defend at all costs the independence of our classrooms, schools, and organizations, we still will be classified, at best, as those queer intellectual critics and, at worst, as draft-dodgers who fear war. On the other hand, if we break the image by refusing the shelter of exemption, the country might more easily take us to mean what we say, and the Government would face the dilemma of whether to silence its intellectual critics in jail or let them break loose from the manageable role [they have played] as the "loyal opposition."

If our revolt needs a political goal, it should be that each individual draftee should have some voice about what he is asked to die for. Therefore, we believe the Selective Service Act should be tested to see if there can be included individuals whose conscientious objection is to particular wars. If not, the law should be changed to include such political objectors and to broaden the forms of alternative service which objectors may perform to include antipoverty or civil rights work in the United States, and other work which builds democracy, in this country and elsewhere—including Vietnam. The basis of objection to war that should become legitimate, in other words, is not pacifist but political.

Our resistance should not be nay-saying alone. We should also affirm the kind of intellectual spirit which ought to flourish in this country, but which exists today mostly at the fringes. We have demonstrated the possibilities for the forming of an authentic intellectual community in the teach-in. Now, ought we not to consider carrying the teach-in into the community, and so completely that a national town-meeting on Vietnam would be virtually created? Could we not make the dialogue in the country drastically different from that at the Defense Department and the LBJ Ranch? In certain places there is going to be violence, for, as Senator Fulbright warns, an atmosphere of war hysteria will grow as the war is escalated but continues to fail. But in other places, and we believe in most places, we might rely on the more generous feelings and serious doubts of the American people to create dialogue rather than domestic civil war. The spirit of a town meeting is that those affected by public decisions meet together to seek common solutions. . . .

Senator Fulbright's "Teach-In"

—JAMES RESTON

Excerpts from statements and testimony before the Fulbright committee can be found in Vietnam Hearings *(New York, 1966), which also contains an introduction by Senator Fulbright. The following evaluation of the hearings is from* The New York Times, *February 13, 1966.*

Senator Fulbright's official "teach-in" on Vietnam has been quite a show—big lights for the TV cameras up front in the Senate caucus room, big shots and their decorative wives out back, and growls of protest from the White House about "the little band of willful men."

There is something to protest about. The Senator's inquiry is very late, as he himself concedes. The timing, in the middle of a new bombing offensive and a new peace offensive, is awkward, but neither the timing nor the theatrical bustle, nor the senatorial posturing is as important as the educational possibilities of this televised debate.

It is years since there has been a serious open debate here on the basic problems of American foreign policy which the public could watch via television. The last one was about the so-called missile crisis, when Lyndon Johnson was still in the Senate.

Meanwhile, the Soviet-Chinese dispute; the rise of nationalism in both Eastern and Western Europe; the Soviet missile crisis in Cuba; the development of nuclear weapons and a military psychosis in Communist China; the outbreak of modern war in Vietnam; and the specter of hunger and political chaos in many parts of the underdeveloped world have transformed the political scene in every major continent.

One reason for much of the misunderstanding in the Fulbright hearings these past few days was that witnesses and senators often differed fundamentally about the implications of these changes, and some of the senators were repeating the old cliches of the Cold War as if the problem of containing China were the same as the old problem of containing the expansion of the Soviet Union.

In this situation, there is much to be said for a series of public, televised hearings by the Foreign Relations Committee on the rising U.S. problems in Latin America, Asia, Europe, and the rest of the world.

The most creative minds in America on most of these questions are not in the Government today, but in the universities, the foundations, and elsewhere in private life. They would respond to an appeal by Senator Fulbright to testify before the cameras and could, in the process, help bring about a much wider understanding in Congress and the nation of the problems facing the President.

The Fulbright committee barely touched on the problem of China, for example, this week. The American experts and scholars on China have not been heard in open hearings on this subject since the Sino-Soviet split. What do the old China hands and the new Orientalists think of this convulsive new force in the world? It is not at all clear that the executive or the Congress knows.

Latin America is another problem that needs much more public understanding. Somehow, the people of the United States would do anything for Latin America except read about it. Yet, problems are building up in this hemisphere that are likely to make Cuba and the Dominican Republic seem like innocent annoyances. . . .

Washington is, for the time being, a one-man and one-subject city. It is almost impossible, even in a social situation here, to talk for ten minutes about anything except Lyndon Johnson and Vietnam, and it is unlikely that the present Administration will be able, in its prevailing mood, to think deeply about anything else.

The Senate, however, is beginning to realize that it, too, has been hypnotized by the power of the President and the problems of Vietnam and has not been meeting its responsibilities to either.

"Maybe if we had held this inquiry earlier," Senator Fulbright said the other day, "the teach-ins on the university campuses would not have been so necessary."

It was the decision of the National Broadcasting Company to televise the Fulbright hearings that gave them so much influence. Open hearings without the TV cameras do not influence the White House to the same extent, do not bring the senators to the caucus room with the same interest, and do not have the same impact on the general public.

The combination of Congress, the television cameras, and the current problems, however, could be a powerful influence for understanding and change, and if he can get continued support of the TV networks, Fulbright is in a mood to continue the inquiry.

The Teach-In Continues

This statement, issued by the Inter-University Committee for Debate on Foreign Policy, appeared in The New York Times, March 6, 1966.

WE COMMEND:

Senators Fulbright, Kennedy, Morse, and dozens of other senators and congressmen who have, in recent weeks, continued the debate begun on campuses last March, and who have carried it to the halls of Congress, where it should have begun. At last, millions of Americans are being confronted with the grave issues and disturbing facts of the Vietnamese tragedy. . . .

WE PROPOSE:

A National Week of Teach-Ins, March 21–26. The teach-in is America's new town meeting. There were scores last year, and there must be hundreds this year, on Vietnam and other problem areas of foreign policy. You and your friends can do it alone. If you ask, the Inter-University Committee will provide documents, speakers, and help of all kinds.

Political Action. Reasoned dissent seeks power, and finds expression, in the normal contests for political office. Primaries and general elections make the case against present Administration policies. All must try to promote the candidacy of opponents to this war, in the political party of their choice. The Inter-University Committee will send documents to help candidates organize effective campaigns and assist the reasoned presentation of dissenting views in any way that is consistent with our basic functions.

A National Dialogue. Continual discussion of foreign policy on the local level is essential to the functioning of a democratic society. The dialogue will provide seminar packets, conference programs, speakers lists, and bibliographies. These resources will be selected for their objectivity and will present opposed points of view designed to stimulate thorough consideration of the issues.

Community Action. We have established a document bank and invite anyone who can make use of these resources to send their requests to the Inter-University Committee. The documents include literature, films, and tapes—the latter two resources available for local showing and radio presentation. We will try to promote congressional hearings at the local level similar to those sponsored by representatives Kastenmeier, Diggs, and Vivian in their respective constituencies.

Mass Media. We are presently exploring the possibilities of reaching a national audience through the purchase of television and radio time. Such ventures are, of course, expensive. Whether we can succeed will depend, in large measure, on your response to this advertisement.

STATEMENT OF PURPOSE:

We are dismayed by the U.S. Administration's failure to generate informed public discussion of foreign policy. Our aim is to counteract the tendencies that have brought about this condition, in ways appropriate to our function as educators and students, so that this country can, for the first time, make foreign policy on the basis of fact and moral principle rather than solely on the basis of myth and exclusive concern with national interest in its narrowest sense.

IN CONCLUSION:

On March 24, 1965, when the Teach-ins began, we were a small band. Today, much of the Congress of the United States, many newspapers, and hundreds of thousands of Americans are in outspoken opposition to the war in Vietnam. But Vietnam is only the most dramatic instance of American inability to cope with a revolutionary world. What has developed there, in recent years, may well develop, tomorrow, in South Africa, Guatemala, and numerous other areas.

It can no longer be said that the actions of a few are meaningless. Those who oppose Administration policy have the responsibility and the power to change it.

If not now, *when?*

If not you, *who?*

Introduction to Teach-In II

—CONSTANCE SUTTON

Professor Sutton teaches anthropology at New York University's University College. Her remarks were delivered at New York University's first-anniversary teach-in, May 3, 1966.

I want to welcome to Teach-In II those of you who attended the teach-in last year and those who are attending a teach-in for the first time. Last year, Professor [Philip] Zimbardo and I were co-chairmen of the student-faculty committee that organized our first teach-in on campus. We felt, therefore, that we would like to make a few introductory remarks to tonight's teach-in, which has been entitled "Vietnam and the College Community: A Look Ahead." Our comments might well be labeled "A Look Behind." . . .

Let us be clear about the functions of a teach-in on a college campus. The faculties of colleges and universities are purveyors of knowledge and understanding. It is their responsibility to examine assumptions, seek and amass information, and point out consequences. It is their responsibility to do so critically and, if necessary, in the face of popular opposition. The teach-in developed when a portion of the academic community felt that this role should not be confined to the classroom. Confronted with a serious issue affecting the lives of people, they felt it their responsibility to bring to students information and viewpoints that were generally either neglected or suppressed. Thus, the teach-in became a vehicle by which faculty could express their deep concern and present the basis for adopting positions of dissent to policies and actions which critically affect us all. As such, it is a form of education, but also a particular form of protest. And, as such, it represents a departure from the more restricted role that faculties played in relation to students during the 1940's and 1950's. Those of us who believe that this new responsibility of the academic community is a strategic part of the total educational process will continue to hold teach-ins as long as there exists the need to present students with information and alternative assumptions for making evaluations of critical situations.

But let us also be clear about what the teach-in is not. It is not, when held on college campuses, a dialogue with the Government.

Rather, it is a dialogue between students and faculty. It is not a debating society. Hence, we do not have, tonight, speakers for the Administration, although the Administration's position is reviewed in an early section of this program. Rather, we believe that it is the argument of the opposition which has not been sufficiently understood or given adequate attention in the mass media. Thus, we have concentrated on presenting criticism and exploring alternatives. Finally, the teach-in is not a form of political action, although it may help provide better guides to political action through deepening and enlarging our understanding.

Last year's teach-ins expressed concern with the morality of this undeclared war and with its consequences. With respect to consequences, the critics of the Administration have predicted more accurately than the Administration. With respect to morality, it is, today, no longer an abstract issue. It has become one which directly confronts students who face the draft and students who engage in protest action, many of whom have already been subjected to punitive measures. Clearly, it takes more personal courage, today, not to go along with the "consensus" Johnson wants than it did a year ago. And, clearly, the situation is many times more serious than it was a year ago.

Since last year, both the war and the criticism and protest over the war have escalated. The fact that the marches, demonstrations, teach-ins, read-ins, congressional investigating committees, et cetera, have not stopped the Administration from pursuing this war has led many people to be skeptical about the effects of opposition. Out of a sense of frustration and impotence, they withdraw to private concerns and seek strictly private solutions. These reactions are understandable—we have all felt them. It was not surprising, therefore, that the idea of holding another teach-in on our campus was initially greeted with doubts: What good would it do? Everyone knows the arguments; no one is interested any more. Some claimed we needed a new gimmick—that great American faith in gimmicks reared its head. Perhaps, however, the source of this sense of helplessness lies elsewhere. Perhaps it's based in not having understood enough or as much as we like to believe we do. The past year should have alerted us to the fact that more fundamental issues are involved, including the nature of political power in our society and the interests the Government represents when it responds to a world in revolution in the fashion that it has. Perhaps our capacity to enhance our understanding of these issues can suggest new modes of action which convert us from becoming *victims* of history into *actors* in history.

Thus, despite doubts concerning the *success* of another teach-in, we felt it a moral obligation to have one, even if only a handful of students turned up. To do less would be to ignore the fear we should all feel in the face of the way events are drifting; to ignore the fact that we continue to face a serious crisis, with the possibility of more of them in the future. But, this time, the teach-in is directed toward broader issues than the Vietnam war itself—issues raised by it and by the efforts to stop it and to prevent other wars like it from occurring. We hope that, tonight, our program of speakers will enlighten on questions which vitally concern us all.

Action Report

Statement issued by the Inter-University Committee for Debate on Foreign Policy (relocated in Ithaca, New York), July 29, 1966. The Inter-University Committee also participated in the work of the November Eighth Mobilization Committee, formed by hundreds of peace, educational, and civil rights organizations "to make sure that the issues of peace in Vietnam and the related issues of economic justice and human rights are forcefully injected as the primary issues of [the 1966] electoral period."

This year, the Inter-University Committee:

CONTRIBUTED to over 100 teach-ins across the country. We furnished over 400,000 pieces of literature and other material. . . .

PROVIDED speakers—from both sides, when possible—for many debates and discussions. We keep a current list of well-informed, articulate speakers who are prepared to lecture or debate on topics relevant to domestic and foreign policies. . . .

DISTRIBUTED tapes of Marshall Windmiller's weekly commentary to contacts in twenty communities for airing on local FM stations. These tapes, and others in our document bank, were also loaned to local groups for seminars and [to serve as] discussion-starters.

SUPPORTED the trip of Howard Zinn, Professor of History at Boston University, . . . to Japan for a speaking tour of Japanese universities and communities. Mr. Zinn's trip was important in influencing Japanese opinion about the war; it has led to the possibility of a conference in Japan at which U.S. scholars would meet representatives of the NLF and North Vietnam. Mr. Zinn's report is available on request.

Sponsored the International Teach-In held in Toronto, Canada, which was made available to campuses and communities through closed-circuit radio. Tapes of this teach-in are available to local groups for a small rental charge.

Financed the printing of a major document, *Citizens' White Paper: The Politics of Escalation*, which received notice in *The Nation, I. F. Stone's Weekly*, and in a major foreign policy address by Senator Vance Hartke. . . .

Sponsored, in cooperation with the National Student Association, a National Dialogue on Vietnam. The National Dialogue makes available packets of information containing various points of view—including those of the Department of State, National SANE, Young Americans for Freedom, the Inter-University Committee, Friends of Vietnam—and reprints from current periodicals analyzing the political, economic, and military situation in Vietnam. . . .

Co-sponsored, with Students for a Democratic Society, the National Vietnam Examination. This exam, with a separate answer sheet, was distributed in conjunction with the Selective Service Qualification Test in 850 communities. A total of over 500,000 exams were distributed. The exam asked critical questions about the history, background, and political complexion of the situation in Vietnam, in a multiple-choice format. . . .

Is Currently Sponsoring a trip to Saigon by Marshall Windmiller, whose political analysis is known to listeners of Pacifica Network in Los Angeles, San Francisco, and New York. Professor Windmiller will talk to people in Vietnam and base his [future] commentary on the information he receives during his stay.

Brought Thich Nhat Hanh to the United States for an extended speaking tour and consultation with officials of the American Government. He made a tremendous impact on all who heard him and brought the message of the Vietnamese Buddhists to the American people for the first time.

Supported an Open Hearing on China, held at Syracuse University. . . . This conference had resource people, including Hans Morgenthau, Jonathan Mirsky, and O. Edmund Clubb, on hand for lectures and discussions.

Contributed to several other major conferences on China and Southeast Asia by providing financial backing and/or literature and speakers. Some of these conferences received national TV and press coverage, and tapes have been made available for groups that cannot hold major conferences in their communities.

We Are Choking with Shame and Anger

— SUSAN SONTAG

*Susan Sontag, critic and essayist, delivered this state-
ment at the Read-In for Peace held in Town Hall
(New York City), on February 20, 1966. The read-in
was organized by the Committee of the Professions,
a group formed to coordinate the protest activities of
writers, artists, and professionals. Excerpts from the
Town Hall read-in, including sections of Miss Sontag's address, are on Broadside Records, BR452,
edited by Rosalind Wells and Louis Menashe.*

I am not going to read from a story or a novel of mine. Whatever I have already written—even if I could conceive it to be relevant, owing to the secret contiguousness of all despair—has to do
with *then*, when it was written, or (perhaps) with *always*.

It does not have to do with *now*. And it is about now, about our
situation, tonight, that I want to speak.

We meet here tonight to bear witness to our sorrow and anxiety
and revulsion at the American war on Vietnam. Most of us have
already signed the petitions and statements that have appeared in
The New York Times, written a senator or congressman, walked
down Fifth Avenue, and picketed in Washington. Some of us have
done more: joined committees, written articles, raised money for
demonstrations, proselytized among friends and, if we are teachers,
among students.

Tonight, we are sitting quietly. One by one, someone up here
reads, recites; you listen, whisper among yourselves, applaud. At the
end, we will all put on our coats, leave with our friends, talk some
more to each other in small groups, then go home—to write in
diaries, have midnight snacks, make love, watch TV, read, or sleep.
We, tonight, are not the makings of a new political movement.
We are not going to immolate ourselves, like Roger La Porte and
Norman Morrison. Nor have we even come together, tonight, to
exchange information about the war or to clarify the arguments
against it.

Why are we here? So far as I can determine, we are here on the
simplest basis: because we are choking with shame and anger, because we are afraid for ourselves and our children, and because we

are profoundly discouraged. Most of us have been deploring this wicked war, in public and private, for at least a year, some of us for much longer. But things go from bad to worse, from crime to greater crime; the stakes mount, the hypocrisy becomes more gross and Orwellian—as when the President of this country declared, the other day, that Americans are in Vietnam "to wage the battle for peace." We are, I repeat, discouraged and we are, or ought to be, afraid at the increasing likelihood of a much wider and more terrible war. And we have come together to renew our capacity to feel and to help each other to go on feeling strongly, to go on protesting, to have the courage to go on being afraid—though, clearly, our feelings, already known to our rulers and written off in advance by them, can hardly halt this crime or count much in the forestalling of even greater ones.

But, if what we are doing tonight is not, in a strict or gratifying sense, a political act—that is, no tangible changes in the behavior of our rulers or the attitudes of most of our fellow citizens will follow from our gathering—it doesn't follow that what we do here is of no use.

As I have indicated: Sociologically, we are not representative Americans. This is neither a mass rally nor a conclave of zealots, but an audience of educated, middle-class, urban intellectuals and professional people, and a stage full of writers and actors. Let's not pretend to be other than what we are—much less apologize for it.

We, as American writers and actors, have no special knowledge of the war on Vietnam. But most of us have made some effort to inform ourselves, to distinguish truth from lies, to tell living voices from the humanoid computers of megadeaths. As writers, guardians of language, and as actors, those who practice the art of speaking with a human voice, we may and should conceive ourselves to have a vocational connection with the life of truth, that is, of seriousness.

Let us be serious.

A small nation of handsome people, ravished by twenty years of civil war, is being brutally and self-righteously slaughtered—in the name of freedom!—by the richest, most grotesquely overarmed, most powerful country in the world. America has become a criminal, sinister country—swollen with priggishness, numbed by affluence, bemused by the monstrous conceit that it has the mandate to dispose of the destiny of the world, *of life itself*, in terms of its own interests and jargon.

Think of it. Fertile land is being drenched with poison, an honorable rural culture is being steam-rollered with asphalt and strung with barbed wire. At this moment, babies are being charred by napalm bombs; young men, Vietnamese and American, are falling like trees, to lie forever with their faces in the mud. And we who are here, not there, and alive, not poisoned or burned, are being injured, morally, in a way that is also profound.

But you know all this. I said that it was about our situation tonight that I wished to speak. One of the most fundamental problems we have is that of finding an adequate response. Our situation, in both its public and private aspects, could be defined as one in which we have *more* than we can handle. We have a surplus of stimulation, a surplus of information, a surplus of provocation. There are too many things, there are too many people, there is too much art. There is too much jazz and too much nightmare.

The honest response to all this tends to be nausea, or moral anaesthesia. The real effort is to invent and sustain *appropriate* responses.

Response does not mean just reaction, acting back, hitting back because someone has assaulted you. Response, intelligent creative action in a situation that is understood, can take many forms. Language supplies words that tend to emphasize the difference between types of response and to value one type of response over another. People talk about *acts* versus *gestures*. About irrational versus rational behavior. I think it would be more useful if we noticed how these distinctions are hardly as fixed as we tend to think.

This meeting is one response—one kind of response possible and, therefore, necessary—to a bad situation. I am sure the people who designed the read-ins that are taking place all over the country right now are aware of the frailty of this response—its inadequacy, if you will, to the situation. But let's not compound the fragility of the act by a too ready labeling—as rhetoric, as mere gesture, or, even, as an act of protest. The response embodied in our physical presence here this evening is more complex than that.

In the endless registry of atrocities which have stunned our hearts in the last thirty years, we, here, now, have—I think rightly —singled this one out. To be sure, there is much else in the world to deplore. Only in the last months, the slaughter of 100,000 or more Indonesian "Communists" went virtually unnoticed—because we are exhausted by vicarious grief and rage, by what seems demanded if one simply reads the newspaper every morning. Indiscriminate compassion is an indulgence; actually, we don't even feel after a while. Every sympathy or hatred that is not soon discharged in an action constitutes a prison. And there is always the danger that one's moral and political opinions, if one does not *live* them in efficacious deeds, are just a form of emotional recreation.

But most of us here have chosen, though I hope not without some awareness of the danger of *having* something called a "position," something that's mainly an affair of living-room talk, of polite, organized strolls under the windows of power, of signing statements and joining committees for the issuing of more statements. Most of us have chosen to oppose this war. For it is not just any war. It is *our* war, and in a double sense. The Government that you and I consent to live under is the principal malefactor in the situation. And the war, as that Government clings to its policy of escalating folly, threatens *our* lives.

I do not doubt that the war on Vietnam can be ended, whenever, and if, the American Government wishes to end it; and I am for all the practical steps to terminate the war—beginning with an unconditional cessation of the bombing of the North—which have been proposed by many eminent figures in this country and abroad. But we, here, can only second these well-known proposals. We can only add our voices. If that is our role, because as writers and actors we already possess a public voice as well as a private one, we must also recognize that whatever authority or influence our voices may command is ours not because we have a special insight into the war that is not available to any well-informed intelligent citizen—we do not—but because of the quality, let me say bluntly, the integrity of our voices.

None of us here, I think, is the worse for being involved in the protest against the war on Vietnam. But many of us could be better as the result of it, and are not.

I'm not suggesting that we, who are neither policy-makers nor academic specialists on political affairs, become more involved in testing our own moral purity than in the practical issues. But it takes a certain spiritual grace, and a continuing questioning of oneself, to be a voice that deserves trust. Conscious virtue is a dangerous trap. And all of us here—whether we are against war generally, or simply protesting this particular war—are consciously, uninnocently virtuous. Therefore, it seems to me important that we know what we are feeling—not just that we have our information straight, our judgment informed. It seems to me important that the pitch and timbre of our feelings be correct, sound.

We may feel anger, compassion, horror, fear—certainly fear. But let's reject that middle-class emotion, indignation. The trouble with indignation is its underlying complacency, its complicity with those respectable-looking people who are instigating the acts we deplore. Let's not bemoan, with an unquenchable surprise, that "our" Government could do what it is doing. We are, most of us, even us, or, should I say, especially us, still dupes of the myth of a special American virtue, of an America that remains, somehow, eternally innocent and forgivable, whatever her crimes. Let us confront the bloodstained face of America. I, for one, feel ashamed of my country, ashamed and anguished to be an American at this moment in world history.

And neither let us allow our condemnation to be bought off by appeals to our "practical" sense, to a phony *Realpolitik*. We are, after all, intellectuals and, therefore, especially vulnerable to the reproach that we are impractical idealists. But it requires no special idealism to be appalled by this war. And, precisely from a practical and historical point of view, the war is nothing less than an insane blunder. Anyway, even if *we* should be bought off, it is unlikely that non-Americans will be appeased so easily. Even if the Johnson Administration decides not to force a war with China, a prospect obviously being seriously considered at this very moment in Washington, even if the Administration begins a genuine bid for negotiations, instead of pressing for the unconditional surrender of the Vietnamese, it is unlikely that America will be let off the hook, that this country will be able to expiate its crimes or repeal its arrogance with aid programs for those who survive American bombs.

Let's be angry, truly angry. Let's be horrified. Let's be afraid.

ABOUT THE EDITORS

Louis Menashe, Assistant Professor of History at the Polytechnic Institute of Brooklyn, is author of a forthcoming study of the Russian bourgeoisie in the revolution of 1905, and editor of several documentary recordings, including *Berkeley Teach-in: Vietnam* and *Town Hall Read-In*.

Ronald Radosh, Assistant Professor of History at Queensborough Community College, City University of New York, has written an analysis of the Negro's status for *Lyndon Johnson's Great Society* as well as articles in *The Nation*, the *Journal of American History*, and other periodicals.